ACUA
Underwater Archaeology
Proceedings
2020

edited by

Victor Mastone and Calvin Mires

Dave Ball and Chelsea Freeland, Series Editors

AN ADVISORY COUNCIL ON UNDERWATER ARCHAEOLOGY PUBLICATION

2020 © Advisory Council on Underwater Archaeology

Made possible in part through the support of the
Society for Historical Archaeology

Cover Image: *Abandonned Fishing Boats, Wellfleet Mass.* Distributed by the Slate Company, Hyannis Mass.

Foreword

Revolution is an elegant word that conjures an immediate singular understanding, yet it encompasses multiple meanings and ideas. As the solitary word theme for the 2020 annual meeting of the Society of Historical Archaeology, based in Boston, there is an inherent association with the American Revolution. However, revolution is not only associated with resistance, physical violence, or violent political change, such as the War of Independence from the British Empire. Rather, revolution can represent sweeping change in the human condition.

The theme of revolution can be characterized as a reshaping of ideas, a shift or transition of theoretical and/or technical approach, or simply an adaptation of new tools. These are the outcomes of the scientific revolution, industrial revolution, technological revolution, and communication revolution. For the science of archaeology, revolution is a coupling of new ideas, a reshaping of old ideas, improvements to precepts and approaches that formed the sweeping changes. It is a change in how the archaeological community views and interprets the world.

The Annual Proceedings on Underwater Archaeology give voice to past, current, and ongoing research that embrace these various underlying meanings of revolution. This volume contains 20 papers presented at the Society's annual meeting, and three memorial essays. While it is beyond the scope to summarize individual Proceedings papers, you will find some papers discussing technological revolutions and approaches to data interpretation and presentation. Some examine environmental revolutions and the influence of climate change and sea level rise on submerged and foreshore archaeological resources. Others resist the artificial boundary between terrestrial and submerged heritage, highlighting maritime landscapes. In some cases, material culture is used as a mechanism to describe social change or revolution. On both the local and global scale, legal transformation on the treatment of cultural resources are described. Revolution often suggests difficult change and as noted above, this volume has three memorials.

In the brief time following the close of the conference, three esteemed colleagues passed away. These colleagues were Richard (Dick) Gould, Pilar Luna, and Roger Smith. In reading the essays on their lives and accomplishments, you will come to know them as colleagues, mentors, and friends. They are often described as pioneers in the field of underwater archaeology, part of Generation 1. As pioneers, they are also revolutionaries. They willingly brought new ideas to the table and invited us to join them. These Proceedings are dedicated to them.

As you read these papers and memorials, the editors offer for your consideration a parting thought from Gloria Steinem (Moving Beyond Words: Age, Rage, Sex, Power, Money, Muscle, Breaking Boundaries of Gender. Simon & Schuster, 1995, p.196):

"…revolutions come from combining what exists into what has never been before."

Archaeologists should never shy away from being revolutionaries.

VICTOR MASTONE
CALVIN MIRES

Foreword..1

Contributing Authors

Integrating Underwater Cultural Heritage into the UN Decade of Ocean Science for Sustainable Development...5
    Ole Varmer, Mark J. Spalding, Alexandra Refosko

The Trials of *Trinité*: the Discovery of and Legal Battle over Jean Ribault's 1565 Flagship....................15
    Chuck Meide

Archaeological Investigations at La Isabela, Dominican Republic...25
    Tori L. Galloway, Charles D. Beeker, Denise Jaffke, Claudia C. Johnson

The Effects of Major Hurricane Events on Shipwreck Site Vulnerability in the Florida Keys..................33
    Airielle R. Cathers

The Bermuda 100 Project: An Island-Scale Digital Atlas for Underwater Cultural Heritage....................43
    Vid Petrovic, Dominique Rissolo, Eric Lo, Scott Blair, Philippe Rouja, Jean-Pierre Rouja, Falko Kuester

The Ancient Mesambria Field School in Underwater Archaeology: Synergy in Benefit of Bulgarian Cultural Heritage 49
    Nayden Prahov, Danny Zborover

Integrated Maritime Cultural Landscape for Management of Vulnerable Coastal Heritage 57
    Sorna Khakzad, Michael Thomin

Shipwreck Tagging Archaeological Management Program (STAMP): A Model for Coastal Heritage Resource Management Based on Community Engagement and Citizen Science......................................69
    Austin Burkhard

Known Sites, Unknown States: Monitoring Activities on Intertidal Sites in St. Augustine......................73
    Allyson Ropp

Privateers on the Mullica River - Mapping Shipwrecks of the Revolutionary War...................................81
    Stephen D. Nagiewicz, Peter F. Straub, Steven P. Evert, Shannon M. Chiarel, Jaymes Swain, Jessica DiBlasi

Loss of USS *Milwaukee* (C-21): An Archaeological Study of a World War I-Era U.S. Navy Disaster in Northern California...91
    Jeffrey Delsescaux

Return to *Portland* 2019: Stellwagen Bank National Marine Sanctuary and Telepresence....................101
    Calvin H. Mires, Evan Kovacs, Kirstin Meyer-Kaiser, Benjamin Haskell

An Investigation of the Microbial Community Associated with USS *Arizona*..111
    Jennifer Clifford, Archana Vasanthakumar, David L. Conlin, Ralph Mitchell

Sparrow-Hawk (1626), the Oldest Shipwreck on Cape Cod, MA: An Analysis of Wooden Artifacts Using X-ray Fluorescence (XRF)..117
    Raymond L. Hayes

The Wreck of HMS *Erebus*: A Fieldwork and Research Update...125
    Jonathan Moore

Seeing Life in 3D: Digital Recording of HMS *Erebus*..135
    Thierry Boyer, Brandy Lockhart

HMS *Erebus* Material Culture: Reaching Out to the Individuals..143
    Charles Dagneau

A Personal Snapshot: An Abridged Comparative Analysis of the Emanuel Point, Padre Island, and *Santa Clara* Shipwrecks (1554-1564)..153
    Brandon L. Herrmann

Aviators Down! Tuskegee Airmen in Michigan..159
    Wayne R. Lusardi

Mystery Rocket Recovered from Lake Ontario: Avro Arrow or Other Cold War Relic?......................165
    Nancy E. Binnie, Erin Gregory

2020 Tributes...175

Memorial: Richard Allan Gould (1937–2020)..177
    David L. Conlin

Memorial: María del Pilar Luna Erreguerena (1944–2020)..185
    Toni Carrell, Margaret Leshikar-Denton, Dolores Elkin, Roberto Junco

In Memoriam - Dr. Roger C. Smith (1949–2020)...193
    Della A. Scott-Ireton, Christopher E. Horrell, Chuck Meide

Integrating Underwater Cultural Heritage into the UN Decade of Ocean Science for Sustainable Development

Ole Varmer, Mark J. Spalding, Alexandra Refosco

The resources that we want to protect and conserve for future generations include both natural and cultural heritage in the ocean. As the United Nations Decade of Ocean Science for Sustainable Development (2021-2030) is to facilitate science-based decision making, it is important to consider underwater cultural heritage (UCH) and the law protecting it. This paper discusses existing law and policy that should be considered with this integration as part of the Ocean Science for Sustainable Development, including recommendations of the recent Report on the UNESCO Evaluation of the 2001 Convention (UNESCO, 2019 and Varmer, 2020) and a panel forum held at the Society for Historical Archaeology 2020 meeting in Boston.

Introduction

This paper discusses what our ocean heritage is, how it is threatened, and some of the laws and organizations that facilitate its conservation. It discusses the importance of integrating underwater cultural heritage (UCH) into the work of the United Nations (UN) Decade of Ocean Science for Sustainable Development (2021-2030) (Decade). Within the UN, this effort is being led by the Intergovernmental Oceanographic Commission (IOC) which is also the lead agency in implementing the Law of the Sea Convention (LOSC) and Marine Scientific Research (MSR).

Our Ocean Heritage (Natural and Cultural Heritage) and Threats

The interest in conservation has existed since the dawn of human civilization and is found in many beliefs and religions. This evolved into a conservation movement in the 1800s - 1900s. The first United States (U.S.) national park was established at Yellowstone in 1872, which addressed threats to our heritage from development. Under the 1906 Antiquities Act (AA), natural and cultural areas were set aside as monuments. (National Park Service. 2020). Threats from war to cultural heritage were first addressed in the U.S. by the Lieber Code during the Civil War which was a precursor to the Convention on the Protection of Cultural Property in the Event of Armed Conflict (known as the "1954 Hague Convention") - the first treaty under the auspices of the United Nations Educational, Scientific, and Cultural Organization (UNESCO). The earliest integration and balancing of economic development with the conservation of our heritage is the 1972 UN Conference on the Human Environment Stockholm Declaration developed under the auspices of UNESCO.

UNESCO and The International Law Protecting Heritage

The 1954 Hague Convention – Protection of Cultural Property in the Event of Armed Conflict

The first treaty protecting cultural heritage under the auspices of UNESCO was the 1954 Hague Convention. It addresses concerns about the war-time destruction of monuments, art, manuscripts, books, and other objects of artistic, historical, or archaeological interest, as well as scientific collections. While it does not expressly refer to UCH, UNESCO interprets it broadly to include UCH (UNESCO Evaluation of the 2001 UCH Convention 2019). There have been discussions about including UCH in the Blue Shield Program, a non-governmental organization designed to protect heritage sites from disasters using emblems that identify the heritage.

The 1972 World Heritage Convention (natural and cultural)

The 1972 Convention Concerning the Protection of the World Cultural and Natural Heritage (1972 Convention) is a merging of two separate movements: the first focusing on the preservation of cultural sites and the other dealing with the conservation of nature (UNESCO #45 2016). A major catalyst was the development of the Aswan Dam in Egypt that threatened nearby cultural sites. The campaign to protect this and other cultural heritage sites led to the establishment of the International Council of Monuments and Sites (ICOMOS) in 1965. Around the same time there were efforts to protect natural heritage such as those under the UNESCO Man and the Biosphere Programme. In the U.S., the concept of a "World Heritage Trust" involving both natural and cultural heritage was raised at a 1965 international meeting held at the White House under the Johnson Administration (Batisse and Bolla 2005). The idea was to stimulate cooperation in order to identify and develop the most beautiful natural and historical sites in the world for the benefit of present and future generations. The 1972 Convention was subsequently adopted by the General Conference of UNESCO on 16 November 1972. The U.S. was the first to ratify on 12 July 1973 under the Nixon Administration. The 1972 Convention entered into force with 20 nations in 1973 and now includes 193 State parties; it is the most widely accepted of the conservation treaties promoting cooperation for the preservation of natural and cultural heritage.

The initial focus of the World Heritage Committee was, understandably, on monuments and sites found on land in the Americas, Africa, and Eurasia. Among the first sites to be inscribed-in 1978-were the remains of an 11th-century Viking settlement at L'Anse aux Meadows National Historic Park in Newfoundland. L'Anse aux Meadows is a maritime heritage site of perhaps the first Euro-American connection through Viking exploration. The Canadian Nahanni National Park Reserve is also inscribed as a natural site because of the outstanding value of the Nahanni River and the four associated canyons and falls that are closely associated with First Nation people who have occupied the land for the last 9,000-10,000 years. The Galapagos Islands were inscribed on the natural list, but the historical significance of the site because of Charles Darwin and the marine component are also noteworthy. Albania was the first nation to have one site, Lake Ohrid, meet the criteria for both natural and cultural resources. At present, there are only 39 sites on this "Mixed List" of sites recognized for their "outstanding universal value" as natural and cultural resources or properties. The first exclusively marine site to be inscribed on the natural list occurred in 1981 in recognition of Australia's efforts to protect and manage the Great Barrier Reef. It is worth highlighting that the U.S. was a leader in the development of the 1972 Convention and its protection of the U.S. national parks in Mesa Verde (cultural) and Yellowstone (natural) were recognized in the 1978 inscription of its first two nominations.

U.S. Leadership In Developing The World Heritage Convention And The Integration Of The Protection Of Natural And Cultural Heritage

As indicated above, the U.S. was a leader in the development of the 1972 Convention and was the first to ratify it. The U.S. already had a few domestic laws that provided authority and examples for the protection of our natural and cultural heritage through the AA and specific Acts establishing national parks. The AA has recently been extended seaward to protect ocean heritage such as Papahânaumokuâkea where it protects both natural heritage and cultural heritage of the native Hawaiian people. The 1966 National Historic Preservation Act was enacted to address threats from federally funded development projects. It was amended in 1980 with a new Section 402 to implement the 1972 Convention for express extraterritorial application in all World Heritage sites and to heritage resources identified by foreign governments in what is the equivalent of the U.S. National Register of Historic Places. Section 402 of the NHPA has a process which is the equivalent of the NHPA Section 106 process that applies in the U.S. Section 402 has been applied by U.S. courts to a federal development project in Okinawa to ensure that there was consideration of impacts on heritage including consultation with Japan which listed the dugong (a marine mammal) as part of its cultural heritage. Other U.S. laws that support integrated protection of our heritage include the 1969 National Environmental Policy Act, the 1972 Marine Protection Research and Sanctuaries Act and the 1972 Coastal Zone Management Act.

The UN Law of the Sea Convention (LOSC)

The public international law of nations involving the sea and private international maritime law involving private activities were part of the earliest development of customary international law that continues to evolve, including the integration of provisions protecting heritage both natural and cultural. The codification of the law of the sea was initially accomplished at the first UN Conference on the Law of the Sea (UNCLOS I) in 1956, which resulted in four conventions regarding the maritime zones of the Territorial Sea, Contiguous Zone, Continental Shelf, and the High Seas. The 1958 Conventions did not address cultural heritage or property, much less a duty to protect it despite the emerging public interest as reflected in the 1954 Hague Convention. The 1958 Convention on Fishing and Conservation of Living Resources is evidence of the public interest in the natural heritage of fish and other living natural resources in the ocean. The international community, however, recognized the need for more work to address these heritage issues. Accordingly, the UN held a second UN Conference on the Law of the Sea in 1960 (UNCLOS II), but it did not result in any treaty. In 1973, on the heels of the 1972 Stockholm Declaration and 1972 Convention, a third conference was called to address certain unresolved issues (UNCLOS III). It took almost a decade, but it did result in the 1982 LOSC which includes a Part XII on the Protection and Preservation of the Marine Environment and several other provisions regarding the conservation and duty to protect the natural heritage of the ocean (United Nations LOSC, 1982). While Articles 149 and 303 of the LOSC are the only provisions regarding the duty to protect the cultural heritage found at sea, the duty is very similar to the duty to protect the natural heritage in the marine environment.

The parties negotiating the LOSC agreed to the duty to protect UCH and recognized the need for more details as is implied in Article 303(4). In response to the continued threats to UCH from looting and salvage, the vagueness of the duty to protect, and the perceived gap in the protection of UCH on the continental shelf, States came together to the Paris headquarters of UNESCO to develop a more specific agreement to protect UCH.

2001 UNESCO Convention on the Protection of Underwater Cultural Heritage

History of the Development of the Convention

While UNESCO's initial focus was on culture sites on land, in 1956 it suggested the Recommendation on International Principles Applicable to Archaeological Excavations be applied to UCH within territorial waters (Dromgoole 2010). With the advent of technology to access the deep seabed, the need for an international agreement for the continental shelf and high seas became apparent. There were studies in Europe in the 1970s, but no text was adopted. The International Law Association (ILA) developed a draft Convention in 1994 that was transmitted to UNESCO. In 1996, ICOMOS adopted its International Charter on the Protection and Management of the Underwater Cultural Heritage. UNESCO convened several meetings of Government experts between 1998 and 2001 that used the ILA draft and ICOMOS Charter as starting points. The Convention on the Protection of UCH was adopted in 2001 by the UNESCO General Conference with 88 votes in favor, 5 against and 19 abstentions (UNESCO Evaluation of 2001 UCH Convention 2019).

The Convention, Purpose, Scope, and its General Principles

The 2001 Convention represents an international response to the concern of looting and the destruction of UCH by unscientific salvage. It contains a few general principles that were agreed to by all the negotiating parties, including the U.S.:

> the obligation to protect and preserve UCH (similar to the duty to protect under LOSC Art. 303(1); 2) the preferred first policy or option of in situ preservation; 3) an agreement on the international standards and requirements for when recovery or salvage is determined to be in the public interest (i.e., consistent with rest of this Convention); 4) no "commercial exploitation" of UCH; and 5) cooperation among States to protect UCH, particularly for training, education, and outreach (also similar to duty to cooperate in LOSC Article 303, Archaeological and historical objects found at sea). UCH is defined to include "all traces of human existence having a cultural, historical, or archaeological character which have been partially or totally under water, periodically or continuously, for at least 100 years." (UNESCO 2002).

It expressly references the 1970 UNESCO Convention on illicit trafficking, the 1972 World Heritage Convention and the LOSC. The 2001 Convention entered into force with the ratification of 20 nations in 2009. At that time, none of the self-named maritime powers that had expressed concerns about consistency with LOSC were among those 20 nations. Since then, France has become a party in 2013, and other maritime powers, such as Germany, are exploring joining due to the primary concerns about upsetting the delicate balance of jurisdiction between flag States and coastal States has not materialized in the past two decades. During the 10th year anniversary of its entry into force the UNESCO Evaluation Office assessed the 2001 Convention, its implementation and its support in order to provide findings, lessons learned and recommendations on its relevance and effectiveness.

UNESCO Evaluation of the 2001 Convention on the Protection of Underwater Cultural Heritage

Methodology

The evaluation involved a desk review, a survey of the 193 UNESCO Member States, to which 93 people from 75 States responded (38% response rate), semi-structured interviews with stakeholders, questionnaires for established partners and observation of three conferences on UCH (UNESCO Evaluation of the 2001 UCH Convention 2019).

Key Findings

The 2001 Convention and the Rules in its Annex have become the world reference for underwater archaeologists. The State Cooperation Mechanism created by the Convention is of interest to States and aspires to become a model for other processes of international cooperation in areas beyond national jurisdiction in a manner consistent with the LOSC. It is relevant in that it complements the existing international framework for the protection of UCH, namely by filling the void left by the LOSC on the continental shelf beyond the 24 nm contiguous zone. However, many viewed the discourse around the 2001 Convention as too narrowly focused on shipwrecks. Some expressed misconceptions on key concepts of the Convention, that *in situ* preservation was a bar to recovery of UCH, creating a museum for recovered artifacts or, even, the removal of human remains from UCH sites. Regarding gender parity, women remain largely underrepresented in this field. The Scientific and Technical Advisory Body to the 2001 Convention (STAB) has been appreciated, but it has focused exclusively on underwater archaeology,

> *overlooking potential ties with other related subjects, e.g. the environment, ocean, and heritage at large. Existing partnerships have been underutilized and potential ones unexploited. There is great potential for UNESCO to explore synergies among its Culture Conventions and with the Man and the Biosphere Programme, and the work of the IOC, particularly in the framework of the upcoming Decade. UNESCO also has valuable expert networks in UCH (NGOs, UNITWIN, Category II centre), whose strength lies in skills development, but they have so far not been very involved in capacity-building initiatives. Several additional partnerships also remain unexplored such as with law enforcement organizations, museums, and organizations working on oceans and the environment more broadly. Finally, UNESCO is not sufficiently present in international development fora in which the protection of UCH needs to be promoted (UNESCO Evaluation of the 2001 UCH Convention 2019).*

Recommendations in the Report of the Evaluation

There are 15 recommendations in total, six for the UNESCO UCH Unit, including the development of a strategic plan and monitoring to support countries in implementing the 2001 Convention that should be articulated in a results framework and linked to all relevant Sustainable Development Goals (SDGs). Among other things, it recommends the STAB broaden its scope include legal and environmental issues in view of strengthening recipient countries' systems of protection. For the Meeting of the States Parties (MSP), the recommendations include integrating UCH into the Roadmap of the Decade, including cooperation between the UCH Unit and the IOC in the implementation of the Roadmap, invite stakeholders from the UNESCO Secretariat (IOC, units responsible for the 1954, 1970, 1972 and 2003 Conventions), DOALOS, NGOs working on oceans and the environment, law enforcement agencies, etc., to MSP meetings in view of clarifying issues related to the law of the sea and broadening discussions to include the larger issues at stake (UNESCO Evaluation of the 2001 UCH Convention 2019). Recommendation 14 is for UNESCO's Culture Sector to ensure that there is regular representation of the UCH Unit in UN Ocean and any other global coordination mechanisms in ocean-related matters in order to clearly reaffirm the contribution of the protection of UCH to the 2030 Agenda. The Cultural Sector should also integrate the protection of UCH and awareness of the 2001 Convention in the mechanisms of other Culture Conventions and UNESCO programmes (e.g. Man and the Biosphere Programme) such as in their site management and conservation plans, broader safeguarding policies, regional consultations, trainings, and meetings of statutory bodies. Collaborate with the IOC in integrating UCH into initiatives such as marine spatial planning, marine scientific research, and capacity building (UNESCO Evaluation of the 2001 UCH Convention 2019). As we look to the future of the conservation of our heritage in the ocean, the focus should include cooperating in protecting our natural and cultural heritage found in the high seas such as RMS *Titanic* and the Sargasso Sea which are both currently beyond the geographic scope of consideration under the 1972 Convention (UNESCO #45 2016).

UNESCO's Hangzhou Declaration: Placing Culture at the Heart of Sustainable Development Policies

The Hangzhou Declaration, adopted in Hangzhou, People's Republic of China on May 2013, affirmed the link between culture and the Sustainable Development Goals (SDGs or the 2030 Agenda). The declaration notes that culture can serve as knowledge capital and a sector of activities. It recognizes that different cultural perspectives will result in different paths to development; this allows enhanced opportunities and human capabilities while promoting mutual understanding and exchange. Further, development is particularly effective when a people-centered and place-based approach is taken to ensure that all programs and policies are inclusive and effective (UNESCO Hangzhou Declaration 2013).

Integrating UCH into the UN Decade of Ocean Science for Sustainable Development

The United Nation's Decade of Ocean Science for Sustainable Development (2021-2030) is intended to be the largest campaign in the history of science and seeks "to support efforts to reverse the cycle of decline in ocean health and gather ocean stakeholders worldwide behind a common framework" (UNESCO Accelerating Ocean Science 2019). The vision for the Decade is defined as "The science we need for the ocean we want." The official mission statement is "to generate and use knowledge for the transformational action we need to achieve a healthy, safe, and resilient ocean for sustainable development by 2030 and beyond" (UNESCO Decade Summary Event 2020).

Preparations for the Decade are led by UNESCO's IOC and brings together governments, scientists, NGOs, and industry. The goals were set during the first planning meetings held in May 2019 (UNESCO First Global Planning Meeting 2019). Twelve archaeologists were invited to participate in the meeting and provided guidance on how to integrate cultural heritage into this effort (Underwood et al. 2020). It was agreed that the focus on heritage should include underwater and coastal heritage which has also been referred to as a maritime cultural landscape approach. During UNESCO's June 2019 meetings in Paris, the Executive Secretary of the UNESCO IOC suggested the group of accredited NGOs develop a workshop highlighting the importance of cultural heritage in the Decade (Underwood et al. 2020). This resulted in the establishment of the Ocean Decade Heritage Network (ODHN 2020).

The Decade hopes to deliver a digital atlas of the ocean, a comprehensive observing system, quantitative understanding of ocean ecosystems, a data portal, an integrated multi-hazard warning system, capacity building and accelerated technology transfer, and an ocean in earth-system observation supported by social and human sciences and economic valuation (UNESCO The Science We Need 2019). Underlying this is the search to increase understanding of the ocean through science-based solutions, achieve the 2030 Agenda and produce the six desired outcomes of the Decade: a clean ocean where sources of pollution are identified and removed, a healthy and resilient ocean where marine ecosystems are mapped and protected, a sustainably harvested and productive ocean ensuring the provision of food supply and sustainable livelihoods, a predictable ocean where society has the capacity to understand current and future ocean conditions, a safe ocean where people are protected from ocean hazards, and a transparent and accessible ocean with open access to data, information and technologies. While none of these specifically mention culture or heritage, one of the Guiding Principles for the Decade calls for "Activities [that] are based on partnerships between many disciplines and sectors. [And which] integrate social and cultural values, and traditional/indigenous/local community knowledge" (UNESCO Ocean Decade Summary Event 2020). According to the IOC Executive Secretary, "we need emotional engagement, as well as a show of how the ocean is part of society's value chain" (Spalding, pers. com. 2020). In framing the case for philanthropic support for the Decade, the IOC wrote:

> *The world is experiencing a revolution in science and technology. In the coming decade, we have a tremendous opportunity to harness advances in ocean science to achieve a better understanding of the ocean system and deliver science-based solutions to achieve the 2030 Agenda . . . To meet this challenge, the UN General Assembly called for an*

acceleration of ocean science and data exchange to reverse declines in the health and functioning of the ocean system and to catalyze new opportunities for sustainable ocean uses. The Decade will bring together scientists and stakeholders from all relevant sectors to generate the scientific knowledge and to develop the partnerships needed for informing policies to support a well-functioning, productive, resilient, and sustainable ocean. The Decade will enable the delivery of timely information about the state of the ocean and articulate development-dependent scenarios and a sustainable pathway into the future (Concept note The Ocean Decade 2020).

Following on the UNESCO *Hangzhou Declaration* consensus, to be successful the Decade must integrate culture, through cultural heritage and creativity, as an enabler of sustainable development while also promoting capacity for science innovation and allowing the world to achieve the benefits contemplated by the SDGs. "Placing culture at the heart of development is the only way to ensure a human-centered, inclusive and equitable development" (Hosagraha 2017). As a result of *The Hangzhou Declaration*, those concerned about culture and heritage are recognized "stakeholders" and are key to the global approach to meet the SDGs. For example, natural and cultural heritage tourism, also known as eco-cultural tourism, is often looked to as a sustainable ocean use when part of a conservation management plan. While the socio-economic benefits of UCH may be relatively less known, historical sites that are responsibly managed, protected, and monitored can be maintained and used to create tourism revenue. For example, the U.S. Florida Keys National Marine Sanctuary plan's *in situ* conservation of natural and cultural heritage was determined to have a more positive impact on the economy than any short-term benefits of the private exploitation of treasure hunting (NOAA Varmer 1997).

While none of the SDG titles directly address culture, the world's natural and cultural heritage is expressly referenced in one of the targets under goal 11 see SDG target 11.4: "Strengthen efforts to protect and safeguard the world's cultural and natural heritage." As explained in the UNESCO Report on the Evaluation of the 2001 UNESCO UCH Convention, "Underwater cultural heritage research, education and protection is relevant to many Sustainable Development Goals" (UNESCO Evaluation of 2001 UCH Convention 2019:15). For example, the benefits from UCH conservation activities and associated tourism revenue can help address SDG 1: no poverty. UCH research can contribute to coastal societies sustainable development, while protecting their heritage. UCH may open opportunities for recreation, cultural enrichment, and economic and social development. For instance, it can provide long-term opportunities for eco-cultural tourism, and promote social well-being in support of SDG 3 on Good Health and Well-being. Public access to UCH, in the form of museums, dive trails, 3D visioning or other means, ensures the conservation of the UCH, and a lasting return on the investment of our heritage. The protection, research, and education of UCH is also relevant to SDG 4: Education as it is part of ocean literacy. The SDG Target 4.7 is particularly relevant to education for sustainable development as it can contribute to highlighting the connections between people and building peace and sustainable development through understanding our shared maritime and cultural heritage. UCH and our maritime heritage are also relevant to SDG 5 Gender Equality in that research and education about our maritime heritage and UCH may also contribute to empowering communities through the telling of stories of women and their traditional knowledge of UCH. UCH is also relevant to SDG 8 on Decent Work and Economic Growth as the protection of UCH has the potential of contributing to the Blue Economy, such as through eco-cultural tourism, touched on above. UCH is relevant to SDG 11 Sustainable Cities and Settlements as SDG target 11.4 seeks to strengthen efforts to protect the world's cultural and natural heritage. Regarding the especially important SDG 13 Climate Change, "UCH can provide vital evidence about how human populations have adapted to, or been affected by, climate changes in the past" (UNESCO Evaluation of the 2001 UCH Convention 2019).

Within the Decade's goals there is ample area to integrate UCH into the science-based sustainable development decision making and to particularly encourage the conservation of both natural and cultural heritage for the betterment of the ocean and human interaction with it. Culture, nature, and science must be considered holistically to provide the most successful development programs and policies incorporating new developments in science-based solutions and emerging technology with the understanding from cultural considerations needed to protect UCH. Because UCH is part of the heart of UN SDGs, the related science-based solutions support the 2030 Agenda.

Recommendations:

- The mapping of the seabed should be done in a manner that can identify natural and cultural heritage so decisionmakers can balance their conservation with sustainable development.
- Include research of UCH in ocean scientific research and marine scientific research.
- Include UCH as part of the marine environment for environmental assessments, marine spatial planning, and the integrated management of human activities.
- The use of a maritime landscape approach is encouraged. This approach considers how humans have used the ocean and coastal environment for their development and how that environment affected their human use. As such, it is part of the cultural heritage that is fundamental to understanding how many coastal and marine ecosystems achieved their present form and understanding the pressures upon them and the possible lessons learned in how to address for sustainable development.
- Recognize that protecting UCH *in situ* may also serve as artificial reefs of potential use in sustainable development as a site for eco-cultural tourism and a fishery enhancement device for recreational and commercial fishing.
- Recognize that sustainable development may include the recovery and conservation of certain UCH in a museum or other institution of public access.
- Support the research and identification of potentially polluting shipwrecks in a manner that surveys the wreck site prior to activities to remove bunker fuel and hazardous material or other activities to prevent or minimize pollution of the ocean and coastal areas.
- Support integration of cultural heritage into Ocean Literacy as human interaction with the historic environment is essential to understanding our present ocean and to forecasting change and its implications for human well-being and livelihoods.
- Support research of cultural heritage that informs the understanding of coastal inhabitation and intervention in the past and present—including the impact of previous catastrophes—to identify risks, present examples of human adaptations, and to encourage resilience; and
- Recognize cultural heritage as a major contributor to the Blue Economy, especially through recreation and eco-cultural tourism in a manner that does not damage the world's irreplaceable cultural heritage.

Conclusion

This paper discussed ocean heritage, the law developed to conserve it, and recommended next steps particularly integrating UCH into all the work of UNESCO. Additionally, this paper focuses on the work of IOC and the Decade, including marine scientific research, environmental assets, planning and management of human activities in the ocean. The significant precedence for the protection of both natural and cultural ocean heritage exists through the Antiquities Act of 1906, the 1972 World Heritage Convention, the 1982 Law of the Sea Conventions, and the 2013 Hangzhou Declaration. This paper not only reinforces the belief the Decade should prioritize the preservation of both natural and cultural ocean heritage but reaffirms the benefits of mitigating risks to the environment and our communities as well as increasing economic opportunities in the process. In sum, the science we need for the ocean we want, includes sustainable development that conserves natural and cultural heritage for present and future generations.

References

Batisse, M. and Bolla, G.
2005 *The Invention of World Heritage,* History Club - Association of Former UNESCO Staff and Members. <https://whc.unesco.org/document/138563> Accessed 28 February 2020.

Dromgoole, S.
2010 *Revisiting the Relationship between Marine Scientific Research and the Underwater Cultural Heritage,* International Journal of Marine and Coastal Law 25(1):33-61

Hosagrahar, J.
2017 *Culture: at the Heart of SDGs,* The UNESCO Courier, April 2017, <https://en.unesco.org/courier/april-june-2017/culture-heart-sdgs> Accessed 28 February 2020.

Ocean Decade Heritage Network (ODHN)
2020 *About the Ocean Decade Heritage Network.* ODHN. <https://www.oceandecadeheritage.org/why-and-how/> Accessed 17 April 2020.

NATIONAL PARK SERVICE
2020   American Antiquities Act of 1906 16 USC 431-433. The National Park Service. <https://www.nps.gov/history/local-law/anti1906.htm> Accessed 17 April 2020.

NATIONAL OCEANIC AND ATMOSPHERIC ADMINISTRATION (NOAA)(VARMER),
1997   Supplement to Final Regulatory Flexibility Analysis for the Final Regulations Implementing the Final Management Plan for Florida Key National Marine Sanctuary: Commercial Treasure Salvors available at https://www.gc.noaa.gov/documents/060197_rfa_keys_salvors.pdf

SPALDING, MARK
2020   Personal conversation between IOC Executive Secretary and Mark Spalding. February 3, 2020.

UNDERWOOD, CHRIS, MARC-ANDRE BERNIER, GARRY MOMBER, PETA KNOTT, JENNIFER MCKINNON, DOLORES ELKIN, AMANDA EVANS, AND DAVE BALL.
2020   *Implementing UCH into the UN Decade of Ocean Science for Sustainable Development*, SHA/ACUA UNESCO Panel: 9 January 2020. Boston, Massachusetts.

UNITED NATIONS LOSC
1982   Convention on the Law of the Sea of 10 December 1982 Overview and Full Text. United Nations Division for Ocean Affairs and the Law of the Sea. <https://www.un.org/depts/los/convention_agreements/convention_overview_convention.htm> Accessed 17 April 2020.

UNITED NATIONS EDUCATIONAL, SCIENTIFIC AND CULTURAL ORGANIZATION (UNESCO)
UNESCO DECADE SUMMARY EVENT
2020   UNESCO Ocean Decade Summary for Foundations Event Partnership Dialogue for the '*UN Decade of Ocean Science for Sustainable Development (2021-2030)*' San Diego, CA 18 February 2020.

UNESCO CONCEPT NOTE THE OCEAN DECADE
2020   Concept note T*he Ocean Decade Alliance: Acting together to build the science we need for the ocean we want.* UNESCO. 12 February 2020

UNESCO ACCELERATING OCEAN SCIENCE
2019   *Accelerating Ocean Science for a Better World: The UN Decade of Ocean Science for Sustainable Development 2021-2030*. UNESCO. May 2019.

UNESCO THE SCIENCE WE NEED
2019   *The Science We Need for the Ocean We Want* UNESCO. May 2019. <https://unesdoc.unesco.org/ark:/48223/pf0000265198> Accessed 17 April 2020.

UNESCO FIRST GLOBAL PLANNING MEETING
2019   *Summary Report of the First Global Planning Meeting: UN Decade of Ocean Science for Sustainable Development*, 13-15 May 2019 National Museum of Denmark, Copenhagen see https://oceandecade.org/

UNESCO EVALUATION OF 2001 UCH CONVENTION
2019   *Report on the Evaluation of the 2001 UNESCO UCH Convention*, Ekaterina Sediakina Rivière, Evaluation Manager, Taipei Dlamini, UNESCO Evaluation Office, Ole Varmer, Legal Expert, Dimitris Kourkoumelis, Underwater Archaeologist.

UNESCO
2016   UNESCO #45, *The Future of the World Heritage Convention for Marine Conservation: Celebrating 10 years of the World Heritage Marine Programme*, <https://whc.unesco.org/en/series/45> Accessed 28 February 2020.

UNESCO
2013   UNESCO, *The Hangzhou Declaration: Placing Culture at the Heart of Sustainable*, Adopted in Hangzhou, People's Republic of China, on 17 May 2013. <http://www.unesco.org/new/fileadmin/MULTIMEDIA/HQ/CLT/images/FinalHangzhouDeclaration20130517.pdf> Accessed 28 February 2020.

UNESCO
2002   *Records of the General Conference, 31st session, Paris, 15 October to 3 November 2001*, v. 1: Resolutions. UNESCO General Conference. <https://unesdoc.unesco.org/ark:/48223/pf0000124687.page=56> Accessed 17 April 2020.

UNITED STATES WHITE HOUSE, OFFICE OF THE PRESS SECRETARY
2002   *Fact Sheet: United States Rejoins UNESCO*, 12 September 2002 <https://georgewbush-whitehouse.archives.gov/news/releases/2002/09/20020912-4.html> Accessed 28 February 2020.

VARMER, OLE
2020   *Ten Years After the 2001 UNESCO Convention Became Law: I'd love to change the world … and here's what you can do.* 11 January 2020, Coastal Processes Management Issues: Boston at SHA annual meeting.

Ole Varmer
Senior Fellow
The Ocean Foundation
1320 19th St NW
Washington, DC 20036

Mark J. Spalding
President
The Ocean Foundation
1320 19th St NW
Washington, DC 20036

Alexandra Refosco,
Research Associate
The Ocean Foundation
Suite 500, 1320 19th St NW
Washington, DC 20036

The Trials of *Trinité*: the Discovery of and Legal Battle over Jean Ribault's 1565 Flagship

Chuck Meide

The 450th anniversary of French colonization at Fort Caroline (Jacksonville, Florida) in 2014 renewed interest in the search for Jean Ribault's four 1565 shipwrecks. It was not archaeologists, however, but treasure hunters who in 2016 found one of them off Cape Canaveral. After an Admiralty claim was filed, France counterclaimed the wreck was Ribault's flagship la Trinité, and therefore French property. The author, among others, assisted in the analysis and compilation of primary source documents to prove the identity of the shipwreck. On 29 June 2018 a federal judge recognized France's ownership, noting the preponderance of evidence indicated the shipwreck was indeed la Trinité.

Introduction

Sixteenth-century France was a vigorous, expansionist nation eager to assert her claims to a New World empire. To that end, an expedition was sent in 1562 to start a French colony made up largely of protestant Huguenots in the land known to the French as *La Floride*, which had already been claimed as *La Florida* by Spain (Figure 1). Led by Jean Ribault and his subordinate René de Laudonnière, the flotilla reconnoitered the Florida coast, setting up a stone monument with the royal arms of France at the River of May (present-day St. Johns River, Jacksonville, Florida) (Figure 2) and another at the eventual site of their settlement, Charlesfort (Parris

Figure 2: A Timucuan elite welcomes Laudonnière in 1564, showing how his people revere the stone column or borne erected during the first French expedition in 1562 at the River of May (present-day St. John's River at Jacksonville, Florida). *Bornes* were used as boundary markers to denote with the coat-of-arms of France the territory claimed by King Charles IX (1560-1574). Two were erected in 1562, and six more were in the hold of *la Trinité* when it wrecked. A portion of a *borne* with the royal arms, seemingly identical to those seen here, was encountered on the seafloor by GME divers. This image is one of the Theodore de Bry engravings, from a watercolor by Jacques Le Moyne, who was with the 1564 expedition. (Image courtesy of the Service Historique de la Défense, Vincennes, France).

Figure 1: Broad perspective view of the Northeast Florida region showing geographic features and sixteenth-century place-names mentioned in the text. LAMP's 2014 survey area focusing on Ribault's remaining three ships was located in Canaveral National Seashore waters, while both DHR and GME concentrated their surveys for *la Trinité* in separate areas off Cape Canaveral. View is facing north (Graphic by Brendan Burke and Chuck Meide, courtesy of LAMP, 2020).

Island, South Carolina). When this first colony ended in failure, Laudonnière returned in 1564 to establish Fort Caroline at the River of May. After a year of hardships, Jean Ribault returned to Florida just in time with a resupply fleet. Almost immediately confronted with a hostile Spanish force commanded by Pedro Menéndez de Avilés, Ribault launched a preemptive attack with his four largest ships on Menéndez' fledgling settlement of St. Augustine on 10 September 1565. A subsequent hurricane destroyed Ribault's fleet, with the flagship *la Trinité* wrecking at Cape Canaveral, and the other three ships lost some distance to the north. This event allowed Menéndez to capture Fort Caroline and secure Florida as a Spanish colony for the next two centuries. More detailed accounts of this history are presented in Lyon (1976), McGrath (2000), and Meide and de Bry (2014).

In 2014, commemorating the 450th anniversary of Fort Caroline's founding, two separate archaeological expeditions were launched to search for Ribault's lost fleet. One was sponsored by the Lighthouse Archaeological Maritime Program (LAMP) and directed by the author (Meide 2015), while the second was sponsored by the State of Florida's Division of Historical Resources (DHR) and directed by the late Roger C. Smith. Neither project resulted in the discovery of sixteenth-century shipwrecks.

GME's Discoveries at Cape Canaveral, 2015-2016

Professional archaeological research institutions were not the only groups seeking the remains of the lost French fleet in time for its 450th anniversary. The treasure hunting company Global Marine Exploration, Inc. (GME) also set out to search the waters of Cape Canaveral. GME, incorporated in Delaware, maintains a field station in Cape Canaveral and its headquarters and conservation laboratory in Tampa. Under the auspices of a 1A-31 salvage exploration permit issued by the State of Florida, GME conducted remote sensing operations off Cape Canaveral in August 2015. They subsequently received an addendum to their permit allowing limited excavation for the purposes of identifying anomalies (Sinclair 2015; Duggins and Price 2016:3-4). This led to the discovery of three to four areas of scattered wreckage they believed dated to the sixteenth or early seventeenth centuries. While no hull remains were observed, sixteen iron verso-type swivel guns, one iron muzzle-loading cannon, six anchors, ballast stones, and cannonballs were observed (Sinclair 2015:4, 16).

GME publicized these discoveries in their September 2015 online newsletter, linking the artifacts to Ribault's lost fleet by announcing that they had found:

> "several shipwrecks which we believe were lost in the area in the 16th and 17th century, one possibility is that two of the sites could be related to the lost 1565 French Fleet of Jean Ribault which was believed to have been lost further north. Several unsuccessful expeditions, both by private companies and taxpayer funded organizations have been mounted in the past, but nothing has been found. "The importance of finding part of this fleet would be significant" says Archaeologist- Jim Sinclair "(GME 2015:1).

After seeing this, the author and former LAMP Associate Director Brendan Burke met informally with Sinclair, GME's chief archaeologist, at a local bar in October 2015. Sinclair discussed some of the findings that were believed to date to the sixteenth century and potentially related to Ribault's fleet. The most diagnostic artifacts were the versos, which were scattered over a wide area; they appeared likely to be sixteenth century, but whose nationality could not be determined in the field.

The following year, GME made even more definitive discoveries. On 30 June 2016, GME reported to DHR that they found ballast stones, cannon balls, assorted wrought-iron objects, a stone grinding wheel, 12 anchors dating to the sixteenth through nineteenth centuries, 2 iron muzzle-loading cannons, 3 iron *bombardeta*-style cannons (likely sixteenth century), 13 verso-type swivel guns (likely sixteenth century), three French sixteenth-century bronze cannon with diagnostic markings, and, most notably, a stone marker or monument bearing the coat of arms of the King of France (Pritchett 2016). This last artifact appeared very similar to the monument erected by Ribault at the River of May famously depicted in the Theodore de Bry engraving, an iconic image readily familiar to most residents in Jacksonville and the surrounding First Coast region (Figure 2). These objects strongly suggested that the remains of one of Ribault's ships, most likely his flagship *la Trinité*, had been discovered.

Word spread quickly, and even before GME's report was submitted to DHR, a letter-writing campaign was initiated by Dr. Jennifer McKinnon of East Carolina University. Condemnation was rapid and widespread from the national archaeological community, including letters from the Advisory Council on Underwater Archaeology (ACUA), the Society for Historical Archaeology (SHA), and LAMP, urging DHR to refrain from granting a salvage permit allowing GME to further disturb the site or recover artifacts. It was pointed out that, in addition to the inappropriateness of allowing treasure hunters to salvage archaeological sites of such importance and retain 80% of recovered artifacts, the almost certain association of the wreckage to Ribault's fleet meant that the sites are sovereign property of the Republic of France and would be protected under the Sunken Military Craft Act. In that case, the State of Florida would not even have the authority to permit either research or salvage on the wreckage sites.

DHR's response was that, while there was yet no definitive proof of the wreck's identity, a 1A-31 recovery permit was not under consideration. Further, this response stated that any:

> *"future determinations or decisions made by the Division of Historical Resources on work conducted in the area will be solely based, and in strict compliance with, all applicable laws and rules. Because of the historical significance of Ribault's fleet and possible implications of the Sunken Military Craft Act, the Secretary of State has reached out to French Consul General Philippe Létrilliart and will maintain open lines of communication with the French Government. The Division has also been in contact with the United States Navy about the find"* (Parsons 2016).

Two days after this response, the U.S. State Department was notified by the French Embassy that given French policies regarding the preservation of underwater cultural heritage "the Republic of France therefore opposes any commercial exploration of the vessel discovered by Global Marine Corporation Inc. [sic] and would be extremely grateful for the State Department's help in insuring that this opposition is respected" (Embassy 2016:2). This diplomatic note also related that GME had approached the French government expressing its desire to work in an area that might contain Ribault's ships and the French responded by asserting their ownership of these vessels and forbidding their salvage.

GME then made their discoveries public when they published their July 2016 newsletter, followed by an online press release published 9 August 2016 (GME 2016a, 2016b). By this time, it was apparent that GME realized that an association with Ribault's fleet, as part of Charles IX's royal navy, would present a legal challenge to their salvage rights, and so their July 2016 newsletter contradicted the potential Ribault identification that had previously been asserted in their September 2015 newsletter

> *"Initial findings suggested the possibility that these were part of the remains of the lost French ships commanded by Jean Ribault in 1565, but subsequent physical evidence and historical research done by the GME archaeological team have ruled out that possibility, the identity of the sunken vessel or vessels may never be known"* (GME 2016a:1).

It has never been made clear what physical evidence or additional historical research would contraindicate the wreckage was from Ribault's fleet. GME did assert that none of the anchors found corresponded in size to any of Ribault's ships (Pritchett 2016:8, 43). GME believed the anchor found closest to the stone monument and bronze cannons was too large for a ship of *Trinité*'s size (150-160 tons), and that another anchor nearby was too small. However, it is well-known that ships carried an assortment of anchor sizes, including small kedge anchors, large bower anchors, and larger sheet anchors. At 3.84 m long, the large anchor found closest to the French material at Canaveral is comparable to the range of those found on the early sixteenth-century vessels at Highborn Cay and Molasses Reef (estimated to be between 90-150 tons), and at the 1554 Padre Island Wreck (estimated to between 123-286 tons) (Arnold and Weddle 1978:Appendices E-F; Nick Budsberg 2 November 2020, elec. comm.). Based on the weight of the Padre Island anchors, weight estimation put this anchor within the range of that suggested by the Spanish writer Escalante de Mendoza in 1575 as appropriate for bowers on a ship of *Trinité*'s size, and its length also roughly coincides with the ca. 1582 "Hawkyns' rule" for the proper size sheet anchor for a English ship of this approximate size (Escalante de Mendoza 1985:43-44; Tinniswood 1945:88; Filipe Castro 28 October 2016, elec. comm.; Chuck Meide 1 November 2016, elec. comm.).

On the other hand, the markings on at least one of the bronze cannons in GME's report and online publications provided indisputable physical evidence that these were French naval weapons dating to the reign of Henri II (1547-1559). While GME (2016a, 2016b; Pritchett 2016:5-7,12-13) acknowledged this in its reports and online publications, GME suggested that the earlier date of the cannons might indicate a pre-1560s French expedition in the region (Pritchett 2016:8); there is absolutely no archival evidence for this assertion (John de Bry, 14 August 2016, elec. comm.).

In late September 2016, the author travelled to Paris to attend the UNESCO International Meeting on Underwater Cultural Heritage and Site Protection. While in Paris, the author and John de Bry of the Center for Historical Archaeology visited the Musée de l'Armée to meet with Sylvie Leluc, Curator of Artillery, and Christophe Pommier, another curator in the Département Artillerie. Pommier drove the researchers to an auxiliary storage area in Pontault-Combault, 23 km east of Paris, where there was a Henri II cannon cast in 1548 with markings identical to those on one of the bronze guns discovered by GME. The author and de Bry inspected this cannon and recorded it through photography and digital photogrammetry (Figure 3).

Both guns featured a cypher that superimposes the letters H, D, and C, which has been interpreted as representing Henri II, his mistress Diane de Poitiers, and his Queen Catherine de Medici. Another symbol featured on these guns is a depiction of two bows with broken strings surrounding a crescent moon, emblematic of the moon goddess Diana the Huntress, which enforces the association with Diane de Poitiers. The crescent moon was adopted by the King when he became Dauphin in 1536 (Blackmore 1976:114-115). Both cannons feature the letter B, which Leluc and Pommier attribute to a gun founder whose identity has been lost to history, but who worked for both François I of France (1515-1547) and Henri II (1547-1559). Both also feature a fleur-de-lys, long the national symbol of France. The Pontault-Combault cannon also features an H surmounted by a crown, another clear reference to Henri II. The GME cannon bears a similar large H, albeit differing somewhat stylistically, though it cannot be observed if there is also a crown above it from the available photographs. Both cannons also have a fenestrated cascabel whose function is not fully understood. The two other bronze cannons discovered by GME were both reported to have fleurs-de-lys on their chases (Pritchett 2016:10).

There is no doubt that the GME cannons are French naval guns which likely were in use in 1565. The length (3 m) and bore diameter (15.24 cm) of the shipwrecked cannon described above indicates to Leluc that it was a *coulevrine moyenne* or *demi-culverine*. This could correspond to the *petite coulevrine* listed as part of *la Trinité*'s bronze armament in the commissioning papers of that ship (Bibliothèque National de France 1565, folio 36 recto; see also Meide and de Bry 2014:Table 1).

Other interested parties in attendance at the UNESCO meeting in Paris, included John de Bry, Florida State Historic Preservation Officer Timothy Parsons, James Delgado (then with NOAA and now with SEARCH), and James Pochurek and Michael

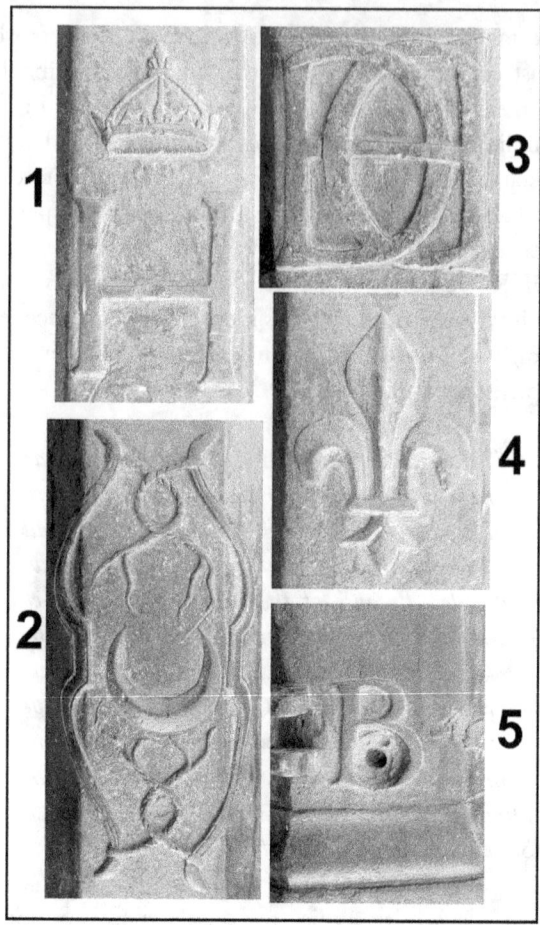

Figure 3: Details of markings cast into a bronze cannon (coulevrine) cast in 1547 and now in the collection of the Musée de l'Armée. At the time the photographs were taken (27 September 2016) this gun was in an offsite storage facility outside of Paris. Virtually identical markings have been observed on one of the three bronze guns from the *Trinité* wreckage. Key to markings: 1. The letter H surmounted by a crown, representing King Henri II (1547-1559). 2. Motif of two bows with broken strings surrounding a crescent moon, emblematic of the moon goddess Diana the Huntress, which enforces the association with the King's mistress Diane de Poitiers. The crescent moon was also a symbol of the King he adopted when he became Dauphin at the age of 17, after he began his long-term affair with de Poitiers. 3. A cypher that superimposes the letters H, D, and C, which has been interpreted as representing Henri II, his mistress Diane de Poitiers, and his Queen Catherine de Medici. 4. Fleur-de-lys, the symbol of France (similar fleurs-de-lys were on the other GME cannons as well). 5. The letter B surrounding the touchhole. This is believed to be the mark of a founder whose name is forgotten but who served both Henri II and his predecessor François I (1515-1547) (Photographs by Chuck Meide, courtesy of LAMP, 2016).

Arbuthnot of SEARCH. This group met with Michel L'Hour of the French government agency Département des Recherches Archéologiques Subaquatiques et Sous-Marines (DRASSM). While all parties understood the identity of the wreckage was not yet settled, it was understood that if the wreckage proved to be that of a sovereign French vessel then an international partnership between France and the State of Florida might be developed, similar to the agreement between France and Texas to manage the 1686 wreck *la Belle*.

The Legal Battle

After the Florida contingent returned home, a letter was sent to DHR on 4 October from the U.S. Navy acknowledging that France made a claim of ownership to the Ribault ships and that, while neither disputing nor endorsing that claim, the Navy "has a strong interest in ensuring the provisions and intent of the Sunken Military Craft Act are respected" and that the disturbance of a foreign military shipwreck "requires the authorization of the foreign sovereign [and] the law of finds does not apply to any foreign sunken military craft . . . and that no salvage rights or award shall be granted without the express permission of the relevant foreign state" (Thomas 2016:1).

On 5 October 2016, GME filed an Admiralty claim with the U.S. District Court in the Middle District of Florida, Orlando Division (Chapman 2015). GME alleged that the shipwreck or shipwreck scatter it had discovered was "subject to maritime peril," and that "any and all efforts by any previous owners and/or other parties and/or other entities to salvage the wreckage have been long since abandoned, with the exception of looters, who make no effort to report or document their work" (Chapman 2015:2, 5). GME sought declaratory judgements that the wreck site was subject to "admiralty laws of abandonment and the law of finds, or the maritime law of salvage," and that no government had the authority to interfere with GME's salvage of the wreck or the recovery of its artifacts (Chapman 2015:6). Further, GME requested the sole and exclusive ownership of the wreck and all recovered artifacts, or alternatively a "liberal salvage award" if it was found that another claimant owned the wreck (Chapman 2015:6).

GME filed the claim, just one day before Florida began to undergo the devastating impact of Hurricane Matthew, when a state of emergency had been declared, and as many as 1.5 million Floridians were evacuating their homes. This timing was quite possibly deliberate as the filing was made when state and private archaeologists were severely distracted, including the author whose home was rendered uninhabitable by flooding. As a result, there was a delay of approximately two weeks before knowledge of the court filing became known to Florida's archaeological community. The news was alarming and word was sent to French embassy officials and DRASSM through both formal and informal channels that there was a legal threat to France's claim to the wreck believed to be *la Trinité*.

There was some delay before France formalized an agreement with the American lawyer James Goold to serve as France's counsel, but France finally filed a verified claim on 22 November. The State of Florida shortly thereafter filed another, subordinate, claim, declaring support of France's claim, but stating that if the court ruled the wreck did not belong to France then it would belong to Florida under the Abandoned Shipwreck Act.

Goold is well-known for successfully representing Spain in a similar case when the treasure hunting company Odyssey Marine Exploration, Inc. attempted to claim the cargo it had salvaged from the warship *Nuestra Señora de Mercedes* lost in 1804. Goold initially reached out to the author on 21 October, which led to four meetings between 25 October and 21 December; these meetings involved Goold, the author, Dr. Sam Turner (at that time with LAMP), John de Bry, and on one occasion Brendan Burke. Turner and de Bry specialize in Spanish and French paleography; their skills were valuable as the group sorted through a variety of documents in order to make the best possible case that the shipwreck remains did indeed represent *la Trinité*.

The most fundamental French documents were the commissioning papers for Ribault's ships, which had originally been located and translated in 1993 by de Bry at the *Bibliothèque nationale de France* in Paris, in the manuscript section (*Département des manuscripts*), under *BnF, français* 21544. Despite GME's suggestion that Ribault's ships might have been privately owned (Pritchett 2016:15), these documents unequivocally proved that *la Trinité* was a crown ship; this was essential to the argument that the remains could only be claimed by France.

Goold believed it was also important to locate a primary document specifying that *la Trinité* wrecked at Cape Canaveral, using that explicit place name. The document in question turned out to be a letter Pedro Menéndez wrote in Cuba to King Felipe II on 5 December 1565, which was re-translated by Turner to clarify a previous error: "I had notice from the Indians that 70 to 80 French were gathered making a fort at Cape Canaveral and a vessel to send to France to ask for aid and that they had much artillery and munitions that they had removed from the flagship of Juan Rribao that was there lost" (Menéndez 1565).

GME's argument in court was that the shipwreck in question was not *la Trinité*, but a privately owned merchant vessel, possibly one belonging to Menéndez lost in 1572 carrying "war booty" from Charlesfort or Fort Caroline to Havana and which wrecked at Cape Canaveral (Pritchett 2016:15,44). The team consisting of Goold, the author, and the aforementioned Florida scholars set out to disprove any arguments that might support this hypothesis. The first goal was to identify the final disposition of any French cannon brought to Florida in the 1562 or 1564 expeditions. Could the cannons found by GME represent the French guns left at Charlesfort? The answer was no. When the beleaguered French settlers abandoned Charlesfort and sailed back to Europe in their makeshift vessel, they took these guns with them, according to Laudonnière's account (2001: 49) and the 1564 report of the Spaniard Enrique de Rojas (Wenhold 1959:58).

Next could the guns have come from Fort Caroline, and been lost on a ship Menéndez was using to transport them to Cuba? It makes little sense that Menéndez would ship cannon from Fort Caroline to Havana, as GME suggested. De Merás' 1567 biography of Menéndez (1964:123) records that Menéndez felt the need to bring more cannons to effectively protect Fort Caroline after its capture. This means he needed, not only the four existing French bronze guns at the fort, but additional artillery; thus, weakening the argument that he would have shipped the French guns elsewhere. Lyon (1976:134) also makes clear that Menéndez had a hostile relationship with Governor Garcia Osorio in Cuba, who refused (despite orders from the King) to give artillery to Menéndez to fortify *La Florida*. Thus, it absolutely makes no sense that Menéndez would be transporting Fort Caroline's captured guns to Cuba.

There was even more definitive proof. In April 1568, the French nobleman Dominique de Gourges attacked Fort Caroline (or San Mateo as the Spanish had re-named it), capturing the cannons there and taking them back to France, where he sold them to help recoup the costs of his expedition (McGrath 2000:164). John de Bry found and translated a letter from King Charles IX written 19 July 1568 explicitly stating these captured guns were the French cannons originally at Fort Caroline, in the form of a rhetorical (and sarcastic) question: "Didn't the artillery which he won over the Spanish bear our fleurs de lis?" (Douais 1897:186).

The other diagnostic French artifact found in the wreckage was the stone monument. The French described these makers as *bornes*, and they served as boundary markers to mark the territory of Charles IX (John de Bry 2016, pers. comm.). Only two *bornes* were erected in 1562. The disposition of the one at the River of May has been lost to history. However, the one at Charlesfort has been accounted for in the 1564 de Rojas report:

> *"By order of the captain this marker was taken down and thrown to the ground. There-upon the captain, in the presence of me, the scrivener, had the stone marker put into the boat to be taken to the* fragata *and carried to the governor at Havana. This was done and witnessed"* (Wenhold 1959:61).

A 14 September 1564 letter to the King indicates that this marker was subsequently transported from Havana to Seville (Christopher Allen 9 March and 12 April 2020, elec. comm.). Thus, it cannot have been lost at Cape Canaveral.

GME and its experts repeatedly asserted that there were no *bornes* or markers listed on *la Trinité*'s manifest (Pritchett 2016:8,43; Spaulding 2018:30), and so the wreck in question must have been carrying the marker presumably captured when Menéndez took Fort Caroline. However, the document they cite is not a traditional cargo manifest; rather, it is a register of artillery, munitions, and related supplies and, thus, it would not be expected to list territorial markers. (BnF 1565; Spaulding 2018:30). There is, however, a document that does indicate that *la Trinité* carried six such stone markers. Originally found by University of La Rochelle historian Mickaël Augeron but misplaced, it was subsequently relocated in the archives by Hélène Lhoumeau and could be presented to the court.

This document was written in code by Francés de Alava, the Spanish ambassador in the French court who served King Felipe II as a spy. Dated 19 January 1566, it relates the arrival from Florida of Jean Ribault's son, and goes on to mention the loss of *la Trinité* along with six *bornes*:

> *"Of the captain [Ribault] who went from Bordeau in the small ship (of which I have written your majesty), to la Florida, it is also understood*

> *here that a Spanish ship sent it to the bottom. And they felt this keenly because it carried six marble columns with the arms of this king and many epitaphs to put them in the fort of la Florida"* (de Avala 1566).

Ultimately these and other data were incorporated by Goold into more than 800 pages of evidence, with declarations from four experts including Leluc, Delgado, the French Embassy's Attaché for Judicial Affairs, and historian Frank Lestringant of the Sorbonne. This was presented to the court to make the case for *la Trinité*.

The Ruling

Judge Karla R. Spaulding issued her 35-page ruling on 29 June 2018 (Spaulding 2018). After conducting a review of the various parties' briefs, along with the substantial evidence filed in support of their motions, Judge Spaulding concluded that the Republic of France had established, through a preponderance of the evidence, that the wreck was indeed *la Trinité*, and therefore a sovereign vessel still owned by France and outside of the court's jurisdiction. With that, the court granted the Republic of France's motion to dismiss GME's admiralty claim and noted that the State of Florida's subordinate claim was rendered moot. The specific finding of the judge was emphatic:

> *"Based on the above evidence, the Court concludes that the res is* La Trinité. *The res is located near Cape Canaveral, which is where* La Trinité *is known to have sunk. The shipwreck site includes cannons that correspond to the artillery register of* La Trinité. *And* La Trinité *was known to be carrying a stone monument similar to the monument found at the shipwreck site. Taken together, these facts establish by a preponderance of the evidence that the res is* La Trinité. *See also Delgado Dec., Doc. No. 75-16 ¶ 56-58 (opining that the res is* La Trinité*). GME has not come forward with sufficient evidence to undermine this conclusion. Instead, GME and its experts rely for the most part on speculation: Maybe some unnamed non-French ship somehow gained control of cannons like those on* La Trinité *and a territorial monument like that on* La Trinité *and then happened to sink in the exact place that* La Trinité *is known to have sunk—all without leaving any documentary evidence that can be presented to the Court. Such arguments, "which simply advance metaphysical doubt," "propos[e] explanations other than the obvious," and suggest pure happenstance as the "more reasonable hypothesis" are not persuasive"* (Spaulding 2018:33).

Conclusion

GME declined to appeal this ruling in the time allowed, rendering this decision the final verdict as to the ownership of the wreckage off Cape Canaveral. GME is currently engaged in a lawsuit against the State of Florida, seeking damages related to the data it turned over to the State as required by its 1A-31 permit. At the time of this writing, this legal action is still underway. In December 2018, it was announced that France and the State of Florida would jointly investigate and manage this shipwreck. In February 2019, a delegation of DRASSM archaeologists, along with the French consulate in Miami, came to North Florida to meet with DHR, SEARCH, and LAMP to discuss how such an investigation might be carried out. Future research goals and activities will be developed by DRASSM and the DHR. This has the promise to increase our understanding of this immensely significant shipwreck and its brief but formative contribution to Florida's history.

Acknowledgments

Thank you to the many individuals and organizations whose efforts led to the positive outcome of the court case, including Jim Goold, counsel for France, John de Bry of the Center for Historical Archaeology, Michel L'Hour and the French agency DRASSM, Florida Secretary of State Ken Detzner, David Fugett, John Glogau, and other Florida state lawyers, SHPO Tim Parsons, Mary Glowacki, Ryan Duggins, and other DHR staff, Sam Turner and Jim Delgado at SEARCH, David Howe at the Institute of Maritime History, Kathy Fleming of the St. Augustine Lighthouse & Maritime Museum, and former LAMP Associate Director Brendan Burke.

References

ARNOLD, J. BARTO III AND ROBERT S. WEDDLE
1978 *The Nautical Archeology of Padre Island: the Spanish Shipwrecks of 1554.* Academic Press, New York.

BIBLIOTHÈQUE NATIONAL DE FRANCE (BnF)
1565   Register of Artillery and Utensils Dependent of the Said Artillery for *la Trinité*, 28 April 1565, Départment des Manuscrits, BnF, français 21544

BLACKMORE, H. L.
1976   *The Armouries of the Tower of London*. Volume I. Ordnance. H. M. Stationery Office, London.

CHAPMAN, BARRY R.
2015   Global Marine Exploration, Inc., v. The Unidentified, Wrecked and (for Finders-Right Purposes) Abandoned Sailing Vessel, Verified Complaint in Admiralty *In Rem*. Case No. 6:16-cv-01742-GKS-KRS, Document 1, Filed 5 October 2016 in U.S. District Court for the Middle District of Florida, Orlando Division.

DE AVALA, FRANCÉS
1566   Letter to King Felipe II, 19 January, AGS, Estado K 1505, Simancas, Spain.

DOUAIS, C. (EDITOR)
1897   *Lettres de Charles IX à M. de Fourquevaux, Ambassedeur en Espagne,* 1565-1572. Paris.

DUGGINS, R. AND FRANKLIN H. PRICE
2016   Underwater Archaeological Site Assessment: Cape Canaveral 1A-31 Permit 2015.03. Bureau of Archaeological Research, Division of Historical Resources, Tallahassee.

EMBASSY OF THE REPUBLIC OF FRANCE
2016   Diplomatic Note to the U.S. Department of State, 8 July, Washington, D.C.

ESCALANTE DE MENDOZA, JUAN DE
1985   *Itinerario de Navegacion de los mares y tierras occidentales* 1575. Museo Naval Madrid, Madrid.

GLOBAL MARINE EXPLORATION, INC. (GME)
2015   2015 GLOBAL MARINE EXPLORATION TEAM DISCOVER FOUR 16TH CENTURY SHIPWRECK SITES OFF CAPE CANAVERAL. *Global Marine Exploration, Inc. Newsletter* 34 (September 2015):1-2.

2016a   *Global Marine Exploration, Inc. Newsletter* 44 (July 2016):1-2.

2016b   Global Marine Exploration, Inc., Discovers Highly Important Shipwreck Artifacts in Waters of Cape Canaveral, Florida. Press release, EIN Presswire, Washington, D.C. <https://www.einnews.com/pr_news/339155600/global-marine-exploration-inc-discovers-highly-important-shipwreck-artifacts-in-waters-of-cape-canaveral-florida>Accessed 8 March 2020.

LAUDONNIÈRE, RENÉ GOULAINE DE
2001   *Three Voyages*. Charles E. Bennett, translator. University of Alabama Press, Tuscaloosa.

LYON, EUGENE
1976   *The Enterprise of Florida: Pedro Menéndez de Avilés and the Spanish Conquest of 1565-1568*. University Press of Florida, Gainesville.

MCGRATH, JOHN T.
2000   *The French in Early Florida: In the Eye of the Hurricane*. University Press of Florida, Gainesville.

MEIDE, CHUCK
2015   The Search for the Lost French Fleet of 1565: Results of the 2014 Survey. In *ACUA Underwater Archaeology Proceedings 2015*, Marco Meniketti, editor, pp. 79-88. Advisory Council on Underwater Archaeology, Seattle, WA.

MEIDE, CHUCK AND JOHN DE BRY
2014   The Lost French Fleet of 1565: Collision of Empires. In *ACUA Underwater Archaeology Proceedings 2014*, Charles Dagneau and Karolyn Gauvin, editors, pp. 79-92. Advisory Council on Underwater Archaeology, Quebec City.

MENÉNDEZ, PEDRO
1565   Letter to the King, 5 December. AGI Santo Domingo 15, 54-1-31. Microfilm copy held in the Stetson Collection, St. Augustine Historical Society, St. Augustine, FL.

PARSONS, TIMOTHY
2016   Letter to Chuck Meide, 6 July. Lighthouse Archaeological Maritime Program, St. Augustine, FL.

PRITCHETT, ROBERT H. III
2016   Final Dig & Identify Report and Request for Rescue Recovery Permit, 08-24-2015 through 06-28-2016, Permit # 2015.03 - Brevard County, Florida. Report to Bureau of Archaeological Research, from Global Marine Exploration, Inc., Tampa, FL.

SINCLAIR, JAMES
2015   Archaeological Research Design Plan Permit # 2015.03 - Brevard County, Florida. Report to Bureau of Archaeological Research, from Global Marine Exploration, Inc., Tampa, FL.

SPAULDING, KARLA R.
2018   Global Marine Exploration, Inc., v. The Unidentified, Wrecked and (for Finders-Right Purposes) Abandoned Sailing Vessel, Order (And Directions to the Clerk of the Court). Case No. 6:16-cv-01742-GKS-KRS, Document 106, Filed 29 June in U.S. District Court for the Middle District of Florida, Orlando Division.

THOMAS, J.B., JR.
2016   Letter to Timothy Parsons, 4 October. Florida Division of Historical Resources, Tallahassee.

TINNISWOOD, J. T.
1945   Anchors and Accessories, 1340-1640. *Mariner's Mirror* 31(2): 84-105.

WENHOLD, LUCY L.
1959   Manrique de Rojas' Report on French Settlement in Florida, 1564. *Florida Historical Quarterly* 38:45-62.

. . . .

Chuck Meide
St. Augustine Lighthouse Archaeological Maritime Program (LAMP)
St. Augustine Lighthouse & Maritime Museum
81 Lighthouse Avenue
St Augustine, FL 32080

Archaeological Investigations at La Isabela, Dominican Republic

Tori L. Galloway, Charles D. Beeker, Denise Jaffke, Claudia C. Johnson

Indiana University (IU) is assisting the Dominican Republic with the assessment of terrestrial and underwater archaeological components of La Isabela settlement. Founded by Christopher Columbus in 1494 on his second voyage, the settlement site has remains of structures from the first European-style colony in the Americas. IU efforts include providing recommendations for long-term stabilization of the eroded cliff, as identified in the UNESCO Technical Assistance Mission Action Plan, as well as continued underwater survey. IU's previous survey has resulted in thirty-one underwater magnetic anomalies adjacent to the settlement that may represent one or more of the ships of Columbus.

Historical Overview

La Isabela, regarded as America's first European town, is an historic settlement on the north coast of Hispaniola, present-day Dominican Republic. The settlement, founded by Christopher Columbus on his second voyage in 1494, is situated on a limestone terrace overlooking Isabela Bay. Historically, Isabela Bay provided relatively secure anchorage, fresh water from the Bajabonico River, a nearby delta plain for agriculture, an abundance of Pleistocene limestone, and an elevated promontory ideal for a fortress (James and Beeker 1994). Columbus was said by Las Casas to have "hasteneded to proceed the building of a fort to guard their provisions and ammunitions, of a church, a hospital and a sturdy house for himself; he distributed land plots, traced a common square and streets; the important people were grouped together in a section of the planned township and everyone was told to start building his own house. Public buildings were made of stone, individuals used straw and wood…" (Collard 1971; Deagan and Cruxent 2002a). Whatever the reason may have been for choosing La Isabela as the first European settlement site in the New World, it is known to have lasted for only a few years (Deagan and Cruxent 2002b; James and Beeker 1994; Sale 1991). By order of the Spanish crown, a new permanent settlement, Santo Domingo de Guzman, was established on the south coast of Hispaniola at the mouth of the Ozama river. By 1498, La Isabela was completely abandoned (James and Beeker 1994).

Before Columbus's arrival to La Isabela, the site was likely inhabited and abandoned by Taíno peoples, though drawing social and cultural distinctions based on imposed geographic boundaries and determining the timespan of occupation between inhabitants is undoubtedly complex (Deagan and Cruxent 2002a). Those claiming Taíno and Dominican heritage continued to occupy the site for nearly four hundred years after Columbus's La Isabela, before being relocated by the government in order to continue archaeological investigations and the designation as a national park (Deagan and Cruxent 2002a). La Isabela is known to have actively-forming reefs, dynamic coastal change, and intense geological processes over the span of the settlement, which have changed the site drastically and must be considered when analyzing the social context over a historical span. The site has been mapped and surveyed by many archaeologists and explorers since 1891, but significant looting and human influence are generally known to have affected Isabela more than the passage of time (Ober 1893).

La Isabela Settlement

As understood today, La Isabela is made up of two colonial sites: El Castillo (Figure 1), which included

Figure 1: Drone photography over El Castillo portion of La Isabela (Jaffke and Kramer 2019).

the fortified house of Columbus, the storehouse (or *alhóndiga*), a powderhouse, a watchtower, and a church, and Las Coles, which is understood to be the portion dedicated to colonial living and service work, according to excavations by Kathleen Deagan and José Cruxent (2002a). Like Deagan and Cruxent's work, a number of archaeological surveys have been done both terrestrially and underwater at La Isabela. Deagan and Cruxent are largely to thank for the most complete compilation and interpretation of La Isabela as a whole. From their discoveries at Las Coles, the theory that materials used to build La Isabela were created in Europe changed to fit a narrative based on evidence (Deagan and Cruxent 1993). With the interpretations that stem from Las Coles and the service work that occurred there, regular loading and un-loading of ships could have occurred at Isabela Bay to accommodate the production and trade happening at Las Coles and El Castillo (Deagan and Cruxent 2002a; James and Beeker 1994). La Isabela provides a unique glimpse into early relations between Columbus's colony and the indigenous people of the Dominican Republic.

The first survey, conducted in 1891 by Frederick Ober, mapped the geography of La Isabela and has continued to provide a baseline for geologic change of the "well-situated rock", or the limestone promontory upon which Columbus founded his settlement (Las Casas 1985; Ober 1893). Since then, no fewer than twelve archaeological surveys have been conducted at La Isabela, yielding information on site layout, indigenous life, and political and natural events that affected the settlement (Deagan and Cruxent 2002a). During this time, the site was turned into *El Parque Nacional Solar de Las Américas*, where multiple efforts have been made to successfully showcase the heritage at La Isabela and generate tourism. None of these efforts have proven sustainable thus far.

In addition to numerous terrestrial surveys, Isabela Bay has been surveyed four times with remote sensing technologies. The first magnetometer data were collected during an underwater survey by the Institute of Nautical Archaeology (INA) in 1983 (INA 1985). In 1996, IU conducted a subsequent magnetometer survey, which provided results consistent with the 1983 INA survey (Panamerican Consultants 1996). IU conducted a third survey in 2006 and recovered a kedge anchor adjacent to a significant anomaly, followed by a fourth magnetometer survey in 2010 in order to confirm the exact location of previously-recorded anomalies before beginning excavation (Figure 2) (Panamerican Consultants 2010).

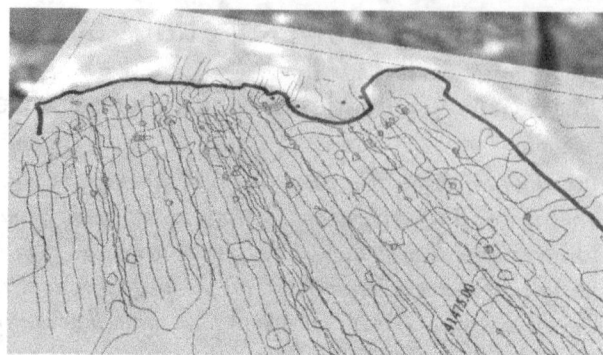

Figure 2: Magnetometer data from the 2010 IU survey, showing thirty-one magnetic anomalies in Isabela Bay (Panamerican Consultants 2010).

All surveys yielded 28-31 anomalies of similar sizes and locations, proving that the data are accurate and reliable.

Excavations were attempted during each of the four magnetometer surveys (INA 1985; Panamerican Consultants 2010). In 1983, INA reached a depth nearly 3.5m below the sapropel, the thick, gelatinous sediment that covers the floor of the bay (INA 1985). The test pit did not yield any archaeological material. During the 2010 survey, IU reached a depth of approximately 3.0m below the seafloor (Panamerican Consultants 2010). While these surveys were unsuccessful in locating a shipwreck associated with La Isabela, it should be noted that an anchor was located and recovered during the 2006 IU survey; it was taken to the *Dirección General de Patrimonio Cultural Subacuático* (DGPCS) laboratory in Santo Domingo, on the advice of the DGPCS's technical director. An additional anchor was reportedly salvaged from Isabela Bay by INA in 1983, though its location is unknown today (Beeker 2020; INA 1985). Future underwater survey will include additional remote sensing methodologies to confirm previously obtained magnetometer data, using new and improved technologies.

Today, the site is still considered valuable for the understanding that continues to stem from archaeological research, especially given the potential for associated shipwrecks. The remains at La Isabela, including possible shipwrecks and their cargoes, could hold information from the time of Columbus, a period of contact that undoubtedly changed the course of history on a global scale. Indigenous people lived at La Isabela before Columbus and continued to do so after Columbus, though claims to heritage and identity changed significantly with the cultural blending that occurred from European colonialism and an expanded economy (Deagan and Cruxent 2002a). Additional value in La Isabela stems from the continued hopes at revenue generated from tourism.

Based upon the 2007 UNESCO Technical Assistance Mission Workshop, held between a number of institutional stakeholders including archaeologists from Indiana University's Center for Underwater Science, a World Heritage nomination should not be pursued until a number of factors have been addressed. The most pressing of these factors is the eroding cliff of El Castillo (Action 4.1: UNESCO 2007). This portion of the site has experienced drastic erosion and disruption from geological processes and anthropogenic factors. Situated on the edge of the cliff face is the eroding house of Columbus, which has continued to deteriorate as materials slip into the sea underneath (Figure 3). This structure, the only remaining intact remnant of El Castillo that survived the site gradings in the 1940s and 1950s, will continue to erode, based on historical knowledge and consultation from geologists and cliff-stabilization specialists (Deagan and Cruxent 2002a; IU 2019). As an original and non-renewable part of La Isabela settlement, the remaining house structure should be the top priority of site managers if they wish to pursue future World Heritage nomination and preserve what remains of La Isabela. This site is inherently important to understanding early Colonial trade and relationships with the Native groups in the Dominican Republic and is a tangible memory for those who identify with heritage of the region or country. To allow this memory to disappear into the ocean would be another trauma inflicted on involved communities.

IU Center for Underwater Science researchers have recommended depositing a large volume of riprap at the base of the calcareous cliff and extending seaward. The riprap will fill a space that supports the steep cliff face and prevents further erosion (see La Isabela Settlement Technical Report 2019 for details). A visual survey was conducted to ensure that biological resources on the terrace would be unaffected by stabilization efforts. To ensure that no underwater cultural or biological resources would be affected by this stabilization effort, IU researchers used SCUBA to survey the area for sensitive materials. No cultural material was located in the immediate area. One ceramic block was found near the historic wharf structure to the north, where it was photographed in-situ.

Work is actively being conducted at La Isabela by representatives from the country's Ministry of Culture. Current activity at La Isabela proves that the settlement site is important to the country's heritage, despite being ignored historically. Should stakeholders invest to make La Isabela a highly visited heritage site, funding is available for site improvement. Ideally, any funding that is brought in to prepare La Isabela for tourism would be focused on cliff stabilization and site maintenance. Any remaining funding should be applied toward existing structure maintenance, site managers, interpretative materials, and collections management, all of which have impeded successful heritage tourism ventures in the past.

Current Investigations

During 2019, IU researchers conducted three surveys at La Isabela. These surveys were largely in preparation for underwater excavation intended for Summer 2021. During the three surveys that were conducted, partners were brought in from California State Parks and Mexico's *Instituto Nacional de Antropología e Historia* to provide consultation on a series of issues concerning La Isabela. During the May survey, researchers documented the house of Columbus and the immediate cliff area. On the return June survey, researchers used drone photography to expand on 3D photogrammetric models made in May. These drone images were used to construct a 3D model of the entire cliff face and settlement site of La Isabela, in order to monitor and visualize the structural integrity of the site and provide recommendations based off of obtained knowledge (Figure 4). During the December survey, IU researchers used SCUBA as a tool to survey the immediate area underneath the cliff to ensure that no cultural or biological material would be affected during cliff stabilization procedures. IU researchers visited the associated stone quarry during these surveys, representative of 15th century limestone processing technologies, to understand the greater site context. By looking at the geological processes that

Figure 3: A 3D photogrammetric model of the eroding cliff face at La Isabela (Indiana University 2019).

Figure 4: Aerial drone 3D photogrammetry of La Isabela (Jaffke and Kramer 2019).

have affected Isabela, researchers may better be able to understand how the underwater landscape has changed since the time of Columbus.

Following 2019 surveys, IU submitted recommendations to involved government agencies in support of required maintenance necessary to advance the condition and interpretation of La Isabela. IU plans to continue working with a number of institutional partners during the next four years to re-survey the underwater landscape of Isabela Bay containing previously confirmed magnetic anomalies and to survey the underwater portion not previously surveyed. In the instance that magnetic anomalies support past data, IU will work with stakeholders to excavate on suspect anomalies.

Photogrammetric Modeling Methodologies

During 2019 surveys, IU collected images at La Isabela in order to create highly accurate 3D models through computer-vision photogrammetry. Images were collected by drone and GoPro photography of the cliff face, El Castillo site, and of individual artifacts. Computer-vision photogrammetry uses two-dimensional images to reconstruct three-dimensional models, which have proven useful for site and artifact monitoring, data collection, and for making heritage accessible to those who cannot see or experience it in person, through virtual reality and online platforms. Images were processed in Agisoft Metashape using a standard workflow to generate a sparse point cloud, dense point cloud, mesh, and texture, in that order (Agisoft 2016). Animation was added in Metashape to 3D models of the cliff and house of Columbus to create a digital tour effect. The digital mapping methodologies employed during 2019 surveys at La Isabela were designed to be time efficient and inexpensive, so that they may be repeated and compared in future surveys.

IU hopes that these models will be used to monitor La Isabela over time and will allow stakeholders to identify and address any deterioration of the site with maximum efficiency.

Heritage Management

While the house of Columbus is undoubtedly the highest concern for the future success and preservation of La Isabela settlement, increased interpretation and maintenance is required in order to support sustainable tourism and accurately represent the history of La Isabela, gathered from both local knowledge and archaeological data. Located on-site in *El Solar de las Americas, El Museo Isabela* currently lacks adequate interpretation to display and promote the site's traumatic history. The museum displays, without interpretation, artifacts excavated or gathered from other sites in the Dominican Republic, including some of the earliest known horseshoes in the Americas (Deagan and Cruxent 2002a). In order to generate revenue, increased efforts to make the site accessible to tourists have contributed to a lack of accurate outreach regarding La Isabela's history. This will only be overcome when a variety of stakeholders urge for a fair and balanced understanding of La Isabela to be displayed and taught to the public. In an effort to do so, IU has continued to facilitate government cooperation between the Dominican Republic's Ministry of Culture, Ministry of Environment, and Ministry of Tourism, along with other stakeholders. With this cooperation, IU continues to facilitate scientific research and community involvement with the assistance of the Dominican non-profit *El Museo Subacuática*, local knowledge, and continued research in order to work through the difficulties and impediments that past heritage management of La Isabela has created.

The Future of Heritage Management at La Isabela

Local communities undoubtedly share a stake in heritage management at La Isabela, evidenced by their heritage, proximity to the site, and knowledge of the land. By relying upon and sharing gained understanding from La Isabela with local communities and stakeholders, archaeologists can work to rewrite the largely one-sided history. While the site is still accessible to local communities and tourists alike, though there are few tourists, the work of heritage managers undoubtedly has implications on the local community. In order for La

Isabela to sustainably support tourism and local heritage stakeholders, the settlement requires maintenance and interpretation, decided upon through consultation and discourse between heritage stakeholders, government entities, and cultural heritage managers. This is an attempt to address the negative ramifications from past archaeological excavations, through organized and systematic methodological approaches for handling previously collected and looted artifacts and public outreach promoting in-situ preservation and common-pool resource management. Archaeological excavation of an associated shipwreck could work to tell both the European and Taíno heritage of La Isabela, as well as answer a number of questions regarding early Iberian seafaring and European colonialism in the Caribbean. IU's Center for Underwater Science has continued discourse with communities in the Dominican Republic promoting in-situ preservation and the importance of heritage management, which local communities are beginning to adopt and view as non-renewable, common pool resources. This work promotes the cooperation of all three government agencies and contributes to a larger dialogue regarding heritage management on a national scale. This shift in resource management is largely due to the work of the Living Museums in the Sea model, developed by IU's Center for Underwater Science for protection and promotion of significant underwater cultural landscapes (Beeker and Hanselmann 2010). The Living Museums in the Sea model, a resource management network dedicated to protecting and promoting underwater cultural heritage and biological resources, is based off of Elinor Ostrom's Common Pool Resource Management Theory (Barbash-Riley 2015; Ostrom 2002). IU first implemented the Living Museums in the Sea model in the Dominican Republic in 2011; there are currently five Living Museum sites in the country, creating a regional network of shipwreck sites that support public visitation, heritage management, and tourism (Beeker et al. 2012).

Ultimately, IU's Center for Underwater Science hopes to continue ongoing archaeological survey of the underwater landscape directly surrounding La Isabela. Beginning in 1983, magnetometer surveys were conducted at least four times (INA 1985; Panamerican Consultants 1996, 2010). The results from these surveys provide fairly consistent data, proving that one or more large shipwreck(s) could lie in the immediate area, under a thick deposit of sapropel that has accumulated over the past hundreds of years. If these data align with the historical descriptions of the sinking events associated with Columbus's second fleet and the 1495 hurricanes, an invaluable glimpse into the first contact at La Isabela could be uncovered. In order to do so, IU will team with the *Instituo Nacional de Antropología e Historia*, Panamerican Consultants, the University of Miami, the Submerged Archaeological Conservancy International, and *El Museo Subacuática* to continue the search for the Lost Fleet of Columbus during Summer 2021. This process involves strenuous permitting requirements from all government entities and importation of infrastructure in order to support a large-scale underwater survey, all of which require extensive planning and take time and political negotiation to implement. All parties are hopeful that this search is productive and that the data that can be understood from an excavation of this type will be informative and meaningful in representing the heritage of the Dominican Republic and colonialism of the New World.

Conclusions

The logistical and survey data obtained during the past decades of research will serve to guide future archaeological efforts at La Isabela. IU's Center for Underwater Science plans to resurvey the entire bay area with the most current remote sensing technologies, covering previously surveyed areas as well as the unexplored portion of Isabela Bay. Test pits will be selected for priority anomalies located during the upcoming survey. The archaeological and historical significance of any 15th-century Spanish vessels cannot be over-emphasized; these ships were some of the first known vessels "capable of making reliable, round-trip, oceanic voyages" (INA 1985). These shipwrecks offer a unique opportunity to understand and interpret this important period in maritime history. Their discovery may provide answers to questions concerning early Iberian ship construction during the "Age of Exploration," the early Spanish colonial economy, and social interactions between European colonists and the Taíno. Although many controversies surround Columbus's colonization of the New World, this contact between distinct cultures undoubtedly affected the globe. By understanding the full context of La Isabela through the settlement site and associated shipwrecks, the conflicted story of Taíno and European colonial heritage can be accurately interpreted and acknowledged.

References

AGISOFT LLC
2016   Agisoft Photoscan User Manual: Professional Edition, Version 1.2. St. Petersburg, Russia.

BARBASH-RILEY, LYDIA
2015   "Using a Community-Based Strategy to Address the Impacts of Globalization on Underwater Cultural Heritage Management in the Dominican Republic," *Indiana Journal of Global Legal Studies:* Vol. 22: Issue 1, Article 11.

BEEKER, CHARLES
2020   Personal Interview. January 10, 2020.

BEEKER, CHARLES D., CLAUDIA C. JOHNSON, LOREN CLARK, EMILY PALMER, AND MATTHEW J. MAUS
2012   "Living Museums of the Sea in the Dominican Republic: Bridging the Gap Between Cultural and Biological Resources." Poster abstract, 46th Annual Conference on Historical and Underwater Archaeology, Society for Historical Archaeology. Leicester, UK.

BEEKER, CHARLES D. AND FREDERICK H. HANSELMANN,
2010   "Living Museums in the Sea: Annual Accomplishments and Accrual Report: Year One." Report submitted to the US Agency for International Development (USAID).

COLLARD, ANDRÉ
1971   *Las Casas: History of the Indies.* Translator and editor. New York: Harper and Row.

DEAGAN, KATHLEEN AND JOSÉ MARÍA CRUXENT
1993   "From Contact to Criollos: The Archaeology of Spanish Colonization in Hispaniola". Proceedings of the British Academy, Vol. 81, edited by Warwick Bray, pp. 67-104. Oxford University Press, London.

2002a   *Archaeology at La Isabela: America's First European Town.* New Haven and London: Yale University Press.

2002b   Columbus's outpost among the Taínos: Spain and America at La Isabela, 1493-1498. New Haven and London: Yale University Press.

INDIANA UNIVERSITY CENTER FOR UNDERWATER SCIENCE
2019   La Isabela Settlement Technical Report. Submitted to: *Ministerio d Medio Ambiente y Recursos Naturales; Ministerio de Cultura; Ministerio de Turismo.*

INSTITUTE OF NAUTICAL ARCHAEOLOGY
1985   "An Archaeological Survey of La Isabela, Dominican Republic". Technical Report. Submitted by: Donald H. Keith and Bruce F. Thompson. Exploration and Discovery Research Team and Morning Watch Research.

JAFFKE, DENISE AND KENNETH KRAMER
2019   La Isabela Coastal Erosion Assessment & Recommendations. Technical Report. Prepared for: Indiana University Center for Underwater Science. Submitted to: *Ministerio de Cultura (República Dominicana).*

JAMES, STEPHEN AND CHARLES BEEKER
1994   "Fifteenth and Sixteenth-Century Spanish Seafaring in the Caribbean". Society for Historical Archaeology.

LAS CASAS, BARTOLOMÉ DE
1985   *Historia de las Indias.* Serie V Centenario de Descubrimiento de las Américas. 3 volumes. Santo Domingo: Edicioned del Continente.

OBER, FREDERICK
1893   *In the Wake of Columbus.* D. Lothrop Company. Boston, Massachusetts.

OSTROM, ELINOR
2002   *Common-pool resources and institutions: Toward a revised theory,* Handbook of Agricultural Economics, Chapter 24. Elsevier, Volume 2, Part A.

PANAMERICAN CONSULTANTS
1996   "Remote Sensing Investigations: La Bahia Isabela, Dominican Republic". Technical Report. Authored by Michael C. Tuttle. Submitted To: Indiana University.

2010   "Submerged Cultural Resources Survey for Columbus Fleet Shipwrecks in La Bahia Isabela, Dominican Republic". Technical Report. Submitted To: Indiana University, *Oficina Nacional de Patrimonio Cultural Subacuático.*

SALE, KIRKPATRICK
1991   *The Conquest of Paradise: Christopher Columbus and the Columbian Legacy.* Alfred A. Knofe Inc., New York.

UNESCO
2007   "La Isabela Historical and Archaeological Site, Dominican Republic: Report of the UNESCO Technical Assistance Mission". UNESCO Regional Bureau of Culture in Latin American and the Caribbean.

Tori L. Galloway
1025 E 7th St, Room 058
Bloomington, Indiana 47405

Charles D. Beeker
1025 E 7th St, Room 058
Bloomington, Indiana 47405

Claudia C. Johnson
001 E. 10th St
Bloomington, IN 47405

Denise Jaffke
1416 9th Street, Rm 905
Sacramento, CA 95814

The Effects of Major Hurricane Events on Shipwreck Site Vulnerability in the Florida Keys

Airielle R. Cathers

Since the 1970s, 163 Atlantic tropical and subtropical cyclones have impacted the state of Florida; eleven were major hurricanes. Hurricanes and other major storm events may cause severe impacts to submerged cultural resources depending upon the resources' characteristics. As the climate continues to change, increasing the severity of these impacts, site vulnerability assessments and post-storm evaluations are important tools for the management of these sites. This study proposes vulnerability criteria and presents four case studies of shipwrecks in the Florida Keys. Investigations of these sites reveal varying impacts from Hurricane Irma and the applicability of the site assessment methodology.

Introduction

In the last three decades, overall hurricane intensity has increased worldwide, most notably observed in the North Atlantic (Lim et al. 2018, Emanuel 2005, Webster et al. 2005). During the 2017 Atlantic hurricane season, meteorologists documented six major hurricanes (Category 3 status or higher on the Saffir-Simpson wind scale), making it the third most active season on record. According to Lim (et al. 2018) and the National Oceanic and Atmospheric Administration (NOAA)'s Geophysical Fluid Dynamics Laboratory (NOAA GFDL 2019), higher sea-surface temperatures in the eastern Marine Development Region combined with record-breaking ocean heat content are linked to expanded tropical cyclones. This is based on models showing an increase in the global proportion of tropical cyclones that reach a Category 4 or 5, not in the overall increase in hurricane numbers. The majority of models show little to no change in the general increase in tropical cyclone frequency, independent of the intensity (NOAA GFDL 2019). As of 2020, there are uncertain predictions regarding the size of tropical storms in response to anthropogenic climate change. Nevertheless, this increase in hurricane intensity will amplify the degradation of submerged cultural resources.

A variety of physical factors exhibit passive and active forces over submerged cultural resources. The theoretical studies of Muckelroy (1978), Murphy (1983), Schiffer (1987), and Gibbs (2006) help with this understanding of the specific forces that transform shipwreck sites over time. In terms of site formation, environmental forces encompass biological, chemical, and physical factors. Physical scrambling devices at the magnitude of hurricanes and major storms are the forces that often pose the most rapid and evident damage to submerged sites. Notable cases of recent hurricane induced site damage can be seen in the coastal Atlantic regions. In 1992, Hurricane Andrew produced strong enough storm surges to shift sediment on the seabed, exposing various historic artifacts and sites (Davis et al. 1993: 36). In 2005, Hurricanes Katrina and Rita caused extensive damage to offshore oil and gas platforms and pipes. The knowledge of these impacts resulted in a cultural impact assessment of ten shipwrecks in the Gulf of Mexico led by the Bureau of Ocean Energy Management, Regulation and Enforcement. Hurricane impacts ranged between sites, with subsurface conditions resulting in structural hull damage to one wreck and complete reburial of another (Gearhart et al. 2011). In Biscayne National Park (BISC), archaeologists noted exposure of the Pillar Dollar Wreck due to shifting sands during Hurricane Wilma in 2005 (Price 2015: 38).

The shipwreck sites presented within this study are located in the Florida Keys. The sites, like the majority of the shipwrecks found here, tend to reside in shallow, high-energy environments and are at an increased risk of disturbance due to such major storms. Post-hurricane resource surveys in the Florida Keys following these major weather events, documented significant damage to both the natural environment and cultural remains. Submerged cultural resources are a finite and nonrenewable resource (Jameson & Scott-Ireton, 2007). Once these sites are gone, the associated cultural heritage is also lost. Federal resource managers from the National Park Service and NOAA's Office of National Marine Sanctuaries (ONMS) are responsible for protecting, managing, and educating the public about submerged cultural resources in the Florida Keys.

Hurricane Irma

Hurricane Irma was a devastating Category 5 hurricane that initially formed on 30 August 2017, over the Atlantic Ocean. Moving north, Irma made landfall on 10 September as a Category 4 hurricane on Cudjoe Key to the lower Florida Keys. As it moved over the lower Keys and up the western coast of Florida, it left a trail of destruction in its path, causing an estimated 50 billion dollars of damage to infrastructure, businesses, and personal property (NOAA 2018). NOAA documented extensive sediment movement along Florida's Reef Track and various levels of biological damage done to the region. Reports from dive community members to resource managers suggested that multiple submerged cultural resources had moved, been buried, uncovered, or otherwise altered due to the storm (Marano 2018, Matthew Lawrence 2018 pers. comm.).

Study Objectives

To address these issues, this study presents a basic methodology for quantifying the effects of non-cultural impacts, principally hurricanes, on shipwrecks within the Florida Keys. It aims to provide a cost effective, quick, and straightforward way for resource managers to assess the current condition and overall stability of the sites within their jurisdiction. This then allows resource managers to prioritize pre-hurricane mitigation and post-hurricane documentation based on overall site vulnerability.

Four sites in the upper Keys region were selected to assess vulnerability: *Nuestra Señora del Populo*, *San Pedro*, SS *City of Washington*, and SS *Benwood*

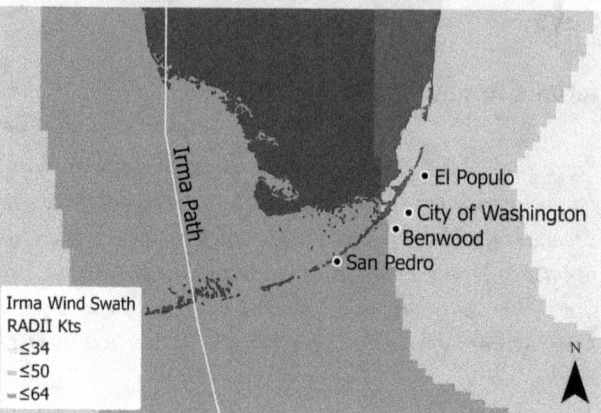

Figure 1: Map of Hurricane Irma's path and wind swath over the study area (Map by author, 2019).

(Figure 1). These sites benefited from previous documentation (prior to Irma in 2017) and exemplified different construction types and stages of site formation. The findings addressed the following questions:

1. Can resource managers, using photogrammetric/ orthomosaic images taken before and after a major hurricane, visually detect archaeological site changes in a quantifiable manner?
2. What factors contribute to site vulnerability?
3. Can cultural resource managers use a Site Vulnerability Classification and Baseline Characterization Assessment to identify resources most vulnerable to storm impacts?

Marine Sanctuary (FKNMS), University of Miami (UM), and Indiana University (IU) dove each site to collect site images and conduct a general Baseline

BASELINE CHARACTERIZATION ASSESSMENT					
Stability	Structural Relief	Distribution	Artifacts	Sediment Type
5 (High Risk)	Extensive structural remains to fully intact > 26 ft	Disordered pattern	Extensive exposure / uncovered or loose objects	Hardbottom, no reef coverage
4	15ft-25ft	> 50% Scattered pattern	Many loose objects exposed	Hardbottom with reef coverage
3	6-15ft	< 50% Scattered pattern	Some loose objects exposed	Hardbottom / Sand
2	1-5 ft	Ordered pattern	Very few loose objects exposed	Sand
1 (Very Stable, Low Risk)	Complete coverage of structural remains 0 ft	Coherent pattern	Objects fully buried / not disturbed or loose	Sand with seagrass coverage

Table 1: Baseline characterization assessment.

Characterization Assessment (BCA). This BCA served as a way to create a baseline for overall site integrity and stability using four variables: Structural Relief; Site Distribution; Artifact Exposure/Movement; and Sedimentary Type (Table 1). BCA was numerically rated on a scale of 1 to 5; "5" represents little to no stability or complete loss of the variable, while "1" represents a very stable site that is at the lowest risk of disturbance of outside forces. This assessment was created to easily and swiftly document the variables most indicative of site stability and coherency.

During post fieldwork, the collected images were run through Agisoft Metashape 1.5.1 software to create photogrammetric and/or photomosaic models. After processing all models, the pre- and post-Irma photogrammetric/photomosaic models were compared for singular event changes in both structural and sediment features. Structural features included hull fragments and associated features related to the shipwreck itself. Sediment features included the surrounding sand, seagrass, rubble, and rock. Points of change were noted between each by outlining areas that showed apparent movement, where the structural/sediment could be tracked in both images, and where the complete absence of a feature could be noted. This allowed for a quantifiable number to be assigned to each wreck, representing the

SITE VULNERABILITY CLASSIFICATION		
Stability	Structural Points of Change	Sediment Points of Change
5 - Low	10+	10+
4	7-9	7-9
3	4-6	4-6
2	1-3	1-3
1 - High	No movement	No movement

Table 2: Site vulnerability classification.

extent of change the event had on the site (Table 2). This was known as the initial Site Vulnerability Classification number (SVC). The higher the number, the lower the site stability. For both the BCA and SVC, a number was assigned to each variable (column) and added up. For BCA, the total number was divided by four (for each variable) to get the average stability score out of 5.00. For the initial-SVC, the structural and sediment point of change total was divided by two for a vulnerability score out of 5.00. When combined, the initial-SVC and BCA scores resulted in a total SVC score out of 10.00

Results

Populo

On 10 September 2017, Category 4 Hurricane Irma passed 93 miles west of *Nuestra Señora del Populo*, an 18th-century wooden-hull merchant vessel that wrecked in 1733 as part of the 1733 Spanish Treasure Fleet. Sustained wind speeds were recorded at 51-63 knots in the area where the shipwreck resides (SCOORA 2017). *El Populo* was the farthest site from the eye of the hurricane and is also the only site that lies in BISC waters. In 2017 and 2018, University of Miami's Underwater Archaeology Program conducted a general site assessment and produced photomosaic site maps. After comparing the two models, the post-Irma site shows very slight shifts of sand along the south end of the ballast pile and within the central holes/patches. The only exposed structural element, a length of timber, was unmoved due to Irma. This may owe to the slight protection of coral and sea fans west/north-west of the feature, which remain undamaged. Not pictured, but noted by BISC staff, a previously unexposed timber with fastener was discovered along the southern end of the site, by the base of the reef (Josh Marano 2018, pers. comm.). It is still unknown if this fragment is part of *Populo*'s structure.

In general, this movement cannot be wholly attributed to Hurricane Irma, as seasonality plays a role in slight sedimentary shifts. Sites are covered or exposed to varying degrees depending on the location and time of the year, so often perceived minor changes in sediment levels can be attributed to these seasonal changes. As such, no movement of either structure or sediment was attributed to Irma. The only exposed features are ballast stones, but this still has a very limited impact on the site's overall vulnerability. Most of the surrounding reef appeared minimally affected as well, with only slight shifts in sediment coverage accounting for negligible change. This data was used to assign an SVC of 1.00/5.00 and a BCA of 2.00/5.00 to the site.

Overall, *El Populo* sustained minimal to no impacts from Hurricane Irma. The site's general location over 90 miles from the epicenter of the hurricane limited its exposure to hydraulic forces and its minimally exposed remains were not impacted. Wind speeds of 34-50 knots were recorded in this area (SCOORA 2017). After the initial wrecking, salvagers and looters produced the majority of the damage, accounting for the patches in the ballast. Comparing the Florida Bureau of Archaeological

Research's site map in 2005 and the site map created by the University of Miami in March 2017, prior to Irma, site change can be observed. The north/northeast end of the site showed significant change as the ballast on this end appeared to be less dense and more sporadic than initially mapped. In addition, the hole in the ballast that connects to the singular timber grew in size. It is difficult to tell without excavation if the sparseness of these sections is due solely to extracting filters such as looters, or natural re-coverage by seasonality shifts. The main factors attributing to the slightly higher BCA score is the scattered pattern of distribution. No structural remains are visible to give the semblance of the vessel, just the exposed ballast stone. This increases the site instability as loss of material decreases the site coherency as a whole and results in loss of archaeological context.

San Pedro

The wreck site of *San Pedro*, another wooden-hulled merchant ship from the 1733 Spanish Plate Fleet, lies 53 miles northeast of Hurricane Irma's path. SCOORA estimated that the sustained wind speeds over the site were greater than 64 knots (SCOORA 2017). The area in which the vessel wrecked is primarily white quartz sand partially surrounded by beds of seagrass. The site itself is quite shallow at only 20ft/6.1m and lacks protection from surrounding reefs. In 2015, IU assessed the site and rendered a full photogrammetric model. IU and ONMS staff then revisited the site in June 2018 to update it. A comparison of these two figures

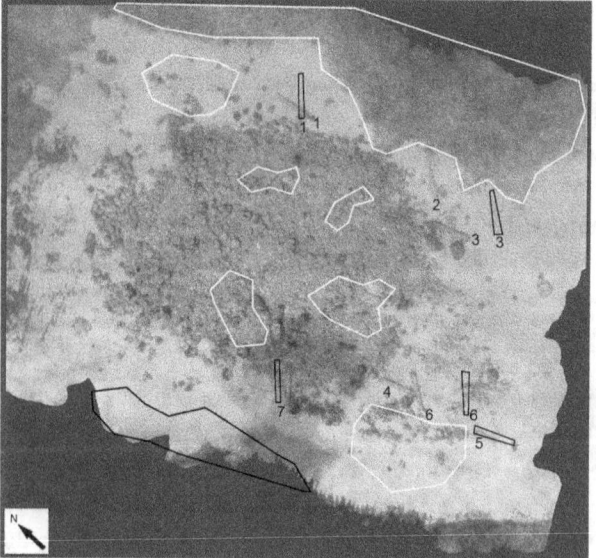

Figure 2: Post-Irma Comparison Model of San Pedro (Model courtesy of Indiana University; Comparison analysis by author, 2019).

exhibited some change in sediment coverage over the general site (Figure 2). More significant shifts were seen in the position of the replica cement cannons and the surrounding seagrass growth. Cannons 1, 3, 5, and 6 all showed general movement, as seen by the black outlines in Figure 2, noting their pre-Irma position. Cannon 7 showed slight sideways movement, but this could be attributed to a minor difference in the top-down angle of the model. In addition, the surrounding seagrass beds exhibited signs of retreat and growth. The eastern section of the site showed a curious increase in coverage of the seagrass between 2015 and 2018. In contrast, the seagrass to the west of the site showed complete retreat and/or sand coverage. Taking into consideration these observations, an SVC of 3.5/5.0 and a BCA of 2.25/5.00 was assigned.

San Pedro, as the closest shipwreck to the direct path of the hurricane, was expected to incur the most impact from the storm. The change exhibited was, in contrast, skewed in terms of historic shipwreck site analysis. The artifacts that exhibited the most change, the cannons, are not of historically accurate material, nor original to the ship. As part of its role as a 'Museum in the Sea,' resource managers placed seven replica cement cannons at the site as interpretation aid for tourism. These were cast from a mold of a 9-pounder cannon that had once been on board San Jose, another member of the 1733 Fleet. Since these cannons were constructed of different and lighter material than the originals (cement vs cast iron), their inclusion in the formation model was initially questioned. However, as it pertains to cultural resource management, these items are now part of the shipwreck and a key component in its educational value. Since researchers know exactly how many were initially placed, where, and in what orientation, they serve as known indicators of significant change on the site. For example, cannon 5 had not been visible since 2004. Hurricane Irma uncovered it providing an indication of sediment movement. The SVC and BCA reflect these.

In general, the cannons moved towards the north/northwest revealing that wave action penetrated to the seabed moving these low-density objects. Sediment movement can be seen around the contour of the ballast piles, as well as its absence in the sparse pockets seen in the pre-Irma model. The surviving hull of *San Pedro* remains buried under the protective layer of ballast stone, sand, and seagrass. Irma did not expose any timbers, nor were artifacts uncovered or moved.

The retreat in the seagrass beds to the west of the site is concerning. This seagrass is a critical natural factor in site formation, as it secures the site underneath and around it, sheltering it from natural forces. By stabilizing the seafloor with a network of roots and thicker horizontal stems (rhizome), seagrass beds dampen wave energy and prevent extensive sediment movement. Seagrass also aids in organic preservation by reducing oxygen concentrations. The retreat of the seagrass, due to physical scour and/or decreased water quality and increased salinity, is a concern for the preservation of the area immediately surrounding the site. Seagrass retreat can mean destabilization of the seabed, place the buried hull at risk for exposure, and increase subsequent impact from chemical, biological, and physical impacts. The main concern is the stabilization of cannon placement, as continued movement due to major storm activity could cause scouring or displacement of the site's coral colonies. A secondary concern is monitoring of seagrass bed retreat and scour of sediment off the site, as increased exposure would result in more physical impacts from future major storms and hurricanes. Increased exposure would also increase possible looting-behavior impacts from tourists or treasure hunters.

City of Washington

City of Washington was a late 19th century iron merchant steamship, later turned into a coal transport barge. Known for its role with the USS Maine and the start of the Spanish-American War, this vessel ultimately wrecked in June of 1917 in FKNMS waters. Just over a century later, on 10 September 2017, Hurricane Irma passed 83 miles west of *City of Washington*, with sustained wind speeds of 51-63 knots (SCOORA 2017). The initial site visit post-Irma by ONMS divers familiar to the site noticed no apparent change. Anecdotal reports expressed to ONMS managers by local dive shops supported this observation (Matthew Lawrence 2019, pers. comm.). After comparing IU's Pre-Irma model done in 2017, and UM's model completed in 2018, the only point of change was a small hull-plate fragment that shifted 25 degrees starboard (Figure 3). Minimal sediment movement occurred. *City of Washington* sits on a bed of coral rubble and coarse sand, with only the lighter sand showing any movement following the storm. Still, this is more likely a standard shift due to the regular bottom current at the site.

With only a single structural point of change and no discernible Irma-induced sediment change, a SVC of 1.5/5.0. In contrast, the BCA for the site was marginally higher at 2.5/5.0. The site itself exhibits

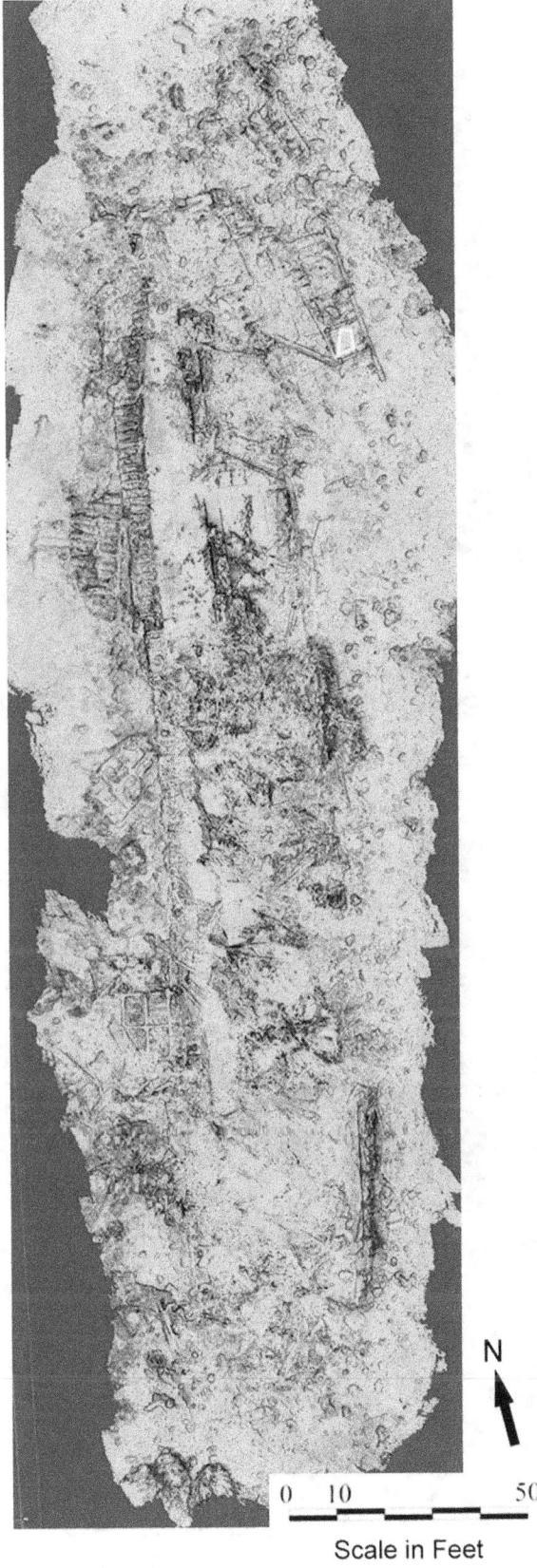

Figure 3: Post-Irma Comparison Model of SS *City of Washington* (Models by author, 2018).

only fragmented structural remains which have eroded in their exposed environment on top of hardbottom. This contributes the most to the increased value, as the overall vulnerability remains high as long as the site stays so exposed to both natural and cultural forces. *City of Washington* does benefit from a robust coverage of calcium concretions over the site, fusing any possible loose structural fragments. In general, *City of Washington* remains relatively stable due to this factor, as it decreases the possible loss of information.

The results of the SVC for *City of Washington* proved surprising. During the initial site visit, researchers could not detect any discernible change, in contrast to Benwood, the other metal hull wreck in the study. Researchers expected the vessel to have sustained at least moderate physical impacts from the hurricane. *City of Washington*'s history and previous site formation processes account for some of this. Prior to the wrecking, the ship was stripped of most of the superstructure and converted into a barge. This reduced the profile and limited any excess or loose materials onboard. During the wrecking event itself, *City of Washington* sustained massive damage to the hull. These two factors helped to minimize the overall profile in the water column and reduce the physical impact it would sustain from waves, currents, and surge action.

As *City of Washington* sits on a coral rubble field on the seaward side of the outer reef, its environment offers little protection. What remains today has been entirely calcified over, covered in various encrusting organisms, and ultimately cementing the wreck and the debris together to its environment. Not only does this provide a relative protective cover for the iron, slowing deterioration due to oxidation and physical abrasion, but it provides a stronger foundation for coral growth. Given the biological cover of this site, a detailed documentation of coral density covering the wreck would have contributed to the analysis of its overall vulnerability and was noted for future studies.

Benwood

With sustained wind speeds close to 64 knots, Hurricane Irma passed 77 miles away from *Benwood*, a 20th Century steel freighter that wrecked in 1942. Almost immediately after the hurricane, dive charters reported significant structural movement on the site to ONMS staff (Matthew Lawrence 2019, pers. comm.). During the initial site visit, the most pronounced change was noted amidship, where a large section of

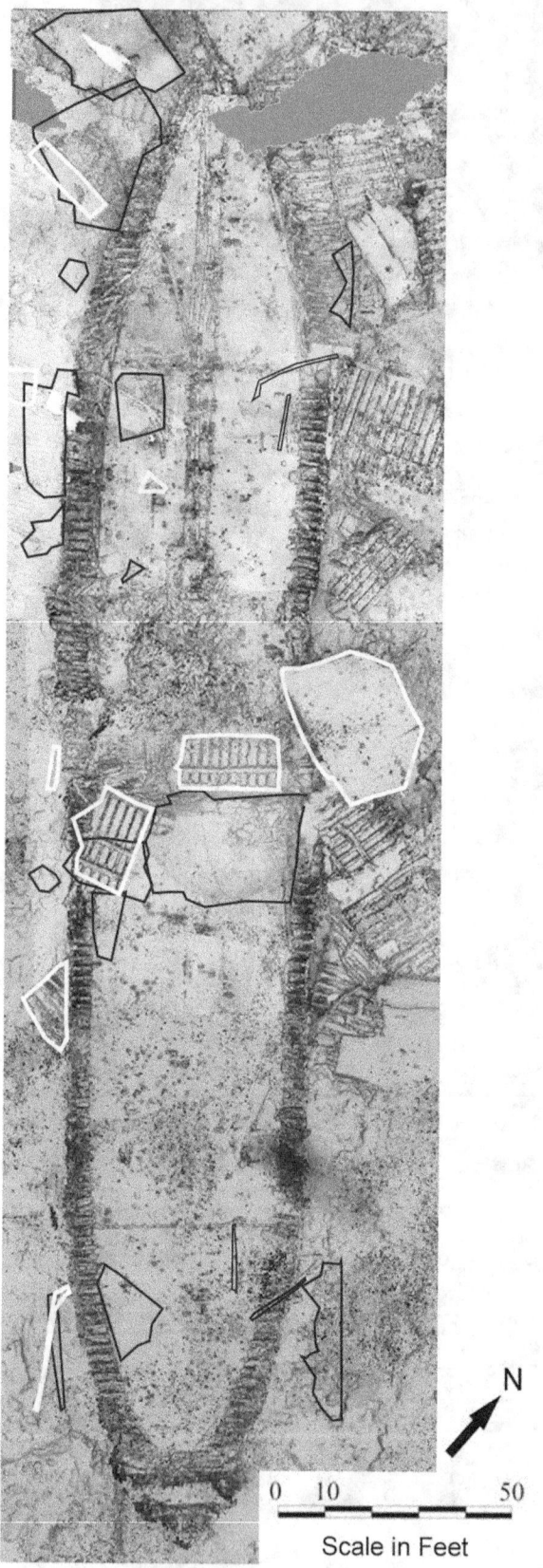

Figure 4: Post-Irma Comparison Model of SS *Benwood* (Model by author, 2018).

the deck plate shifted over the portside bracket frames and settled partially on a section of the interior hull plate and the sand. Comparison of pre- and post-Irma photogrammetric models allowed researchers to conduct a more detailed assessment of the changes occurring at this site. By overlaying the pre-Irma model from the summer of 2017 and the post-Irma model done in late 2018, twenty-five points of specific change can be distinguished, giving *Benwood* an SVC of 4.0/5.0 (Figure 4). This includes:

1. Hull plate shifted up and off the top of the wreck
2. Interior hull-plate segment at the starboard bow disappearance
3. New interior hull-plate segment located starboard just forward of amidships, resting between the hull and sand
4. Movement of exterior hull-plate once located port side of the bow
5. General movement of multiple pieces of iron debris across the deck, mainly seen at the stern and bow
6. Arrangement shifts of interior hull plates located on the sand, starboard of the stern
7. Removal/disappearance of an exterior hull-plate segment once located starboard side, just aft of midships.

Much of the area off the port side of *Benwood* was not captured in the 2017 pre-Irma model and, therefore, could not be used as part of the analysis. Still, some apparent shifts in the exterior and interior hull plates located on the seabed northeast of the portside can be discerned. In addition, some scouring can be observed in the exposure of rubble underneath the sand. The area just off the starboard side shows obvious signs of material transportation and sediment deposition. In addition, an anchor near *Benwood* (not included in this study) had been completely uncovered, another example of sediment removal across the site (Matthew Lawrence 2019, pers. comm.). *Benwood*'s BCA also showed decreased stability regarding the site as a whole. The extensive structural remains and exposure of loose objects show a very high risk for decreased stability. The surrounding sedimentary characteristics only exacerbate these factors. *Benwood* currently rests on shallow fore-reef hardbottom with some sand, leaving the wreck exposed with limited to no coverage from hydraulic forces. As the wreck itself is relatively young, there is still a reasonably ordered pattern to the site distribution. These factors result in a BCA of 3.50 / 5.00.

Benwood was the closest metal hulled wreck to the hurricane's path. Multiple points of significant change were noted in the form of movement of hull plate segments, iron debris, and sediment. Structurally, *Benwood* is the most exposed. The nature of the grounding, combined with the construction as a steel freighter, preserved much of the structural integrity. The majority of the changes show location shifts in hull-plate segments both on top of the wreck and those smaller pieces resting on the seabed to the port side. A powerful northward force would be needed to move a segment of this size. *Benwood* exhibits the highest vertical profile, as well as the largest intact structural segments, not otherwise attached to the ship itself. In the case of the hull-plate and deck-plate segments, their overall flat and large shape lends itself to increased impact from hurricane-force currents and surge. As it resides in an area that experienced direct hurricane-forces of a lower end Category One hurricane, it is expected that *Benwood* experienced sufficient storm-force currents to shift large sections of steel debris. The increased surface area of these sections is a contributing factor in their general movement during the storm. The shape allowed for greater surface friction and upward force due to currents and wave action. This accounts for the portions of hull and deck-plates to 'flip' or shift up and over. In contrast, City of Washington, resides in a mostly fragmented and concreted state, with few large sections with enough surface area to allow for extensive outward or inward force.

Due to the extensive movement of large sections of structural pieces, shifts of smaller artifacts/items and structural fragments, and overall exposure on the seafloor with limited sand cover, this site exhibits greater site vulnerability. As cultural resource managers have noticed obvious, large scale change, priority for yearly documentation of the site is high. This includes detailed mapping of hull and deck-plates, calculation over time of metal deterioration, and monitoring of coral both on and nearby the wreck. With the recorded extensive movement of sections of the wreck, the risk of damage to the associated biology is also a considerable concern.

Discussion

The effects of hurricane forces on shipwreck sites found in this study corroborate other recent studies on hurricane impacts on cultural resources. One of the main findings, damage potential in relation to time submerged and construction, is critical for resource managers. In terms of damage and site mitigation loss, exposed wooden wrecks have the greatest potential for total loss if in the path of a major storm, whereas metal wrecks are still relatively stable and fall in earlier stages of site formation. This also makes any sudden, extreme force more likely to show substantial structural damage to metal hull wrecks as compared to their wooden counterparts that are often buried. The longer a vessel has been submerged, the greater the number of hurricanes has already affected the structural integrity of the site. Younger vessels are more likely to show sudden changes following a singular event. Extreme examples of this can be seen in artificial reef wrecks where lateral and vertical displacement or rolling have occurred, as well as structural failure (Gearhart et al. 2011; Emmons 2018). *Benwood* follows this logic and presented the study's highest SVC and BCA numbers.

This study sought to answer three key questions. Utilizing historical information and site formation theories, each shipwreck in the study underwent analysis to determine Irma's overall impact. This analysis informed the following answers.

   1. Can resource managers, using photogrammetric models taken before and after a major hurricane, visually detect archaeological site changes in a quantifiable manner?

Researchers compared Pre-Irma and post-Irma photogrammetric models and were able to discern even small site changes. Low-quality images and their resulting models could also be used by researchers to distinguish substantial, general changes over each site. High-quality images and, therefore, high-quality models allowed for a more detailed analysis of general change. Details such as the movement of smaller artifacts, intricate site scatter, environmental scour, and biological assessments can be addressed at this level. The drawback of larger scale, higher-quality models proved to be the computing power needed to process them fully.

   2. If change is apparent, what forces are hypothesized to have acted upon the wrecks to cause the specific change and contribute to site vulnerability?

Site changes were determined to be the result of wave, surge, and current action. Severity of the damage depended directly on the prior condition and overall stability of the site in question, distance from the eye of the storm, years submerged, site depth, substrate composition, site construction material, presence of encrustations, and other biological cover. Each site in this study exhibited varying stages of change. *San Pedro*, the site nearest to the eye of the hurricane, exhibited significant movement to the replica cannons. The wreck itself has reached equilibrium with the environment, but the cannons, which have a different construction and have been submerged for a shorter period of time, exhibited movement in contrast to the rest of the site. On the other hand, *El Populo* exhibited no markable change. This raises another question, if *San Pedro* lacked the educational aids present, would Irma have affected the site less, more similar to *El Populo*? *Benwood* ultimately showed the most storm-induced change as compared to the Pre-Irma models, contrasting starkly against the lack of change seen at *City of Washington*.

This susceptibility for or resistance to movement is dependent on various factors on the site and through the environment. In terms of the wreck, the extent of the vessel surface area determines how much exposure it will have to wave and surge energy. This also applies to the vertical rise or profile of the ship, size of intact components, and weight of the vessel and individual components resisting vertical lift. The deck plates on *Benwood* provided a larger, flat surface for external storm forces to cause vertical lift and horizontal shifts. *City of Washington* has fewer substantial pieces with enough flat surface area to assist with these movements. Concretions also act as friction forces that dampen overall movement. The strength of the environmental forces such as wave height, surge, and currents mandate the extent of their effect over the site. As subsurface conditions were not able to be utilized in this study, these forces are not touched on in great detail.

   3. Can cultural resource managers use a Site Vulnerability Classification [SVC] and Baseline Characterization Assessment [BCA] to identify resources most vulnerable to storm impacts?

While limited, the sample sites presented in this study provide an example of what may be achieved through vulnerability analysis of submerged cultural resources in hurricane-impacted areas. Divers, both cultural resource management and citizen scientists/volunteers, have the ability to quickly assess sites in a single dive by utilizing BCA. This analyzes visible site characteristics such as wreck scatter, vertical relief, sediment type, and artifacts. These factors all affect the level of preservation expected after a storm. The BCA provides a starting point when addressing rapid damage assessment protocols by assigning a numerical value to general site stability. With over 2,000 shipwrecks in the Florida Keys, knowing which shipwrecks are the most susceptible to damage from extreme forces will aid the decision-making process of which sites to visit first. With limited time, resources, and staffing, this could also mean that only 2 or 3 percent of sites could be investigated immediately after a storm. This allows for the most vulnerable sites to be addressed and increases the chance of damage mitigation measures to be implemented following a major storm.

By utilizing the SVC, cultural resource managers can also easily track site stability. While not as quick or efficient as a basic baseline check, SVC allows for cultural resource managers to track storm-induced change on a site in a systematic manner. Photogrammetry, while time-consuming for large vessels such as *Benwood*, is much more time efficient than hand-mapping whole sites. Image-based analysis also reduces the amount of 'interpretation' between two time-frames. Hand-drawn maps are often based around the interpretations of the mapper; this may result in discrepancies if another researcher uses said map for comparative analysis later on.

Conclusion

Overall increases in global warming, specifically higher ocean temperatures, are fueling stronger hurricanes. This increase in hurricane intensity, when combined with the biological and chemical-related effects of climate change, will amplify the degradation of submerged cultural resources. These archaeological sites are unique and often represent or reflect moments in history. As such, they are irreplaceable and non-renewable. Maritime archaeologists have a responsibility to engage in such discussions on climate change related impacts, as well as lead proactive measures in the understanding of how these forces are affecting submerged cultural resources. This research attempts to develop a specific methodology for quantifying the effects of these forces on various shipwreck sites in the Florida Keys. By creating a Baseline Characterization Assessment and a Site Vulnerability Classification, cultural resource managers can more quickly assess the current condition and overall stability of the sites within their jurisdiction. This then allows resource managers to prioritize pre- and post-hurricane efforts based on overall previous site vulnerability. In short, this research aims to contribute to the overall protection and management of these archaeological sites.

References

Davis, Gary E., Mark Flora, Lloyd L. Loope, Brian Mitchell, Charles T. Roman, George Smith, Michael Soukup, and James T. Tilmant
1993   Assessment of Hurricane Andrew's Immediate Impacts on Natural and Archaeological Resources of Big Cypress National Preserve, Biscayne National Park, and Everglades National Park. The George Wright Forum, U.S. National Park Service, Washington, D.C.

Emanuel, Kerry
2005   Increasing Destructiveness of Tropical Cyclones over the Past 30 Years. *Nature* 436(7051). August 4:686–688.

Emmons, Mary F.
2018   How Hurricane Irma Radically Shifted South Florida Wrecks. March 11.

Gearhart, Robert, II, Doug Jones, Amy Borgens, Sara Laurence, Todd DeMuna, and Julia Shipp
2011   *Impacts of Recent Hurricane Activity on Historic Shipwrecks in the Gulf of Mexico Outer Continental Shelf*.: U.S. Dept. of the Interior, Bureau of Ocean Energy Management, Regulation, and Enforcement. https://www.boem.gov/ESPIS/4/5111.pdf.

Gibbs, Martin
2006   Cultural Site Formation Processes in Maritime Archaeology: Disaster Response, Salvage and Muckelroy 30 Years on. *International Journal of Nautical Archaeology* 35(1). April:4–19.

Jameson, John H., and Della A. Scott-Ireton
2007   *Out of the Blue: Public Interpretation of Maritime Cultural Resources*. Springer Science & Business Media, April 15.

Lim, Young-Kwon, Siegfried D. Schubert, Robin Kovach, Andrea M. Molod, and Steven Pawson
2018   The Roles of Climate Change and Climate Variability in the 2017 Atlantic Hurricane Season. *Scientific Reports* 8(1). November 1:16172.

Marano, J. L.
2018   Research Design for the Non-Disturbance Digital Documentation of Several Submerged Cultural Sites Affected by Hurricane Irma in Biscayne National Park. Cultural Resource Management, Homestead: Biscayne National Park.

MUCKELROY, KEITH
1978   *Maritime Archaeology.* Cambridge University Press.

MURPHY, LARRY
1983   Shipwrecks as Data Base for Human Behavioral Studies. *Shipwreck Anthropology.* University of New Mexico Press Albuquerque:65–89.

NOAA
2019   Global Warming and Hurricanes. November 25. https://www.gfdl.noaa.gov/global-warming-and-hurricanes/.

NOAA GEOPHYSICAL FLUID DYNAMICS LABORATORY (NOAA GFDL)
2018   Costliest U.S. tropical cyclones tables updated. Internal Report. National Hurricane Center. January 26, 2018. National Hurricane Center, Department of Commerce. https://www.nhc.noaa.gov/news/UpdatedCostliest.pdf

PRICE, MELISSA RAE
2015   Intellectual Treasure Hunting: Measuring Effects of Treasure Salvors on Spanish Colonial Shipwreck Sites. Thesis in Maritime Studies, East Carolina University.

SCHIFFER, MICHAEL B.
1987   *Formation Processes of the Archaeological Record.* University of New Mexico Press, Albuquerque.

SOUTHEAST COASTAL OCEAN OBSERVING REGIONAL ASSOCIATION [SCOORA]
2017   Hurricane Irma Wind Swath. *Hurricane Irma Data Resources.* September 6. https://secoora.org/hurricane-irma-data-resources/.

WEBSTER, P. J., G. J. HOLLAND, J. A. CURRY, AND H-R CHANG
2005   Changes in Tropical Cyclone Number, Duration, and Intensity in a Warming Environment. *Science* 309(5742). September 16:1844–1846.

. . . .

Airielle R. Cathers
33 East Quay Road
Key West, FL 33030

The Bermuda 100 Project: An Island-Scale Digital Atlas for Underwater Cultural Heritage

Vid Petrovic, Dominique Rissolo, Eric Lo, Scott Blair, Philippe Rouja, Jean-Pierre Rouja, Falko Kuester

The Bermuda 100 Project is creating a comprehensive, online, interactive digital atlas, representing a broad range of sites surrounding Bermuda – from shipwrecks to the marine habitats they support – as well as deploying the tools required to document, analyze, manage, and virtually explore them. The reefs surrounding Bermuda are home to a remarkable diversity of shipwrecks. We are using digital documentation techniques to record sites and associated benthic features while developing custom point-based visual analytics tools to facilitate multi-resolution data fusion and visualization across land and sea. Associated web-based scientific storytelling allows the public to fully engage and become active stakeholders.

Overview

The Bermuda 100 Project is a collaboration between faculty, researchers, and students from University of California, San Diego (UCSD) and colleagues from Bermuda's Department of Environment and Natural Resources, LookBermuda and Nonsuch Expeditions. Together, the partners are bringing the power of student-driven engineering and citizen science to the study and conservation of Bermuda's underwater ecosystems. The project aims to document 100 or more historic shipwrecks and distinct natural habitats in the waters surrounding Bermuda in order to enhance conservation efforts and open the sites to both physical and virtual visitation from interested scholars, students, and supporters from around the world. Local divers, marine scientists, and archaeologists have teamed with UCSD's Cultural Heritage Engineering Initiative (CHEI) to document and disseminate digital reconstructions of shipwreck sites and marine conservation areas using digital workflows to acquire, process, analyze, visualize, and disseminate 3D data and visualizations from known shipwrecks and reef sites.

For marine archaeologists, documenting the location and assessing the integrity of wrecks, with respect to individual deposits and overall site morphology, is essential to reconstructing the natural and cultural processes that resulted in the formation of wreck sites and provides both spatial and temporal contextual information. From the perspective of underwater cultural resource management, each model (point cloud) can serve as a synchronic baseline to better characterize and assess the condition or "state-of-health" of individual wreck sites. In particularly dynamic environments, digital tools can be used to detect or quantify change over time at those sites where multiple image-sets (or time series data) are available.

The Bermuda 100 website (http://bermuda100.ucsd.edu) is intended to function as an online resource for a broad range of users and to facilitate documentation, dissemination, and preservation efforts. It provides locations, images, interactive digital models, and fly-through videos of major shipwrecks and other sites in Bermuda waters (Figure 1). An initial 35 wreck sites are featured (including recent 3D digital content for four shipwrecks) with a goal of expanding to 100 sites. Much of the descriptive content draws from the general literature (e.g. Berg and Berg 2006; Gillies 2007; Hume 1995) as well as published reports (e.g. Delgado et al. 2016). A future goal is to provide online access to relevant publications and reports.

Each shipwreck's page consists of historical information, vessel description, the current condition of the wreck, detailed location, and a multimedia archive including new and existing 3D digital models, videos, fly-throughs, photographs, and historical documents (Figure 1). The "Technologies" section of the website provides detailed information on techniques for acquisition, processing, analysis, and dissemination of the interactive 3D models and videos, including techniques such as structure-from-motion (SfM) photogrammetry. It should be noted that the photogrammetric models are not the result of a consistently applied image acquisition protocol. Rather, the authors have aggregated "legacy" image data and worked with a variety of practitioners to bring site-specific image-sets into our processing pipeline. Future efforts call for greater consistency as best practices and standards for SfM photogrammetry are adopted.

Technical Approach

The 3D model generation follows an SfM photogrammetry workflow (Drap 2012), with some accommodations for more variable data quality from older video or imagery datasets acquired for other purposes, and imagery acquired from divers without extensive experience with underwater photogrammetry.

In general, the process begins with divers capturing a set of hundreds to thousands of overlapping images of the shipwreck from different points of view to allow the SfM algorithm to estimate the geometry of the scene. Once captured, the imagery is uploaded to servers in our lab and processed. First, the image alignment is attempted on all the images from each site. This produces an estimate of where each image was taken and a sparse 3D point cloud with the geometry of the scene. If the majority of the cameras are not successfully aligned, this step is repeated with different reconstruction parameters until a satisfactory result is obtained. Especially with legacy datasets, the image acquisition pattern is sometimes insufficient for most of the images to align into one consistent model. In those cases, the images are grouped to reconstruct different areas of each site separately. Once the reconstruction has completed with as many cameras as possible, both the camera positions and the geometry are evaluated for consistency with the rest of the model, and erroneous camera position estimates are reset and re-estimated. Before the dense point cloud computation is started, the remaining outlier and noisy points are subsequently removed manually. In cases with substantial noise in the dense point cloud, the corresponding points can be manually removed. The dense point cloud models are then exported and placed on the appropriate shipwreck pages for public access via Potree (Schuetz 2016) web viewer (Figure 1).

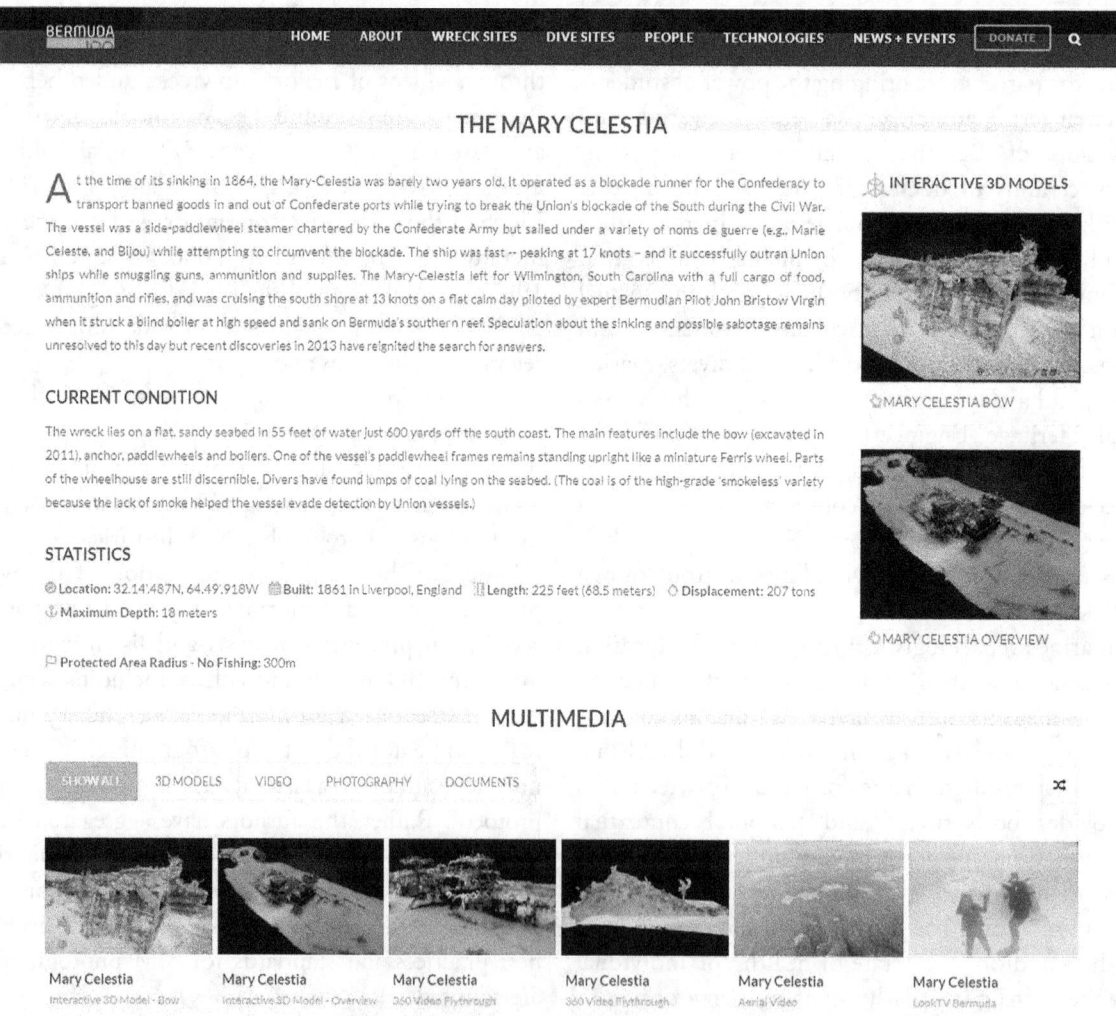

Figure 1: Example of a Bermuda 100 website wreck page, featuring *Mary Celestia*. Note the graphics (upper right), which link to interactive 3D models via Potree.

In parallel, multiple derivative data products such as maps, resampled point clouds or meshes, fly- and swim-through videos, as well as 3D VR-360 content, are then created with our Viscore visual analytics framework. Using Viscore, the individual point cloud models are reassembled into a spacio-temporally referenced representation of the shipwrecks surrounding the island. For each shipwreck, the point clouds corresponding to different wreck parts or different time snapshots are first co-aligned into a composite shipwreck model. As an example, the composite *Mary Celestia* model comprises four point clouds (totaling 1.7 billion points), with one point cloud covering the bow, another the amidships wheels and stacks, one covering the entire site (bow-to-stern) and one again covering the stern. Later, a storm had exposed more of the stern structure, for which we now have additional image data (Figure 2). Simple color-adjustment is performed to remove the blue cast from the images and the point clouds and to reconcile the colors between parts of a composite model — currently a manual process, though we are investigating alternatives — both with and without requiring changes to the imaging protocol (Figure 3).

Figure 3: Point cloud of the bow section of *Montana*. Upper image represents color adjustment to remove the blue cast. Lower image represents the application of a light-scattering model to simulate an in-water viewer experience.

The next step is to place the composite shipwreck models into geographic context, provided by a combination of low-resolution bathymetry and a high-resolution 5.7-gigapixel aerial photo map covering the Bermuda atoll. The aerial imagery is draped onto the idealized ocean surface plane when viewed (virtually) from above-water, and onto a bathymetry-derived seafloor mesh when underwater (Figure 4). The initial placement of shipwrecks is provided by the field-recorded GPS coordinates and site depth, then adjusted to maintain compatibility with the bathymetric mesh and aerial view. Note that the quality of the georeferencing information varies from dataset to dataset (just as the coverage pattern and image quality do, as discussed above). As a result, the alignments are considered tentative and subject to improvement as more data are collected. To this end, the individual point clouds that make up the composite representations of the wreck sites are maintained as separate layers and can be realigned at any time within Viscore.

With the full virtual georeferenced representation of the shipwrecks, one can fly from site to site (viewing the aerial imagery), then dip underwater and inspect the

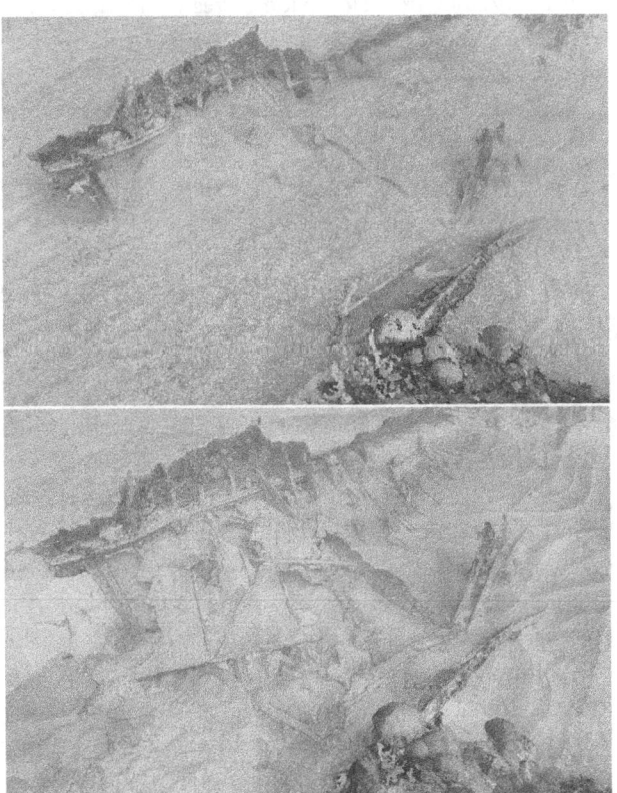

Figure 2: Point cloud of the stern section of *Mary Celestia*, before (upper image) and after (lower image) storm-induced scouring event.

Figure 4: Island-scale interactive 3D model comprised of bathymetry, aerial imagery, and geo-referenced shipwreck point clouds.

point clouds placed onto the bathymetric mesh. When rendering underwater views, a simple light-scattering model is optionally applied to simulate the view-dependent effects of the intervening water and increase the apparent "realism," accounting for both attenuation (out-scatter) and veiling light (in-scatter, from depth-dependent downwelling irradiance) along the viewing ray, and (in the limit) producing the blue-gradient background one expects to see underwater (Figure 3). However, whenever useful for analysis, this effect can be turned off — "draining" the water — and the estimated white-light colors can be viewed.

The Bermuda 100 website was designed to showcase the project visuals, including 3D models, immersive video, and photography, in a minimal aesthetic that streamlines the content for easy navigation and optimal engagement. The site was built in HTML5 and CSS3, which offers several improved features such as better accessibility, cleaner code, mobile optimization, and improved video support, all of which are utilized to achieve a positive user experience.

Results and Broader Impacts

The tourism value of this type of public interface cannot be overstated and has far exceeded our expectations. The decision to initiate this project by cataloguing *Montana* (1863) was largely based on its historic significance and dimensional attractiveness. The wreck lies in shallow water on the western edge of Bermuda in only 26 feet of water. As an iron side-paddle steamship, many key features are still prominent in situ. Boilers, paddlewheel frames, iron hull and bow and stern are all very prominent and recognizable. Now covered in hard and soft corals with several swim-through areas (where the wreck is complete enough to be penetrated), *Montana* is particularly attractive and challenging to catalogue in detail using traditional 2D photomosaic techniques. Given its shallow location, the wreck is also bathed in natural light eliminating the need to add artificial light to the data collection process.

As one of the few remaining side paddlewheel blockade runners in the world in shallow clear blue water, it is extremely popular as a dive, snorkeling, and glass-bottom boat site and is visited by close to 100 people daily at the height of the summer tourist season. Cataloging this shallow wreck was prioritized as an opportunity to not only monitor its condition and the condition of the reef on and around the wreck, but also to explore all avenues for expanding its heritage value. The site impacts that we were interested in monitoring were primarily anthropogenic and caused by the heavy visitations, which can be up to five tour boats a day. Impact appears to be progressive. This may be linked to chemical damage from sunscreen and sloughing boat-bottom paint, but also to some nitrification and direct minor damage to the site from tourists holding on to the wreck or reef and moving small artifacts and the like.

While we were conducting our post-hurricane surveys of the shipwrecks on the dynamic south coast of Bermuda, Hurricane Humberto struck Bermuda in September 2019. This inspired an initial deep shipwreck scanning effort on the Civil War blockade runner, *Mary Celestia*. Reports were received that *Montana* had been heavily impacted with the bow section being completely flattened and all the attached coral smashed. The descriptions of the damage to *Montana* were accurate. What began as a "monitoring exercise" on *Montana* turned into a high-priority heritage conservation exercise. Based on the project's earlier work, the entire bow of the ship (as it was, pre-hurricane) can still be visited virtually and analyzed. Following Humberto, the team immediately collected a post-hurricane image/dataset over three dives and then a few weeks later created another image/dataset, following the rescue of the hundreds of corals that were displaced and buried under the iron plate of the bow. These corals have moved and there is now a record that can be evaluated and monitored as part of their recovery plan. In communicating about the wreck, one can now share its heritage value as well as discuss the impact of climate change on hurricane frequency and intensity providing a reliable baseline for coral recovery efforts and coral recruitment in the highest resolution possible.

The lateral value of developing these data-rich capture techniques, the accompanying interdisciplinary nature of the work, and the creation of a wide network of added capacity led to some interesting add-on project opportunities, such as using photogrammetry to collect important baselines for ongoing analysis of sea-level rise at Bermudian dock faces. The initiation of the project also coincided with the amateurization of image capture by drone and the advent of consumer-accessible professional quality drones with imaging capabilities. Workflow for data collection came to include image capture of wreck and reef sites by drone; today, a georeferenced drone image of a reef can be used to perfectly indicate the location of a known wreck and the location of specific features and even associated artifacts. In this way, heritage managers cannot only easily geographically relocate the sites they manage, but can also include and monitor specific items and objects of concern. Of great importance is the replicability and transferability of these capture techniques and data handling methods that can be easily applied and understood by other managers or scientists from any discipline, even if unfamiliar with the site.

Bermuda's shipwreck heritage attracts very specific and specialized attention from professional and amateur marine archaeologists, historians, and divers. Inevitably, it also attracts attention from a less academic sector regarding the myth of the Bermuda Triangle. The Bermuda 100 web interface has saved heritage managers a significant amount of time processing inquiries from global media about the rich history of Bermuda shipwrecks and seeking information that would allow them to plan segments featuring Bermuda shipwrecks as they relate to their various Bermuda Triangle productions. Any significant shipwreck inquiry to a heritage manager can be answered initially with a recommendation that they visit the Bermuda 100 website and then get back in contact if they have a more specific question. Filmmakers can access most available and recent images, videos and related stories of all publicly-open shipwrecks and determine what fits their needs and, then, contact the heritage manager with more specific and useful questions. This has been an unforeseen and extremely useful feature.

In Closing

These shipwreck sites – many surrounded by myth and mystery – are integral to the cultural patrimony of this Atlantic outpost. Underappreciated by many is the fact that shipwrecks become naturalized components of the benthic ecology. They are, in fact, unique biological communities that function as time capsules for the study of natural systems. Their stories tell of human misadventure and tragedy, yet they create new worlds of discovery for marine scientists and the interested public. Bermuda is a world leader in the incorporation of shipwrecks into marine protected areas, yet much documentation needs to be done in order to understand and assess the state-of-health of these unique places. The Bermuda 100 Project hopes to better coordinate and accelerate efforts to preserve and share the region's rich underwater cultural heritage.

Resources

The Bermuda 100 Project has been conducted in cooperation with the Government of Bermuda, Department of Environment and Natural Resource and in collaboration with LookBermuda and Nonsuch Expeditions. We acknowledge the National Museum of

Bermuda, Dive Bermuda, NOAA Maritime Heritage Program, Waitt Institute, UC San Diego Jacobs School of Engineering, and Qualcomm Institute. Special thanks to James P. Delgado, Kevin Kinsella, the late Teddy Tucker, and the following individuals: Piotr Bojakowski, Derrick Burgess, Chris Burville, Tane Casserley, Michael Dessner, Mark Diel, Edward Harris, Geoff Gardener, Chris Gauntlet, Stuart Joblin, Joe Lepore, Wayne Lusardi, Dominique Meyer, Christopher McFarland, and Anson Nash.

References

BERG, DANIEL AND DENISE BERG
2006 Bermuda Shipwrecks. Aqua Explorers, Inc., Baldwin, New York.

DELGADO, JAMES P., PHILIPPE M. ROUJA, DOMINIQUE RISSOLO, RHONDA K. ROBICHAUD, DAVID PYBUS, TANE CASSERLEY, ISABELLE RAMASAY-BRACKSTONE, JEAN-CLAUDE DELVILLE, LIONEL NESBITT, AND WAYNE LUSARDI
2016 Archaeological Excavation of the Forepeak of the Civil War Blockade Runner *Mary Celestia*. Maritime Heritage Program Series, 2, Office of National Marine Sanctuaries, National Oceanic and Atmospheric Administration, Silver Spring, Maryland.

DRAP, PIERRE
2012 Underwater Photogrammetry for Archaeology. In *Special Applications of Photogrammetry*, Daniel Carneiro Da Silva, editor, pp. 11-136. Intech Europe, Rijeka, Croatia.

GILLIES, WILLIAM B.
2007 Reefs, Wrecks & Relics: Bermuda Underwater Heritage. Print Link, Bermuda.

HUME, IVOR NOËL
1995 Shipwreck! History from the Bermuda Reefs. Capstan Publications, Hamilton, Bermuda.

SCHUETZ, MARKUS
2016 Potree: Rendering Large Point Clouds in Web Browsers. Diploma Thesis, Faculty of Informatics, Vienna University of Technology, Vienna, Austria.

Vid Petrovic
Qualcomm Institute
University of California, San Diego
9500 Gilman Drive
La Jolla, CA 92093-0436

Dominique Rissolo
Qualcomm Institute
University of California, San Diego
9500 Gilman Drive
La Jolla, CA 92093-0436

Eric Lo
Qualcomm Institute
University of California, San Diego
9500 Gilman Drive
La Jolla, CA 92093-0436

Scott Blair
Qualcomm Institute
University of California, San Diego
9500 Gilman Drive
La Jolla, CA 92093-0436

Philippe Rouja
3 Evans Bay Road
Southampton, Bermuda

Jean-Pierre Rouja
LookBermuda | LookFilms
P.O. Box HM 878
Hamilton, Bermuda

Falko Kuester
Qualcomm Institute
University of California, San Diego
9500 Gilman Drive
La Jolla, CA 92093-0436

The Ancient Mesambria Field School in Underwater Archaeology: Synergy in Benefit of Bulgarian Cultural Heritage

Nayden Prahov, Danny Zborover

Since 2018, the Balkan Heritage Foundation and the Bulgarian Center for Underwater Archaeology, in collaboration with New Bulgarian University and the Institute for Field Research, have been conducting an annual field school in underwater archaeology in Nesebar's peninsular Old Town Quarter, ancient Mesambria, a UNESCO World Heritage site on the Bulgarian Black Sea coast. While teaching, studying, and training, the scientists and students are actually participating in ongoing field research projects and are contributing to the study, conservation, and promotion of underwater and maritime cultural heritage. Thus, the field school creates a synergy in benefit of the cultural heritage.

Introduction

Since 2018, the Balkan Heritage Foundation and Balkan Heritage Field Schools (BHF/BHFS), the Bulgarian Center for Underwater Archaeology, and the Institute for Field Research (IFR), have been conducting an annual field school in underwater archaeology in Nesebar, ancient Mesambria, on the Bulgarian Black Sea coast. The field school enables students, heritage specialists, the partnering institutions and local communities to interact, collaborate with and benefit from each other. As a result, BHFS participants receive a quality practice-based education and intercultural experience; specialists and their heritage projects receive funding, volunteers, advocacy and other kinds of support; local communities generate income for providing their products and services to the field school, and have the shared Bulgarian heritage promoted and supported. The goal of the project is to create a synergy between all involved parties, achieving sustainability and providing a wide impact from its results. Thus, the Ancient Mesambria Field School in Underwater Archaeology becomes a platform for solidarity in benefit of cultural heritage.

Nesebar, ancient Mesambria and its underwater cultural heritage

Founded in the early Iron Age by a Thracian tribe, Nesebar, ancient Mesambria, is considered one of the oldest towns on the Western Black Sea Coast. Today, it is situated on a small peninsula (about 0.5 sq. km) that is connected to the mainland by a narrow isthmus. According to ancient sources, the first Greek settlers there were of Dorian origin who established their colony at the end of the 6th century BCE. Due to its strategic position, favorable landscape and two natural harbors, the town grew quickly and became one of the most powerful Greek colonies along the Western Black Sea Coast. The peak of its prosperity was in the 3rd–2nd centuries BCE. Commercial links connected it to towns from the Black Sea, the Aegean, and the Mediterranean. After the Classical and Hellenistic periods, the town consecutively became part of the Roman, Byzantine, Bulgarian, and Ottoman empires and, now, the modern Bulgarian state. The legacy of Nesebar is derived from its rich history. The numerous monuments on land and underwater, along with its unique landscape, were the reasons for the inclusion of the town in the list of UNESCO World Heritage sites in 1983.

Underwater archaeological studies in Nesebar began in 1960 under the directorship of Mrs. Liuba Ognenova, one of the pioneers on the Bulgarian underwater archaeology. Fifteen campaigns were conducted up to 1983. During these surveys, it was determined that significant parts of the ancient town are below sea level. Ruins of fortification walls, towers (including a hexagonal one), staircases, gates and other structures from the pre-Greek (Thracian) time, Classical and Hellenistic era, Late Antiquity and the Middle Ages, were traced in various sectors around the peninsula – northwest, north, northeast, and east. The traced layout of the fortification walls of Mesambria leads us to conclude that Nesebar has lost a significant internal part of its territory, approximately one third of its ancient expanse, due to marine transgression, landslide activity, sea abrasion and a series of earthquakes. Today, it lies underwater at a depth up to -5 meters and up to a distance of approximately 160 meters from the present shore.

The work of Liuba Ognenova's team was exceptional. During 15 field seasons most of Nesebar's underwater heritage were carefully studied. The surveyed areas were divided by a 50 square meter grid. The squares were marked on the sea surface and investigated by divers who used the method of the parallel strips. The discovered structures were carefully recorded in a 1:100 scale and plotted on a map. Hundreds of stones which were part of preserved or destroyed structures were measured, drawn, and geodetically positioned on survey plans. The studied area was scanned by a Singlebeam Echosounder and a bathymetric map in 1:2000 scale was produced on which the underwater monuments were plotted. The work and discoveries of the underwater archaeologists had an important impact on the decision for inclusion of Nesebar in UNESCO's list of World Heritage sites.

Unfortunately, the impressive discoveries were not published properly or in a timely fashion. Only an overview of the underwater monuments was published in several articles, containing very limited photographs and only general plans (Ognenova-Marinova and Preshlenov 2004; Preshlenov 2008a, 2008b, 2010, 2012). Most of the information remained in the archives of the Liuba Ognenova's expedition and, for decades, have been waiting to be processed and published.

In 2017, after a gap of 33 years, the Bulgarian Centre for Underwater Archaeology resumed the regular archaeological research in Nesebar with the support of the Ministry of Culture and, from 2018 onwards, of the Balkan Heritage Foundation and the Institute for Field Research. The main scientific and research questions are:

1. What was the evolution of the maritime and terrestrial landscapes of the Nesebar peninsula?
2. What was the sequence, time period and the volume of the marine transgression and regressions that affected the ancient town?
3. What was the layout, construction, and function of the submerged archaeological structures?
4. Where were the harbors of the town and what was their construction?
5. What is the perseveration state of the submerged archaeological structures?
6. What are the possibilities for the exhibition and inclusion of underwater structures in cultural tourism?

The research on Nesebar's submerged and maritime heritage addresses some general scientific problems and topics, such as the evolution of the Black Sea basin and the stages of the sea level fluctuations, the harbors building traditions along the Western Black Sea Coast, the shipbuilding, seafaring and trade.

The field approaches applied in the ongoing project include a multifaceted survey of Nesebar and identification, exploration and documentation of its underwater cultural heritage. Field and lab methods include a geophysical and remote survey with Multibeam Echosounder and a side scan sonar, aerial photogrammetry, electric resistivity survey, dive survey, excavations, 3D photogrammetry recording, photogrammetry mosaics recording, photography, scale drawing, and creating a GIS database.

The ultimate goal of the project is publication, presentation and communication of the submerged and maritime heritage of Nesebar with the academic and non-academic public, including peer-reviewed scientific and popular publications, establishment of Nesebar Maritime Museum, touristic underwater archaeological tours, a virtual reality recreation of ancient Nesebar, delivering public lectures and presentations.

Since 2017, the multifaceted archaeological survey has been quite successful and rewarding. It revealed previously unknown components of the fortification system including: massive block walls dating probably from the Hellenistic period; stone and mortar as well as opus mixtum walls from the Byzantine period; three massive stone jetties which are the first structures that could be associated with the ancient harbors of the town found so far. These newly discovered monuments as well as those found by Liuba Ognenova have been cleaned, partly excavated and recorded with Multibeam Echosounder scanning, photogrammetry 3D models, photomosaics, and technical drawings. The research team is continuing the studies of the underwater and the maritime heritage of Nesebar and is working on its publication and information dissemination.

The Underwater Archaeology Field School

The Ancient Mesambria Field School in Underwater Archaeology was established in 2018 to increase the resources available for the achievement of the set goals and tasks, raise awareness to the rich Bulgarian submerged cultural heritage, provide training opportunities which are rare in underwater archaeology. This was implemented in partnership of four organization:

1. The Balkan Heritage Foundation (BHF), a Bulgarian charity organization, whose mission is the preservation, study and promotion of the

cultural heritage of South East Europe. BHF committed to the organization of this project as part of its existing educational program, the Balkan Heritage Field School (BHFS) established in 2008. The BHFS provides practice-based education in the fields of archaeology and conservation. It annually organizes various field schools around the Balkans.
2. The Institute for Field Research (IFR), a US-based nonprofit academic organization whose mission is to transform individuals and communities through experiential education and field research. The IFR conducts annual peer-reviews of all its field schools.
3. The Bulgarian National Center for Underwater Archaeology (CUA), under the Ministry of Culture, whose mission is to protect, study and promote the underwater and maritime heritage of Bulgaria.
4. The New Bulgarian University, along with its Center for Vocational and Continuing Education and the Department of Archaeology, is the largest private university in Bulgaria.

The concept of the field school is based on a symbiosis between an ongoing research project and an experiential academic program. The scientific and research team members are instructors and supervisors in the field school with the students participating as active contributors to the research and dissemination process (see also Baxter 2009; Mandal et al. 2019; Mytum 2012). This field school is suitable for beginners in the field and aims to broaden knowledge, refine skills and propel students to further their career in maritime and underwater archaeology. The requirements for students are to have a strong motivation and interests in the field, and to hold a SCUBA Open Water Certificate issued by any worldwide recognized training organization. The field school combines elements of theoretical, practical and intercultural education and experience such as lectures and instructions, field and lab work, and field trips. The focus of the program is the hands-on experience and learning through practicing concept. The agenda of the one-month program includes learning and practicing of various underwater archaeology and interdisciplinary practices such as: underwater reconnaissance survey, archaeological excavations, underwater photography, photogrammetry and 3D modelling, mapping and recording of submerged archaeological structures and monuments, marine geophysical survey, creating a GIS database, conservation of underwater sites and artifacts, reflectance transformation imaging (RTI) of graffiti of ships in Medieval churches in Nesebar.

Nesebar as a venue offers ideal conditions for the implementation of field school in maritime archaeology, including ongoing research projects for the study of submerged heritage and of ships' graffiti in medieval churches in the historical town; accessible underwater sites, easily reachable from the shore and at a depth of up to -5 meter; numerous facilities as accommodation and food options, emergency and health services, available diving centers and a unique historical environment.

A key component of the scientific and academic projects is raising the public awareness to the local archaeological heritage in order to facilitate and gain support for its protection, study and presentation. This component will be achieved through developing a project for the establishment of a museum of underwater and maritime archaeology as well as diving sightseeing tours showcasing the submerged heritage and landscapes. Students will help with the development of such programs, individual idea proposals (student assignments), communication with local people, diving centers, tourists and local archaeologists.

The program is accredited by the New Bulgarian University and by Connecticut College through IFR. The students are able to receive credit units transferable to their home academic institutions through official university transcripts. They all receive a Balkan Heritage Field School Certificate specifying the topics and the hours of the educational activities (fieldwork, lectures, workshops, study trips). Thus, the ultimate goal of the field school is to create synergy between involved parties and to foster the achievement of their goals and responsibilities, and thus to create a sustainable project.

The Beneficiaries

The main beneficiaries of the field school are the students (Figure 1). They receive a quality practice-based education in the field of underwater and maritime archaeology. Such practical aspects are quite often lacking in university programs that are usually theoretically oriented. The field school objectives are to:

- Present Bulgarian underwater archaeology to students, in the context of world maritime archaeology (history, sites, projects).
- Train students in developing diving skills in a manner that allows scientific research – establish

and maintain neutral buoyancy, work upside down, avoid contaminating the water and use of proper communication signs.
- Introduce students to basic underwater excavation methods and practices, including preparation and work with ejectors, trowels, identify artifacts, features and structures (Figure 2).
- Teach students how to recognize and evaluate stratigraphic relationships and contextual information, generate and test site formation hypothesis.
- Develop capabilities to perform underwater documentation tasks using measuring and documentation devices, creating written, graphic, photographic, and photogrammetric records (Figure 3).
- Introduce students to advanced underwater documentation techniques – photogrammetry and 3D modeling of underwater structures (McCarthy and Benjamin 2014).
- Introduce students to basic finds processing methods – initial desalination, cleaning, sorting, labeling, drawing, photographing and description.
- Introduce students to the basic principles of artifact conservation from a salty water environment.
- Introduce students to geophysical prospection techniques – scanning with Multibeam Echosounder, side scan sonar, sub-bottom profiler as well as data processing and results interpretation (Plets et al. 2013).
- Introduce students to remote sensing prospection and documentation techniques using ROV, bathymetric aerial LIDAR, and aerial photography (theoretical).
- Introduce students to Reflection Transformation Imaging (RTI) technique for documentation of epigraphic monuments.

The students also receive a unique intercultural experience by working and living with colleagues with similar interests, but often with different cultural and educational backgrounds. Together with the team members, they experience the rich Balkan culture. Participants have the opportunity to establish contacts with specialists in the field of their interests and research, and with other students with similar educational and professional plans and intentions. Most of the students

Figure 1: Field school students and their instructors (Photo by Nayden Prahov, 2019).

take advantage of the university credits awarded by the program which they transfer to their home universities. Some of the participants join the field school before the beginning of their graduate studies in order to assess whether underwater and maritime archaeology is what they imagine it to be and to decide whether to continue their studies and future career in this field. In student evaluations of both the 2018 and 2019 field seasons, participants expressed high satisfaction with the academic quality of the program and the metrics showed an increase in the subject interest after the completion of the field school. Another positive index was the large percentage of these students who applied to university programs in maritime archaeology.

Equally important is the students' awareness that they are not just participants in a field school, but are, also, members of the research team and participate in real scientific projects. They find out that their work is a real

Figure 2: A student excavating an Early Byzantine wall in opus mixtum (Photo by Nayden Prahov, 2019).

Figure 3: Students working on a technical drawing of a Hellenistic period fortification wall (Photo by Nayden Prahov, 2019).

contribution to the study, protection and promotion of cultural heritage. They are aware that part of their participation fee directly supports the local cultural heritage and they act as its donors. This creates an even stronger motivation and stimulates their empathy to the local cultural heritage.

Other project beneficiaries are the scientists and heritage specialists whose projects are connected to and supported by the field school. Currently these projects include: The Complex Archaeological Survey of the Submerged Mesambria; and the Study and Documentation of Ships Graffiti on Medieval and Post Medieval Churches in Nesebar. Both are implemented by archaeologists from CUA, the Bulgarian National Archaeological Institute with Museum, the Archaeological museum in Nesebar and the Balkan Heritage Foundation. Through the field school, these scientific projects receive additional funding from student participation fees, organizational and technical support by the field school team, and voluntary field and lab work by the students and their supervisors. A field school season generates more resources for the scientific projects compared to the annual funding by the Ministry of Culture. So far the results of the field school contribution to the scientific projects could be summarized as follows:

- Surveyed vast areas of Nesebar's underwater heritage;
- Discovered and documented unknown parts of submerged Early Byzantine fortification walls;
- Excavated and documented with photogrammetry Early Byzantine fortification walls (Figure 4);
- Cleaned and recorded with photogrammetry significant parts of the Hellenistic stone fortification structures;
- Recorded with Reflectance Transformation Imaging of dozens of ships graffiti in two medieval churches in Nesebar - St. Spas and St. Stefan;
- Conducted geophysical surveys with Multibeam Echosounder and sub-bottom profiler.

The participants in the field school also contribute to the project and cultural heritage promotion through dissemination of information to their universities and colleagues. They also participate in think-tanks and brainstorming about the establishment of exhibitions and a museum dedicated to the maritime heritage of Nesebar, as well as organizing diving sightseeing tours showcasing the submerged heritage and landscapes.

The local people are the other beneficiaries from the project implementation. They provide accommodation, food, transport and other services. The local diving centers also support the project by providing gear, tanks and air, additional training, and other support. Their major business in Nesebar is summer tourism, with the high season from late June to early September. The field school takes place in late May – middle June and, thus, extends the season for our local partners. For most of them who run a small or family business, a project with up to 8 participants and a team of 6 members makes an important impact on their incomes and the local economy.

The ultimate beneficiary of the field school implementation and the collaboration of all involved parties is the cultural heritage. It is studied, preserved and promoted. The project partners and the students interact with a strong motivation and create a synergy that makes the project sustainable. All this makes

Figure 4: Photogrammetric photomosaic of Early Byzantine walls excavated during the field school (Model by Pavel Georgiev, 2019).

the Ancient Mesambria Field School in Underwater Archaeology a platform in solidarity with the cultural heritage.

Conclusions

If run properly, a field school could create a valuable synergy between all involved parties and have a significant impact on the study, preservation and promotion of the underwater cultural heritage. It is an ideal solution for funding and realization of various underwater research or conservation projects. Unfortunately, such educational programs are quite limited worldwide and the number of underwater field schools is insignificant compared to terrestrial field schools. The Archaeological Institute of America Field School Database shows a steady increase in the number and locations of underwater and maritime archaeology programs over the last decade; in 2018, there were 16 programs in the US, Bulgaria, Spain, Italy, Israel, Dominican Republic, and Netherlands Antilles. These still represent only 5% of the total archaeological field schools offered that year (Zborover et al. 2019). As a corollary, publications on training and experiential learning in underwater archaeology are still scarce in the professional literature (see for example Bratten 2012; Corscadden Knox and Smith 2012).

The reasons behind this fact are various. The main issue is that the implementation of an underwater archaeological project is quite a complicated task. Adding a field school component makes the organization of both projects a real challenge, even a burden. In the case of the Nesebar Underwater Field School, the solution is that the Balkan Heritage Foundation handles the bulk of the field school management, including involvement of participants (in cooperation with the Institute for Field Research) and recruitment of their supervisors, organization of accommodation and food for the students and the entire team, technical and logistical support, and fundraising responsibilities. This allows the scientific team to focus on their field research and their educational responsibilities to the students.

Another reason for the lack of popularity of underwater field schools is that many universities and scientific and research institutes, have various provisions for running such practical courses: specialized and expensive insurance, large safety team, high technical requirements, specialized training, and certification for the field school staff. These prerequisites often make the implementation of such practical courses much more expensive and difficult tasks (see also Bratten 2012; Corscadden Knox and Smith 2012).

The field school in Nesebar complies with the general requirements for diving activities of the worldwide recognized diving training organizations: the field work is supervised and secured by experienced divers (mostly instructors or dive masters), all the students are obliged to have DAN diving insurance, and the field school has a strict safety policy, rules and daily safety practices (Bowens 2009).

An important prerequisite for implementation of a good field school is that it should be technically equipped with secure diving gear, boat and geophysical equipment, pumps and ejectors for the underwater excavations. All these facilities are provided by the Centre for Underwater Archaeology and the local diving centers.

Last, but not least, is the importance of a suitable archaeological site. It should be appropriate and safe for educational and training purposes. It should be easily accessible and should be suitable for excavation by untrained hands. It has to provide good opportunities for practice of various underwater archaeology techniques – diving reconnaissance survey, excavations, underwater photography and photogrammetry modeling, drawing of sites and features, exercising diving skills (see also Corscadden Knox and Smith 2012).

The field school in Nesebar combines all these prerequisites: suitable venue and archaeological site, technical and organizational support, motivated team and partnering organizations which collaborate in a sustainable way, creating a beneficial synergy. Nevertheless, the project still faces its difficulties and obstacles. Its results and the impact it has on the cultural heritage, on the generation of future underwater and maritime archaeologists, and on the sustainable development of the local society is rewarding enough and motivates the team to press on.

References

BAXTER, JANE EVA
2009   *Archaeological Field Schools: A Guide for Teaching in the Field*. Routledge, New York.

BOWENS, AMANDA
2009   *Underwater Archaeology: The NAS Guide to Principles and Practice, Second edition*. Blackwell Publishing, Portsmouth.

Bratten, John R.
2012 The University of West Florida's Maritime Field School Experience. In *Global Perspectives on Archaeological Field Schools: Constructions of Knowledge and Experience*, edited by Harold Mytum, pp. 147-164. Springer, New York.

Corscadden Knox, Anne, and Sheli O. Smith
2012 Freshwater Underwater Archaeology Field School, Good Practice, Good Science. In *Global Perspectives on Archaeological Field Schools: Constructions of Knowledge and Experience*, edited by Harold Mytum, pp. 165-177. Springer, New York.

Mandal, Stephen, Ran Boytner, Denis Shine, Danny Zborover, and Madeleine Harris
2019 The Carrig Field School: A Model for the Benefits of Field-School Education. In Carrick, County Wexford: Ireland's First Anglo-Norman Stronghold, edited by Denis Shine, Michael Potterton, Stephen Mandal, and Catherine McLoughlin, pp. 198-212. Four Courts, Dublin.

McCarthy, John, and Jonathan Benjamin
2014 Multi-image Photogrammetry for Underwater Archaeological Site Recording: An Accessible, Diver-Based Approach. *Journal of Maritime Archaeology* 9:95-114.

Mytum, Harold
2012 The Pedagogic Value of Field Schools: Some Frameworks. In *Global Perspectives on Archaeological Field Schools: Constructions of Knowledge and Experience*, edited by Harold Mytum, pp. 9-23. Springer, New York.

Ognenova-Marinova, Liuba, and Hristo Preshlenov
2004 Past and Future of the Underwater Archaeological Research in Nesebar, Bulgaria. In *Mediterraneum. Tutela e valorizzazione dei beni culturali ed ambientali*, edited by Fabio Maniscalco, vol. 4, pp. 263-269. Napoli, Italy.

Plets, Ruth, Justin Dix, and Richard Bates
2013 *Marine Geophysics Data Acquisition, Processing and Interpretation: Guidance Notes*. English Heritage Publishing, Swindon.

Preshlenov, Hristo
2008a Withdrawing Coasts. Geomorphology, Bathymetry and Archeological Cartography in Nessebar. In *Bulgaria Pontica Medii Aevi, VI-VII. Mesambria Pontica*, edited by Iv. Karayotov, pp. 51-67. Studia in Honorem Professoris Vasil Giuzelev, Burgas.

2008b Morphodynamics of the coastal zone of the Nessebar Peninsula (Bulgaria): archaeological and geological benchmarks. In *Geoarchaeology and Archaeomineralogy. Proceedings of the International Conference, Sofia*, edited by R. Kostov, B. Gaydarska, and M. Gurova, pp. 305-307. Publishing House St. Ivan Rilski, Sofia.

2010 Coastal Instability and Urban Changes: The Case of the Nessebar Peninsula. *Geologica Balcanica*, 39(1-2):325.

2012 Mesambria Pontica in orbis Romanus. In *Roman Cities*, edited by Rumen Ivanov, pp. 493-536. Prof. Marin Drinov Academic Publishing House, Sofia.

Zborover, Danny, Ran Boytner, Breann Hall, and Miriam Bar-Zemer
2019 Making the Most of Field Schools: Education, Training, and Experiential Learning in Historical Archaeology. Presentation given at the Society for Historical Archaeology 52nd Annual Conference, St. Charles, Missouri.

· · · · · · · · · · · · · · · ·

Nayden Prahov
National Institute of Archaeology
with Museum – BAS
2 Saborna str., 1000 Sofia, Bulgaria
Balkan Heritage Foundation
7 Tulovo, 5th Floor, Apt.7, 1504 Sofia, Bulgaria

Danny Zborover
1401 E. Girard St.
Englewood, CO 80113, USA

Integrated Maritime Cultural Landscape for Management of Vulnerable Coastal Heritage

Sorna Khakzad, Michael Thomin

In this paper, we applied the concept of Maritime Cultural Landscape (MCL) as a tool to evaluate the maritime heritage of Northwest Florida for a National Heritage Area (NHA) designation. NHAs in the USA are lived-in landscapes where historic, cultural and natural resources form cohesive, nationally important landscapes. We hypothesized that integration of MCL concept and NHA criteria offers a better management tool for the protection of coastal cultural heritage against the adversities of natural disasters. This will ultimately help in designing a management plan that will protect our cultural and natural resources for the benefit of local communities.

Background

A study and assessment of Northwest Florida cultural and natural resources between 2016 to 2018 revealed that this area encompasses a great number of sites and entities such as museums, state parks, national parks, archaeological and historical sites that are significant in understanding the maritime history and cultural landscape of Northwest Florida (Khakzad and Thomin 2019). The results of the study revealed that the maritime landscape of Florida panhandle, including its rivers, coasts, bays and sounds, helped develop the United States' national defense, industry, economy, tourism and innovation into what it is today. The study also highlighted that inadequate level of attention and knowledge to these resources have prevented the area from maximizing the use and benefit from their resources.

The Florida Panhandle is continuously prone to suffer from natural and anthropogenic disasters. Numerous hurricanes and storms that hit the area each year with evidences since the prehistoric era to present have been a major factor in the destruction and alteration of the coastal areas and well inland. In fact, more storms hit Florida than any other state in the U.S (National Hurricane Center 2006). In addition to natural disasters, Northwest Florida has also suffered from anthropogenic factors such as the BP oil spill in 2010. These natural and anthropogenic disasters continuously affect both the historical, archaeological and natural resources, as well as people and communities. The study also highlighted that despite all the disasters in the area, the residents of Florida Panhandle have remained in the area and always rebuild their towns and cities; they helped to revive the area. Making this area unique is a strong connection between people and the landscape in Northwest Florida.

Approach

With the goal of cultural and natural resources preservation and management, promoting diverse tourism—such as eco-tourism and cultural tourism—benefiting from our diverse resources in a sustainable way for present and future generation, we started looking at different strategies to manage the area. Considering the size and nature of the area and involving different stakeholders, we realized that we needed an integrated approach for the management of this landscape and its cultural-natural resources.

The waterways of Northwest Florida, coastal dynamics, and the Gulf of Mexico have had major roles in shaping the maritime landscape of Northwest Florida. Therefore, in this study we apply the concept of maritime cultural landscape to identify themes of the area and retain a degree of integrity that supports interpretation.

Maritime Cultural Landscape Concept

Maritime cultural landscape with all its definitions and uses of the term has been an object of scrutiny (Westerdahl 2011:733-758).

> *Maritime Cultural Landscapes (MCLs) are the product of collective human use of marine and coastal environments across time. Areas of geographic space become "places" only when people give them meaning and value for the resources and qualities they possess. They are places where we work and recreate, and many are deeply connected physically and spiritually. MCLs provide a record of human use of these places throughout history, demonstrating how humans have shaped and been shaped by these places (Delgado 2015).*

Cultural landscape is an in-between-space, where sea and land meet and the activities of humans on both affect and harmonize the space (Khakzad 2009). Understanding the extent of these activities, the resources that humans used over time, and the value of these activities and resources that influence the geography and landscape of a place shapes our concept of maritime cultural landscape.

A maritime cultural landscape can be characterized as the sum of "human utilization of maritime space by boat, settlement, fishing, hunting, shipping and its attendant subcultures" comprising the "whole network of sailing routes, old as well as new, with ports and harbors along the coast, and its related constructions and remains of human activities, underwater as well as terrestrial" (Westerdahl 1992). It includes not only this cultural history of the physical environment, but also how humans who have lived and worked there over time perceive this place at a deeper level. As the history of a place is a tapestry woven over time, the study and characterization of Northwest Florida's maritime landscape provides an opportunity to recognize, understand, and appreciate the threads each culture who called this place "home" contributed to what we observe today. Characterizing MCLs and pursuing a deeper understanding of these important places may be a useful tool to inform contemporary marine and coastal preservation and management. It also provides a way to answer fundamental questions such as "what makes a place special?", "what can we do to highlight and recognize its values?", and "what we can do to keep it that way?" (Penkiunas 2015). By understanding our maritime cultural landscape, we can better understand resources within their evolving environmental context and their many-layered cultural context. The goal is to incorporate this landscape into development of contexts and evaluation of significance for all properties (Wyatt 2015). Each major era of the Florida Panhandle maritime culture and its maritime cultural landscape offers a unique contribution to the nation's history.

Maritime Cultural Landscape of Northwest Florida

The concept that most comprehensively captures and depicts the natural and cultural resources of Northwest Florida is a Maritime Cultural Landscape. The maritime landscape and natural resources of the West Florida Panhandle has been instrumental in its development. This landscape of Northwest Florida provides insights into the evolution of this environment over time. It depicts how the humans who lived here found and used important resources that sustained them physically and spiritually. In addition, there are lessons that the history of this place and people can provide for contemporary and future human uses. The maritime landscape of Northwest Florida has had a significant role in shaping the culture, identity, traditions, and activities of its settlers, and shaping a unique cultural landscape that tell a significant story and contributes to the American history.

Originally, during the Ice Age, many prehistoric Native Americans lived on the then exposed continental shelf and kept using its natural resources and transforming this landscape (Dunbar and Webb 1996; Milanich 2017). For at least six thousand years ago, the native people of Florida traveled the waterways and coasts by canoe, facilitating communication and trade among the tribes. About three hundred prehistoric canoes have been found in more than two hundred sites in Florida, among which there are some of the earliest proven native sites and settlements (Dunbar 2014).

Throughout history, rivers have played a fundamental role as transportation corridors, sources of resources and work, as means for cultural exchanges, as loci of industrialization (water, energy) and as favorable environments for diverse types of settlements from small villages and towns up to big cities (Haslam 1997). The earliest human settlements in the Apalachicola Valley are mostly clustered along the Chipola River, the largest tributary to the Apalachicola (Faught 2004). Today, the Chipola is a beautiful clear blue stream with white limestone banks and many sinks and springs along its course.

As early as the 1500s, Spanish explorers realized the value of the deep-water bay at Pensacola and this site was contested by Spain, France, England, and the United States during centuries of borderlands warfare (Hudson 1988; Worth 2018). By the 1820s, a U.S. Navy Yard was established in Pensacola Bay (Shettle 1995). Coastal live oak trees in the panhandle were utilized in the nation's first experimental forestry station with the Naval Live Oaks Plantation (Snell 1983). These trees were used to build numerous wooden ships (USS *Constitution* 2020). In addition, the region's huge stands of virgin longleaf yellow pines and the clays along the waterways provided income for numerous settlers in the 1800s as the brick industry and the lumber industry boomed (Rucker 1988). Utilizing the swift moving streams and the numerous bays, hundreds of water-powered and later steam-powered sawmills were constructed across the Panhandle from the 1800s to the early 1900s (Ross 2014). In the 20th century the area's beaches, rivers, and bays created attractions for a new tourism industry.

The maritime history of Florida describes significant past events relating to the U.S. state of Florida in areas concerning shipping, shipwrecks, and military installations and lighthouses constructed to protect or aid navigation and development of the Florida peninsula. The maritime landscape of Florida has contributed to industrial development, tourism promotion, innovation, and military and defense of the American nation. Abundance of natural resources, also, contributed to creating a resilient community that survives, revives, and thrives despite the many natural disasters that occur in this coastal area. All this not only tells a significant story about the area's past, but also provides knowledge for present and future generations to learn from the past, act in the present, and plan for mitigating future disasters to come.

Integrated Management Tool: National Heritage Area

A significant maritime cultural landscape, such as Florida Panhandle with its cultural and natural resources, requires a proper valorization in order to play its role in sustainable development (Campbell 2000; LGA Report 2002). An integrative management plan that can maximize the use of all resources in the area, guarantee participation of variety of stakeholders, and considers the socioeconomic and political dimensions into its management, is a necessity (Khakzad 2015 et al.).

The result of a two-year heritage tourism assessment in the Panhandle area demonstrated there is a need for a management plan that ensures continued preservation of the area's natural, cultural and historical resources. This management plan should include providing opportunities for well-planned industrial, tourism and urban development, as well as community and stakeholders engagement. Following an assessment of existing management programs in state and federal levels, and a collaborative agreement among major stakeholders, it was determined that an NHA designation will meet the goals (Barton 2016).

NHAs are designated by Congress as places where natural, cultural, and historic resources combine to form a cohesive, nationally important landscape (National Park Service 2020). The root of these areas is in their communities, as an NHA provides a foundation upon which communities can develop a vision, based on a shared heritage, which addresses opportunities for conserving natural and cultural resources while enhancing economic vitality. "NHAs are lived-in landscapes. Consequently, NHA entities collaborate with communities to determine how to make heritage relevant to local interests and needs" (National Park Service 2020). One of the latest reports on NHA (Alliance of National Heritage Areas 2019) highlights the significant achievement of different NHAs in the country. Examples includes, but not limited to, achieving a healthy, nature-based tourism economy and environment (Mississippi Gulf Coast National Heritage Area), creating innovative educational programs to learn about history (New Jersey, Crossroad of the American Revolution NHA), reinvigorating a passion for learning about the environment (New York, Erie Canalway NHA) and many more.

NHA are required to have specific themes that are relevant to the history and heritage of the area. Themes are the unifying ideas that, when woven together, make up the fabric of NHA. They are a way of presenting and organizing the essential aspects of a region's heritage that demonstrate their national distinctiveness. The National Park Service (NPS) recommends the identification of themes to illustrate the unique qualities of the heritage area and to provide a broad conceptual framework under which to interpret natural, historic, cultural, and recreational resources (Mountains to Sound Greenway Trust 2012).

Themes for the proposed heritage area help to organize the presentation of the region's stories. They can be used to support the organization of interpretive materials, to group destinations for theme-based itineraries, and to identify where there are strengths and weaknesses in telling the region's stories (Tilden 1957). Most importantly, they help to provide a structure for visitors to understand the different aspects of the region's maritime heritage and understand it in the context of the diverse information and experiences available. These potential themes are illustrative of one potential approach for telling the region's stories (Mayo et al. 2015).

Themes

Based on the study and public input, we have developed an overarching theme: "The maritime landscape of the Florida Panhandle—its rivers, coasts, bays, and sounds—helped develop the United States national defense, expansion, industry, tourism, and innovation into what it is today" (Khakzad and Thomin 2020). Four sub themes under the maritime cultural landscape concept also support this theme and help with identifying and interpreting the resources (Figure 1). In the following sections, we will describe the area and specific sites and entities that are associated with these themes and contribute to telling a compelling story about Northwest Florida, revealing its rich maritime culture.

Description of the case area

The study area covers from Perdido River (Florida and Alabama Stateline) in the West to parts of Leon and Jefferson Counties (National Forest line) on the East, Florida Stateline on the North and to the Gulf coast in the South (Figure 2). This area is known locally as the Florida Panhandle, but historically in colonial time periods it was called West Florida. In more recent times, the region is referred to as Northwest Florida.

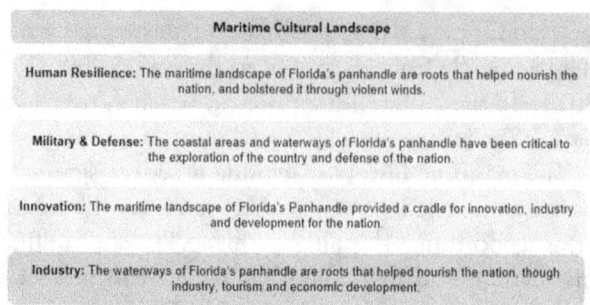

Figure 1: Area's overall concept and teams.

Sites and Entities

Maritime cultural heritage covers a range of different activities, sites and artifacts. The maritime cultural landscape of Northwest Florida comprises many archaeological sites, trails, and historical buildings that are evidence of rich maritime activities in this area from

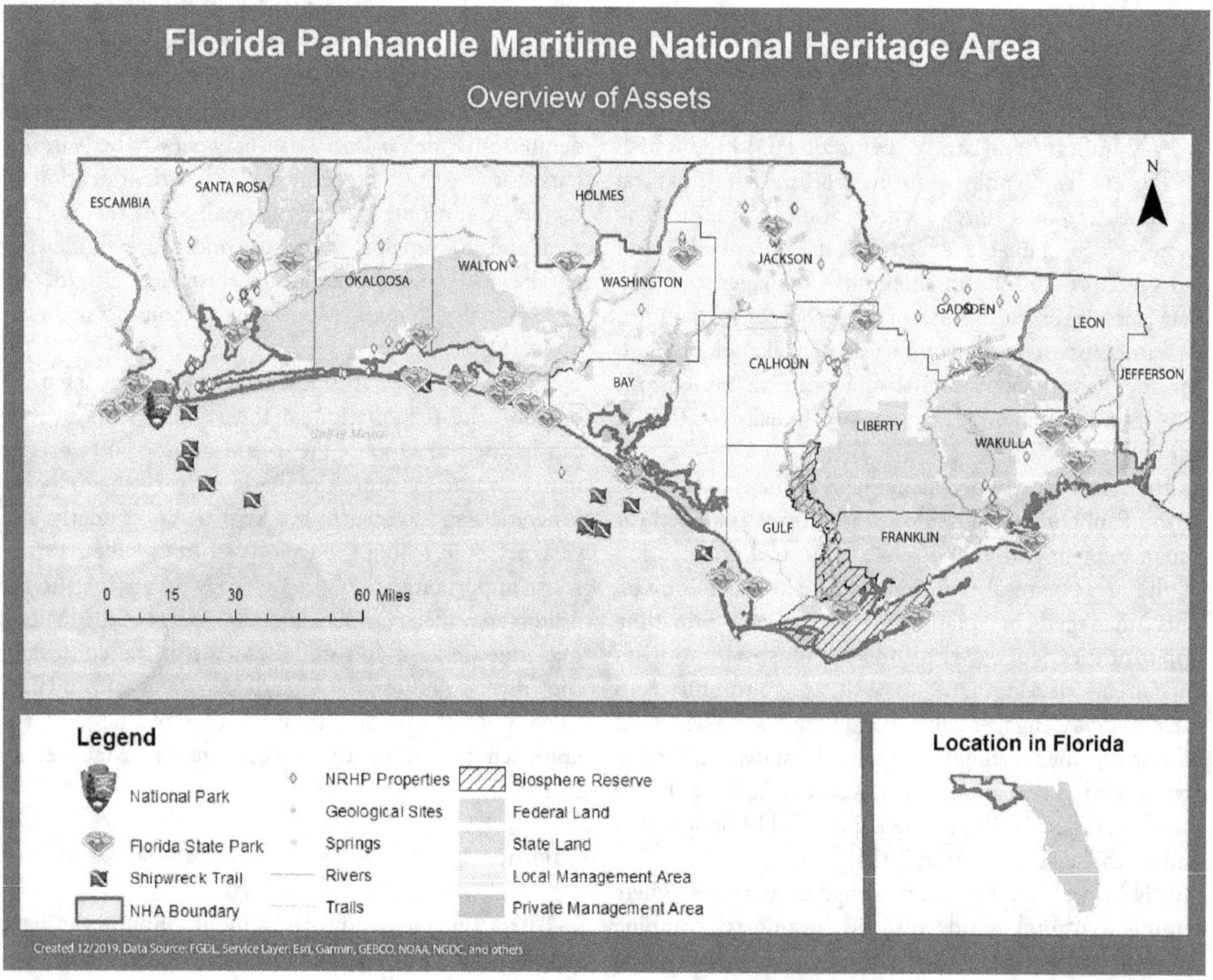

Figure 2: Map of the study area. Prepared by Rachel Hines.

prehistory to present time. The significance of this landscape is that it portrays an image of the past that can be seen today and has many lessons to be learned for present and future generations.

Northwest Florida encompasses specific maritime focused entities, such as museums and trails that highlight naval activities, shipbuilding, sailing, and maritime innovation aspects. They are listed here separately, as they fall under specific themes and highlight the contribution of Northwest Florida in the expansion of U.S. maritime activities.

Numerous museums are highlighting the maritime history of Northwest Florida. Among them are Man in the Sea Museum, Apalachicola Maritime Museum and several lighthouses. In addition, according to the Florida Master Site File the coast of the Florida Panhandle has at least 58 recorded historic shipwrecks, ranging from early European colonial ships to modern casualties of World War II. However, this is probably an underestimate and there are likely hundreds unrecorded in the area. Nevertheless, the recorded sites are evidence of the national (and international) importance of this stretch of the northern Gulf Coast to commerce, trade, travel, and control. Today, these shipwrecks are loci for heritage tourism in the form of snorkeling and scuba diving, as well as contribute to sport fishing by serving as artificial reefs and habitat. The world's largest artificial reef, USS *Oriskany*, is located offshore of Pensacola. It is part of the Florida Panhandle Shipwreck Trail.

In addition to the shipwreck trail, there is the De Luna maritime landscape that is a unique site where there are evidences of colonial exploration, their settlement and shipwrecks still exist. This includes the remains from the terrestrial settlement and the discovery of three shipwrecks that are under study (Worth et al. 2017; Bense 1986). This site is an exceptional example of an MCL that encompasses the remains of an early settlement along with the ships that came to the New World (Cook et al. 2016).

Hundreds of different cultural sites along Northwest Florida's coast and numerous rivers are related to maritime activities. A few examples are especially noteworthy given their existing recognition as being nationally significant sites, such as the National Historical Landmarks San Carlos de Barrancas, Fort Walton Mound, San Marcos de Apalachee, Negro Fort, *Governor Stone* Schooner, and Pensacola Naval Air Station Historic District. Furthermore, these examples demonstrate how they are connected to the four sub themes and the underlying concept of MCL.

Military & Defense

Since the beginning of New World exploration in the 16th century of what is now the southeastern United States, Northwest Florida has held a strategic significance for military expeditions and installations. This is largely due to Northwest Florida's coastline along the Gulf of Mexico and numerous bay systems that provided different cultural groups access to inland waterways and their abundant marine resources. When Spanish Conquistador Tristan de Luna attempted to colonize the area in 1559 as part of a wider plan to prevent competing European colonial powers from influencing the region, the site of Pensacola was selected due to its proximity to a naturally deep water port that was well protected and its connection to the Gulf of Mexico. Although Luna's attempt ultimately failed after two years mostly due to a hurricane, the Spanish eventually returned to the area by the end of the 17th century to establish a series of fortifications (presidios) and missions as a way to protect Spanish interests. These presidios and missions were established along the coast and rivers, and several have been located across the region archaeologically (Bense 1999). Visible remains of other Spanish fortifications along coasts and major river systems are interpreted today at Gulf Islands National Seashore Fort Barrancas Area and San Marcos de Apalache Historic State Park.

A number of other Spanish, British, French, and American forts were also constructed along the Florida Panhandle's coast, as well as river and bay systems for defensive measures because they provided a connection to waterways that empty into the Northern Gulf of Mexico. During the American period starting in 1821, fortifications were constructed and used especially during the Seminole Wars and Civil War. In 1822, the U.S. Congress created the West Indies Squadron as piracy and the illegal slave trade spiraled out of control in the waters of the Gulf of Mexico and Caribbean Sea. Originally stationed in Key West, by 1826 the West Indies Station was relocated to the newly constructed Naval Yard in Pensacola, Florida where the squadron of warships operated until the 1840s (Gough and Borras 2018). Fort Pickens, built in 1834 on Santa Rosa Island as part of the U.S. government's third system of coastal defense, was the only federal fortification in the south to never fall to the Confederacy (Guardian of the Gulf 2020). During the Second Seminole War, which was part of the U.S. government's longest Indian conflict, the Apalachicola Arsenal was constructed along the confluence of the Apalachicola and Chattahoochee

Rivers, where it was used as a major supply depot for the American military (Boyd 1956). Both forts remain standing today and are preserved and interpreted.

In the early 20th century, the area remained strategically important for the American military, especially for training and testing purposes. The Navy's first aviation school was established in Pensacola in 1914 to train pilots to fly on aircraft carriers. The National Aviation Museum today celebrates this fact as the world's largest Naval Aviation Museum that receives over 1 million visitors per year. It is also home of the Navy's Blue Angels (Goodspeed 2011) (Figure 3). A number of other large U.S. bases (Hurlburt Field, Eglin, and Tyndall) were established along Northwest Florida's landscape to train pilots in the Army Air Corps (what later became the United States Air Force) to fly missions in the Pacific and European theaters during World War II (Wynne and Moorhead 2018). The Air Force Armament Museum features this history and over 29 different military aircraft used historically in the region. The large swaths of land owned by the federal government in Northwest Florida made it ideal for gunnery and bomb ranges for aircraft. The maritime landscape also benefited training needs of the U.S. Army's sea and land forces. Camp Gordon Johnston was established along the beaches of Northwest Florida in 1942 to train soldiers in amphibious assaults. The site was selected because of its maritime landscape with its "ability to train year-round there… the quality of the coastline, and access to offshore islands for use in conducting amphibious training" (Lewis and Beach 2001). A year later, many of these military personnel received vital training exercises at Carrabelle, Florida used to storm the beaches of Normandy, France (Lewis and Beach 2001).

Figure 3: The National Naval Aviation Museum in Pensacola. Photo courtesy Michael Thomin.

The Camp Gordon Johnston Museum celebrates and preserves this history today. Several of these key military installations remain in Northwest Florida and are still critically important for training soldiers, airmen, sailors, and marines, and for testing military equipment and munitions. The Northern Gulf of Mexico is one of the largest military testing areas in the continental United States and is considered "an irreplaceable national asset" by the Department of Defense for preserving military readiness (Office of the Secretary of Defense 2018).

Human Resilience

The MCL of Northwest Florida is also evident in the human resilience of the area's diverse cultural groups. One of the best examples of this is an archaeological site located along the Apalachicola River, historically referred to as "Negro Fort." Originally constructed by the British during the War of 1812, this small fortification was manned by hundreds of fugitive slaves by 1816. The position of the fort was chosen strategically for the maritime landscape since it provided direct access to the Apalachicola River. At the time, the fugitive slaves were attracted there because it was Spanish territory and by joining British forces meant that they would become free. In fact, this maroon settlement was the "largest independent community of fugitive slaves in the history of the present-day United States (Clavin 2019). Although the fortification was destroyed during a raid by U.S. soldiers and their Native allies under orders of General Andrew Jackson and many of the inhabitants were killed, several members of the community survived and fled South to resettle in other maroon communities in Florida. Today, this site is preserved as a National Historical Landmark located within the Apalachicola National Forest.

The Apalachicola River was a critical waterway for many of the communities in the region as well. The town of St. Joseph was an important port for shipping in the southeastern United States. Cotton was a product of worldwide economic significance that was shipped north up the Apalachicola River during the time the town was founded in 1835. The location of the town and its economic importance along the maritime landscape is a major reason why St. Joseph was selected as the site to host Florida's first constitutional convention. However, by 1842 a yellow fever epidemic and a series of hurricanes hit the town. The community was devastated, but eventually the town was rebuilt north of the original settlement and renamed Port St. Joe (Hunt 2014).

Hurricanes and disease epidemics continuously struck communities within Northwest Florida, but the people who lived there always found the resilience to survive and rebuild.

Innovation and Industry

From Pensacola to Port St. Joe, yellow fever epidemics remained a constant threat to communities living along the Northern Gulf of Mexico well into the end of the 19th century. Despite this, the people of Northwest Florida innovated and prospered through it. In the 1830s, Dr. John Gorrie moved to the third largest port on the Gulf of Mexico, where he treated the sick in the community. Several years prior to his arrival to Apalachicola, Florida, Dr. Gorrie dedicated his life work to understanding the causes of tropical diseases. To help treat patients stricken with diseases like yellow fever and malaria, Dr. Gorrie advocated for cooling sickrooms; one common theory during the time for the cause was that it was due to "bad air." To help procure enough ice quickly, Gorrie began experimenting with artificial refrigeration and, by 1851, was granted the first U.S. patent for a machine to make ice (Taylor and Gorrie 1935; Sherlock 1982). Gorrie died and was buried in Apalachicola; a state park named after him is dedicated to interpreting his life and invention. Although he was never able to capitalize financially on this Northwest Florida invention, other industries in the region boomed following the end of the American Civil War. The lumber and fishing industries were the economic engine of Northwest Florida during Reconstruction.

At one time Northwest Florida was dominated by the longleaf pine ecosystem. This made the area attractive for the logging and naval store industries. The different colonial powers who inhabited West Florida since the 16th century valued the timber in the area. Not only did they use it to build the many different fortifications along the coastline and near the entrance of bays and key rivers, but the large pine trees were used in shipbuilding (Grinnan 2013). However, the lumber industry exploded right after Florida became a state in 1845. Only ten years after becoming a state, 18 million board feet of lumber were shipped from the port of Pensacola per year (Grinnan 2013). By the 1870s, Northwest Florida's lumber industry was booming, and the port of Pensacola became the lead producer in the state (Drobney 1999). Although longleaf pine dominated the Gulf Coastal Plain, only about three percent of it remains due to deforestation caused by the lumber industry and development (Jose et al. 2006). However, efforts by private and public sectors have tried to replant this ecosystem. The E. O. Wilson Biophilia Center in Freeport, Florida is an internationally recognized non-profit educational and conservation facility. Their goal is to protect and reestablish this once dominate ecosystem that was nearly destroyed by over logging.

The flowing river systems were integral to this logging industry, since logs were cut locally by water powered mills. In fact, during Florida's Territorial Period (1821-1845) there were thirty-seven water powered mills in West Florida (Grinnan 2013). The Arcadia Mill Archaeological Site located in Milton, Florida was one of these mills. This site is interpreted and open to the public. A History of Industrial Power in the United States, 1780-1930, suggests that the rural water-powered mill represented one of the first steps in settling the American frontier (Hunter 1979). These early industries followed closely on the heels of the pioneer and persisted long after the community was established. Often, the gristmill and sawmill preceded even the church and school and usually established before the wagon road. These mills provided meal for the settlers' bread and the lumber for their houses. They became the community centers where settlers gathered to visit and exchange news. The community mill determined the placement of early roads; other commercial ventures such as the blacksmithy, livery and general store soon sprang up nearby.

The water-powered mill was a founding element of a community (Benchley et al. 1993; Little 1988a, 1988b, 1989). The water-powered mill also introduced the age of machines. The sawmill and gristmill gave the colonial and early American settler some familiarity with mechanization and the processes of industry paving the way for the Industrial Age. With the invention of more complex forms of waterpower, such as the turbine engine, and the development of steam power in the mid-nineteenth century, the Industrial Revolution began in earnest; manufactured products became widely available and the American farmer began to lose his self-sufficiency. Simple country water mills and the early turbine and steam powered mills dotted the landscape. They were an integral part of the development of northwest Florida and the nation. The many swift creeks that drain the panhandle provided countless mill seats, or favorable settings for water-powered mills.

As the vast longleaf pine forests were settled, numerous small water-powered sawmills and gristmills were built along these streams. Small communities developed around them. Some of these mills, such as Arcadia, became large industrial complexes; others remained small operations, like Carpenters' Mill in Escambia County, Jernigan's Mill in Santa Rosa County and Milligan Mill in Okaloosa County. A number of these small water-powered mills persisted into the twentieth century as gristmills, ice plants or electrical generators.

As the lumber industry grew in importance, however, the small water-powered mill was gradually replaced by large steam powered lumber mills. The steam-powered engine enabled the lumbermen to move the mills to the bays and rivers near the shipping lanes that provided the country with goods such as lumber, turpentine, and cotton. These steam powered mills along the rivers and bays gave rise to mill towns such as Century, Bagdad and Milton. Scores of mill sites, both small and large, water-powered and steam powered, cover the panhandle. These unique and extremely valuable historical sites define settlements that either no longer exist or live on only in the memories of a few former inhabitants. The majority of the mills, however, have not been recorded. Furthermore, development threatens these sites.

Northwest Florida's inhabitants have always valued the rich marine resources the area offers. The Northern Gulf of Mexico, estuaries, and riverine systems within the region provide an abundance of both salt and freshwater marine life. Large prehistoric Native American settlements relied on fish and shellfish to sustain their population, and this evidence is still visible today in the many prehistoric shell mounds and shell middens that line the coast. Some of these archaeological sites from both the Woodland and Mississippian time periods include the Fort Walton Mound, the Butcherpen Mound, the Chattahoochee Landing, and Hawkshaw (Ashley and White 2012; Anderson and Mainfort, Jr. 2002). Historical and archaeological evidence from colonial sites in the region also shows an abundance of evidence of utilizing these maritime resources, especially through fishing (Benchley et al. 2007). However, fishing was not fully commercialized in the region until the arrival of New Englanders following the American Civil War.

Though New Englanders traveled to the Northern Gulf of Mexico during the 1840s and 1850s to take advantage of the warmer climate, the commercial fishing industry did not hit its peak until the post-bellum years. Fish houses began to spring up in areas like Pensacola in the 1870s. Ties to the New England fishing industry remained strong through contracting seasonal crews and their vessels for fishing operations, eventually fisheries

Figure 4: Red snapper fishing smacks at a wharf in Pensacola Bay circa 1920. Courtesy of University Archives and West Florida History Center, UWF Libraries, Pensacola.

in the Gulf found it cheaper to purchase their own vessels. Despite this, northern fishing methods remained a unique characteristic of Pensacola fishing operations (Bucchino 2014). The Red Snapper fishing industry and oyster fishing were of particular significance to the region both economically and culturally. The Destin History and Fishing Museum and Apalachicola Maritime Museum both interpret and preserve this regional story of Northwest Florida today (Figure 4).

Discussion and Conclusion

The account of Northwest Florida's history reveals that, although the Panhandle provides an array of resources from its yellow pine to red snapper, the area's greatest quality lay in its physical location. The contested Florida territory was a struggle for power as displayed by the rotation of European might over centuries. Despite these turbulent encounters, each ancestral nation featured in the Northwest region persisted, overcoming physical and environmental barriers bent on their destruction. Yet, it was the disintegration and redevelopment of relationships which proved vital in establishing control over the area.

This study highlighted that a thorough study and evaluation of an area's cultural and natural resources can justify planning and actions for promoting preservation and interpretation of these resources. These types of evaluation can help develop policies or use programs that are already in place to manage the area and resources in a more sustainable manner.

By utilizing the NHA designation as a tool for preparing management plans for Northwest Florida, the importance of an integrated management strategy was highlighted. An integrated management plan relies on theories, previous best practices and an interdisciplinary approach. Through an integrated approach, the voices of different stakeholders and communities can be heard and included in the management plan.

NHAs expand on traditional approaches to resource stewardship. They typically support community-based initiatives that connect local citizens to the preservation and planning process. By embracing a community-based approach, NHAs can bring together diverse efforts such as education, recreation, heritage tourism, and historic preservation. Committed to both protecting and promoting the natural, cultural, historic, and scenic assets of a specific area, NHAs play a vital role in maintaining both the physical character and cultural legacy of the United States.

This study highlights the overlooked and forgotten history of Northwest Florida and promotes its unique maritime landscape to local and national audiences. In doing so, communities in the Panhandle can achieve a better understanding of the region's cultural and natural resources, which affect them on a grand scale. Fostering personal connections with valuable historic sites through the themes of national defense, industry, economy, innovation, and human resilience, encourages community members to find the most effective means to sustain and preserve these sources of heritage for generations to come, along with integrated long-term management plans.

References

ALLIANCE OF NATIONAL HERITAGE AREAS
2019 Connecting the Heart and Soul of American Community, Vol. 3. Alliance of National Heritage Areas Publication.

ANDERSON, DAVID G., AND ROBERT C. MAINFORT, JR.
2002 *The Woodland Southeast*, University of Alabama Press, Tuscaloosa and London pgs. 330-331.

ASHLEY, KEITH AND NANCY MARIE WHITE.
2012 *Late Prehistoric Florida: Archaeology at the Edge of the Mississippian World*. University of Florida Press, Gainesville., pgs. 233-237.

BARTON, ALAN
2016 From Parks to Partnerships: National Heritage Areas and the Path to Collaborative Participation in the National Park Service's First to Collaborative Participation in the National Park Service's First 100 Years 100 Years. *Natural Resources Journal*, Vol. 56: 1 National Parks at the Centennial.

BENCHLEY, ELIZABETH D., R. WAYNE CHILDERS, JOHN JAMES CLUNE, CINDY L. BERCOT, DAVID B. DODSON, APRIL WHITAKER, AND E. ASHLEY FLYNT.
2007 The Colonial People of Pensacola: History and Archaeology of the Community Associated with Spanish San Miguel de Panzacola (1754-1763) and British Pensacola (1763-1781) Volume 1. University of West Florida, Archaeology Institute, *Report of Investigations* 107.

BENCHLEY, ELIZABETH D., F. COPES, M. KOLB, N. LASCA, P. PORUBCAN, M. SCHABEL AND L. WHITMAN
1993 Investigations of the Influence of Late 19th-Early 20th Century Logging on Fluvial Geomorphology and Fisheries Habitat on the Indian River, Hiawatha National Forest, Michigan. University of Wisconsin-Milwaukee, Archaeological Research Laboratory, *Report of Investigations* 113.

BENSE, JUDITH
1986 Report of the Pensacola Archaeological Survey, 1986 Season. *Report of Investigations Number 10*, University of West Florida Archaeology Institute, Pensacola.

1999 *Archaeology of Colonial Pensacola*. University Press of Florida

BOYD, MARK
1956 The Apalachicola or Chattahoochee Arsenal of the United States, *Apalachee* 4: 29-43.

BUCCHINO, NICOLE
2014 *Talking Smack: The History and Archaeology of Pensacola's Red Snapper Fishing Industry*, p.28. University of West Florida.

CAMPBELL, HEATHER
2000 Sustainable development: Can the Vision be Realized? *Planning Theory & Practice*, Vol. 1:2, 259-284.

CLAVIN, MATTHEW
2019 *The Battle of Negro Fort: The Rise and Fall of a Fugitive Slave Community*. New York University Press, p. 181.

COOK, GREGORY, JOHN BRATTEN, AND JOHN E. WORTH
2016 Exploring Luna's 1559 Fleet: Final Report for Florida Division of Historic Resources Special Category Grant SC 503. *Report of Investigations* #202, Archaeology Institute, University of West Florida, Pensacola.

DELGADO, JAMES
2015   NOAA Perspective on Maritime Cultural Landscape, In *Proceedings of the Maritime Cultural Landscape Symposium*, B. Wyatt and Dietrich-Smith, D. editors, pp. 14-17. University of Wisconsin-Madison.

DROBNEY, JEFFREY
1999   *Lumbermen and Log Sawyers: Life, Labor and Culture in North Florida Lumber Industry* 1830-1930. Mercer University Press, Macon.

DUNBAR, JAMES S.
2014   The pre-Clovis occupation of Florida: The Page-Ladson and Wakulla Springs Lodge Data. Archived from the original on October 12, 2014. Retrieved 2 march 2020.

DUNBAR, JAMES S. AND S. D. WEBB
1996   Bone and ivory tools from submerged Paleoindian sites in Florida. *The Paleoindian and Early Archaic Southeast*, Anderson, D. G., and K. E. Sassaman. Tuscaloosa (Editors), pp. 331–353. AL: University of Alabama Press.

FAUGHT, MICHAEL
2004   The Underwater Archaeology of Paleolandscapes, Apalachee Bay, Florida. *American Antiquity*, Vol. 69, No. 2, pp. 275-289, Society for American Archaeology

GRINNAN, JOSEPH JAMES
2013   *Molino Mills: The Maritime Cultural Landscape of a Reconstruction Era Sawmill in Molino, Florida*. Pgs. 20-22, The University of West Florida.

GOODSPEED, M. HILL
2011   *U.S. Naval Aviation*, Naval Aviation Museum Foundation.

GOUGH, BARRY AND CHARLES BORRAS
2018   *The War Against the Pirates*, Palgrave Macmillan, p. 48.

GUARDIAN OF THE GULF
2020   Guardian of the Gulf: Fort Pickens, February 19, 2020. https://www.nps.gov/guis/learn/historyculture/fort-pickens.htm

HASLAM, SYLVIA.
1997   *The River Scene: Ecology and Cultural Heritage*, p. 243. Cambridge: Cambridge University Press.

HUDSON, CHARLES
1988   A Spanish-Coosa Alliance in Sixteenth-Century North Georgia. *The Georgia Historical Quarterly* 72(4), pp: 599-626.

HUNTER, LOUIS C.
1979   *A History of Industrial Power in the United States*, 1780-1930. The University Press of Virginia, Charlottesville.

HUNT, CHRISTOPHER
2014   "A Forgotten Community: Archaeological Documentation of Old St. Joseph, Gulf County, Florida," University of South Florida.

JOSE, SHIBU, ERIC JOKELA, AND DEBORAH MILLER.
2006   *The Longleaf Pine Ecosystem: Ecology, Silviculture, and Restoration*. Springer.

KHAKZAD, SORNA
2009   An Interdisciplinary Approach Towards Underwater Cultural Heritage Conservation and Management. In The 1st WTA-International PhD Symposium on 'Building materials and Building Technology to Preserve the Built Heritage, Vol. 1: 43-61

KHAKZAD, SORNA, M. PIETERS, M. AND K. VAN BALEN
2015   Coastal cultural heritage: a resource to be included in integrated coastal zone management, *Journal of Ocean and Coast Management*, V. 118: B, pp. 110-128.

KHAKZAD, SORNA, M. THOMIN
2019   Moving towards a sustainable heritage tourism management: An assessment of Northwest Florida, *Journal of Museum Review*, Vol. 4:1.

2020   Report of Florida Panhandle Maritime National Heritage Initiative (Not published), University of West Florida.

LEWIS, ADRIAN AND OMAHA BEACH
2001   A Flawed Victory, University of North Carolina Press, p. 71. Chapel Hill

LITTLE, KEITH J., C. CURREN, AND L. MCKENZIE
1988a   A Preliminary Archaeological Survey of The Blackwater Drainage, Santa Rosa County, Florida. The University of West Florida, Institute of West Florida Archaeology *Report of Investigations* 19.

1988b   A Preliminary Archaeological Survey of The Perdido Drainage, Escambia County, Florida. The University of West Florida, Institute of West Florida Archaeology, *Report of Investigations* 20.

1989   Arcadia: An Archaeological Evaluation of a Nineteenth-century Industrial Complex, Santa Rosa County, Florida. The University of West Florida, Institute of West Florida Archaeology, *Report of Investigations* 21.

LOCAL GOVERNMENT ASSOCIATION (LGA)
2002   On the Edge- the Coastal Strategy. A Report Prepared by the Local Government Association Special Interest Group on Coastal Issues. LGA, London.

Mayo, Corky, David Larsen, Stephen Wolter, Beth Barrie and Katie Bliss
2007   *Foundation of Interpretation Competency Narrative*, the Trustees of Indiana University, Eppley Institute for Parks & Public Lands,

Milanich, Jerald T.
2017   *Florida Indians and the Invasion from Europe*, p. 96, Library Press@UF

Mountains to Sound Greenway Trust
2012   *Mountains to Sound Greenway National Heritage Area Feasibility Study.*

National Hurricane Center
2006   National Hurricane Center, 2006 https://www.nhc.noaa.gov/climo/

National Park Service
2020   National Heritage Areas. 2020 https://www.nps.gov/subjects/heritageareas/index.htm

Office of the Secretary of Defense
2018   *Preserving Military Readiness in the Eastern Gulf of Mexico*. Report to Congress. https://www.iadc.org/wp-content/uploads/2018/05/DOD-Offshore-Report.pdf

Penkiunas, Daina
2015   SHPO Perspective on Maritime Cultural Landscape, In *Proceedings of the Maritime Cultural landscape Symposium*, p. 19. University of Wisconsin-Madison

Rucker, Brian
1988   Arcadia and Bagdad: Industrial Parks of Antebellum Florida. *The Florida Historical Quarterly* 67(2):147-165.

Ross, Charles
2014   Water-Powered Mills. Florida Watermill Survey, Charles Ross, Maitland, Florida.

Sherlock, V.M.
1982   *The Fever Man: A Biography of Dr. John Gorrie*. Tallahassee, Medallion Press.

Shettle, Jr., M. L.
1995   United States Naval Air Stations of World War II, Volume I: Eastern States, p. 178. Schaertel Publishing Co., Bowersville, Georgia.

Snell, C. W.
1983   *Special History Study, A History of the Naval Live Oaks Reservation Program, 1794-1880: A Forgotten Chapter in the History of American Conservation. Denver: Gulf Islands National Seashore*, National Park Service.

Taylor, Marshall and John Gorrie
1935   Physician, Scientist, Inventor Birmingham, *Southern Medical Journal.*

Tilden, Freeman
1957   *Interpreting Our Heritage*. Chapel Hill: University of North Carolina Press

USS Constitution
USS *Constitution*. (2020, March 03). Retrieved from Boston National Historical Park: https://www.nps.gov/bost/learn/historyculture/ussconst.htm

Westerdahl, Christer
1992   The maritime cultural landscape. *The International Journal of Nautical Archaeology* 21.1: 5-14

2011   Maritime Cultural Landscape, In *Oxford Handbook of Maritime Archaeology*, A. Catsambis, A., Ford., B., and Hamilton, D. editors, Oxford University Press, New York, NY.

Worth, John
2018   Archaeological and Documentary Insights into the Native World of the Luna Expedition. *Paper presented at the 75th Annual Meeting of the Southeastern Archaeological Conference.* Augusta, Ga.

Worth, John, Elizabeth Benchley, Janet Lloyd, and Jennifer Melcher
2017   The Discovery and Exploration of Tristán de Luna's1559-1561 Settlement on Pensacola Bay, *Paper presented at the 69th Annual Meeting of the Florida Anthropological Society,* Jacksonville, Florida, May 6, 2017.

Wynne, Nick and Richard Moorhead
2018   *Florida in World War II: Floating Fortress*. Charleston: The History Press.

Wyatt, Barbara
2015   NPS Perspective on Maritime Cultural Landscape. In *Proceedings of the Maritime Cultural Landscape Symposium*, B. Wyatt and Dietrich-Smith, D. editors, pp. 20-23. University of Wisconsin-Madison.

. . . .

Sorna Khakzad
207 E Main Street, FPAN Office
Pensacola, Florida 32502

Michael Thomin
207 E Main Street, FPAN Office
Pensacola, Florida 32502

Shipwreck Tagging Archaeological Management Program (STAMP): A Model for Coastal Heritage Resource Management Based on Community Engagement and Citizen Science

Austin Burkhard

The Florida Public Archaeological Network began the Shipwreck Tagging Archaeological Management Program (STAMP) in 2019. STAMP utilizes citizen scientists to assist archaeologists in tracking the movement and degradation of beached/coastal shipwreck sites and disarticulated timbers. Historically Florida's coastal regions have been some of the most treacherous navigable waterways for mariners due to high wave turbidity, oceanic currents, and meteorological phenomena. As such, thousands of ships have ultimately met their demise along Florida coasts. The program, partnering with the National Park Service at Gulf Islands National Seashore, has collected data in the continued enhancement of public archaeological programs.

Introduction

Cultural resource managers have a professional responsibility to protect, document, and interpret their materials in a timely, scientific manner. More importantly, cultural resource managers must also educate and share findings with the public. As Jameson and Scott-Ireton (2017) explain, archaeologists and cultural resource managers endeavor to develop more holistic interpretations in which the values of sustainable environment and heritage are linked. "The values of these sites and features often are not readily obvious in the material fabric or surrounding geography, but they must be identified and they require a narrative for the fullness of their meaning to be properly conveyed to local people, site visitors, and the public at large" (Jameson 2006:2). Coastal regions, in particular, make these professional responsibilities more difficult for cultural resource managers because coastlines are unique environmental areas often densely populated with people whilst also being an area of abundant archaeological resources. Bensley and Mastone (2012:63) state, "Coastal regions are rich archaeological landscapes imbued with material records that reflect high concentrations of diverse human activity over a wide swath of time." Coastal lands were used widely throughout time by different groups of people, prehistorically, historically, as well as present day. The wide array of cultural material, both modern and historic, are found along coastal regions creating difficulties in documentation (and possible redocumentation as resources move), interpretation, and monitoring of cultural resources.

To further the difficulties of resource management in coastal regions, recent trends in archaeology require heritage managers to acquire additional knowledge and skills in such areas as heritage resource management and the negotiation of heritage resources, local and regional planning and development, tourism development, advocacy, and public participation and collaboration (Shakel 2004). Archaeologists are called upon to collaborate and participate directly in activities pertaining to community and regional development and in the public negotiation of heritage and tourism resources (Shakel 2004). These new additions to an archaeologist's job title illustrate the need for cultural resource management citizen science-driven programming (Stottman 2010; Ackerman 2014; Timothy 2014; Miller 2019). "Citizen science programs are cost effective and provide an enormous return on investment by sheer numbers of participants" (Susan B.M. Langley 2019, elec. comm.).

To help alleviate the difficulties for resource managers of coastal regions, the Shipwreck Tagging Archaeological Management Program (STAMP) was started by the Florida Public Archaeology Network (FPAN) with the National Park Service (NPS) at the Gulf Islands National Seashore in the spring of 2019. The purpose of STAMP was to create a cultural resource management strategy for coastal and beached shipwreck sites utilizing citizen scientists. The program was based off another shipwreck tagging program that began in the summer of 2013 for the Fish and Wildlife Service (FWS) at the Chincoteague National Wildlife Refuge, Virginia. This program, although successful, was not set up to become a large-scale cultural resource management strategy for beached shipwreck sites. The following paper addresses the shortcomings of the shipwreck tagging program which began for the FWS at the Chincoteague National Wildlife Refuge in 2013 and shows the development and implementation of STAMP in Gulf Islands National Seashore.

The STAMP program works on the same premise as the Fish and Wildlife Shipwreck Tagging Program. The program consists of two distinct phases: tagging and recordation. In the tagging phase, a Plexiglas tag is affixed onto a previously undocumented shipwreck site or disarticulated shipwreck timber. This Plexiglas tag is equipped with a quick response code (QR) which allows the pubic to scan and submit data to the archaeologist's database. To assist staff and trained volunteers in the tagging phase, three forms of documentation are used. First, a standard operating procedure helps users properly affix tags onto shipwreck sites and disarticulated shipwreck timbers. Second, a deployment form acts as a data sheet for deploying new tags. Third, an instruction sheet (used in conjunction with the data sheet), is used to assist the staff member or trained volunteer in providing a standard for filling out the data sheet.

In the recordation phase, public participants that find tagged shipwreck sites or disarticulated shipwreck timbers use their smart phone to scan the QR code or to enter the uniform resource locator (URL) found on the tag. This action will automatically take the user to an online submission form. This form invites the user to answer a series of questions, but most importantly, allows the user to upload global positioning system (GPS) coordinates and photos. The submission is immediately sent to an online database and alerts the project archaeologists. The archaeologists can then log into the online database to view the submission, compare and then analyze data. A feedback form is then sent to the public participant thanking them for their contribution and support of our shared maritime resources.

Since the summer of 2013, the Fish and Wildlife Service shipwreck tagging program has reported that 175 tags have been deployed including tags on two intact beached shipwreck sites. The public has submitted 183 forms that correlate to 90 different tagged resources. The data set may seem small for the length of the program; however, the beaches along Chincoteague Island are closed half the year during the spring and summer months due to endangered bird nesting. Thus far, the program data has provided results showing an individual timber moving over 100 miles south after storm events in a matter of three months, traversing the mouth of the Chesapeake Bay, moving to Virginia Beach, Virginia, and eventually Corolla, North Carolina (Burkhard 2016). These results provided new potential interpretations for resource managers.

Typically, the appearance of a disarticulated piece of wreckage that appears is thought to be from a wreck just offshore which is breaking up. The data provided from this program show that although this interpretation might be true, resource managers now need to take into account how far the timber could have moved since its initial deposition. The program has also experienced one of its tagged intact beached shipwreck sites to become completely besieged and disappear after a major winter storm. Tagged components of that wreck have yet to become re-exposed. The results of degradation and movement will be interesting for comparative analysis when the tagged components become re-exposed.

Despite success, a few shortcomings have been identified with the program. The shortcomings included a non-automatic feedback loop and cumbersome forms that lacked an automatic GPS location. This created limits to the capability of the program.

The first shortcoming preventing the Fish and Wildlife Shipwreck Tagging Program from becoming a cultural resource management strategy on a large scale was the lack of automatic feedback to the submitter by the online database. The Fish and Wildlife Service utilized a third party online database to house all data needs (Burkhard 2013). Each time a public submission was received, an archaeologist had to log in to the database and create a feedback form that was manually sent to the public participant. Feedback for public participants is a necessity for continued public participation and involvement. "Public involvement makes individual stakeholders and induces a level of pride of possession or ownership that makes citizens care more deeply about the resources and stimulates a desire to learn more and spread knowledge" (Susan B.M. Langley 2019, elec. comm.). Since the Fish and Wildlife Shipwreck Tagging Program was small geographically and had a low volume of submissions, this was manageable for one archaeologist to review the data and respond with feedback to the submitters. If this program were to grow and become a management strategy for a large geographic area, the potential for a high volume of submissions would place an increasing need for an automatic feedback capability to be built within the online database.

STAMP addressed these shortcomings within its development phase by creating a large-scale geographic management strategy for beached shipwreck sites and disarticulated shipwreck timbers. FPAN, with the assistance of the NPS Submerged Resources Center (SRC), built a database from the ground up specifically coded for the needs of the program. Foremost, STAMP will house the data on the FPAN server. Not only does the coded database address the need for automatic feedback, it also allows for a more streamlined and effective form for the public to fill out.

The recordation phase of the STAMP program is similar to the Fish and Wildlife Shipwreck Tagging program, but differs with the added modifications of the automatic feedback system. When a member of the public scans a QR code or enters the URL found on the tag, their device will be sent to an online form. This form asks the user basic questions regarding the tagged resource at hand and prompts the user to gather pictures and enter the GPS coordinates of the site. If a submitter desires to include GPS coordinates, they can be automatically uploaded via the pictures of the resource being submitted. The submission allows resource managers to see how the shipwreck has changed and timbers have moved over time. When the public user is finished, they submit the form and are then directed to a map. This map illustrates locations where the timber was recorded previously. The public user can click on the dots to see where the timber has been and access a picture (taken at the time of submission) to see how the timber may have changed or degraded.

Analogous to the Fish and Wildlife Shipwreck Tagging program, STAMP requires the same materials for tag and kit manufacturing. Two plexiglass sheets, a piece of Mylar® waterproof paper, and dichloromethane (sealant) were used to create each tag. To affix the tag onto a shipwreck timber, two stainless steel nails with two stainless steel washers are used. The shipwreck tagging kits are composed of all the necessary materials needed to properly document and tag previously untagged shipwreck sites/timbers. The kit includes tags, stainless steel nails, stainless steel washers, hammer, measuring tapes, photocards, and a camera. All of these materials are kept in toolboxes at FPAN offices or NPS visitor service offices to be checked out by trained volunteers or staff.

At the launch of the program, a one-day STAMP training workshop was held to train interested volunteers as well as FPAN and NPS staff in the methodologies and techniques of the program. Workshop topics included a brief history of STAMP, program purpose, ship timber/wreck identification, timber/site documentation, and proper tag deployment. The workshop had 20 public participants from all ages and backgrounds. Three of the participants were already NPS volunteers that wanted to assist the park in a different way. The morning of the workshop encompassed the series of lectures and the afternoon was spent actively deploying tags onto identified disarticulated timbers within the park boundaries. Unfortunately, at the time of the workshop, no beached sites or disarticulated timbers were exposed for documentation. Fortunately, FPAN had access to a few disarticulated timbers which were collected previously by the public and given to the University of West Florida. The workshop participants were able to document, handle, and affix tags onto two different shipwreck timbers.

The University of West Florida and Gulf Island National Seashore allowed one of the timbers to be left near the new ferry pier at Fort Pickens after the workshop. The purpose of this was to stress test the STAMP database. The database needed to be able to handle a large volume of submissions. To date, the public has responded 35 times to the tagged timber and the database has met expectations. Gulf Islands National Seashore and FPAN have only gotten the opportunity to tag that one timber. Unfortunately (or fortunately), no other beached shipwreck sites or disarticulated timbers have been exposed since the onset of the program. The next step is to deploy more tags when cultural resources are exposed along the shores of Gulf Islands National Seashore, and to begin to expand the program across other geographic areas. In the future FPAN plans to expand STAMP to encompass the entire state of Florida and, eventually, create a cultural resource management strategy for other states and federal agencies to replicate and incorporate into their cultural resource management plans.

References

Ackerman, Lisa
2014 The Evolution of Heritage Management: Thinking Beyond Site Boundaries and Buffer Zones. In *Public Archaeology: Special Issues: Archaeology and Economic Development*, Peter G. Gould and Paul Burtenshaw, editors, pp. 113-123. Maney Publishing, Hanover, UK.

BENSLEY, JUSTIN J. AND VICTOR T. MASTONE
2014   Shifting Sand: A Model for Facilitating Public Assistance. In *Between the Devil and the Deep: Meeting Challenges in the Public Interpretation of Maritime Cultural Heritage*, Della A. Scott-Ireton, editor, pp. 63-72. Springer, New York, NY.

BURKHARD, AUSTIN
2016   From Sea Turtles to Shipwrecks: A Program to Monitor the Movement of Marine Cultural Resources in Coastal Virginia and Maryland. *Horizon and Traditions* 58(2):13-18.

JAMESON, JOHN H. JR.
2006   Values and Connections: Toward Holistic Interpretation and Ename Charter Initiative. Revised paper originally delivered at the November 2004 Australia ICOMOS "Loving it to Death" Conference on Heritage Tourism, Port Arthur World Heritage Site, Tasmania.

JAMESON, JOHN H. JR., AND DELLA A. SCOTT-IRETON
2017   Introduction: Imparting Values / Making Connections. In *Out of the Blue: Public Interpretation of Maritime Cultural Resources*, John H. Jameson, Jr. and Della A. Scott-Ireton, editors, pp. 1-6. Springer. New York, NY.

MILLER, SARAH E.
2019   Community Engagement in the 21st Century. In *Handbook of Global Historical Archaeology*, Charles Orser, Pedro Funari, Susan Lawrence, James Symonds, and Andres Zarankin, editors, pp. xx-xx Routledge, New York, NY

SHACKEL, PAUL A.
2004   Working with Communities Regional and Individual Archaeological in the Contemporary Politics of Indian Heritage. In *Places in Mind: Public Archaeology as Applied Anthropology*, Paul A. Shakel and Erve J. Chambers, editors, pp. 1-19. Routledge, New York, NY.

STOTTMAN, M. JAY
2010   Introduction: Archaeologists as Activists. In *Archaeologists as Activists: Can Archaeologists Change the World?*, M. Jay Stottman, editor, pp. 2-3. University of Alabama Press, Tuscaloosa.

TIMOTHY, DALLEN J.
2014   Contemporary Cultural Heritage Tourism: Development Issues and Emerging Trends. In *Archaeology and Economic Development*, Peter G. Gould and Paul Burtenshaw, editors, pp. 30-48. Maney Publishing, Hanover, UK..

• • • • • • • • • • • • • • • •

Austin Burkhard
St. Augustine Lighthouse Archaeological Maritime Program (LAMP)
81 Lighthouse Ave
St. Augustine, FL 32084

Known Sites, Unknown States: Monitoring Activities on Intertidal Sites in St. Augustine

Allyson Ropp

Over the last decade, the St. Augustine Lighthouse Archaeological Maritime Program has documented several intertidal sites and shipwrecks. With the increased sea level rise arose an interest to reassess sites and to proactively evaluate their condition. Four of these sites were visited by the 2019 LAMP Field School to document the current state and note changes. This paper explores the way this exercise acted as an opportunity for students to experience leading a project. It demonstrates a method to proactively document changes to known sites and begin a program to monitor the array of sites in St. Augustine.

In 2019, as part of the annual field school by the St. Augustine Lighthouse Archaeological Maritime Program (LAMP), an effort was made to reevaluate sites that had originally been documented in the last two decades. This effort developed in part from an archaeological understanding of temporal change to sites, in part from a heritage at risk standpoint of increased tidal surge and storms, and in part from an educational stance of teaching project planning and management. The following paper addresses the archaeological results for these sites, the current climate threats to these sites, and the methodological findings for an educational resource and management practice.

Program Layout

The program took place over a four-week period, part of LAMP's annual field school. The first item that needed to be established was the sites for the program. In choosing the sites, various criteria were accessed. The criteria aimed to find easily accessible sites that were previously known and documented by LAMP, that were within the coastal environment, and that were potentially subject to climate change. The sites chosen exhibited all these facets. Lincolnville Landing, Shell Bluff Landing, the Old Spanish Watchtower, and the U.S. Army Corps of Engineers Groin and Bulkhead exhibited all the criteria and were chosen for the pilot program.

The field school students were split into four groups for the series of sites that were picked for this program. Each group received the existing Florida Master Site File form for the site and access to the original research on the site available in the LAMP archives. From this information, each group made a project plan and list of items they needed to complete the work they wanted to accomplish on their assigned sites. Fieldwork for each group varied between one- and two-days dependent on weather and tidal changes. Each group processed their data and presented their findings to the public in a symposium-style format. The program aimed to provide an environment in which the students could work through the steps of running and organizing a field project, conducting fieldwork within an allotted time frame, and disseminating their research to their peers and the public.

Case Studies

The sites chosen for the program were Lincolnville Landing (8SJ5020), Shell Bluff Landing (8SJ0032), the Old Spanish Watchtower (8SJ3702), and the U.S. Army Corps of Engineers Groins and Bulkhead (8SJ4874, 8SJ4875, 8SJ4876, 8SJ4877, 8SJ4878). The four projects, their methodologies, archaeological findings, and site impacts are described in the following section.

Lincolnville Landing (8SJ5020)

Located on the foreshore of Maria Sanchez Creek, the Lincolnville Landing site was encountered in the early 2000s and initial observations included heavy timbers laid out in the mud parallel to shore and running down towards the water. Their impression was of a ramp-like timber structure that might have been used to launch boats or pull them from the creek. The site was reported to the Florida Master Site Files as the Lincolnville Landing and assigned site number 8SJ5020 (Meide et al. 2010:162-167; Meide et al. 2011:71-77).

2019 Field Research

The goal of the 2019 visit was primarily to ascertain the current state of the site after a decade. To do this, the team aimed to create a site plan for comparison to previously gathered data, probe to identify furthest extents of the site, and document any surface artifacts. The team of five students and a staff archaeologist, accomplished these goals during their day of fieldwork.

To ascertain the state of the site following several major storms, the previously known timbers were identified first. The four previously identified large timber running parallel to shore were found and marked with fiberglass rods at either end. This allowed their length to be visible as the tides rose throughout the day. A baseline was stretched perpendicular across these timbers. From west to east, the timbers were labeled Timbers 1 through 4 (Figure 1). Timber 1 measured 3.71 m (12.17 ft) in length and 26 cm (10.24 in) in width. Timber 2 measured 2.05 m (6.73 ft) in length and 41 cm (16.14 in) in width. Timber 3 was 3.5 m (11.48 ft) in length and 80 cm (31.50 in) in width. Timber 4 was 3.67 m (12.04 ft) in length and 12 cm (4.72 in) in width.

Five vertical timbers were observed and recorded into the site plan using the baseline. Four of these vertical posts were rounded off and cylindrical. The fifth vertical post was a rounded square as compared to the other cylindrical posts. These vertical posts have been interpreted as support timbers or pilings for the activities occurring historically in the area. Other timbers were noted in between the four known timbers. These timbers were sketched into approximate locations, as time and tide constraints shortened the day. These timbers were running parallel to shore and the four main timbers buried underneath approximately a foot of marsh mud.

Any loose artifacts encountered were photographed on-site and returned to their original location. Three artifacts of interest were noted over the course of the day. The first is a fragment of a brick. The brick fragment measured 10 cm (3.94 in) in length, 8.5 cm (3.35 in) in width, and 5 cm (1.97 in) in thickness. The brick has distinct parallel lines running across on face of it. This decoration indicates that it is likely an architectural brick made with a purpose, as compared to a plain or scored brick. The brick was discovered on the eastern portion of the site between the third and fourth timber from shore. The second artifact is a sherd of whiteware. The 7 cm (2.76 in) long sherd has a white paste and a white cracked glaze. It is the rim of a small plate or platter. This sherd was found on the western side of the site right to the east of the first timber from shore. The third was a full glass bottle. The glass bottle was not photographed. It was found to the east of the four timbers. The bottle was inscribed with "ABCo 41," which indicates it was manufactured by the American Bottle Company. Currently, it is unknown if these artifacts are of direct relation to the site or intrusive in a highly active environment.

Over the last decade, there has been a limited amount of change that has occurred. The 2010 site plan and the 2019 plan show the same four main timbers that are parallel to the shore. The site sits in approximately the same amount of mud and level of submersion that it faced a decade ago. The most dramatic environmental change is the expansion of the marsh grasses across the wooden structures. There is also an expansion of oyster beds in the area over the last decade.

Shell Bluff Landing (8SJ0032)

Shell Bluff Landing is a site that provides an in-depth look into almost all of Florida's history. Located on the eastern edge of the Tolomato River in what is now the Guana Tolomato Matanzas National Estuarine Research Reserve (GTM), the site has produced artifacts that range from the Archaic Period (7000-1000 BC) through the 19th-century American period including the natives of Northeast Florida and the multitude of Florida's colonial powers. Based on the quantity and the time frame, this site is a record for over 5,000 years of human contact and connection with maritime Florida (Goggin 1952:45, 59; Weisman and Newman 1991).

2019 Field Research

The goal of the 2019 site visit was to document the exposed artifacts and the eroding bluff line. Various artifacts ranging from prehistoric and historic eras of the site's use were observed during the documentation. The principle methodology for site documentation consisted of baseline-offset recordation of the current coastline, photography of visible artifacts along the eroding coastline, and a photomosaic of the eroding bluff.

Figure 1: Lincolnville Landing at low tide. Three of the four main timbers are marked by the red lines.

To document the erosion, the team used a baseline-offset method. As the coastline had been documented twice before, the baseline was laid in the same location as the one established in 1988. The two tapes were stretched for a total distance of 100 m (328.08 ft) running north to south. Offsets were taken every 5 m (16.40 ft) on the baseline out to the edge of the bluff. At the S20m spot on the baseline, a second baseline was stretched perpendicular to the first. This baseline stretched 11.2 m (36.75 ft) in length running east to west. This secondary baseline was used to measure the bluff line as it turned east-to-west to ensure that the offsets were still measured correctly. This recordation was transferred on to a preexisting site plan to understand the extent of coastline erosion.

In comparing data gathered during the 2019 fieldwork with previous field explorations, a vast amount of change is visible. The most apparent changes are the eroding coastline. Since the bluff line was first mapped in 1988, the bluff line has receded significantly. The average bluff change between 1988 and 2019 is 5.67 m (18.6 ft), while the maximum change is 22 m (72.18 ft) at the southernmost end. However, this change is over thirty years.

Over the last three years, there has been significant change. Since 2016, the site has been impacted by three major hurricanes that have significantly altered the coastline. The well has become an icon of the site due to erosion. The well has gone from being buried upon the bluff line in 2016 to now fully exposed and at tide line in 2019. Between Hurricane Matthew, Hurricane Irma, and the 2019 work, the bluff line exposed the well and the line sits 2.5 m (8.20 ft) to its east side. Between 2017 and 2019, the bluff line has shifted almost 2.5 m (8.20 ft) east in some places (Figure 2). These are drastic changes in just over three years. Such changes not only impact the natural environment of the island but the cultural heritage. While the well is the most visible threatened aspect of the site, each day the shell midden and its artifacts are washed into the Tolomato River and never recorded.

Old Spanish Watchtower (8SJ3702)

Before the current St. Augustine Light Station, completed in 1874, a previous tower stood acting as the primary lookout for St. Augustine. This was the Old Spanish Watchtower on present-day Anastasia Island. The tower complex was constructed by the Spanish and at its fullest extent by the 1730s. The site included a watchtower, guardhouse, well, and an ammunition storage house surrounded by a wall 104 ft. in length and 42 ft. in width. The complex was constructed predominately from natural coquina rock from nearby quarries (Lidh 2004:3-5). Facing active erosion, the tower collapsed in the 1880s due to wave and current action (Lidh 2004:5, 7-8).

The site of the Old Spanish Watchtower underwent archaeological investigations in 2001 as part of a public archaeology opportunity by LAMP. In 2019 as part of LAMP's annual Field School, the site was revisited to monitor the site and establish any change that the site has undergone since 2001 (Morris et al. 2002:23-28).

2019 Field Research

Two days were spent determining the extent of the site and mapping the cluster of coquina foundation stones. The team used fiberglass rods to probe along the known cluster to locate a larger area of coquina slabs. No such slabs were discovered. The amount of time limited the amount of work that could be completed, which included clearing off oyster beds.

Using information from the previous survey, the team established a baseline along the abandoned dock to the north of the site. The baseline, lying west-to-east, was stretched 20 m (65.62 ft) in length. Measurements were taken from the baseline to the corners or perceived corners of each of the coquina blocks. As the tide receded, a second 10 m (32.81 ft) baseline running north-south was stretched across the coquina cluster from the original baseline. Twelve broken coquina slabs were recorded (Figure 3).

Figure 2: Shell Bluff Landing bluff line with Menorcan-era well. The well is located just behind the falling tree in the center of the image.

Figure 3: Visible coquina foundation stones of the Old Spanish Watchtower at low tide.

In comparing the investigation conducted in 2001-2002 and the investigation in 2019, there are a few notable differences. The first notable difference was the number of blocks. While the blocks were discovered in the same shape and location, the 2001-2002 survey identified a larger quantity. The survey conducted in 2001-2002 included extensive hydraulic probing in the surrounding area as compared to the fiberglass rods used for probing during the 2019 investigation. The methodology of the 2019 investigation limited the ability to physically determine the difference between the oysters and the coquina with a fiberglass rod. The 2001-2002 investigation furthermore extended their survey area beyond the known blocks. That survey documented additional coquina blocks scattered in the surrounding landscape to determine the extents of the site. The 2019 investigation focused solely on the known stones and submerged extents.

The other major difference between the two investigations was the treatment of oysters. In 2001-2002, the oyster beds and tidal mud were removed from the stones. This allowed the blocks to be recorded and any details noted including the cross and "NE."

During 2019, the oysters and mud were not removed. No markings were noted on any of the blocks. The lack of these known markings could be that they were indeed covered by the oysters and mud. It could also be an indication of erosion of the coquina blocks. When coquina is exposed to weathering, it begins to disintegrate as well as cause the surface to blacken and case-harden (Scott 2002:6). Further mechanisms for coquina erosion and deterioration are chemical agents causing a chemical reaction; mechanical disruption through salts crystallizing in pores beneath the surface of the stone called subflorescence, water inundation into the pores followed by freezing, and corrosion of metal embedded in a coquina structure; abrasion, attrition, and stress cracking; and biological growth such as fungi and mosses that lead to water retention and accelerated soiling (Bischoff 2000:24-31). While the coquina blocks of the Old Watchtower are not exposed to metal corrosive mechanical deterioration, they are susceptible to the other forms. This deterioration will continue and may be a factor in the noted differences over the last decade.

The Salt Run Groins (8SJ4874, 8SJ4875, 8SJ4876, 8SJ4877) and the Corps Bulkhead (8SJ4878)

Between 1889 and 1893, the US Army Corps of Engineers (USACE) constructed a series of seven coastal groins. The groins were constructed to counter heavy erosion affecting the Atlantic shoreline of Anastasia Island and the southern tip of North Beach. Additionally, the USACE installed a bulkhead along part of the island to combat further erosion. The groins are still present along the western shores of the lagoon. Three groins (8SJ3536 was previously recorded, and two other could not be located) built on the North Beach peninsula, are now completely landlocked within the dunes of the peninsula across the lagoon that was created by the sediment accumulation resulting from the 1940 USACE dredge project (Morris et al. 2002:34-36).

<u>2019 Field Research</u>

Two days were spent examining the remains of the four groins and the Corps Bulkhead. As fieldwork was dictated by tide changes, the goal focused on full documentation of the Coquina Groin (8SJ4875) as well as updated locational information, overall length (if determinable), and degradation of groins since the last full survey of the remains during the 2001-2002 survey.

The Conch House Groin, named for its proximity to a popular restaurant on Salt Run, is fully submerged at high tide and partially submerged at low tide. Moving from shore, portions of the groin are still visible along with the marsh grasses. As the groin continues to the channel, it becomes fully submerged. A full length of the groin was taken, and it measured 168.73 m (553.58 ft) in length (Figure 4). Additionally, measurements were taken along the coquina blocks visible in the marsh grasses. These stones measured 17.53 m (57.51 ft) in length. Visual observations and photographs were taken of the visible portions of the groin. The individual blocks that were used to construct the groin are no longer visible due to oyster growth.

The Coquina Groin, the groin to the immediate south of the Conch House Groin, is fully visible at both low tide and high tide. It is now situated on what is known as Little Beach with marsh grasses. The groin is constructed to twenty-two coquina blocks sitting above the water line and two that sit at or below the waterline. In comparison to the nineteen originally counted in 2002, the increased number may have occurred due to cracks in the coquina blocks. As the groin was fully exposed while the team was in the field, a full site plan was created. The groin measured 30.8 m (101.05 ft) in length (Figure 4). The coquina blocks varied in width from 72 to 161 cm (28.35-63.39 in) and in thickness from 42 to 186 cm (16.54-73.23 in). The blocks furthest east had a distinct trapezoidal shape with the thinner portion on top and getting wider towards the base of the stone. Two notches are cut in the butting ends of many of the stones, which meet up with corresponding notches in the abutting stones. No additional material was noted in these notches. These notches measured 12 cm (4.72 in.) in width and 4 cm (1.57 in) in depth. These notches likely served as a means for affixing the coquina blocks together. Additionally, these notches could represent a precautionary cut for the expansion and shrinking of the stones as a means for them to lock together.

The other two groins and the Corps Bulkhead, due to incomplete information from previous work and tidal changes, only had the geographical information gathered and refined. The Sandspur Groin (8SJ4876) was exceedingly difficult to locate from the site file information and a visual survey. After discovery, the current location was taken and updated with the Florida Master Site File. The footprint is visible on Google Earth in this location. Based on visual observations in the area, the site is currently totally submerged. It is possible some coquina blocks may be above water in the marsh grass, but this was not explored. Stokely's Groin (8SJ4877) is completely submerged. Only a small portion of the groin is visible at low tide and this is marked by a hazard sign for boaters in the waterway. This location was recorded. From previous investigations, the site is covered with oysters.

The U.S. Corps Bulkhead (8SJ4878) has now been joined with additional bulkheads along Salt Run. The difficulty in locating the bulkhead was the description did not stand out from the other bulkheads in between Coquina Groin and Sandspur Groin. After creating a photomosaic of a portion of the bulkhead, additional research was conducted and determined this was not the correct bulkhead. The team went back out to find the site and record the geographical information. The current location was recorded and updated with the Florida Master Site File. While photographs were taken, the bulkhead was not recorded.

In comparison to the previously conducted research on the sites, there are a few noted differences between the data collected in 2002 and the data collected in 2019. As only two of the four groins were recorded, the data is only comparing the Conch House Groin (8SJ4875) and the Coquina Groin (8SJ4876). The

Figure 4. Images of the Conch House Groin, 8SJ4874, (top) and Coquina Groin, 8JS4875, (bottom) at low tide.

2020 Underwater Archaeology Proceedings

most distinct observations were changes in size from the originally built compared with the measurements from the two field seasons. The original length for the Conch House Groin was 159.56 m (523.49 ft). During the 2002 season, only a portion of the site was measured, the main section in the waterway and the break between shore and the groin. This measured to 62.94 m (206.50 ft). As part of the 2019 fieldwork, the entirety of the groin was measured. It measured to 168.73 m (553.58 ft). The apparent main difference is the discrepancy between the overall lengths with the original measured length being shorter than the length measured in 2019. This difference likely is caused by the inability to find the true end of the groin in the waterway in 2019. As the investigation was conducted by probing, the difference between coquina and oyster beds is difficult to ascertain at the east end of the groin. With that in mind, the entirety of the Conch House Groin may still be present in some form. It is unknown in the break between the west section and the east section if there are any blocks present as neither field season fully explored that area for any blocks.

The Coquina Groin has changed since the 2002 field season. This change is noted by two distinct aspects: length and block count. The 2002 team documented the groin as having nineteen blocks with an overall length of 35.97 m (118.01 ft). The 2019 team documented the groin as having twenty-two blocks with an overall length of 30.8 m (101.05 ft). The differences between the two seasons are likely caused by erosion and human impacts. As the main foundation for the blocks is coquina, coquina is susceptible to the environment. Coquina can disintegrate and blacken when exposed to weathering (Scott 2000:6). Coquina can further erode through chemical agents causing a chemical reaction; mechanical disruption through salts crystallizing in pores beneath the surface of the stone called subflorescence, water inundation into the pores followed by freezing, and corrosion of metal embedded in a coquina structure; abrasion, attrition, and stress cracking; and biological growth such as fungi and mosses that lead to water retention and accelerated soiling (Bischoff 2000:24-31). These natural processes, like subflorescence, account for the breaks in the blocks. In looking at the blocks, it is apparent where these breaks occurred in the original blocks. In accounting for the missing 5.17 m (16.96 ft.) documented in the 2002 season, the loss may be a condition of natural processes as well as human influence. The stones could have been removed for access to the beach. Additionally, the difference in length could be attributed to human error. The stones may well be on the west end of the site hidden further in the marsh grasses than what was encountered by the 2019 team.

Noted Climate Effects

The sites monitored during this program exhibit similar trends in climate effects. All four sites are primarily affected by the increased sea level rise and increased storm and tidal surge. As the sites are distinct from one another, they are impacted and reacted differently. For example, Lincolnville Landing is relatively protected from the surge and changes between exposure and submersion due to its muddy layer, while Shell Bluff Landing is significantly eroding due to the tidal surge. Sea level rise will eventually affect all the sites. According to the National Oceanic and Atmospheric Administration these sites will be submerged completely with a 3 ft sea-level rise (National Oceanic and Atmospheric Administration 2019).

Some sites also face similar issues that others do not. The coquina sites are under a different threat than wooden sites. The groins and the Old Spanish Watchtower are facing coquina erosion. They are exposed to different processes that cause the coquina to break and erode leading to site loss. The wooden sites, on the other hand, are experiencing increased growth of the marsh environment on top of them. This process both causes the wooden sites to disintegrate as well as protects them from human threats. The variety of impacts of climate and the natural environment changes are evident and these sites are at risk.

Effectiveness of the Program as a Monitoring Device

Beyond identifying the climate effects and conducting a follow-up investigation for the sites, the program was designed to create a learning environment for project planning and management as well as site monitoring and evaluative skills. Overall, the student feedback for the program was positive and aided in, as one student said, the program "allowed them to lead which is important in blossoming archaeologists." The feedback was also positive from the public perspective. As the pilot year, there is still work that can be done to improve the program as an educational tool for project planning and management. More time for teaching recording methods and planning would aid in student understanding of such topics. The public enjoyed and was very much impressed by the research conducted by the students over the course of four weeks. Through the lens of learning about project planning and management, the program served as a conduit for gathering data to understand site changes and the effects of climate change. The successes of the program reflect the ability to use an educational exercise to further manage and assess sites.

Conclusions

The 2019 LAMP Field School's expanded the idea of what can be provided by a field school. Beyond teaching students the practices of underwater archaeology and investigation, the field school brought in a new component through the group projects that are much more commonplace than shipwreck excavation. The practices and skills the students learned through project planning and management, as well as recordation and dissemination, are required in every facet of the field, while excavation opportunities are limited. Further, the program also served to provide monitoring efforts for these unfrequented sites and assess climate impacts. As the threats of a changing natural environment continue, reevaluating sites and continual monitoring is essential to understanding the impacts faced by these resources.

Acknowledgments

The author would like to extend a sincere thanks to the St. Augustine Lighthouse Archaeological Maritime Program, the St. Augustine Lighthouse & Maritime Museum, and the Florida Public Archaeology Network. Most importantly the author would like to express her undying gratitude to the LAMP Field School class of 2019 for being receptive to the project and being the first of its kind to conduct this work with LAMP.

References

Bischoff, Judith J.
2000 "Current Coquina Conservation and Preservation Technology." In *The Conservation and Preservation of Coquina: A Symposium on Historic Building Material in the Coastal Southeast*. Florida Bureau of Historic Preservation, Tallahassee, Florida. 19-35.

Goggin, John M.
1952 *Space and Time Perspective in Northern St. Johns Archaeology*. Yale University Publication in Anthropology 47. Yale University Press, New Haven, Connecticut.

Lidh, Rosalinda
2004 *St. Augustine Lighthouse: A Short History*. Historic Print & Map Company, St. Augustine, Florida.

Meide, Chuck, Samuel P. Turner, P. Brendan Burke and Starr Cox
2010 *First Coast Maritime Archaeology Project Research Design 2010-2011*. Lighthouse Archaeological Maritime Program (LAMP), St. Augustine Lighthouse & Museum, St. Augustine, Florida.

2011 *First Coast Maritime Archaeology Project 2010: Report on Archaeological Investigations*. Lighthouse Archaeological Maritime Program, St. Augustine Lighthouse & Museum, St. Augustine, Florida.

Morris, J.W. III, J.M. Burns, R.E. Moore
2002 *The St. Johns County Submerged Cultural Resources Inventory and Management Plan 2001-2002: Phase 1*. Lighthouse Archaeological Maritime Program, Inc. St. Augustine, Florida.

National Ocean and Atmospheric Administration
2019 Sea Level Rise Viewer. NOAA Office of Coastal Management. <https://coast.noaa.gov/digitalcoast/tools/slr.html>. Accessed 15 Nov 2019.

Scott, Thomas M.
2000 "The Coquina Resources of Florida's East Coast." In *The Conservation and Preservation of Coquina: A Symposium on Historic Building Material in the Coastal Southeast*. Florida Bureau of Historic Preservation, Tallahassee, Florida. 1-8.

Weisman, Brent and Christine Newman
1991 National Register of Historic Places Nomination Form: Shell Bluff Landing 8SJ32. Prepared for National Park Service. Prepared by Florida Bureau of Historic Preservation, Tallahassee, Florida.

. . . .

Allyson Ropp
Program in Maritime Studies
East Carolina University
302 E 9th Street
Greenville, NC 27858

Privateers on the Mullica River - Mapping Shipwrecks of the Revolutionary War

Stephen D. Nagiewicz, Peter F. Straub, Steven P. Evert, Shannon M. Chiarel, Jaymes Swain, Jessica DiBlasi

This obscure historical battle along the Mullica River in Port Republic, New Jersey, was one of the first documented amphibious assaults by a foreign nation in South Jersey. Side scan sonar systems were deployed to collect imagery on these shipwrecks, providing visual references and data to the State of New Jersey Office of Historic Preservation and help identify, document, and preserve the importance of privateers during the Revolutionary War. This study will also provide the State with benchmark data going forward about how shipwrecks deteriorate due to both environmental and man-made factors over time in coastal environments.

Introduction

New Jersey was an important battleground state in the Revolutionary War, located between the major colonial cities of New York and Philadelphia. While the fledgling colonial navy was greatly outgunned by the British fleet, much of the supplies came from local privateers operating under letters of marque who served as important adjuncts to the colonial naval attacks on British and French shipping (Shomette 2016). Throughout the conflict, 1,697 letters of marque were issued by the Continental Congress, making British transport and supply lines slower and riskier (Howarth 1991). Privateers were so successful that supply shortages of lumber, and dry goods for both citizens and British Troops were common in the New York area. This forced the British Admiralty to devote most of their efforts to defeating the privateers. One capture, involving the luxury merchantman *Venus* in the late summer of 1778, so outraged General Sir Henry Clinton that he decided to move quickly against the particularly troublesome southern New Jersey coast from his base in New York City (Kemp 1966).

The captured supplies and vessels were transshipped up the river and overland to Philadelphia and even to Valley Forge. General George Washington valued this area for its remarkable ability to secure goods according to a letter from Benedict Arnold to George Washington (Shomette 2016). By 1776, the Continental Navy

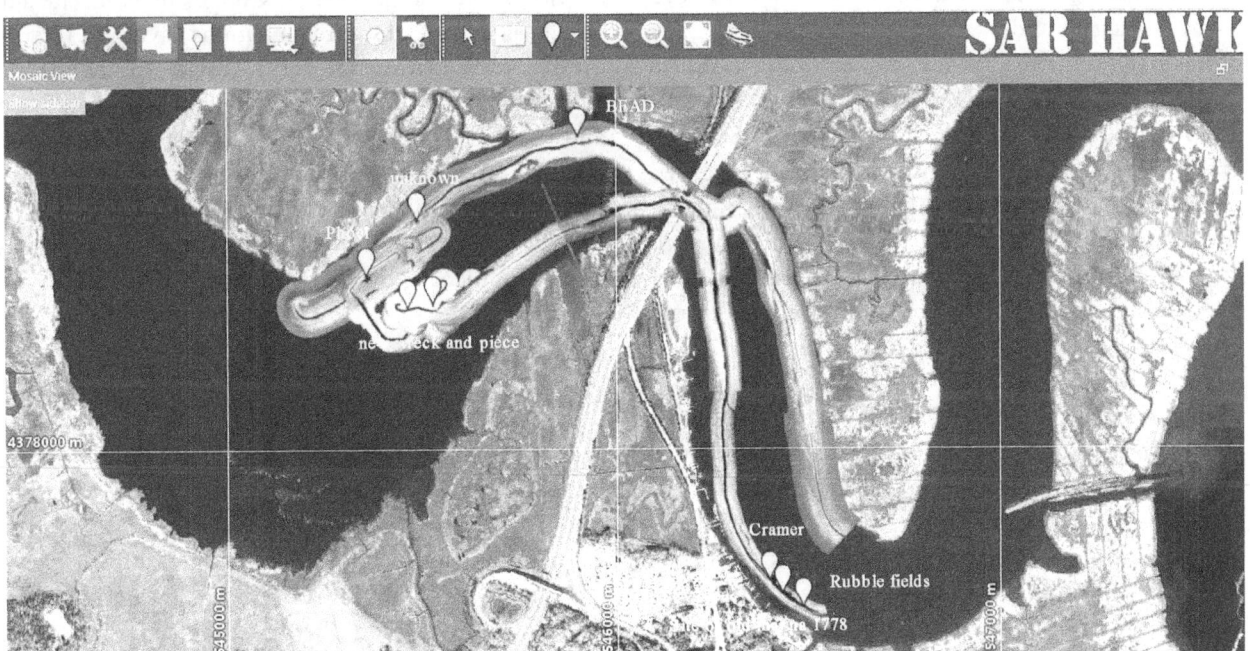

Figure 1: Historic District Labeled. Google Earth image of Chestnut Neck overlaid using with SAR HAWK software creating a sonar mosaic, labeling known shipwrecks and potential new targets in relation to the Mullica River. The Battle of Chestnut Neck was fought on either side of what is now the New Jersey Garden State Parkway, which bisects the river in this image. Credit: Stockton University.

Commanders were instructing privateers to take their prizes into either Cape May or Little Egg Harbor to "seek safety from either inclement weather or enemy forces of superior size" (Shomette 2016). By late-September, a British Squadron of nine vessels and over 200 British Marines left New York Harbor to destroy the village of Chestnut Neck upriver from Little Egg Harbor.

The British expedition to Little Egg Harbor led by Commander Henry Collins, and consisted of HMS *Zebra*, HMS *Nautilus*, HMS *Greenwich*, HMS *Dependence* and five smaller vessels. After delays due to weather, on the morning of October 6th, the British attacked the village after moving a large military force of Royal Marines upriver in small boats. The colonial militia who were poorly trained and equipped were little deterrence to the British Marines, who captured the Chestnut Neck, massacred 50 sleeping militia, and burned its warehouses and the 10 prize vessels at anchorage in the Mullica River (Figure 1). This engagement is referred to as the Battle of Chestnut Neck and the Massacre of Little Egg Harbor (Kemp 1966). The site is commemorated with the Chestnut Neck Battle Monuments built and dedicated by the Daughters of the American Revolution and the Sons of the American Revolution.

Two wreck sites, the Bead wreck (Figure 2) and the Cramer wreck (Figure 3), had previously surveyed by archaeologists. In 1975, the Bead wreck was surveyed by archaeologists and New Jersey wreck divers in 2.5 m of water and was largely intact but buried in marsh sediment (Watts 1976; Mathewson 1985; Fullmer 1998). The Bead wreck is listed on the New Jersey State and National Parks Historic Register. The Bead wreck was named for the glass beads found on the wreck by divers in the early 1970s. These beads are on display at the State of New Jersey's Museum in Trenton. It is likely these beads were used for jewelry and for trading with Native Indians (Marcoux 2012).

The second is the Cramer wreck which is also linked to the engagement and lies in shallow water close to the former village site and has been regularly sighted at extreme low tide. The Cramer wreck was mapped and surveyed in 1985 by the non-profit group Atlantic Alliance, which is a group of local New Jersey wreck divers who provided support to archaeologists Duncan Matthewson and James Sinclair to map the Bead wreck at the same time (Watts, 1976; Mathewson 1985; Fullmer 1998). This entire area of the marina and the river are part of the Mullica River/Chestnut Neck Archaeological Historic District, State of New Jersey. This includes the wreck of the Cramer as well as all the others. All the wrecks have local names, as their original identities remain unknown. In 2008 a third vessel was discovered, the Phoel wreck. This site had not been previously documented and may be the most intact vessel in the historic district.

The Chestnut Neck Historic District (Figure 1) was placed on the State Register of Historic Places in 1976 by the State of New Jersey's Office of Historic Preservation (NJSHPO 2020). This entire area was incorporated into the Jacques Cousteau National Estuarine Research Reserve (JCNERR 2018) in 1997 and is administrated by the National Oceanic and Atmospheric Administration (NOAA), and thus receives additional protection. The purpose of this study was to locate and assess the condition of the existing shipwrecks within the historic district and to use this information for the development of a management plan for these cultural resources using the following suggested guidelines: (1) Locate and identify shipwrecks; (2) Determine which shipwrecks are abandoned and meet the criteria for assuming title under the Abandoned Shipwreck Act; (3) Determine which shipwrecks are historic; (4) Identify recreational and other values that a shipwreck may possess and the shipwreck's current and potential uses; (5) Provide for the long-term protection of historic shipwrecks; (6) Protect the rights of owners of nonabandoned shipwrecks; (7) Consult and maintain a cooperative relationship with the various shipwreck interest groups; (8) Cooperate with state and federal agencies and sovereign nations having an interest in shipwreck management; (9) Provide for public appreciation, understanding, and enjoyment of shipwrecks and maritime history; (10) Conduct archaeological research on shipwrecks where research will yield information important to understanding the past; and (11) Provide for private sector participation in shipwreck research projects (NPSA 2020).

Methods

In 2008, using a Klein 2000 side scan sonar system, Stockton researchers William Phoel, Peter Straub, Steven Evert, and sonar consultant Vince Capone, mapped the Mullica River for remnants of the battle of 1778; they discovered a previously unknown third shipwreck potentially from this battle. The wreck was found opposite Collins Cove along the marsh on the north shore of the Mullica River and was named the Phoel wreck in honor of William Phoel, a former NOAA Fisheries Scientist and Adjunct Stockton Professor who passed away during an expedition in the Amazon rainforest several years ago.

Stephen Nagiewicz, Stockton Adjunct Professor who is now teaching the underwater archaeology course that once was taught by Dr. Phoel, re-discovered the wreck in 2016 while teaching students about sonar mapping applications in underwater archaeology. The Stockton Marine Field Station uses three sonar systems for wreck and bathymetric mapping: a Klein 3900 (Salem, NH) side scan sonar towed array system; an Edgetech 6205 (West Wareham, MA) multiphase echosounder (MPES); and the Humminbird Helix 12. Due to its ease of deployment and use by non-technical users such as students, the Humminbird was the most frequently utilized side scan sonar.

Echo81, a prominent hydrographic consulting firm, lent their expertise and their R2Sonic 2024 Wideband Multibeam Echosounder (WMBES) for very detailed image of the position of the Cramer along an underwater ridge as seen in Figure 3. This system was utilized to provide a better look at the positioning of the Cramer wreckage perched atop a sediment ridge to determine what possible environmental or anthropogenic events could affect the wreck (Brisson and Hiller 2015). The image clearly shows the wreck ready to slide off the ridges and shows its sonar shadow beneath and became disarticulated in much the same manner as did the Bead wreck.

The data collected was primarily processed using SAR HAWK software (Skatmanm 2019) for Humminbird platforms. Additionally, Klein Sonar Pro 12.0 software, SonarWiz by Chesapeake Systems, Edgetech Discover software, and HYPACK by xylem brand were also used. These systems provided students with a broad education in data processing, allowing them to measure, understand, and produce images for analysis.

Team members, Chiarel, DiBlasi and Swain, developed an operational sonar and multibeam mapping methodology which began in late 2017. These students identified potential wreck sites using possible wreck locations from historical records, maps, and local knowledge of possible anchorages that could be used today as they might have been used in 1778. Students then overlaid a survey grid of GPS waypoints that allowed for various transects of the wreck sites for sonar passes. This not only highlighted the wreck's geographical orientation, but also provided intricate details on specific features of interest.

The physical sonar survey expeditions started in 2018. The team then assigned two site surveys for each of the three sites every six-months to provide benchmark comparison data on site conditions. The first of these survey maps was the Phoel wreck, as the least is known of this wreck. Early images indicated it may be the most intact

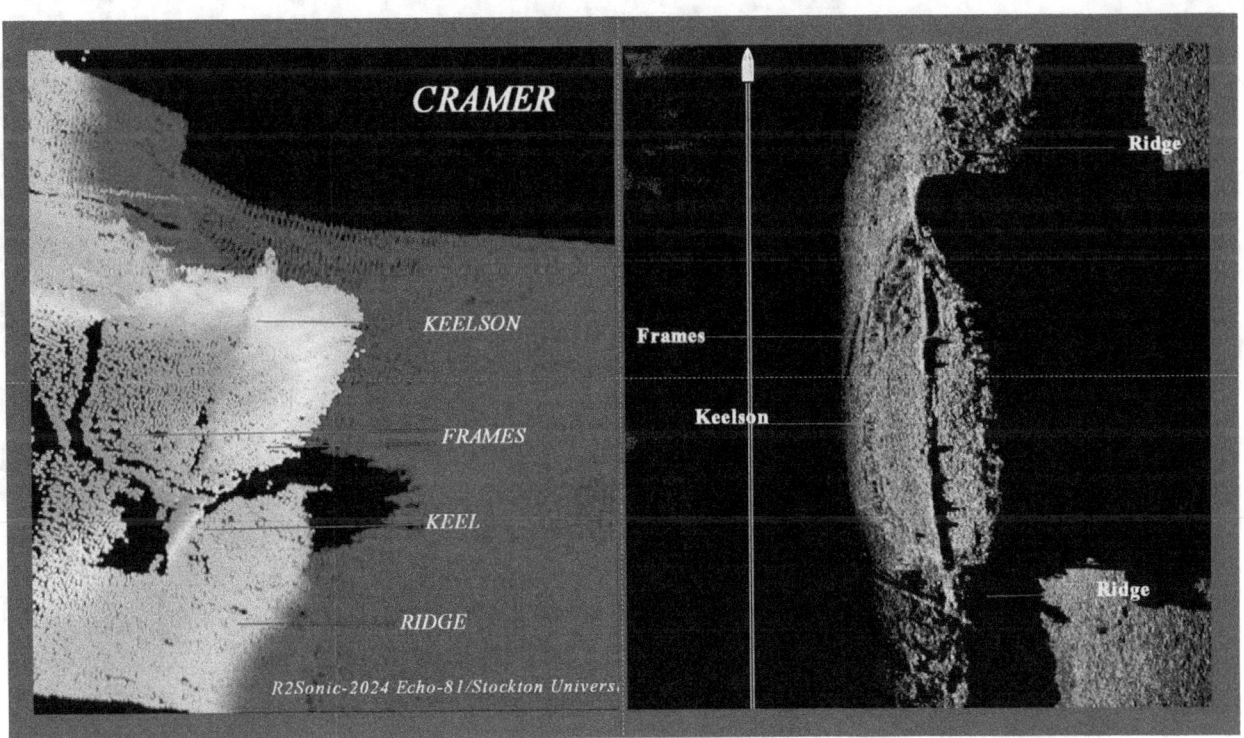

Figure 2: Cramer ridge labeled. Image on the left produced by R2Sonic Wideband MBES clearly show a shadow beneath the hull on the ridge, the Humminbird side scan image shows the wreck site and ridge. Credit: ECHO-81 & Stockton University.

wreck, allowing for better understanding of the type of ship and its construction. The surveys also provided data to the NJSHPO as part of the management plan for this Historic District and for future nominations of the Cramer and Phoel to the State and National Registers (NJSHPO 2020).

Results

Two years of sonar data has helped the team assemble a great deal of information about the shipwrecks including their geographical positioning, orientation, water depth, and by utilizing post processing software, basic measurements of each wreck's dimensions. The sonar data also revealed several potential shipwreck sites that will be studied once work on the three current sites is complete. The Bead wreck currently rests in 11.8 m of water and is quickly migrating towards the marsh ledge into the deeper water of a man-made borrow pit used for the construction of the Garden State Parkway Bridges a few decades ago. Figure 3 shows how the wreck is being undercut by tidal and river currents. In the image, the dark shadow along the straight line is the shipwreck's extant keelson. The shadow's slight bowing indicates that it is raised off the marsh shelf, allowing river and tidal currents to pass underneath, further destroying what is left of the structure. The image also shows that a small section of the keelson overhangs the drop-off, which supports the hypothesis of the movement of the wreck due to environmental causes. The wreck lies in an area where it is vulnerable to anthropogenic damage like frequent fishing and anchoring. It should be noted that the Bead wreck was placed on the State and National Registers of Historic Shipwrecks in 1988 and National Register of Historic Places. Tidal flow and marsh drainage, primarily through intersection of both the Loveland Thorofare and Wading River, create severe outflowing currents into the Mullica River proper. These currents undercut the wreck, which have caused it to break apart over time, and slip deeper into the river. It is now in danger of total break-up, and its historical significance could be lost into the deepest part of the river.

The Cramer wreck lies within 12.2 m of the Chestnut Neck Boatyard's main docks. The site gets its name from the previous boatyard which was owned by Stan Cramer. The current boatyard is almost in the same location of the one which existed in 1778. Residents tell of blowout tide sightings of the wreck and residents have been able

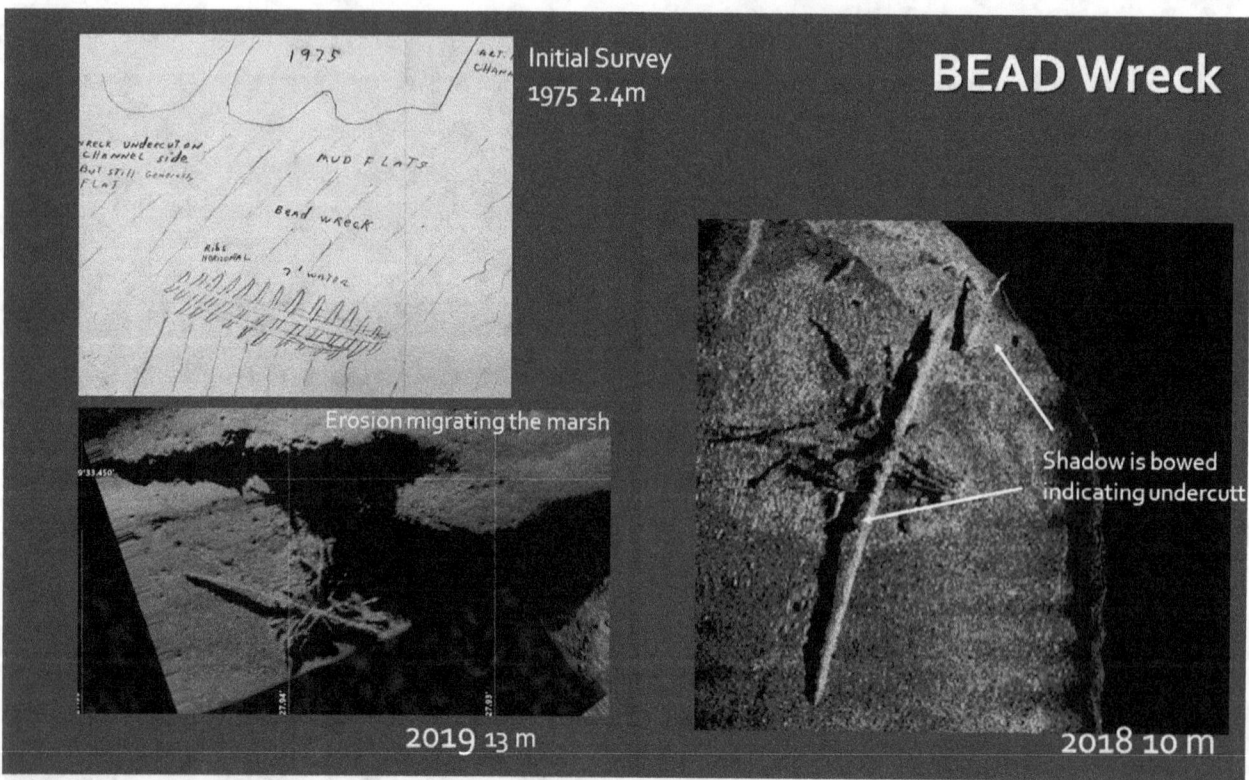

Figure 3: Bead Comparison. Three views of the Bead Wreck from its initial survey by archaeologist Gordon Watts in 1975 and sonar images by Stockton in 2018 and 2019 show the environmental deterioration of the wreck from water current and some evidence of commercial dredging. Credit: Stockton University.

to walk out to the wreck during those periods. A kedge or stream type anchor recovered at the marina site is now part of Monument to the Battle. Figure 3 indicates that the Cramer wreck is intact and similar in size, construction, and measurements to what a merchant schooner might have been built like (VanHorn 2004). There is much research on naval shipbuilding of the time, but scant published information on the development of merchant ships. VanHorn in her 2004 thesis was one of few available sources about merchant ship construction. The wreck is partially broken up at both bow and stern and heavily sedimented. What remains is about 1.5 meters of keel, keelson, first futtocks, partial frames, and ceiling planking and some of the out hull (Kenchington 1993). Two different sonar views show the wreck sitting atop a ridge, gradually slipping into deeper water and, perhaps, facing more break-up. The Cramer appears to be heavily sedimented. There are several areas where the wreck has broken up and debris is scattered. Further complicating the area, the Cramer lies along a ledge for her entire length and is gradually slipping off this ridge into deeper water, and there is a lengthy debris field, extending from the Cramer about 70 m to the East. Preliminary sonar imagery suggests these are pieces of ships broken up over time and possibly burned in the raid on the port in 1778. While the wreck has been accurately mapped, it has not been nominated to the State or National Register, in part because it lies just outside a working marina, although at some point its designation will happen. The surveys that Stockton students conducted were coincidentally beneficial to the marina, who could use this sonar data to help them obtain dredge permits for access to their docks. NJSHPO was able to allow permitting as the surveys provided critical positioning not before available.

The Phoel wreck site is the most complete of the three shipwrecks discussed here and represents the best opportunity to study and document its construction and its impact on local, state, and national history. As a result of Stockton's work on the Phoel, NJSHPO has approved the Phoel Archaeological Site (28-Bu-950) (ID#5660) and COE: 6/28/2018 (NJSHPO 2020). After several sonar surveys there was enough data to conclude this was a wooden sailing ship, with construction typical of the time for merchant ships (VanHorn 2004; Chiarel 2018). The keelson, with two cutouts for the mast steps, is clearly visible as are ceiling planks and frames, all of which can be accurately measured for length and spacing in post-processing software. The wreck measures 19.1 m long with a 5.2 m beam and what is left of her hull measures 2.1 m high. The keelson measures 14.5 m and seems truncated compared to wreck length and has two roughhewn tapered rectangular holes for the insertion of masts. Researchers using sonar software to calculate size and number measured 42 frames of various lengths with 30-40 cm (12-16 inches) spacing among the frames. The frames thickness is approximately 5 cm. The wreck has an NE - SW orientation and lies within 50 m from the shoreline on a 15-degree incline. Based solely on sonar measurement in software processing, it is believed at this time that the Phoel wreck shown in Figure 4 may be a schooner or brig sloop due to its two mast steps and rise in keelson (Fullmer 1998). It has been surmised that based upon the overall length and construction that the Phoel wreck could be 20-25 m long as a fully rigged two-masted sloop.

Comparing these wrecks, both the Phoel and Cramer wrecks are relatively intact. We have measured the Phoel wreck as 3 m longer than Cramer wreck with roughly the same beam, allowing for wreck site deterioration however, no conclusions have been made to determine if both ships are of the same type or construction based upon date collected thus far.

The Bead wreck is the most disarticulated of the three. The wreck's partial keelson is half the measured length of the Phoel at 9.3 m. There are no reliable measurements for the beam. Is the Bead wreck a smaller vessel or has the disarticulation made accurate measurements impossible? There is no way to be certain.

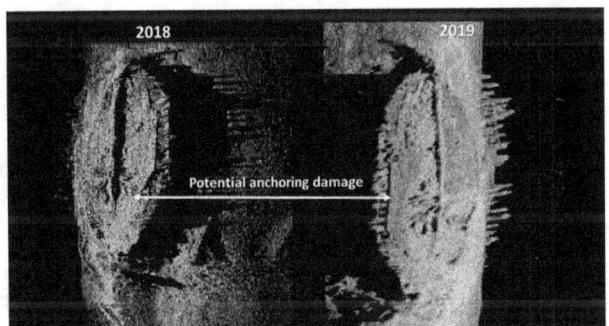

Figure 4: Phoel Comparison. Recent sonar scans of the Phoel wreck, seen mirrored here due to direction of travel, comparing the wreck from 2018 to 2019. The 2018 image is our benchmark data, clear debris is seen off the bow with the faint image of school fish. Noticeable damage near the keelson in the 2019 image, probably due to anchoring (commercial or recreational)

Credit: Stockton University.

Discussion

What researchers have yet to learn is whether these vessels sailed here from England or were built along the American coastline. Sonar data has taken the analysis of the wreck sites only so far. Scuba diving will be the next aspect of this survey. River water is extremely turbid, affected by both river flow and tidal effect as visibility is typically only 20 to 60 cm under optimal mid-tidal conditions. Planned research dives are expected to be undertaken in the summer of 2020-21 to test the wreck's construction, classify the type of wood used in the hull, record how the vessel was constructed, and identify types and quantities of fasteners. This information could indicate the location where the ship was originally built. Additionally, our future dive plans are to grid search the wreck sites to find and record artifacts that will aid in this identification effort. While we prefer to leave artifacts *in-situ*, extremely turbid visibility makes photography difficult so artifact removal for interpretation will be on a case-by-case decision.

The hypothesis of the team based upon earlier archaeological surveys in the 1980's and current research is that the ship would have been built for merchant trade either locally or in New England. New England-built ships make sense as it had prime forests and shipbuilding ports and was controlled by the British. Economically, building merchant ships in New England or locally would seem to make more sense to frugal ship merchant owners than building and sailing hundreds of vessels across the Atlantic Ocean from England, especially if these were for short-term service as some of the evidence suggests.

There is anecdotal evidence of shipbuilding in this southern part of New Jersey during the period, using the available timber, much like those in New England, such as white cedar, white oak, birch, pine even red cedar. Shipbuilding along the Mullica is mentioned in many sources, but no definitive references of a major shipbuilding port capable of producing great quantities of ships have been found to date. The priority of the scuba diving aspect of exploration and mapping, will be getting samples of the ship's construction materials which could be dated by tree-ring analysis to determine the age of the wood and, thereby, help date the ship (Miles 1997; Baillie 2016).

Magnetometry data indicates low metal readings from the wreck site. Certainly, the salvage and removal of anchors, cannons, and any valuable and saleable items would be expected by both privateers and British Marines before these ships were destroyed. The low metallic magnetometer results also add to speculation that perhaps construction is by treenail as opposed to iron fasteners.

The high-resolution sonar images created by advanced post-processing software enables researchers to obtain estimated physical measurements of the wrecks, but on-site visual examination and measurement by research scuba divers will help augment the sonar data. Divers can identify the physical condition and fastening of the ceiling planks and determine the construction of the frames, hull, and keelson. Utilizing the sonar software's capabilities, allows researchers to collect data remotely that would be difficult if based solely on diver measurements in turbid conditions, and can be used in conjunction with diver measurements to calibrate remote methods. In addition, these images allow for historical interpretation (Davis, 2017; Desmond, 1997) and reconstruction of the actual vessel from the sonar record.

Of these three wrecks, the Phoel wreck provides the most complete underwater archaeology field laboratory for study by marine science students and faculty. Remote sensing technology allows researchers and students to accurately measure components of the wreck and 'see' the wreck as an image in its completeness, something impossible to visualize in river conditions. The increased use of remotely operated vehicles (ROV's) is planned and will supplement data collection with aspects of river biology and submerged aquatic vegetation (SAV) which seasonally effectively obscures the wreck.

Multibeam mapping shows bathymetric or depth data and could indicate how river flow might be impacting the wreck site. With this bathymetric data and sonar mapping mosaics, we can view the seafloor and begin to understand the dynamic relationship of environmental deterioration as well as helping to define the battlefield and look for additional shipwreck targets. These shipwrecks are among the oldest known in New Jersey dating back to 1778. If these are indeed merchant ships, the study of them will give marine archaeologists and historians insights into colonial shipbuilding, commerce routes and local history.

All three wrecks are likely the "prizes" of local privateers, or pirated vessels captured by colonial captains, who were issued letters of marque by the Continental Congress. All indications are these shipwrecks are probably merchant ships and most likely, British merchant ships. The thesis "Archaeological Investigation of the Submerged Hull Referred to as the Phoel Wreck" (Chiarel 2018) outlined much of the history of the

Battle, but also undertook exhaustive archival research to try to identify all the possible merchant ships that would have passed this part of the South Jersey Coast and could be one of the ten shipwrecks burned and sunk in 1778.

No record remains thus far in the research conducted of the prize vessels that were wrecked at Chestnut Neck. Two vessels that have been frequently mentioned in this archival research are the great merchant ship *Venus* of London and the schooner *Fame* (Shomette 2016). Chiarel identified over 85 possible ships that likely transited this area between 1777 and 1779 that were mentioned in newspaper records, appeared in auction transactions, or shipping reports and looked to see which of those ships again appeared in similar publications the following year to 1779, eliminating all but 30 ships. Of course, not appearing later in time is not an indication a ship being part of the ones at Chestnut Neck and could be more a function of different routes or newspaper reporting. However, it is believed that ten of these thirty vessels may be the wrecks that lie in the Mullica River from the Battle of Chestnut Neck. Only by closer examination by scuba diving and finding/identifying artifacts from these wrecks will the research team possibly be able to put an actual name on these shipwrecks.

The collection of the data reported here brings to light issues common with shipwrecks, they will deteriorate due to environmental and man-made interactions over time. This is of major concern as these wrecks represent an historical focal point in American and southern New Jersey history. Current sonar data indicate that all three wrecks have shown signs of deterioration over the period during which we have collected data.

Erosional forces from moving water will impact these wrecks as it does with marshes and the riverbanks. However, based upon research so far, most of the damage has been done by river and tidal currents. The Bead wreck is a good example of this. Documented in 1975, the Bead wreck lies on a ledge in 3 meters of water, today it has slid down this ledge to a depth of nearly 12 meters.

It is likely that anthropogenic damage of the wreck sites can be linked to heavy construction in the area of a major river crossing highway. Dismantling of an old bridge and creation of a deep borrow pit for sediment material used in the newer bridge construction has deepened the river near the Bead wreck.

The Bead wreck also lies on a marsh ledge located near very dynamic water flow locations of both the river and man-made marsh drainage canals. Local fishing both commercial and recreational have harmed these wrecks by creating small dredges and anchoring near or directly on the wrecks.

The Phoel wreck, which has always been a popular fishing site, now shows signs of damage, probably due to anchoring. Most wrecks provide habitat for marine life and these revolutionary war wrecks are no different. Large fish schools hover around the wreck, something fishermen will see on their fish-finders, even if they do not know a 241-year old shipwreck is part of the bottom profile. Nominating these wrecks to the National Register is one way we can educate the users of the river to understand the maritime heritage it contains.

The wrecks are too delicate and in poor condition to be raised. If it were possible to raise the Bead wreck as was recently proposed, it would require that the wreck be fully conserved in a lab and eventually be placed in a museum. None of which is in the budget of Stockton, NJSHPO or the New Jersey State Museum. As a result of the conservation, it would then lose its National Register designation.

More work needs to be done mapping these sites. This will include additional scuba diving and sonar mapping. It is hoped that the collected data will be useful in nominating the Phoel and the Cramer wrecks for addition to the State and National Registers of Historic Places, and to install markers and additional historical interpretation near all the wreck sites, detailing their roles in the Battle of Chestnut Neck on 6 October 1778.

Acknowledgments

The authors acknowledge the professional advice and support by James P. Delgado, Vincent Capone of Black Laser Learning, Richard Veit, PhD, Professor of Anthropology and Chair of the Department of History and Anthropology at Monmouth University. and Stockton's Marine Field Station staff, Nate Robinson, and Elizabeth Bick-Zimmermann. Stockton University students: Thomas Barrett, Travis Nagiewicz, Elizabeth Klein, Christina Price, Ashlyn Rowe, Jason Sass, who have helped research this project.

References

Baillie, M. G. L.
2016 *Tree-Ring Dating and Archaeology.* Routledge, London.

Brisson, L. and T. Hiller.
2015 Multiphase Echosounder to Improve Shallow-Water Surveys. *Sea Technology*, 56:10–14.

CATSAMBIS, ALEXIS, BEN FORD, AND DONNY LEON HAMILTON.
2014   *The Oxford Handbook of Maritime Archaeology.* New York: Oxford University Press.

CHIAREL, SHANNON, M.
2018   "An Archaeological Investigation of the Submerged Hull Referred to as the Phoel Wreck." Doctoral dissertation. Monmouth University. Long Branch, NJ.

COOK, E.R. AND W.J CALLAHAN.
1992   *"The Development of a Standard Tree-Ring Chronology for Dating Historical Structures in the Greater Philadelphia Region."* New York: Lamont-Doherty Geological Observatory, Columbia University.

DAVIS, CHARLES GERARD, AND IRVING RAMSEY WILES.
2017   *American Sailing Ships: Their Plans and History.* New York: Dover Publications, Inc.

DESMOND, C.
1997   Wooden Shipbuilding. Lanham, MD: Vestal Press.

FULLMER, JACK.
1998   "The Mullica River Wrecks." Privately printed. New Jersey Historical Divers Association Vol 4 No. 1. Wall, NJ

HOWARTH, STEPHEN.
1991   *To Shining Sea: a History of the United States Navy, 1775-1998.* Norman, OK: University of Oklahoma Press.

JACQUES COUSTEAU NATIONAL ESTUARINE RESEARCH RESERVE.
2018   Accessed April 11, 2020. https://jcnerr.org/JCNERR_REVISEDMGMTPLAN%202018.2022.pdf

KEMP, FRANKLIN W.
1966   *A Nest of Rebel Pirates: The Account of an Attack by the British Forces on the Privateer Stronghold at Little Egg Harbor* Batsto, NJ: Batsto Citizens Committee.

KENCHINGTON, T.J.
1993   "The Structures of English Wooden Ships: William Sutherland's Ship, Circa 1710." *The Northern Mariner* 3:1-43.

MATHEWSON, R. D.
1985   Survey of the Mullica Shipwrecks. Atlantic Alliance for Maritime Heritage. Washington DC.

MARCOUX, JON BERNARD.
2012   "Glass Trade Beads from The English Colonial Period in The Southeast, Ca. A.D. 1607–1783." *Southeastern Archaeology* 31, no. 2: 157–84. https://doi.org/10.1179/sea.2012.31.2.003.

MILES, DANIEL.
1997   "The Interpretation, Presentation and Use of Tree-Ring Dates." *Vernacular Architecture* 28, no. 1: 40–56. https://doi.org/10.1179/030554797786050563.

NATIONAL PARK SERVICE ARCHEOLOGY
2020   "NPS Archeology Program: Sites and Collections." National Parks Service. U.S. Department of the Interior. Accessed April 18, 2020. https://www.nps.gov/archeology/submerged/NRShips

NJDEP-HISTORIC PRESERVATION OFFICE (NJSHPO)
2020.   Accessed April 18, 2020. https://www.nj.gov/dep/hpo. https://www.nj.gov/dep/hpo/1identify/nrsr_lists/Burlington.pdf

SKATMANM.
2019   "SAR HAWK® Humminbird® Sonar Target Acquisition Software." Black Laser Learning, Inc. https://blacklaserlearning.com/2018/03/18/sar-hawk-software-humminbird-sonar-target-acquisition-program.

SHOMETTE, DONALD G.
2016   *Privateers of the Revolution: War on the New Jersey Coast, 1775-1783.* Atglen, PA: Schiffer Publishing, Ltd.

VANHORN, KELLIE MICHELLE.
2004   "Eighteenth-Century Colonial American Merchant Ship Construction," Doctoral dissertation. Texas A&M University Office of Graduate Studies.

WATTS, GORDON P.
1976   "Underwater Archaeological Reconnaissance Survey: Report of an Archaeological Reconnaissance Survey of Several Shipwreck Sites in the Mullica River near Chestnut Neck, New Jersey." State Museum of New Jersey.

· · · · · · · · · · · · · · · ·

Stephen D. Nagiewicz
Marine Archaeologist
School of Natural Sciences and Mathematics
Stockton University
101 Vera King Farris Drive
Galloway, New Jersey 08205

Peter F. Straub Ph.D
Dean
School of Natural Sciences and Mathematics
Stockton University
101 Vera King Farris Drive
Galloway, New Jersey 08205

Steven P. Evert
Director
Marine Field Station
Stockton University
101 Vera King Farris Drive
Galloway, New Jersey 08205

Shannon M. Chiarel
School of Natural Sciences and Mathematics
Stockton University
101 Vera King Farris Drive
Galloway, New Jersey 08205

Jaymes Swain
School of Natural Sciences and Mathematics
Stockton University
101 Vera King Farris Drive
Galloway, New Jersey 08205

Jessica DiBlasi
School of Natural Sciences and Mathematics
Stockton University
101 Vera King Farris Drive
Galloway, New Jersey 08205

Loss of USS *Milwaukee* (C-21): An Archaeological Study of a World War I-Era U.S. Navy Disaster in Northern California

Jeffrey Delsescaux

The semi-armored cruiser USS Milwaukee *(C-21) went aground on 13 January 1917 during a failed attempt to pull the submarine USS H-3 (SS-30) off Samoa Beach near Humboldt Bay, California. More than 100 years later and remnants of* Milwaukee *can still be seen during low tide. In June 2019 archaeologists conducted a survey of the exposed wreckage and adjacent sand dunes and recorded what remains of* Milwaukee *and its associated salvage camp to see if enough archaeological material remains to warrant further research.*

Introduction

An intensive archaeological pedestrian survey of Samoa Beach in Humboldt County, California was conducted between 04 June 2019 and 06 June 2019 during the morning low tides. The pedestrian survey covered an area between the Pacific Ocean on the west, New Navy Base Road on the east, and the areas north and south of cruiser USS *Milwaukee* Memorial. The purpose of the survey was to record what remains of USS *Milwaukee* (C-21) and its associated salvage camp to see if enough archaeological material remains to warrant further research. The survey resulted in the recordation of a new archaeological site, USS *Milwaukee* Disaster Site CA-HUM-1751H (P-12-003897).

Setting

USS *Milwaukee* (C-21) grounded on the west side of North Spit, a 1 km (0.5 mi) wide sandy peninsula that demarcates the northern entrance to Humboldt Bay. North Spit is bordered by the Pacific Ocean on the west and Humboldt Bay to the east (Figure 1).

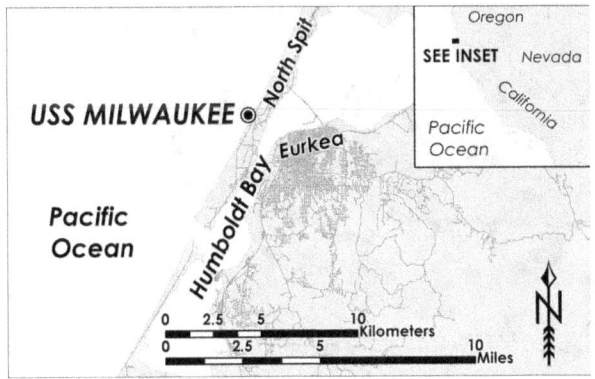

Figure 1: Map of project location. (Map by author).

Humboldt Bay is the most important commercial harbor between San Francisco Bay, California and Coos Bay, Oregon, a distance of 700 km (435 mi). It is approximately 23 km (14 mi) long and varies in width from 1 km (0.5 mi) to 7 km (4 mi).

The North Spit features transverse ridge sand dunes that have been shaped through a combination of northwestern winds, winter storms, storm surf, and vegetation (Cooper 1967:109). The height of the landscape immediately around the project area varies from 0 m (0 ft) to about 7 m (23 ft).

The offshore underwater landscape of the western side of North Spit where *Milwaukee* grounded is a gentle sandy slope. The 10 m (33 ft) depth line is approximately 1 km (0.5 mi) offshore.

Historical Context

USS **Milwaukee** *(C-21)*

During the period after the Spanish-American War, the United States (U.S.) began annexing overseas territories. The U.S. Navy needed large and fast cruisers with extended coal endurance (Friedman 1984:45). Sacrifices were made to the armament and protection for the sake of speed and endurance. Originally envisioned with 8-inch guns and heavier armor, the guns were replaced with 6-inch guns and armor was reduced to 4 in (10 cm) at its thickest (Friedman 1984:49-50).

Only three semi-armored cruisers were ever built, *Milwaukee*, *St. Louis* and *Charleston* (Friedman 1984:50). They were a unique hybrid that were officially rated as protected cruisers, but semi-armored cruisers occupy an area between protected cruisers and armored cruisers. *St. Louis* class were large cruisers with speed and endurance but lacked heavy armor and armament (Alden 1972:157).

USS *Milwaukee* (C-21) was a *St. Louis* class semi-armored cruiser built by Union Iron Works in San Francisco, California between 30 July 1902 and 10 December 1906. She was launched on 10 September 1904 and sponsored by Miss Janet Mitchell, daughter of U.S. Senator John L. Mitchell of Wisconsin.

St. Louis-class of semi-armored cruisers were criticized as being obsolete even before they were commissioned, which might explain why a few years after being commissioned *Milwaukee* was decommissioned and placed into a reserve fleet (Alden 1972:157). The last *St. Louis*-class cruiser was scrapped in 1930 due to limits imposed by the Washington Naval Treaty, leaving *Milwaukee* as the sole surviving example of this type of cruiser that was "among the earliest, well-documented examples of creeping growth in warship design" (Friedman 1984:49; Alden 1972:376).

On 25 April 1908, less than a year and a half after being commissioned, *Milwaukee* was placed in a reserve fleet in Puget Sound Navy Yard in Washington. Decommissioned 3 May 1910 and recommissioned on 17 June 1913, *Milwaukee* was not officially taken out of the reserve fleet until being stationed in San Diego on 18 March 1916. *Milwaukee* was extensively overhauled at Mare Island Naval Shipyard to facilitate its new role as a tender to destroyers and submarines (Dictionary of American Naval Fighting Ships 1969). After its refurbishment, *Milwaukee* left Mare Island Naval Shipyard on 5 January 1917 on its last voyage to Humboldt Bay to pull the stranded submarine USS *H-3 (SS-30)* off Samoa Beach. In temporary command was Lieutenant William F. Newton, U.S. Navy. Newton had never commanded anything larger than a submarine before and he and Lieutenant William B. Howe, commander of *Cheyenne* and senior officer present of the salvage operation, planned on executing a dangerous salvage plan (Hillman 1994:17; Haislip 1967:37).

The idea behind the plan was to use the powerful engines of *Milwaukee* to pull *H-3* off the beach during high tide while lines connected to the tug *Iroquois* and the monitor *Cheyenne* would keep *Milwaukee* from being forced ashore. Three previous attempts had failed. On the morning of 13 January 1917, Newton decided to try again and raised anchor.

After beginning their attempt, things immediately began to go wrong. *Cheyenne* had run over their line during a previous attempt and was not attached to *Milwaukee*. *Cheyenne*'s commander, Lieutenant Howe, was the senior officer in charge and unaware *Milwaukee* was making another attempt in the thick fog (Record Group 125, Spot Files, Box 13, Court of Inquiry Case Number 6779, National Archives and Records Administration). Then *Milwaukee* began to be forced ashore, dragging the tug *Iroquois* with it. The crew of *Iroquois* began to hack away at the line with axes, freeing themselves from *Milwaukee* to prevent their ship from being forced ashore too (Haislip 1967:46).

Milwaukee had secured the towline around the superstructure and it could not be slipped. They tried to use hacksaws to cut through the four thick steel cables wrapped together, but it was too late. A simple pelican hook would have allowed the crew to slip the thick 18.5 in (47 cm) cable before being forced ashore but this was the final mistake in a series of errors (Hillman 1993:24-25; Haislip 1967:47).

Despite their efforts to cut through the steel cables with hacksaws, *Milwaukee* was forced ashore broadside, south of H-3 (Figure 2). Although the Navy was surprised, the Humboldt Bay community was not. Both the Mayor of Eureka and commander of the Humboldt Bay Lifesaving Station saw the dangers and warned Newton (Haislip 1967:43-44). Residents even set up a pre-arranged signal, five blasts of the Hammond lumbermill's steam whistle, to notify the community when *Milwaukee* was aground. They also gathered driftwood for bonfires as they anticipated a disaster (Haislip 1967:45).

The rescue efforts of the crew of 438 men was observed by thousands of spectators, some who captured photographs and film footage. The most recognizable photos of the disaster published in newspapers was captured by Emma B. Freeman. She became known as

Figure 2: USS *Milwaukee* aground in January 1917. (Photo courtesy of the Naval History and Heritage Command. NH No. 46151).

the "pluckiest photographer in the world" and became the "official Government photographer." She even managed to photograph Admiral William B. Caperton, Commander-in-Chief of the Pacific Fleet, who was said to be "strongly prejudiced against being photographed" (San Francisco Chronicle 1917:1).

A Court of Inquiry was held finding Lieutenants Newton and Howe at fault for the disaster. They were to be court martialed for the loss of *Milwaukee*, but they got lucky. Four months after *Milwaukee* went aground, America entered World War I and their court martial was put on hold. By the time the war was over and the Navy got around to pursuing the charges again in 1919, the Navy had lost the motivation to proceed and dropped the charges, citing the "inconvenience and expense to the government entailed by assembling them for the trail is not warranted" (Record Group 125, Spot Files, Box 13, Court of Inquiry Case Number 6779, National Archives and Records Administration).

The Navy decided to abandon *Milwaukee*. They had the Northwestern Pacific Railroad build a spur connected to a trestle built by Mercer-Fraser in February 1917. The trestle extended over the intertidal zone to *Milwaukee*'s portside to facilitate the removal of the heavy guns and equipment (Hillman 1993:31-33). The Navy also constructed a salvage campsite known as "Camp Milwaukee" to house and feed workers and store equipment. Camp Milwaukee was continually occupied until 14 August 1919 when the hulk of *Milwaukee* was sold by the Navy for $3,000 to I. Schneider (Hillman 1993:33). In June 1920, the smokestacks were removed, and Schneider tried to remove the engines and/or boilers. It is unclear if he was successful, but there are reports of boilers being incorporated into the local lumber industry (Simpson 1998:138). A photograph in Humboldt State University's Humboldt Room Photograph Collections (Boyle and Boyle 1999) shows a boiler said to be from *Milwaukee* made into equipment used by the Little Redwood Company in Crannell, California.

After 1919, *Milwaukee* was frequently visited by locals and opportunistic salvage started occurring. Anything of potential value was removed, including the teak deck for woodshop classes at local high schools (Rohde 2013:24). *Milwaukee* remained mostly intact, except for being broken amidships and the forward half of the hull began to settle into the sand almost to the gunwales with only the masts and superstructure protruding.

About twenty-five years later World War II created an incentive for scrap metals and *Milwaukee* was again subjected to salvage efforts. Representatives of the U.S. Marine Salvage Company arrived at *Milwaukee* in August and September 1942 and detonated dynamite to look at the possibility of salvaging metal for scrap (*Humboldt Standard* 1942). They returned and, between 20 May 1943 and 24 May 1943, *Milwaukee* was dynamited between 7 am and noon (*Humboldt Standard* 1943). This salvage episode removed most of the surviving hull structure that remained above the sediment and *Milwaukee* began to obtain its current appearance and configuration. It is not known how successful this salvage effort was.

In addition to the two known secondary salvage periods, there has been multiple incidents of tertiary salvage, dating from the disaster until today. Using the term as defined by Richards (2008:115), tertiary salvage is the post depositional intermittent and opportunistic salvaging that occurs on wrecks. Early tertiary salvage focused on reusable material, such as the teak decking and copper alloy metal. While most tertiary salvage was focused on the monetary value of the metal or material removed, there was a shift in the late-1970s and 1980s when residents began to salvage material from *Milwaukee* for its historic value. While focus remained on copper alloy metals, they also salvaged iron plates and other artifacts. While some might still salvage copper alloy metals from the wreck for its scrap value, most tertiary salvage today is for its historic value.

Field Methods

A pedestrian survey was conducted between 03 June and 06 June 2019 by archaeologists with the goals of conducting an intensive survey of the study area that included the remains of USS *Milwaukee* (C-21), the railroad trestle, and associated salvage camp, Camp Milwaukee. The pedestrian survey examined the ground surface within the study area for the following:

- Artifacts
- Soil discoloration that may indicate the presence of subsurface cultural material
- Soil depressions and features which may indicate the former presence of structures of buildings
- Historic sites, features, and elements of local historical interest
- Historic debris

The survey had complete coverage of the 8.2 ha (20.3 acres) study area through an intensive and mix survey strategy. Field crew walked in parallel transits at intervals between 2 m (6.5 ft) and 10 m (33 ft). Spacing was dependent on landform and density of vegetation. Areas of poor ground visibility were subjected to tighter transit spacing.

The ground surface in the study area is composed of sand. Cultural deposits within a sandy matrix (i.e. unconsolidated sediment) are easily buried and there are rarely any surface manifestations of subsurface archaeological deposits. This is especially true in shallow high energy intertidal zones, where through a process of scouring, heavy objects tend to settle deeper into the unconsolidated sediment until they encounter a layer of cohesive sediment or bedrock.

A recreational metal detector (Harbor Freight 9-Function Metal Detector Model 67378) was used to identify buried archaeological deposits within the study area. The metal detector was used in parallel transits during the pedestrian survey in all areas that were not submerged. Anomalies were examined by careful excavation to investigate. Contemporary debris (e.g., beer cans) were not recorded. For all other anomalies the depth of the artifact, GPS location, and a description were recorded. Temporally diagnostic artifacts and unique or significant artifacts were photographed. Artifacts were then placed back into their test units and reburied.

While investigating magnetic anomalies within the sand dune, buried redwood timbers were encountered. Seven Shovel Test Units (STUs) were excavated around the anomaly to determine its constituents and significance. STUs were approximately 50 cm by 50 cm (20 in by 20 in) and to a depth of approximately 15 to 20 cm (6 in to 8 in).

Although the field dates corresponded to some of the lowest tides of the year that ranged from -47.2 cm to -51.2 cm (-1.551 ft to -1.682 ft), *Milwaukee* was still within the surf zone due to a large offshore swell. This made it difficult to accurately map and recorded all the exposed surviving ship structure above the sediment. GPS points were taken only of the northern and southern extremities and two pieces of miscellaneous wreck structure in between. GPS points were taken of all surviving pylons that were part of the railroad trestle built to *Milwaukee* in 1917. The GPS unit was a Trimble Geoexplorer 6000 series. Accuracy of points varied, but were within half a meter or less.

Study Findings

This study resulted in the identification of a previously unrecorded historical archaeological resource,

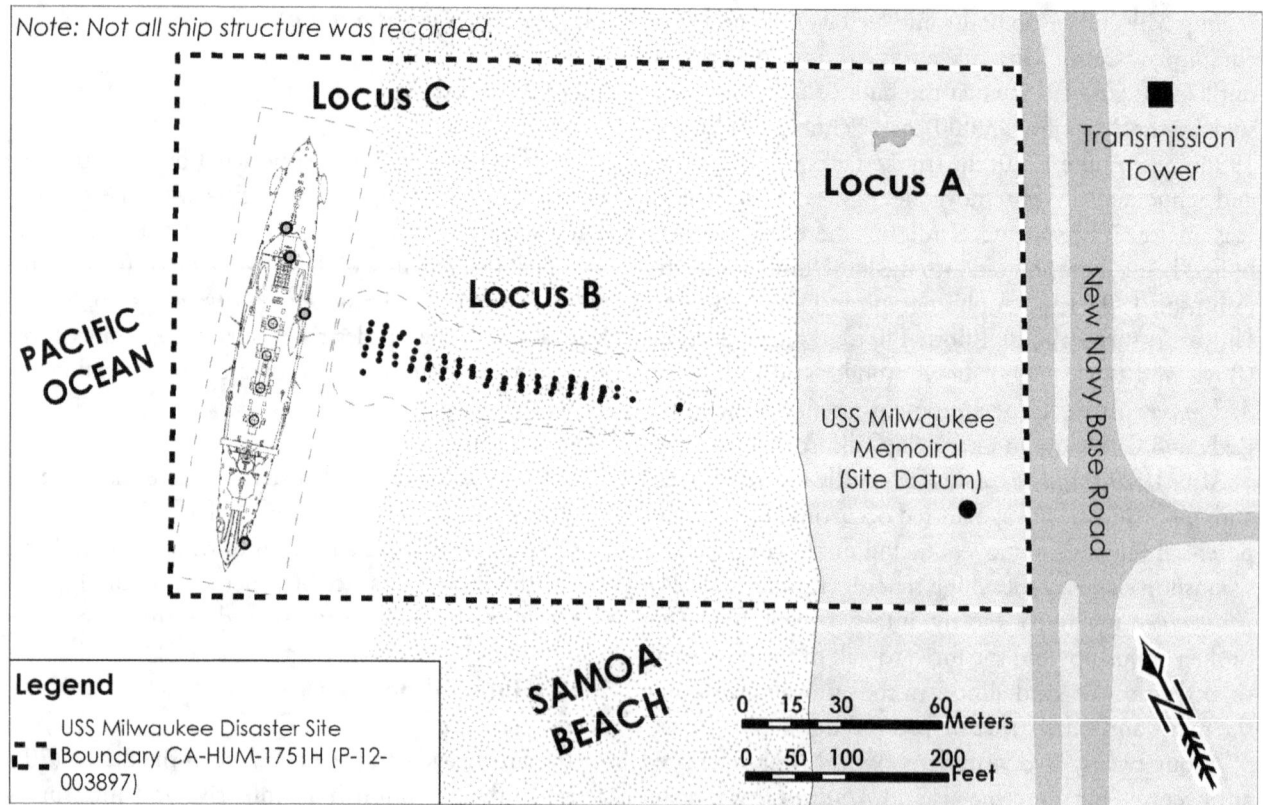

Figure 3: USS *Milwaukee* Disaster Site CA-HUM-1751H (P-12-003897) general site map. (Map by author).

USS *Milwaukee* Disaster Site CA-HUM-1751H (P-12-003897).

USS *Milwaukee* Disaster Site CA-HUM-1751H (P-12-003897), lies in Humboldt County on Samoa Beach in Samoa, California. Samoa Beach is on the westside of the North Spit approximately 6.5 km (4 mi) north of the entrance to Humboldt Bay. The City of Eureka lies on the opposite side of Humboldt Bay approximately 3 km (2 mi) east of the survey area. The site covers an area of 10.11 acres (40,938 m²) and contains three separate constituents (or loci): Camp *Milwaukee* (Locus A), railroad trestle (Locus B), and the wreck of USS *Milwaukee* (C-21) (Locus C) with artifacts scattered in between loci (Figure 3). Additional studies will probably identify new loci and current loci will be refined.

USS Milwaukee (C-21) – Locus C

The remains of USS *Milwaukee* (C-21) are within the intertidal zone and exposed only a few days a year during the summer minus tides (Figure 4). Most of the surviving ship structure lies buried in the sand with only a few dozen pieces of surviving ship structure protruding from the sediment.

During field work in June 2019, an offshore swell diminished the minus tide and all pieces of ship structure were within the surf zone. GPS points were taken at the most northern and southern ship structure. Two data points were taken of ship structure in between these north and south limits; surf conditions were too difficult and no other points were taken.

The southern point appears to be the bow chocks. A chock is an opening in the ships bulwark for mooring lines. The northern point is a bulkhead with a passageway, listing about twenty-six degrees to starboard. Pictures of *Milwaukee* prior to the 1943 blasting and salvaging show what appears to be that bulkhead behind the aft military mast on the lower decks. The stern and propellers are buried farther north.

Discussions with local divers revealed that the wreck can be dived with SCUBA equipment, usually during the winter months. One must wait for the perfect combination of a large winter storm that has removed the overburden of sand, a high tide, and a low swell. Depth is typically between 4.5m to 7.6m (15 ft to 25 ft) with 6m (20 ft) visibility. A dive on *Milwaukee* is described as very dangerous. Divers said they have been able to penetrate the hull of *Milwaukee* and salvage metal from within.

Some ordinance remained on board *Milwaukee*. One diver related a story of 3 shells being recovered by another diver and examined by an Explosive Ordnance Disposal (EOD) team from the U.S. Army, after being reported to the Arcata Police Department. This story was collaborated by a local newspaper article (*Times Standard* 1998).

The area around the surviving ship structure, where *Milwaukee* remains are believed to be buried, was designated Locus C.

Site Formation Process

USS *Milwaukee* (C-21) is one of the most photographed naval disasters. Thousands of residents visited the ship, and many took photographs and film footage. In the years that followed, hundreds more visited and salvaged material from the wreck. They also captured photographs of the remains of *Milwaukee* as she deteriorated through time. These photographs assist in developing an informed understanding of what happened to *Milwaukee* over the past 100 years.

On the morning of 13 January 1917, *Milwaukee* was pushed broadside onto the sands of Samoa Beach. The ship began to rock back and forth, working its way into the sand before becoming firmly imbedded and listing approximately twenty-six degrees to starboard. The amidship settled into more consolidated sediment, while the bow and stern settled into a more unconsolidated sediment. As the bow and stern began to subside, a crack formed between the 3rd and 4th funnel. By 1919, the bow had subsided to its gunwales while the stern had subsided slightly less. The area near the crack had only subsided to about the waterline.

Following work done by Nathan Richards (2008), salvage activity of *Milwaukee* can be broken up into three phases: primary, secondary, and tertiary salvage.

Figure 4: Remnants of the USS *Milwaukee* visible in the surf, view looking south. (Photo by author, 2019).

According to Richards (2008:155) "...*primary salvage* is a term that aptly describes the salvage of materials of shipwreck remains...by the 'owners, insurers or their agents,' and that secondary salvage describes work activities by 'professional salvers or sport divers.'... Tertiary salvage encompasses attempts at salvage that occur through time following abandonment. These activities are intermittent and opportunistic..."

It was clear that *Milwaukee* was beyond saving. The Navy was quick to begin salvaging, starting the primary salvage period. A railroad trestle was built to the wreck (Locus B) to facilitate the offloading of equipment, particularly the guns.

After the Navy had completed their salvage efforts, they sold the hulk in August 1919 to a San Francisco scrap dealer named I. Schneider, starting the secondary salvage period. Less is understood about what was salvaged during this period, but Schneider appears to have removed three smokestacks, the boilers from *Milwaukee*, and possibly even the engines. Schneider eventually completed his salvage efforts and *Milwaukee* began to deteriorate and collapse.

America was dragged into World War II in December 1941 by the attack on Pearl Harbor, Hawaii. Patriotic sentiments combined with the need for scrap metal started another secondary salvage effort. In May 1943, the remains of *Milwaukee* were dynamited and hauled away as scrap metal. The sand dunes were also searched for metal that could be used in the war effort.

Tertiary salvage began shortly after the Navy left and continues to take place on the wreck. Items taken during these tertiary salvage episodes included the teak deck, which was removed and used in wood shop classes at local high schools and other woodworking project (Rohde 2013). Later divers would scavenge copper alloy metals from the wreck for scrap and in the 1980s members of the Humboldt Bay Maritime Museum went out at minus tides to salvage metal for their museum collections (Carranco 1981:226). Tertiary salvaging continues as residents reported seeing individuals within the last few years scavenging during low tides. The focus has shifted from salvaging metal as scrap for its monetary value towards salvaging material from the wreck for its historic value.

Long Term Stability

Despite the tertiary salvaging by locals, the site of *Milwaukee* appears to be stable. Photographs from 1969 show wreckage similar to what is seen today at a minus tide. The periodic cycle of submergence and exposure is starting to show on the bulkheads, but they are remarkably intact for being exposed to saltwater for over 100 years.

Located in the intertidal zone, the processes of scouring during the winter months and redistribution of sediment during the summer months mean that the site is always changing what is exposed. Sand redistribution was significant and within the 3-days of fieldwork at least 1 m (3.3 ft) of sand had already been redeposited on the beach and buried several pylons. While there was no way to quantify the preservation of the lower portions of the hull, historic photographs and the surface manifestations of the wreck suggests that large portions of the lower hull are preserved below the sands, including most of the bow and the propellers in the stern.

Railroad Trestle – Locus B

Due to a deep scour on the eastern side of *Milwaukee* between the wreck and shoreline, 79 pylons were visible and recorded during the survey. The pylons suggest that the trestle was approximately 3.8 m (14.42 ft) wide at the eastern end, expanding to approximately 14.42 m (47.32 ft) wide at the western terminus near Milwaukee. The scouring was approximately 1.37 m (4.5 ft) deep, which helped expose these pylons. The 79 pylons were grouped together into an area designated Locus B.

Camp Milwaukee – Locus A

The coastal sand dunes are a dynamic environment that have changed significantly since 1917. Any surface magnifications of Camp Milwaukee have been buried and are difficult to locate. A recreational metal detector (Harbor Freight 9-Function Metal Detector Model 67378) was used to assist finding remains of Camp Milwaukee within the sand dunes. One promising area where remains of the camp might be located were found at Locus A.

Locus A was a concentration of buried disarticulated milled redwood timbers that was located using STUs. Originally identified through a magnetic anomaly using the metal detector, soil changes were noticed while excavating down to investigate the anomaly. The typical sandy matrix became a dark, reddish color and was infested with ants, possibly thatch ants (*Formica obscuripes*). It was soon realized that these were decomposed redwood timbers, possibly from a structure. The five positive STUs and artifacts found during an intensive pedestrian survey of the area helped delineate the boundaries of Locus A.

In one STU, three fragments of redwood siding were located. One of these fragments has an approximately 0.5cm x 0.5cm (0.20in x 0.20in) depression and hole that had linear groves surrounding it. It appeared this is where a nail was used to secure the redwood siding to a structure and the linear groves are scratches caused by its removal at some point. The milled redwood timbers identified in Locus A appeared to be disarticulated and not laid out in any linear fashion.

USS Milwaukee *Memorial*

USS *Milwaukee* Memorial was a project initiated by the community, particularly William Zerlang and Fred Bott, founders of the Humboldt Bay Maritime Museum. The rock came from a Mercer-Fraser quarry and was placed there in the early 1980s (Leroy Zerland, 2019, pers. comm.). They wanted to honor *Milwaukee* and hoped it would serve as a reminder to the community. Today, the memorial is overrun with ice plant (*Carpobrotus Chilensis* or *C. Edulis*) and the rock has been vandalized with graffiti. Otherwise it retains its integrity and has not changed in the past three decades. Its permanence made it ideal for use as the site datum.

Conclusions and Recommendations

Milwaukee disaster is a significant event for the Humboldt Bay community. Thousands of residents witnessed and partook in the rescue of sailors and salvaging of both USS H-3 (SS-30) and USS *Milwaukee* (C-21). The wreck of *Milwaukee* became a favorite location for recreation where residents could catch crab and fish or use the wreckage as a diving platform. Material salvaged from *Milwaukee* was incorporated into the homes of residents and remains well known today in the collective memory of the Humboldt Bay community.

The introduction of steam technology was an important contributor to the increased output of the Humboldt Bay lumber mills. There is historical evidence that the boilers or pieces of *Milwaukee* were incorporated into the local lumber industry, contributing to this important industry (Simpson 1998:138). It is possible that a boiler was used at Korbel Mill (now Green Diamond Lumber Company) at Blue Lake, California. It is also possible that the boilers were "sold to the Hammond Lumber Company and converted into steam locomotives Nos. 8, 9, and 11 of the Oregon & Eureka Railroad for the transport of timber to mills and milled lumber to the Port of Eureka" (Simpson 1998:138). A photograph in Humboldt State University's Humboldt Room Photograph Collection (Boyle and Boyle 1999) shows a boiler from *Milwaukee* being used by the Little River Redwood Company in Crannell, California, suggesting that Schneider's post-1919 salvage efforts were at least partially successful in removing the boilers.

Milwaukee is the only surviving example of a "semi-armored cruiser" that was "among the earliest well-documented examples of creeping growth in warship design" (Friedman 1984:49; Alden 1972:376). The cruiser resulted from the post Spanish-American War naval build up and was intended to patrol the expansive Pacific Ocean. This is reflected in *Milwaukee*'s design where priority was given to range and speed at the expense of armor and armament. The integrity and amount of hull structure surviving below the surface could not be determined but pictures and limited amount of archaeological data suggests that the lower portions of the hull are intact, especially in the bow area where *Milwaukee* is buried up to the chocks.

In addition to the wreck itself, there are possibly intact archaeological depots related to the salvage camp, Camp Milwaukee. The limited number of STUs conducted at Locus A suggests the deposits retain their archaeological integrity and data potential. More testing is necessary.

Lack of Metal at USS *Milwaukee* Disaster Site

There was a surprising lack of metal identified outside Locus C (USS *Milwaukee* wreck). Contemporary photographs show substantial occupation at Camp Milwaukee for years. There should be archaeological remains of the camp in the form of nails, structures, refuse scatters, and other miscellaneous metal debris.

Throughout the pedestrian survey of USS *Milwaukee* Disaster Site CA-HUM-1751H (P-12-003897), only five metal artifacts were identified. Of those five artifacts, two were identified as probably relating to Camp Milwaukee, and one was possibly relating to Camp Milwaukee. The other two metal artifacts identified were determined to be modern (dating post-1969) and were not related to the *Milwaukee* disaster or Camp Milwaukee. Obvious modern debris (e.g. beer cans) were not recorded. There are various reasons for this disparity of metal artifacts, including: 1) Removal through previous unauthorized metal detecting; 2) Artifacts too deeply buried to be identified with recreational metal detectors; or 3) Removal through metal salvage activity during World War II.

The piece of redwood siding with evidence of a removed nail suggest the camp was disassembled at some point and the metal removed. This might correlate with World War II when metal salvaging was a popular activity. The wreck of *Milwaukee* was extensively salvaged during World War II for metal, it makes sense the adjacent sand dune would also have been scavenged for any metal. The lack of metal could also be the result of recreational metal detecting. Newspaper articles report the "demonstration" of reactional metal detectors at the site of *Milwaukee* on 06 June 1981 for the first "*Milwaukee* Day" (Time-Standard 1981:2).

There are probably intact subsurface archaeological deposits within the site boundary that relate to Camp Milwaukee and USS *Milwaukee* shipwreck. Significant portions of the lower hull of the *Milwaukee* appear to be preserved below the sediment. Salvaging of *Milwaukee* had an impact on the Humboldt Bay community and local lumber industry. The wrecking event had an impact on the U.S. Navy with the loss of a multi-million-dollar asset and the spending thousands of dollars in salvage costs months before entering World War I. In a bit of irony, USS *San Diego* (ARC-6) was the flagship of the Pacific Fleet and visited *Milwaukee* when she took Admiral William B. Caperton, the Pacific Fleet Commander-in-Chief, to Eureka to assess the disaster. In a little over a year, *San Diego* would strike a mine laid by a German submarine off New York on 19 July 1918 and sink into the Atlantic Ocean. She was the only major warship lost by the U.S. Navy during World War I.

Acknowledgements

This paper would not have been possible without the generosity and support of many individuals and organizations. They include the Humboldt Bay Maritime Museum, specially Don Hofacker, Jeff Hood, and Joe Polos; Whitney Petrey; Raymond Hillman; Leroy Zerlang; Humboldt County Historical Society, specifically Jim Garrison; and all the property owners who gave their permission for the study, specially the Naval History and Heritage Command, California State Lands Commission, and Samoa Pacific Group, LLC. And to anyone else who contributed, thank you! The author is also grateful for the helpful comments by Victor Mastone on the manuscript.

References

ALDEN, JOHN DOUGHTY
1972 *The American Steel Navy: A Photographic History of the U.S. Navy from the Introduction of the Steel Hull in 1883 to the Cruise of the Great White Fleet, 1907-1909*. Naval Institute Press, Annapolis, Maryland.

BOYLE, WILLIAM AND KATIE BOYLE
1999 *Boiler on railcar (1999.03.1280)*. n.d. Photograph. *The Library, Special Collections/Humboldt State University*, Arcata, California. Humboldt Room Special Photographic Collection. http://library.humboldt.edu/humco/holdings/boyle.htm

CARRANCO, LYNWOOD
1981 Maritime Fiasco on the Northern California Coast. *California History* 60(3):210-227.

COOPER, WILLIAM S.
1967 *Coastal Dunes of California. Geological Society of America Memoir* 104. Geological Society of America, Boulder, Colorado.

DICTIONARY OF AMERICAN NAVAL FIGHTING SHIPS
1969 *Milwaukee*. Volume 4, pp. 362. Government Printing Office, Washington, D.C.

FRIEDMAN, NORMAN
1984 *U.S. Cruisers: An Illustrated Design History*. Naval Institute Press, Annapolis, Maryland.

HAISLIP, HARVEY
1967 The Valor of Inexperience. *U.S. Naval Institute Proceedings* 93(2):34-49.

HILLMAN, RAYMOND W.
1993 *Shipwrecked at Samoa, California: The Loss of the Navy Cruiser U.S.S.* Milwaukee. Pride of the River, Eureka, California

HUMBOLDT STANDARD (HS) [EUREKA, CALIFORNIA]
1942 *Milwaukee* Salvage Work Planned. 31 August. Eureka, California.

1943 *Milwaukee* Blasting Continues Here. 24 May. Eureka, California.

RICHARDS, NATHAN
2008 *Ships' Graveyards: Abandoned Watercraft and the Archaeological Site Formation Process*. University Press of Florida, Gainesville.

ROHDE, JERRY
2013 Decking from the Disaster: A Memorial to the USS Milwaukee. *Humboldt Historian* 61(1):20-25

SAN FRANCISCO CHRONICLE [SAN FRANCISCO, CALIFORNIA]
1917 U.S. Rewards Plucky Woman Photographer. 31 January: 1 San Francisco, California.

SIMPSON, GLENN D.
1998 Wreckers on the Bay: The Archaeological Potential of Historic Shipwrecks in the Humboldt Bay Region. *Proceedings of the Society for California Archaeology* 11:135-140. Fresno, California.

TIMES STANDARD [EUREKA, CALIFORNIA]
1981 '*Milwaukee* Day' is scheduled. 20 May:2. Eureka, California.

1998 WWI shell found near shipwreck. 25 June. Eureka, California.

. . . .

Jeffrey Delsescaux
Associate State Archaeologist
California Office of Historic Preservation
1725 23rd Street, Suite 100
Sacramento, CA 95816

Return to *Portland* 2019: Stellwagen Bank National Marine Sanctuary and Telepresence

Calvin H. Mires, Evan Kovacs, Kirstin Meyer-Kaiser, Benjamin Haskell

In 2019, an interdisciplinary team from Woods Hole Oceanographic Institution, Marine Imaging Technologies, and NOAA Stellwagen Bank National Marine Sanctuary explored and documented shipwrecks within Stellwagen Bank National Marine Sanctuary. This first year of a multi-year project included archaeological and biological analyses of the shipwrecks, PS Portland *and schooners* Frank A. Palmer *and* Louise B. Crary. *Sites were surveyed using custom-made ROVs that collected 4K motion video and 3D photogrammetry. The project was broadcast to schools, museums, and individuals around the country and world using telepresence technology. This paper presents results from 2019 field research and goals for future investigations.*

Introduction

In 2019, an interdisciplinary team from Woods Hole Oceanographic Institution (WHOI), Marine Imaging Technologies, and National Oceanic and Atmospheric Administration (NOAA) Stellwagen Bank National Marine Sanctuary (SBNMS) set out to explore, survey, and provide telepresence outreach of biological and cultural sites within SBNMS, utilizing some of the most cutting-edge underwater technology available to date. This was the first year of a multi-year project funded through NOAA's National Ocean Service (NOS) and the Office of National Marine Sanctuaries (NMS). Additionally, collaborating partners from University of Rhode Island's (URI) Inner Space Center (ISC), University of Connecticut's R/V *Connecticut*, and Exploring by the Seat of Your Pants provided their expertise, equipment, and experience.

The 2019 expedition returned to the paddle steamer, *Portland*, and the coal schooners *Frank A. Palmer* and *Louise B. Crary* to assess the changes on all three shipwrecks since the last expedition ten years ago. Second, the project sought to explore and find undiscovered shipwrecks using high-resolution multibeam. Next, it leveraged telepresence technology to interact with school learners of all ages across the country. Finally, it supported critical research needs for SBNMS. The results of the 2019 expedition already had an immediate impact on SBNMS policy and decision making for future protection of its underwater cultural heritage.

Project Overview: Rationale and Objectives

Designated in 1992 as the 10th National Marine Sanctuary, Stellwagen Bank National Marine Sanctuary is the only sanctuary in New England and encompasses more than 842-square miles of Gulf of Maine waters at the mouth of Massachusetts Bay (Figure 1). Its shallow banks and deep basins provide feeding and nursery grounds for 22 species of marine mammals, such as the humpback, northern right, sei, and fin whales, more than 80 species of fish, invertebrates, and 55 species of seabirds. This richness of marine life attracts over 300,000 people each year hoping to see whales and

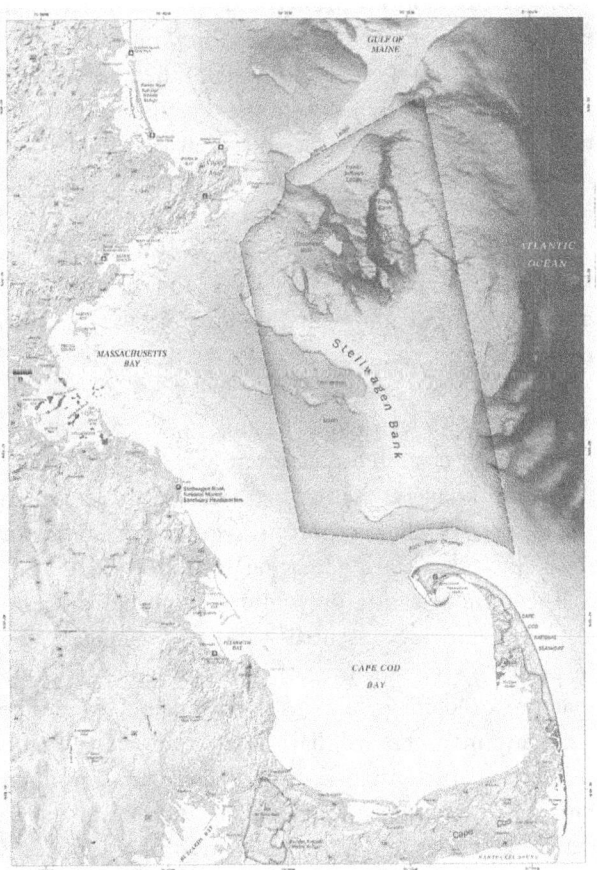

Figure 1: Map of Stellwagen Bank National Marine Sanctuary (courtesy of NOAA).

other animals in the natural environment (Stellwagen Bank National Marine Sanctuaries 2020a).

It also protects an estimated 200 historic shipwrecks. Since 2000, SBNMS staff have documented 47 vessels, twelve of which have been identified with seven of those listed on the National Register of Historic Places (NRHP), in accordance with the mandates of the National Historic Preservation Act (NHPA). These vessels represent more than 400 years of maritime history, architecture, technology, industry, and culture (SBNMS 2012; Lawrence et al. 2015). They are also part of an environmental and ecological system, and serve as island-like biological habitats, colonized by anemones, sponges, ascidians, bivalves, sea stars, and fish. It is the mission of SBNMS to conserve, protect and enhance the biological diversity, ecological integrity, and cultural legacy of the sanctuary while facilitating compatible use (SBNMS 2020a).

To achieve this mission, it is important to have the best and most recent data possible, but much of the sanctuary's information is almost ten years old. It is unlikely that the fishing activities reported on these sites abated over the past decade – activities such as "commercial bottom trawls and gillnets [that] have ensnared portions of the wrecks, breaking pieces from them" (Lawrence et al. 2015:62). Therefore, it was important to acquire new site assessments and new data that could help scientists and managers understand on-going site formation processes by utilizing the latest advancements in underwater documentation.

New technology developed at WHOI and Marine Imaging Technologies was used to capture high-definition video and ultra-high-definition 4K video recorded from the remotely operated vehicle (ROV) *Pixel*. ROV *Pixel* is a custom built, cinema-class vehicle designed for undersea imaging and documentation with a proprietary custom camera array. Using this ultra-high-definition imagery, the research team is building high-resolution 3D photogrammetric volumetric models of the shipwrecks (Marine Imaging Technologies 2020).

These models not only inform archaeologists but also can provide essential data for managers. For instance, by visualizing and comparing any cultural material or damage that has accumulated over time, sanctuary managers will have a better understanding of the impacts of human activity. These digital products, ranging from digital models on the Internet or mobile devices and apps to a scaled 3D print of the shipwrecks, can also be rendered for public outreach and education in various formats. This will allow students and the public to engage with tangible representations of the sanctuary's submerged sites in new, innovative, and exciting ways, and reinforce the sanctuary's commitment to "preservation through education."

In addition to developing 3D models for formal and informal learning, the team provided a series of outreach events using telepresence technology, which is a means for ship-to-shore live programing. By partnering with NOAA's ONMS and SBNMS, URI's Inner Space Center, and Exploring by the Seat of Your Pants, scientists, engineers, and NOAA managers connected with schools, museums, various venues, and over 9,400 individuals across the United States and from 12 other countries. They were to able explain the mission and answer questions in real time while aboard University of Connecticut's R/V *Connecticut*. Additionally, live programs were recorded and made available on-line for further viewings.

Acquiring new archaeological and biological data, applying cutting-edge technology, and engaging new audiences and life-long learners were also the bases for planning the 2019's expeditions goals:

Archaeological Objectives: (1) To conduct an archaeological assessment survey of ongoing site formation processes for PS Portland *and coal schooners* Frank A. Palmer *and* Louise B. Crary; *(2) to compare new video documentation with previously acquired video footage to determine any cultural impacts to submerged cultural resources; and (3) to explore and document deep-sea habitats and cultural sites in the northeast quadrant of SBNMS, known as the "Tuning Fork," using high-resolution multi-beam in order to locate new shipwreck sites and other submerged cultural resources that exist and have not previously been discovered.*

Biological Objectives: (1) to document and quantify invertebrate and fish species inhabiting PS Portland *and coal schooners* Frank A. Palmer *and* Louise B. Crary *from ROV footage; (2) to compare present video to past ROV recordings and characterize changes in the species composition and relative abundance (community structure) of shipwreck communities over time; and (3) to determine the influence of fishing gear on the biological community, including any change over time.*

Technological Objectives: (1) to acquire high-resolution 4K video and high-resolution images that can be used to derive essential product, such as 3D photogrammetric volumetric models, site plans, and photomosaics; and (2) to develop a methodology for high-resolution survey with small boat and observation class vehicles.

Educational Objectives: (1) to provide live-broadcasts from ship to shore using telepresence technology; (2) to engage school children across United States and Canada; (3) to produce lesson plans for classrooms on biodiversity of shipwrecks; and (4) to provide informal programming for audiences during day and evening broadcasts at public venues.

As planning progressed, it was decided to focus most efforts on documenting the paddle steamer *Portland* due it its iconic status with SBNMS and the tragic conditions surrounding its sinking which earned it the ominous sobriquet, "New England's *Titanic*" (Conway 2019).

Historical and Archaeological Background of the Paddle Steamer *Portland*

The story of the paddle steamer *Portland* and the eponymous storm that sank it, the *Portland* Gale of 1898, has been well told. Several books have tackled the ship's history specifically (Bachelder and Smith 1998; Lawrence et al. 2015; Milmore 2019). In 2003, the Discovery Science Channel made the documentary, The Wreck of the *Portland*. Compendiums of New England shipwrecks, journal articles, and newspaper reports discuss it as well. Therefore, only a brief synopsis of the ship's history and the fateful events surrounding its last voyage and eventual discovery will be provided here.

Built in 1889 by the New England Shipbuilding Company of Bath, Maine, the wooden-hulled, sidewheel steamship, *Portland*, was one of the most luxurious night boats to travel on New England waters during its near ten-year career. During the mid- to late-19th century, night boats dominated coastal travel in New England. They provided a comfortable, relaxing, and inexpensive way to travel from Boston to various Maine ports. For only a dollar (or approximately $30 today), passengers enjoyed fine dining, music, and company before going to sleep in comfortable staterooms and berths to wake at their destination the following morning. *Portland* was built to serve the demands of this clientele. Measuring 291-feet in total length and with a maximum breadth of 65-feet from sponson to sponson, the steamship contained a 225-foot long main saloon, skylights, 167 cherry-paneled staterooms, and 514 white-pine berths. Its single-cylinder, walking-beam engine was powered by two boilers built by Bath Iron Works that provided enough steam pressure to move its 35-foot, 10-inch diameter paddle wheels at 20 times per minute for a top speed of 15 miles per hour (Lawrence et al. 2015:27-29).

On 26 November 1898, *Portland* left Boston at 7:00 pm with reports of severe weather moving up the Atlantic coast. Captain Hollis Blanchard was aware of the incoming weather but decided to leave with nearly 200 passengers and crew. He did not realize, however, that the storm with hurricane gusts and heavy snows was moving as fast as it was. Sea conditions worsened rapidly and, at 11:00 pm, *Portland* was reported struggling against the wind and waves. Sometime around 9:00 am, the vessel succumbed to the storm and sank almost 500-feet to the ocean floor. Bodies and artifacts started to wash ashore at Cape Cod on 27 November (Lawrence et al. 2015:31-34). The disappearance and location of *Portland* became a mystery for the next 100 years.

In 1989, the location of *Portland* was found through the efforts of two Massachusetts residents, John Fish and Arne Carr, who had spent years using side-scan sonar to search for the vessel. They were aided by Richard Limeburner from WHOI, who calculated possible search areas based on historic currents and the fact that the watches washed ashore read 9:30. Limeburner correctly hypothesized that this meant 9:30 in the morning. Based on this information, Fish and Carr soon had an image of a shipwreck, but the data were inconclusive, and confirmation of this wreck's identity had to wait.

In 2002, Fish and Carr revealed the wreck's location to SBNMS; the vessel sat within the established boundaries of the sanctuary. With advanced technology, SBNMS and collaborators conclusively identified the vessel as *Portland*. For the next eight years, archaeologists at SBNMS returned to *Portland* at least five times to acquire new data and to assess if there had been any changes the site. Most of these surveys were conducted using the latest side scan sonar and ROV equipment available. When possible, they recorded high definition video and photographic images. In 2004, they created a photomosaic of the main deck at the bow to the steamship's boiler uptakes on the port side. They were unable to document more of the ship due to overhanging nets and the danger of entanglement to the

ROVs (SBNMS 2012, 2020b; Lawrence et al. 2015). In 2005, their research and documentation led to PS *Portland*'s listing on the National Register of Historic Places (SBNMS 2012; Lawrence et al. 2015).

The final mission in 2010 produced a high-quality, synthetic aperture sonar image of *Portland*. Afterwards, archaeologists disseminated their findings through reports, educational materials, a book, and an interactive website that allowed visitors to track not only the ship's journey and discovery, but provided information about some of the passengers and crew, and excellent discussions of the wrath and havoc the *Portland* Gale of 1898 caused (Lawrence et al. 2015; Marx 2017).

Return to *Portland* 2019: Expedition Technology and Methodology

In 2019, WHOI received funding to return to *Portland* and other underwater cultural sites in SBNMS with new, cutting-edge technology to document the cultural and biological changes (if any) that may have occurred over the ten years. A new cinema-class ROV, called *Pixel*, was developed by Marine Imaging Technologies to carry 40,000 Lumens of lights and up to eight cameras including large format and panoramic cameras. *Pixel* was also designed to be used for small boat operations and with an aesthetic that gave it anthropomorphic characteristics to help connect with young audiences (Figure 2).

Pixel carried several high-definition cameras, including a Sony 4k and Nikon 45MP Z7 still-camera, used for acquiring photomosaic sequences, and was deployed from a 31-foot lobster boat, *Dawn Treader*. Several days of learning how to maneuver *Pixel* and *Dawn Treader* while documenting *Portland* 450-feet below produced a successful anchoring system that handled several on-site environmental challenges. First, currents on site were regularly over one knot and shifted with the tides. Although *Pixel* had six thrusters, the trade-off of its small size meant it was not as powerful as a larger class of ROV. With that factor, the team decided to work down current to avoid being thrust into the wreck or one of its several nets unintentionally, which provided the second challenge. Previous projects had reported on the abundance of nets and fishing gear on *Portland* (Lawrence et al. 2015), but the team encountered heavier coverage in areas that had not been impacted previously. Therefore, a full systematic recording methodology was initially not possible. Through initial reconnaissance and site characterization surveys that provided beta-testing for survey lanes and capabilities of *Pixel* in such hazardous environmental and cultural conditions, the system was modified. Transects were run along each side of the wreck and along the top of the wreck, recording plan and profile views. All cultural and biological material was recorded including abandoned gear and netting, as these articles are part of the site formation process (Figure 2). The team successfully covered and recorded 85%-90% of *Portland* visually on HD and SD video and photographs. This accomplishment was a testament to both *Pixel*'s size and maneuverability as well as the skill of the ROV pilot.

While most of the time for data collection was spent on recording *Portland*, the remains of two coal schooners, *Frank A. Palmer* and *Louise B. Crary* that collided bow to bow racing to the Boston market in the winter of 1902 were also documented (SBNMS 2012; Lawrence et al. 2015). Due to the redesign and adaptions made to the stabilizing and recording methodologies on *Portland*, the efficiency of the visual and site characterization survey of the *Palmer* and *Crary* archaeological site was greatly

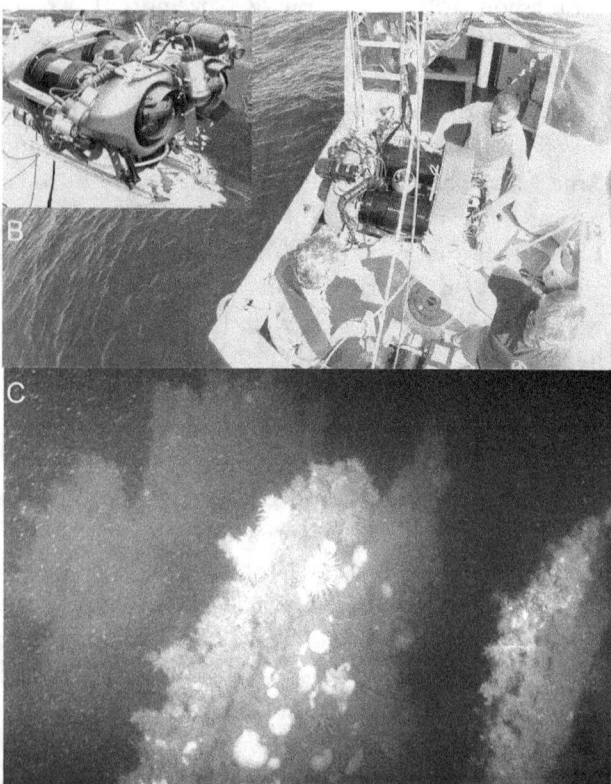

Figure 2: Sampling operations in summer 2019. A) ROV Pixel; B) Kovacs, Mires, and Mike Skowronski (ROV pilot) recovering Pixel on the deck of R/V *Dawn Treader*; C) anemones (*Urticina felina*) and sponges (*Mycale lingua*, *Axinella infundibuliformis*) cover the paddle wheel on the *Portland* wreck (courtesy of Marine Imaging Technologies).

increased. Within two days, the team covered nearly 100% of both wrecks, except where nets and fishing gear made it impossible to document safely.

While the predominant data collection at the sites was performed over the summer months of 2019, the team returned in the fall on R/V *Connecticut* to fill in missing areas, provide live ship-to-shore programming, and to conduct multi-beam operations. However, due to bad weather ROV operations were suspended. Instead, efforts focused on public engagement and outreach during the day. At night, a high-resolution, multi-beam survey was conducted to locate new shipwreck sites and other submerged cultural resources in the northeast quadrant of the Sanctuary, known as the "Tuning Fork" because it features a south-facing Y-shaped valley.

Post-processing and Preliminary Results

As of this writing, much of the data collected on the 2019 expedition is being processed, cataloged, and indexed for further rendering towards the objectives of producing 3D photogrammetric volumetric models, site plans, and photomosaics. These products will provide opportunities for further scientific information, management decision making, and public engagement and outreach. The video footage that was collected has already provided the team with visual and qualitative results and analysis. Further, some preliminary 3D photogrammetric models were able to be rendered from the raw footage of PS Portland – providing the first 3D image and partial model of the vessel as it rests on the ocean floor.

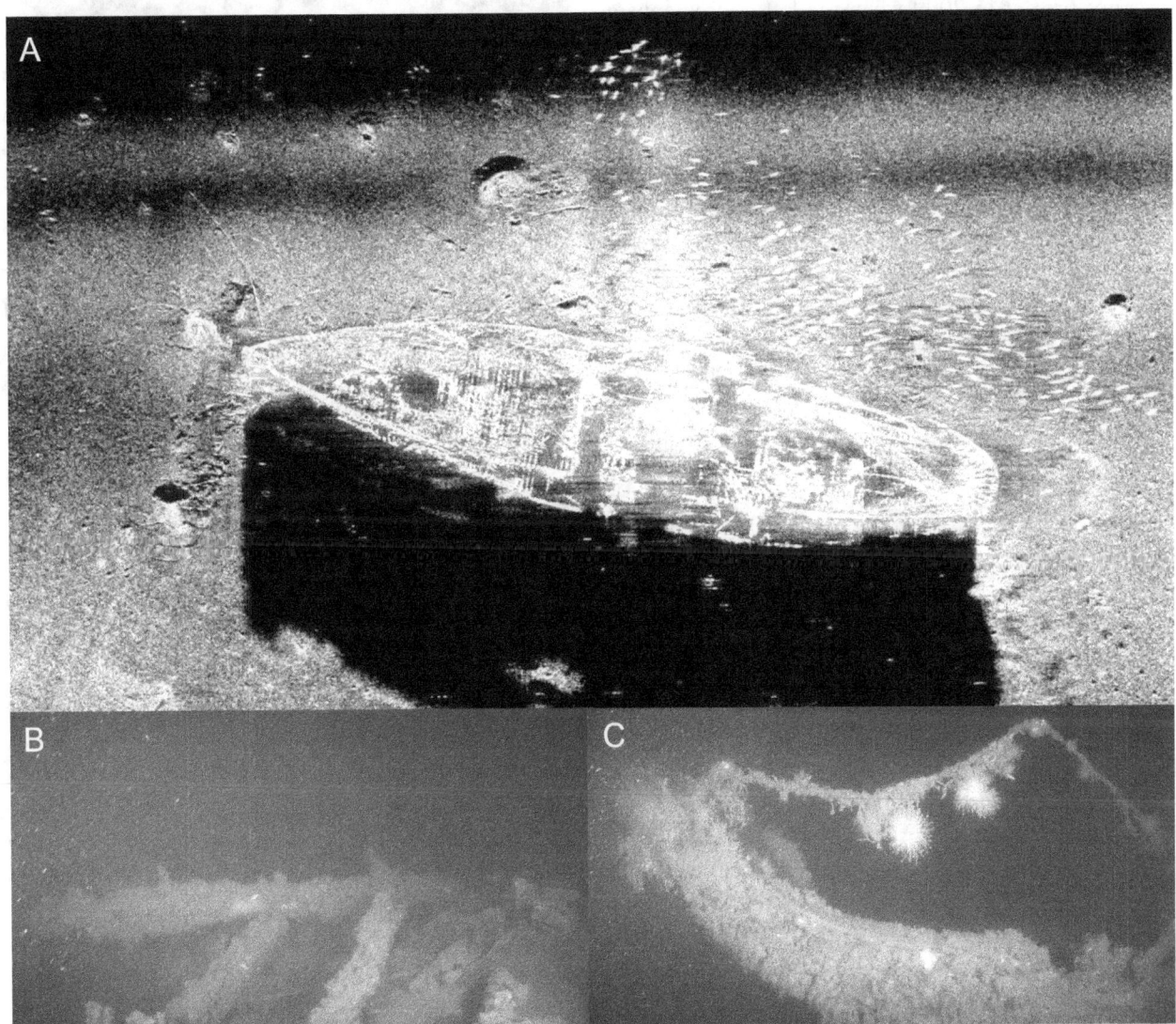

Figure 3: A) 2010 synthetic aperture sonar image of *Portland* B) stern timbers and main rail on seafloor; C) exposed stern frames (courtesy of NOAA/SBNMS/Applied Signal Technology, Inc. and Marine Imaging Technologies).

Archaeological Analysis

For the preliminary archaeology analysis, raw video footage from the 2019 expedition was reviewed and identifiable features and artifacts on *Portland* – both historic and contemporary – were labeled through editing software and then saved as their own files. As the video was reviewed, two research questions representing SBNMS critical management priorities focused the preliminary observations: 1) What is the archaeological integrity of known maritime archaeological resources, and how is it changing?; and 2) What are the levels of human activities that may adversely influence maritime archaeological resource quality, and how are they changing? The answers to these questions were immediately apparent.

A large trawl net on the port bow was recorded that was not present in 2009 when the last photographs of the bow were taken. The exact date of the entanglement is unknown, but it has caused physical damage to the site where the net cables have cut into the bow's cutwater. It also has caused biological impacts through scarification of the dense anemone community growing at top of the cutwater and along the port bow gunwale. Further, the net rises in the water column by floats used to keep it open while fishing. This presents an entanglement hazard to ROVs, which prevented further documentation of the bow's freight deck. In fact, this net was not the only new entanglement noticed on the bow. Other netting that was not present when the first photomosaic project occurred in 2004 inhibited efforts to document cultural material recorded at that time.

Another significant discovery was the collapse of the stern fantail. In 2010, synthetic aperture sonar showed the fantail intact and a shadow of the stern still standing above the seafloor. In 2019, we found the fantail railing and timbers completely detached and disarticulated from the wreck (Figure 3). Remnants were strewn around the stern. While there were gillnets entangled around the rudder and collapsed fantail, it has not been confirmed whether cultural processes or natural processes, or a combination of both, were the cause of collapse.

Finally, a preliminary 3D model developed by Marine Imaging Technologies has provided some first impressions and site integrity of *Portland*'s profile on its starboard side (Figure 4). This model highlights net entanglements over the bow and sponson that were documented in previous expeditions and made recording the starboard side difficult. It reveals artifacts and timbers *in situ* that collapsed outside of the hull

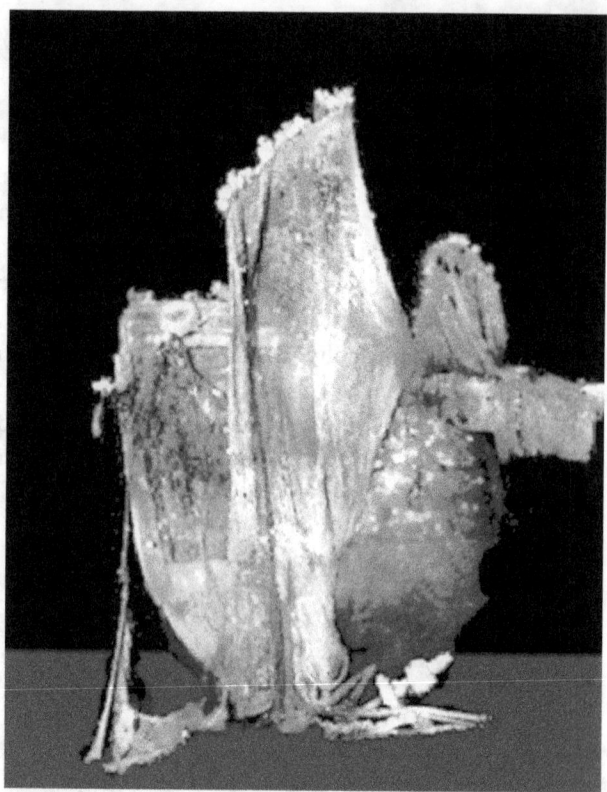

Figure 4: Partial 3D model of PS *Portland* (courtesy of Marine Imaging Technologies).

and scattered in a debris field on the starboard side of *Portland*. As the model-processing proceeds, more visual and qualitative analysis will occur.

Biological Analysis

For the biological analysis, ROV data was converted into frame grabs anytime the ROV had a clear view of the wreck at a distance that allows the invertebrate species to be counted and identified. Frame grabs were categorized by their position on the wreck (bow/stern/amidships and port/starboard/mid), altitude above the seafloor (top/middle/bottom of the wreck), and surface orientation (vertical/horizontal/complex). A sub-set of frame grabs representing different parts of the wreck were selected and treated as independent replicates for analysis. All invertebrates visible in the frame grab were counted and identified, and the percent cover of fishing gear was estimated. Fish communities were characterized by direct count from ROV video.

The invertebrate communities on *Portland*, *Palmer*, and *Crary* are dominated by sponges and anemones (Figure 2). The most common taxa are the plumose anemone (*Metridium senile*), and the breadcrumb sponge (*Halichondria sp*). Larvae of these species' taxa are fed by yolk from their mother and disperse in the water column for only a few days (Bergquist and Sinclair 1968, Bucklin 1987). The stalked tunicate (*Boltenia ovifera*) is also common on both wrecks, but this species has a pelagic larval duration of just 36 hours (Lacalli 1980). Isolated, island-like shipwrecks would not be expected to be colonized by species with short pelagic larval duration, because these larvae usually settle close to their parents. It is hypothesized that populations on shipwrecks could have been founded by just a few individuals which then came to dominate the wreck community through asexual reproduction or philopatry (that is, recruitment of larvae back to the same wreck over many generations).

In previous investigation years (2002 and 2010), fish communities on both wrecks were dominated by Atlantic cod (*Gadhus morhua*) and pollock (*Pollachius virens*). In 2019, Acadian redfish (*Sebastes fasciatus*) had replaced them as the dominate community. The reason for this change is currently unknown, though the accumulation of fishing gear on the wrecks suggests it may be related to fishing activity. Spiny dogfish (*Squalus acanthias*) were also observed near the *Portland* wreck in 2019.

Photogrammetric Analysis

The photogrammetry process is well underway for *Portland* and in initial phases for the *Palmer* and *Crary* site. While there was 85%-90% video coverage on *Portland*, only 45% of collected data was satisfactory for 3D modeling. This required extensive post-processing due to the numerous breaks in usable footage. A planned survey for photogrammetry, or even mosaicking, typically requires running overlapping and perpendicular lanes over and around the site. Metashape is the software commonly used, and like all photogrammetry software, it works well with a continuous stream of images that build upon each other. The environmental conditions on the wrecks made this type of planned pattern survey impossible to do and therefore, the wrecks were recorded as conditions permitted. Additionally, the amount of nets on each site posed significant challenges in model rendering but were included to illustrate current and on-going cultural site transformation.

The methodology for producing the models involves pre-processing all the images collected to even out exposure, color and image quality. Next, images are collated into numerous groups that could be built up as "mini models." Through Metashape, the sparse point clouds of approximately a dozen mini models are aligned and merged together over time. This works reasonably well, but there is still much refining and manual aligning required. In the next field season, *Portland* and *Palmer* and *Crary* sites will be revisited to acquire data required to complete the models. As there are numerous areas on each wreck that are inaccessible for larger ROVs, a small penetration ROV will be deployed to fill in gaps where possible. Additionally, stadia will be added to the site to confirm measurements and scale by calibrating the software to known shapes on the stadia, and augment incorporated laser scales for verification analysis of accuracy.

Telepresence and Public Outreach

During September, the team connected with learners of all ages from around the world using telepresence technology. Nine programs were offered from R/V *Connecticut* that reached schools, museums, and venues across the United States. Programs were organized by a combination of hosts at URI's Inner Space Center, who explained to the audience the format of the program, introduced scientists and short films, and facilitated questions from those watching to those onboard the ship. After an introductory video, Mr. Haskell, Dr. Meyer-Kaiser, and Dr. Mires discussed the history, biology, and archaeology of *Portland* respectively. Mr. Kovacs also joined some of the programming to discuss technology and its application for the project.

The 2019 project connected to 1,415 students in 28 schools. During direct interactions with classrooms, the crew answered enlightening questions from students. Why do organisms colonize shipwrecks? What is the significance of the *Portland* tragedy? How are underwater habitats sampled and understood? In one particularly proud moment for the outreach team, a group of students who had participated in a broadcast during the day at school logged on to view an evening broadcast and ask the rest of their questions. Two students from another state connected to the broadcast from their home after school was cancelled for inclement weather. In addition to this informal education programming, lesson plans were developed and made available online, covering topics such as larval dispersal, shipwreck biodiversity, critical thinking exercises about the colonization of shipwrecks, and the process of investigating shipwrecks.

Beyond the classroom setting, public broadcasts were streamed to 21 venues with an in-person audience of 647. Another 9400 viewers joined online from 12 different countries. Volunteer sanctuary ambassadors reported that many members of the public stayed long after the broadcast had concluded to continue asking their questions.

Discussion

While current results are limited, they have already proved impactful. An archaeological priority was to establish a contemporary baseline for on-going site formation processes, including cultural transformations (c-transforms) such as fishing gear and marine debris, and natural transformations (n-transforms) such as colonization by benthic organisms. While n-transforms are present, it is apparent that the greatest transformations to *Portland* are cultural. The presence of new nets and the potential for human activities causing the collapse of the fantail stern offer significant concern for the overall site stability.

The results of the 2019 expedition have already had far reaching implications for management of maritime heritage resources in the National Marine Sanctuary System. The location of most historic resources in most national marine sanctuaries are not made public to protect them from human impacts primarily looting by wreck divers. However, results from this expedition have made it clear that the impacts of commercial fishing are a much greater threat than looting in SBNMS. This points to the need for a more tailored, case-by-case approach to management that considers the risk profile of each historic resource. As a result, the practice of non-disclosure of historic resources is being reevaluated by the Office of National Marine Sanctuaries.

Future Research

As the second year of the project commences, needed data will be acquired at *Portland* and *Palmer* and *Crary* shipwreck sites to fill gaps for the 3D models and photogrammetric site plans. Laser scales and stadia for scaled imagery and models will also be calibrated and deployed. With a year of experience, 2020 will provide opportunities for testing archaeological hypotheses involving reasons for *Portland*'s loss by documenting areas of the ship that have not yet been recorded. Focus of research will shift from these two sites, however, and more sites throughout the sanctuary will be analyzed such as a mystery collier in the north east section of the sanctuary. Shipwrecks are also powerful natural experiments for biology, and observation of the communities inhabiting them can lead to significant insights for benthic ecology, fisheries management, and for understanding changes in marine ecosystems over time. Therefore, the team will start sampling benthic communities on shipwrecks to identify species taxonomically and compare these communities to natural hard-bottom reefs in SBNMS. For both archaeological and scientific observations, enhanced imaging and modeling will continue.

These new models will provide greater opportunities for engaging audiences in the second year of the project. For instance, 2020 broadcast plans will be built on a new type of Microwave system developed by AVWatch and heavily utilized by military, Coast Guard and other first responders. It creates a closed network up to 30 miles away that supports sustained throughput of 20-30MB bandwidth, which is over 10 times what the sustained bandwidth was during 2019 broadcasts and should open numerous possibilities. Boat testing of the network is about to begin with antennas already placed in Provincetown, Gloucester and Scituate. With this new technology in combination with established telepresence, children and adults are brought to the shipwrecks providing them an engaging, indelible experience to learn about SBNMS's underwater cultural heritage. Finally, in accordance with the NHPA, Stellwagen Bank Sanctuary has a responsibility to inventory, understand and protect its historic resources (SBNMS 2012, 2020a). Therefore, searching for and documenting new historic shipwrecks in the northern quadrant of the sanctuary is a priority in the second year of the project.

Conclusion

The first year of the "Return to *Portland* 2019: Stellwagen Bank National Marine Sanctuary and Telepresence" research and exploration expedition has provided learning opportunities, successful research, and engaging outreach. It has already helped sanctuary staff at SBNMS and the National Marine Sanctuary system re-evaluate their management strategies for underwater cultural heritage on a case-by-case basis. The upcoming project season will further help the sanctuary provide the best preservation for these non-renewable cultural resources. The project is evolving and improving its methods and programming to ensure the highest quality data is acquired and the highest quality of outreach possible to engage the public around the world on the scientific and social significance of shipwrecks in Stellwagen Bank National Marine Sanctuary.

References

Bachelder, Peter D. and Mason P. Smith
1998 *Four Short Blasts: The Gale of 1898 and the Loss of the Steamer* Portland. Provincial Press, Portland, ME.

Bergquist, Patricia R, and Mary E. Sinclair
1968 The Morphology and Behaviour Of Some Intertidal Sponges. *New Zealand Journal of Marine and Freshwater Research* 2(3): 426-437.

Bucklin, Ann
1987 Growth and Asexual Reproduction of the Sea Anemone *Metridum*: Comparative Laboratory Studies of Three Species. *Journal of Experimental Marine Biology and Ecology* 110:41-52.

Conway, J. North
2019 *The Wreck of the* Portland. Lyons Press, Lanham, MD.

Lacalli, Thurston
1980 Annual Spawning Cycles and Planktonic Larvae of Benthic Invertebrates from Passamaquoddy-Bay, New Brunswick. *Canadian Journal of Zoology* 59:433-440.

Lawrence, Matthew, Deborah Marx, and John Galluzzo
2015 *Shipwrecks of Stellwagen Bank: Disaster in New England's National Marine Sanctuary*. The History Press, Charleston, SC.

Marine Imaging Technologies
2020 Remotely Operated Vehicles. Marine Imaging Technologies <https://marineimagingtech.com/rov/>. Accessed 25 February 2020.

Marx, Deborah
2017 Portland Gale of 1898. National Oceanic and Atmospheric Preserve America Initiative <www.Portlandgale.com>. Accessed 3 February 2020.

Milmore, Art
2019 *And the Sea Shall Have Them All*. Art Milmore, Whitman, MA.

Stellwagen Bank National Marine Sanctuary (SBNMS)
2012 Maritime Heritage: Maritime Heritage Management. PDF Brochure, Gerry E. Studds Stellwagen Bank National Marine Sanctuary, National Oceanic and Atmospheric Administration's Office of National Marine Sanctuaries, United States Department of Commerce, Scituate, MA.

2020a Welcome. Stellwagen Bank National Marine Sanctuary <https://stellwagen.noaa.gov/welcome.html>. Accessed 16 January 2020.

2020b Projects. Stellwagen Bank National Marine Sanctuary. <https://stellwagen.noaa.gov/maritime/projects.html>. Accessed 16 January 2020.

•••••••••••••••••

Calvin H. Mires, Ph.D.
5 Bunker Hill Road
Plymouth, MA 02360

Evan Kovacs
Marine Imaging Technologies, LLC
1227 Route 28A
Pocasset, MA 02559

Kirstin Meyer-Kaiser, Ph.D.
Woods Hole Oceanographic Institution
266 Woods Hole Road
Woods Hole, MA 02543

Benjamin Haskell
Stellwagen Bank National Marine Sanctuary
175 Edward Foster Road
Scituate, MA 02066

An Investigation of the Microbial Community Associated with USS *Arizona*

Jennifer Clifford, Archana Vasanthakumar, David L. Conlin, Ralph Mitchell

USS Arizona contains crude oil, which continues to leak slowly into Pearl Harbor. The use of a remotely-operated vehicle provided a unique opportunity to investigate, and collect samples from, the ship's interior. We evaluated bacterial communities in sediment collected from interior and exterior sites. The data provided an initial estimation of the bacterial community associated with the interior. Bacterial phyla appeared to differ in abundance between interior and exterior samples. Continued research is needed to develop targeted long-term strategies for protecting both the ship and the surrounding ecosystem.

Introduction

USS *Arizona* is an American naval memorial and National Historic Landmark submerged in Pearl Harbor, Hawaii, USA and entombs more than 1,100 officers and crew. The ship also contains approximately 2400 tons of Bunker C grade crude oil, which has been slowly leaking from the corroding hull for more than 75 years (Russell et al. 2004). Not only is the preservation of USS *Arizona* as a national shrine important, but so too is the health of Pearl Harbor.

Previous investigations into the structural stability of USS *Arizona* report corrosive activity on the external surface (Makinson et al 2002; Wilson et al 2007). The potential for further metal corrosion and subsequent oil leakage could impose a serious environmental hazard, placing the surrounding ecosystem in jeopardy.

We are interested in increasing our understanding of the microbial community composition of USS *Arizona*. Such analysis can provide insight into the potential influence of microbes on metal corrosion and the stability of the sunken structure. Understanding the bacterial community composition will help in developing methods to manage corrosion, thereby protecting the integrity of the USS *Arizona* and the surrounding ecosystem of Pearl Harbor. Our initial investigation was centered on determining the bacterial community associated with USS *Arizona*, and making preliminary comparisons of these communities across different locations along the exterior and the interior of the ship. Ultimately, we are interested in evaluating whether the bacterial community in the interior of the ship differs from that of the exterior and the influence that this community has on metal corrosion.

The bacterial community was investigated using high-throughput gene sequencing technology targeted to specific sequences of nucleic acids isolated from sediment samples. This study presents preliminary data on composition, distribution, and activity of the bacterial population that is associated with USS *Arizona*. The potential differences in those communities between locations were also explored.

Other studies have investigated the microbial community composition associated with USS *Arizona*. Due to sampling and social limitations, these were confined to samples associated with the exterior of the ship (McNamara et al 2009; Graham et al 2006). Development of a remotely operating vehicle (ROV), the 11th Hour (Figure 1), by Marine Imaging Technologies (https://www.marineimagingtech.com) and the Woods Hole Oceanographic Institution (https://www.whoi.edu), has enabled unprecedented access to the interior of the vessel. We now have the opportunity to not only have visual representation of these areas, but can also collect various sample types in order to evaluate the microbial communities associated with several locations around USS *Arizona*.

Figure 1: A remotely operated vehicle (ROV), the 11th Hour, developed by Marine Imaging Technologies and the Woods Hole Oceanographic Institute, was used to collect the sediment samples from various locations around the USS *Arizona*. Photo courtesy of Brett Seymour, National Park Service.

This 'snapshot in time' will help us to better understand the biology of the microorganisms associated with USS *Arizona* and the potential of these microbial communities to contribute to metal corrosion. Long-term goals for this research include aiding in the development of targeted strategies for protecting USS *Arizona* and the surrounding ecosystem of Pearl Harbor.

Methods

The sampling sites where sediment was collected for analysis were located at several locations at varying water depths. Exterior samples were collected by divers at both bow and stern mudlines and along the upper deck of the ship. The interior sample was collected by the ROV within a third deck stateroom. Once the samples were collected, they were shipped to Harvard University for analysis. Analysis involved extracting all the genetic material (DNA and RNA) from each sediment sample using commercially made kits specific for this process (Qiagen). A very specific region, V4 of the 16S rDNA gene, that is unique to bacterial species was targeted and amplified to determine the unique genetic sequence using Illumina MiSeq, a high-throughput sequencer. The University of Connecticut Microbial Analysis Resources and Services Center performed the sequencing, using protocol and primers adapted from Caporaso and colleagues (2012) for use with the Illumina MiSeq protocol. The DNA sequence of the V4 region provides a unique marker, much like a fingerprint, that has sufficient differences in its sequence that allows a software program to place each sequence in a specific bacterial grouping. Analysis for taxonomic association was performed using the mothur software program (Schloss et al 2009) and a formatted version of a database from the Ribosomal Database Project (RDP, Univ. of Illinois; Maidak et al 1994). The result is the frequency of sequence that is categorized into specific bacterial taxonomic groups. This simply refers to the number of times a specific target sequence is identified to a particular group. In this study, we report taxonomic classification at the level of bacterial phyla.

Results and Discussion

Community quantification and distribution

Figure 2A shows the distribution of the eight bacterial phyla and the broader grouping of the Bacteria_unclassified that were represented by at least 1% of total reads in at least one of the sediment samples. The number of times that a specific sequence was identified, the clone frequency, is shown along the

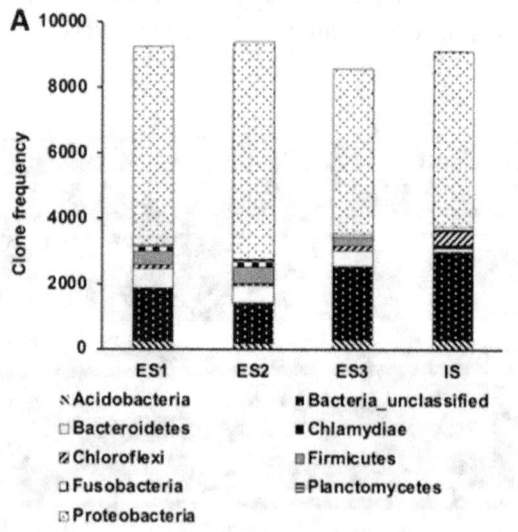
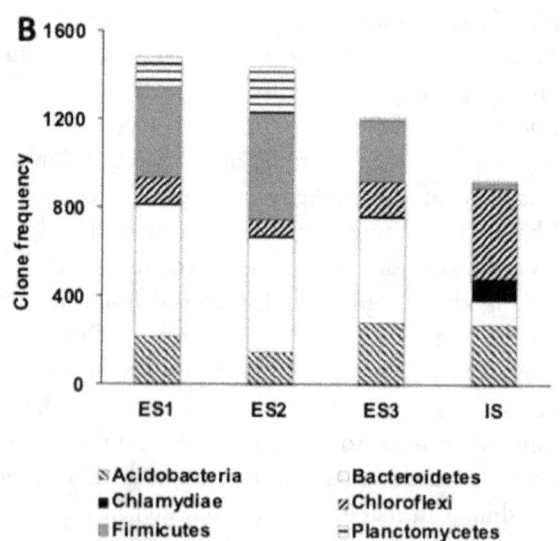

Figure 2: The bacterial phyla with representatives identified in the sediment samples belong primarily to the Proteobacteria, Bacteroidetes, and Firmicutes, in addition to the broader taxonomic grouping of the Bacteria_unclassified. The number of times that a specific sequence was observed (clone frequency) is shown on the y-axis. The primary distribution of these bacterial communities from each sample is shown (**A**). The remaining phyla are represented differently (**B**), suggesting that bacterial composition differs between the interior and exterior populations.

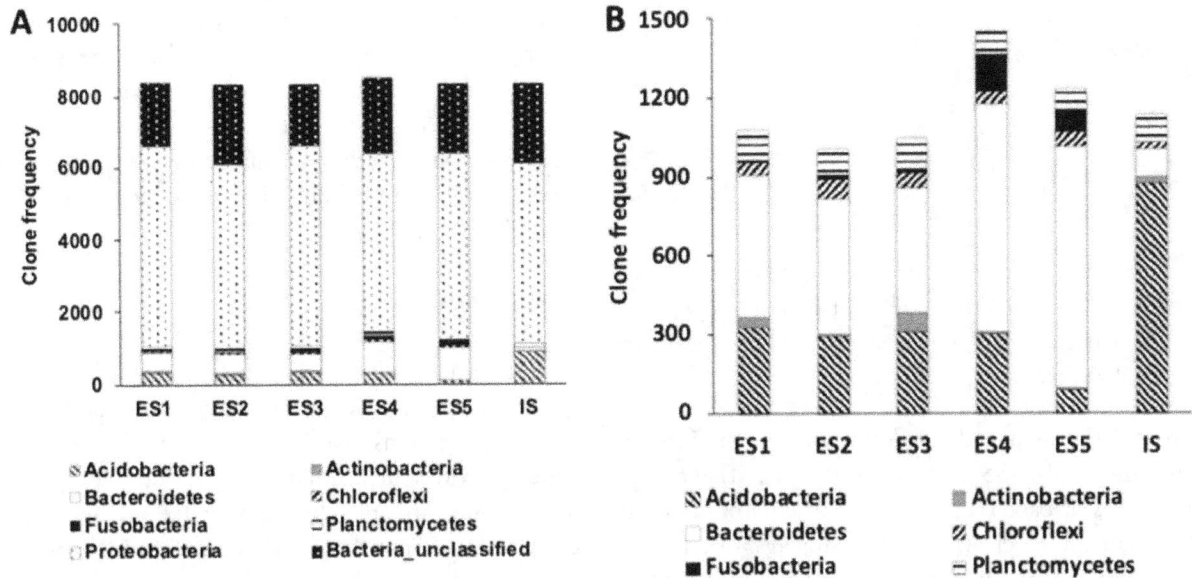

Figure 3: The bacterial phyla with representatives that are metabolically active in the locations sampled belonged primarily to the phyla Proteobacteria, in addition to the broader taxonomic grouping of the Bacteria_unclassified. The primary distribution of these bacterial communities from each sample is shown (A). Some variation in representation among the remaining phyla was observed, particularly with regard to the bacterial distribution in the interior sediment sample (B). The number of times that a specific sequence was observed (clone frequency) is shown on the y-axis.

y-axis. The greatest proportion of sequences found in the exterior sediment samples belonged to the phyla Proteobacteria, Bacteroidetes, and Firmicutes, as well as those representatives from the general taxonomic grouping of Bacteria_unclassified. These data support previous findings of bacterial communities associated with concretions formed on USS *Arizona* where analyzed strains belonged to the phyla Firmicutes, Bacteroidetes, and Proteobacteria (McNamara et al 2009). This suggests that the bacterial community exterior to the ship has changed little over the last decade.

Sequences of bacteria preliminarily identified in the interior sediment belonged primarily to the phlya Proteobacteria, Chloroflexi, and Acidobacteria and also included representatives in the Bacteria_unclassified grouping. The remaining phyla are also represented differently (Figure 2B). The observed distribution suggests that the bacterial community composition differs between the interior and exterior populations. These data must be confirmed and its significance remains to be determined. However, this does provide a glimpse as to which organisms are present in these locations.

Initial insight into metabolically active bacteria

Figure 3A shows those bacterial phyla with representatives that are most active; in other words, those bacteria that are growing, replicating, and metabolizing in the sampled locations. In the sediment samples collected from both the exterior and interior locations, the most abundant phylum identified was that with representatives from Proteobacteria. All sampled locations also had a greater abundance of the representatives from the Bacteria_unclassified compared to the remaining phyla. In this analysis, some variation was observed in representation among those phyla that have fewer representatives, particularly those within the phyla Acidobacteria and Bacteriodetes (Figure 3B). These data continued to give the sense that there are differences in populations between the exterior and interior samples.

Implications for metal corrosion and biodegradation

The implication of further metal corrosion and increased oil leakage from USS *Arizona* on the ecology of Pearl Harbor is a concern, particularly with regard to the interior of the structure. Within these phyla reported above are bacterial species with potential to influence corrosion, particularly the sulfate-reducing bacteria that belong to the Proteobacteria (Enning and

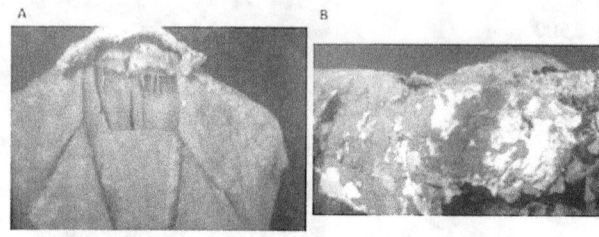

Figure 4: Images captured by the ROV show lack of biodegradation as evidenced by an intact uniform (**A**) and pages of a book (**B**). Photos courtesy of Brett Seymour, National Park Service.

Garrelfs 2014; Kip and van Venn 2015). The interior environment of USS *Arizona* is unique. The overall populations of bacteria in the interior environment are lower than the exterior (data not shown). In addition to low bacterial populations, oxygen levels recorded by the ROV were consistently low: ~4%. We assume that there is little microbial activity in the interior, because there are small populations, hypoxia, and observed lack of biodegradation as evidenced by images of intact textiles and paper (Figure 4). The potential for corrosion exists in the interior environment, but the severity of the threat is unknown. Is the rate of corrosion slowed because there are fewer bacterial populations with a lower overall metabolic activity in this environment?

Currently, there is no information as to the extent of metal corrosion in the interior of the ship. Our investigation provides additional evidence that the environmental conditions and microbial activity in the interior sediment provide a situation where microbially-induced corrosion may occur on the steel surface of USS *Arizona* in a hypoxic marine environment (Atkas et al. 2013; Enning and Garrelfs 2014; Little and Lee 2014; Kip and van Veen 2015).

Preservation of the undegraded textiles and paper could be happening strictly as a consequence of low oxygen, supporting lower bacterial populations with reduced metabolic activity. We speculate that certain bacteria with distinctly increased representation in those environments could possibly be contributing to preservation of these items in other ways, perhaps via metabolic by-products. Based on small populations and hypoxia, and assuming there is little microbial activity in the interior, our data suggest differences in community composition between the exterior and interior areas of USS *Arizona*. We observed overlap in communities by location, which might be expected, even though water exchange is very limited. However, bacterial families with distinctly reduced representation in the interior environment could explain the lack of microbial activity on those organic materials. More sampling and further study of the internal and exterior locations of USS *Arizona* is critical for contributing to a greater level of understanding in differences between bacterial communities and their influence on metal corrosion and biodegradation.

Conclusion

To our knowledge, this is the first analysis of bacterial species that comprise the communities associated with the sub-ecosystems that lie internal to USS *Arizona*. This paper provides preliminary data on the composition, distribution, and metabolically active members of the bacterial communities in these locations. This initial data suggests that there are differences in community composition between the exterior and interior areas of USS *Arizona*. Some represented bacterial phyla have members that are involved in metal corrosion, but further study is required to better understand these populations. With this 'snapshot', we aim to provide researchers with information to begin making comparisons of these communities and to better understand how that information can be utilized to develop strategies aimed toward reducing or eliminating undesirable changes to USS *Arizona* memorial and the surrounding ecosystem of Pearl Harbor.

Much remains to be done to develop a thorough understanding of the microbial community role in the structural stability and biodegradation phenomenon observed on USS *Arizona*. More sampling is required to provide the number of replicates needed to confirm and report, with significance, on the composition of the bacterial community. There are several questions and lines of investigation that can potentially be addressed: What is the role of these bacteria in a low oxygen environment? Are there unique members or a consortium of bacterial species that are contributing specifically to the preservation of the organic materials observed in the staterooms on the third deck of USS *Arizona*? What is the role of the bacteria in this environment, what contribution do they make toward corrosion, and what, if any, are the mechanisms that influence corrosion? Continued research is necessary to support development by providing areas of focus as to where to implement management strategies used to preserve USS *Arizona* and Pearl Harbor

Acknowledgements

The authors wish to thank Brett Seymour, Marc Mittelman, and Julianna Braun for technical assistance, advice, and administrative support. The United States National Park Service, Department of the Interior, provided support.

References

Atkas, Deniz F., Jason S. Lee, Brenda J. Little, Kathleen E. Duncan, B. Monica Perez-Ibarra, and Joseph M. Suflita
2013 Effects of oxygen on biodegradation of fuels in a corroding environment. *International Biodeterioration and Biodegradradation* 8:114-126.

Caporaso, J. Gregory, Christian L. Lauber, William A. Walters, Donna Berg-Lyons, James Huntley, Noah Fierer, Sarah M. Owens, Jason Betley, Louise Fraser, Markus Bauer, Niall Gormley, Jack A. Gilbert, Geoff Smith, and Rob Knight
2012 Ultra-high-throughput microbial community analysis on the Illumina HiSeq and MiSeq platforms. *The ISME Journal* 6:1621-1624.

Enning, Dennis and Julia Garrelfs
2014 Corrosion of iron by sulfate-reducing bacteria: new views of an old problem. *Applied and Environmental Microbiology* 80(4):1226-1236.

Graham, Amanda, T. McDonald, K. Blair, K. Crawford, M. Russell, L., and Pamela J. Morris
2006 The USS *Arizona*: Microbial degradation of Bunker C crude oil. Abstracts of the General Meeting of the American Society for Microbiology. Volume 103:Q-048.

Kip, Nandy and Johannes A. van Veen
2015 The dual role of microbes in corrosion. *The ISME Journal* 9:542-551.

Little, Brenda J. and Jason S. Lee
2014 Microbiologically influenced corrosion: an update. *International Materials Review* 59(7): 384-393.

Maidak, Bonnie L., Niels, Larsen, Michael J. McCaughey, Ross Overbeek, Gary J. lsen, Karl Fogel, James Blandy, and Carl R. Woese
1994 The Ribosomal Database project. *Nucleic Acids Research* 22(17): 3485-3487.

Makinson, John D., Donald L. Johnson, Matthew A. Russell, David L. Conlin, and Larry E. Murphy
2002 *In situ* corrosion studies on the battleship USS *Arizona*. *Materials Performance Materials Selection and Design*: 56-60.

McNamara, Christopher J., Kristen B. Lee, Matthew A. Russell, Larry E. Murphy, and Ralph Mitchell
2009 Analysis of bacterial community composition in concretions formed on the USS *Arizona*, Pearl Harbor HI *Journal of Cultural Heritage* 10: 232-236.

Russell Matthew A., Larry E. Murphy, Donald L. Johnson, Timothy J. Foecke, Pamela J. Morris, and Ralph Mitchell
2004 Science for Stewardship: Multidisciplinary research on USS *Arizona*, *Marine Technology Society Journal* 38:54-63.

Schloss, Patrick D., Sarah L.Westcott, Thomas Ryabin, Justine R. Hall, Martin Hartmann, Emily B. Hollister, Ryan A. Lesniewski, Brian B. Oakley, Donovan H. Parks, Courtney J. Robinson, Jason W. Sahl, Blaz Stres, Gerhard G. Thallinger, David J. Van Horn, and Carolyn F. Weber
2009 Introducing mothur: open-source, platform-independents, community-supported software for describing and comparing microbial communities. *Applied and Environmental Microbiology* 75(23): 7537-7541.

Wilson Brent M., Donald L. Johnson, Hans Van Tilburg, Matthew A. Russell, Larry E. Murphy, James D. Carr, Robert J. De Angelis, David L. Conlin
2007 Corrosion Studies on the USS *Arizona* with Application to a Japanese Midget Submarine *JOM* Archaeotechnology: 14-18.

....

Jennifer Clifford
Harvard University
Pierce 100E (Mitchell Group)
Cambridge, MA 02138

Archana Vasanthakumar
Harvard University
Pierce 100E (Mitchell Group)
Cambridge, MA 02138

David L. Conlin
National Park Service Submerged Resources Center
12795 W. Alameda Parkway
Lakewood, CO 80228

Ralph Mitchell
Harvard University
Pierce 100E
Cambridge, MA 02139

Sparrow-Hawk (1626), the Oldest Shipwreck on Cape Cod, MA: An Analysis of Wooden Artifacts Using X-ray Fluorescence (XRF)

Raymond L. Hayes

In 1626, a sailing ship carrying European adventurers to Jamestown was blown off course, beached, and abandoned at Nauset, MA. A storm in 1863 exposed Sparrow-Hawk, *the oldest shipwreck on Cape Cod. An Olympus x-ray fluorescence (XRF) instrument was used for elemental chemical analysis of ship artifacts, lumber for ship building, and marine sediment from the stranding site. Histograms, Principal Component Analysis, Bray-Curtis Similarity Coefficients, and Cluster Analysis were computer-generated for multivariate statistics. Results show that wooden ship timbers vary in chemistry and differ from sediment and lumber. XRF data document alterations that parallel physical degradation of the shipwreck* in situ.

Introduction

As one of six historic wooden ships ranging from 1626 to 1921 and chosen for chemical analysis with x-ray fluorescence, *Sparrow-Hawk* (1626) is the oldest and most unique shipwreck evaluated. Foundered in December 1626 on the shores of Cape Cod, MA, after a perilous mid-winter Atlantic crossing, that sailing ship was abandoned on a sandbar in Nauset (Figure 1). After six weeks at sea, the adventurers and their Irish crew had exhausted all provisions, and their captain had been incapacitated by scurvy (Bradford 1647).

Fortunately, by reaching landfall on a desolate sandbar, all were rescued, and their personal belongings were salvaged. The landing was witnessed by Native Americans of the Nauset Wampanoag tribe, who greeted the survivors in English and alerted Governor Bradford of Plymouth Colony of their arrival. Attempts were initiated to repair the ship, but these failed. The Plymouth colonists hosted the travelers until the end of the summer of 1627 (Bradford 1647). Efforts were soon abandoned due to wintry weather that prevented work on the badly damaged and unseaworthy wooden ship. The English and Irish adventurers, farmers and merchants resumed their journey to Virginia with two borrowed barks and under fair summer weather conditions (Wilkins 2011). They eventually settled near the Jamestown colony to farm tobacco.

Sparrow-Hawk was abandoned and buried in marsh meadow mud of Pleasant Bay and shifting sands of Nauset Beach. The wreckage was virtually forgotten at the "old ship" harbor, but re-surfaced in 1863 after a series of intense storms struck Cape Cod. *Sparrow-Hawk* had been lost for 237 years, when it was discovered by local residents. Encapsulation in thick mud and packed sand sustained the integrity of the ship's hull and preserved component wood. Geological forces kept the wreckage intact as the sandbar shifted its original configuration westward toward Cape Cod Bay and the mainland at Plymouth (Wilkins 2011).

During prolonged burial, wooden timbers of *Sparrow-Hawk* were scoured and re-shaped. Since construction, only wooden treenails, gluts (chocks), and notches secured the ship framing. The compact marine sediment preserved the form of the ship and stabilized

Figure 1: Map of Cape Cod showing the original recovery site for *Sparrow-Hawk* at Nauset (Nawset) Beach in 1865 (Livermore and Leander 1865, Modified By Author).

individual wooden frames for over 200 years. Following re-discovery in 1863, *Sparrow-Hawk* was exhumed, transferred, and assembled for public viewing on Boston Commons. For display, drift bolts, metal spikes and nails were added to assure the integrity of the wreckage and to minimize looting from the wreckage. No other efforts to conserve the ship were attempted. So for several years, the ship timbers were exposed to harsh and bitter winters and hot summers that typify coastal New England weather. Between scouring during burial and weathering of the wooden frames during prolonged exposure, fine details of construction were lost. In 1869, the historic *Sparrow-Hawk* was disassembled, removed from Boston, and donated to the Pilgrim Hall Museum in Plymouth, MA. Since then, the timbers have been in storage or on display for public viewing at the Pilgrim Hall Museum and at the Cape Cod Maritime Museum at Hyannis, MA (Figure 2).

Sparrow-Hawk is a unique and historic Cape Cod treasure. Many of its secrets are yet to be discovered. The original sail configuration, the date and place of

Figure 2: The display of *Sparrow-Hawk* at the Cape Cod Maritime Museum, Hyannis, MA, in 2011. View looking toward the stern; the bow is missing. Floor and futtock timbers are shown. Keel and keelson are not visible, but are centered under the floor planks (photo by author).

construction, and the age of the wood used for building the ship have been debated since its discovery. Several reports have been written (Otis 1864; Livermore and Crosby 1865) and books published (Holly 1969; Wilkins 2011), addressing construction details which may date to the mid-16th century Tutor era of medieval England. Recently, dendrochronology has been initiated to determine the vintage of the wooden keel assembly (Daly 2020). In 2011, chemical analysis of *Sparrow-Hawk* was begun while on display at the Cape Cod Maritime Museum in Hyannis, MA. X-ray fluorescence analysis was used to determine whether sub-molecular data might reveal additional details about the wreckage. The entire keel assembly was reported to be made from English Elm, and the floor planks and futtocks from English Oak (Wilkins 2011). The elemental chemistry of the ship wood was compared to types of lumber used in the original construction of *Sparrow-Hawk*. Sand and mud sediment from the Nauset Beach site where the ship was exhumed was analyzed for comparison to the artifacts. Those sediments would likely transfer elements to the frames during the prolonged period of contact between 1626 and 1863. The overall objective of this study was to analyze, compare, and contrast components of the wooden frames from the ship.

The comparison of chemical signatures from these sets of wood, sediment, and ship artifacts has resulted in detailed descriptions of the elemental composition of several frames. Not only have chemical differences been identified, but the database suggests where replacements or repairs to the ship were introduced, and how burial and exposure may have impacted the wooden artifacts. The hypothesis for this study was that chemical data at the elemental level would provide previously unknown details about the wreckage, thereby extending or enhancing information from historical documents about the historic shipwreck.

Methods

X-ray fluorescence (XRF), an emerging technology for archaeological investigations, is a portable, convenient, rapid, and precise tool that is standardized for elemental chemical analysis. This technology detects elements between Magnesium (Mg) and Uranium (U) as listed sequentially in the Periodic Table of chemical elements. XRF detects qualitative and quantitative elemental content of a specimen. It has found widespread application for analysis of clay pottery, artistic paints, geological specimens, and metals. The technology is non-invasive, reproducible, and can be applied to wet specimens. However, XRF does not read compounds or molecules such as $CaCl_2$ or SiO_2. Also, it does not detect elements that form the bulk of organic or biological specimens, namely Carbon (C), Hydrogen (H), Oxygen (O), and Nitrogen (N). Thus, there are limits to the application of XRF (Thermo Fisher Scientific 2015).

However, for the determination of heavy metal content, the characterization of soils and sediments, and the detection of mineral deposits, XRF is an excellent

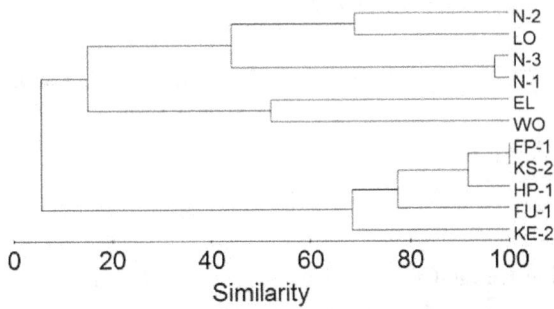

Figure 3: Cluster Dendrogram of an assortment of specimens grouped according to Bray-Curtis Similarity Coefficients. N-1-3 = Nauset sediments; LO = live oak, EL = elm, and WO = white oak wood; FP = floor plank, HP = hull plank, KS = keelson, FU = futtock, and KE = keel. This graphic shows relationships among an assortment of ship timbers, sediment cores, and ship building wood, based on Bray-Curtis Correlation Coefficients. The historic wooden frames are different from the wood lumber and sediment cores (only 5% similarity). The sediment cores differ from the elm and white oak lumber (only 15% similarity).

analytical tool. The expectation that XRF would be of use in wooden ship analysis is justified because of the porosity and adsorptive qualities of wood. Chemical elements in minor quantities that are trapped in wood generate elemental arrays or "fingerprints" that should be specific to a site. Unknown structural components, personal items, and cargo from a shipwreck would be important to describe. Elemental chemistry should be retained, even though the physical integrity of artifacts that were submerged in seawater would have deteriorated beyond recognition (Fors et al. 2014).

Due to the complexity of elemental arrays from the timbers of *Sparrow-Hawk*, computer-based multivariate statistical analysis was selected for this analysis. Bray-Curtis Similarity Coefficient Analysis (BSCA), Cluster Dendrogram Analysis (CDA), and Principal Component Analysis (PCA) were the multivariate algorithms selected for statistical treatment of these archaeological data. These statistical procedures provide numerical and graphic presentations of the chemical database that substantiate and validate differences between or among fingerprints. The computer software used for these statistical analyses was PRIMER-5, an analytical software created for ecological assessment at the Plymouth Marine Laboratory in England. PRIMER is an acronym for Routines in Multivariate Ecological Research. Version #5 was originally developed by Clarke and Gorley of PRIMER-E, Ltd. for biological monitoring of marine environmental impacts. This software contains an array of uni-variate, graphic and multivariate analytical routines for laptop computers. Published ecological research applying PRIMER-5 software is cited in several references (Warwick et al. 1990; Warwick and Clark 1995; Clarke and Warwick 1998a, 1998b; Clarke and Gorley 1999).

The specific statistical treatments listed above were selected for this study to compare and contrast elemental chemistry of wooden ship artifacts, wood lumber, and marine sediment. The graphics and tables generated indicate statistically significant comparisons among these chemical arrays. Specific combinations of elements and ratios of elements provide unique information about these specimens.

Results

XRF analysis detects 34 elements in the Periodic Table between atomic number 12 and 92, namely Magnesium and Uranium (Thermo Fisher Scientific 2015). A single specimen, however, rarely shows all of these elements and the ones displayed are standardized qualitatively and quantitatively for reliability. The elements in serial order that are detectable in XRF records when above minimal limits are Magnesium (Mg), Aluminum (Al), Silicon (Si), Phosphorus (P), Sulfur (S), Chloride (Cl), Potassium (K), Calcium (Ca), Titanium (Ti), Vanadium (V), Chromium (Cr), Manganese (Mn), Iron (Fe), Cobalt (Co), Nickel (Ni), Copper (Cu), Zinc (Zn), Arsenic (As), Selenium (Se), Rubidium (Rb), Strontium (Sr), Zirconium (Zr), Molybdenum (Mo), Silver (Ag), Cadmium (Cd), Tin (Sn), Antimony (Sb), Iodine (I), Barium (Ba), Mercury (Hg), Bismuth (Bi), Lead (Pb), Thorium (Th) and Uranium (U). K, Ca, Rb, and Sr are alkali earth metals. Transition elements (non-metals to metals) are Ti through Zn and Zr through Cd, as listed above. In this study, XRF analyses for each specimen were conducted in duplicate with the Olympus Delta XRF instrument operating first in the soil mode and then the mining mode. Many elements are commonly found in marine sediments. Among those are chlorine and calcium. Other elements in the marine sediments are iron, copper, nickel and zinc. Different wood species contain enrichments of several elements, such as potassium, sulfur, silicon and iron.

Wooden artifacts adsorb elements that bind to the organic wooden matrix or are sealed within porosities within the mural structure of the wood. The assortment of elements and the proportions of those elements constitute the XRF "fingerprint." These fingerprints are specific for both the sediment type and the wood species. Wooden ship artifacts have fingerprints that reflect the wood species, environmental exposures to sediment, as well as applications of caulking, paint, oil, and tar.

Graphic displays indicate that only a few elements are detected in each specimen. Only 6 elements were detected in three Nauset Beach sediment cores, while the elm wood lumber analysis reveals 9 elements (with 3 at concentrations of 10ppm or less). The keel of *Sparrow-Hawk* contains 22 elements (with 5 at 10ppm or less). While beach sediment cores contain no iron, the elm wood lumber contains 10ppm of iron, and the keel artifact, 10,000ppm. These values suggest that iron spikes or bolts may have been located near the area analyzed on the keel, since the sediment and the wood lumber do not account for the high iron content. The high levels of K, S, P and Cl in the keel suggest that seawater or marine organisms may have concentrated in the artifact. Elemental analyses of three Nauset Beach sediment cores indicate a composition of Ba, Ti, Si, Pb, Zn, and Zr. The elemental fingerprints for elm lumber show P, S, K, Ca, Mn, Fe, As, Rb, and Sr. The elemental fingerprints from the keel assembly of *Sparrow-Hawk* contain a complex array of Si, P, S, Cl, K, Ca, Ti, V, Mn, Fe, Co, Ni, Cu, Zn, As, Se, Rb and Sr.

In order to develop more detailed analysis of the complex data, multivariate statistics were applied. The Bray-Curtis Similarity Coefficient (B-CSC) matrix for the marine sediment, wood type, and ship artifact indicates the degree of similarity between any two specimens (Table 1). These coefficients are read as percentages, so the floor planking of *Sparrow-Hawk* shares a 15.1% similarity to Nauset Beach sediment and a 20.4% similarity to oak wood. The Nauset Beach sediment shows a 17.8% similarity to oak wood. A PCA plot of the sediment, wood and ship artifact data from Table 1 reveal wide separation of the data points, confirming the disparity among the respective fingerprints of these three specimens. Had they been identical or similar, the 2D-PCA data points would be superimposed or closely clustered, respectively. The graphic separation of any two marks represents their degree of difference, based upon comparison of up to ten principal components. Hence, the 2D-PCA analysis of the data in Table 1 substantiates the unique chemical compositions of sediment, wood lumber and ship artifact.

B-CSC data were used to display a Cluster Dendrogram Analysis (CDA) for an array of samples (Figure 3), including several sediment cores, wood used in ship construction and components of the historic

BRAY-CURTIS SIMILARITY COEFFICIENT MATRIX

	SHIP TIMBER (Floor)	MARINE SEDIMENT	WOOD (oak)
Ship Timber	0	0	0
Sediment	15.1	0	0
Wood	20.4	17.8	0

Table 1: Bray-Curtis Similarity Coefficient Matrix comparing a floor planking from *Sparrow-Hawk*, a Nauset Beach sediment core, and oak wood used in ship building. The coefficients indicate similarities between any two specimens as a percentage. Sediment and wood are only 15.1% similar, the ship floor planking and wood are only 20.4% similar, and the sediment and wood are only 17.8% similar. These three fingerprints reveal distinctive elemental arrays for each specimen without significant overlap. The corresponding Principal Component Analysis indicates wide separation (no clustering) among these three specimens.

ship framing. The cluster dendrogram of an assortment of specimens shows their organization and relationships according to Bray-Curtis Similarity Coefficients. The codes are N-1-3 for Nauset sediment cores, LO, EL, and WO, for live oak, elm and white oak wood species, and FP, HP, KS, FU, and KE, for floor planking, hull planking, keelson, futtock and keel artifacts.

The similarity scale along the x-axis of the graphic is in percentage. The CDA data range from 0 to 100% and specimens are grouped according to their degree of similarity. This provides a statistical comparison of how components of any set of samples relate to one another. The ship timbers group together in the dendrogram and show similarities of 70% or greater. They share only 5% similarity with the specimens of wood and sediment. This indicates that the wooden artifact fingerprints are minimally contaminated by sediment and that they also differ significantly from the ship building lumber. The sediment cores (N-1 and N-3) are 90% similar and share only 15% similarity to the wood (EL and WO).

So comparative analysis of XRF chemical data from wood used in ship building, marine sediment and wooden artifacts from *Sparrow-Hawk* indicate that these fingerprints differ as to the specific elements represented and their respective quantities. Shown separately, the marine sediment consists of a very few elements, with silicon and titanium predominating. The wood analyses show that phosphorus, sulfur, potassium, and calcium are in highest concentrations. The keel, known to be of elm wood, shows high levels of the same four elements as the wood lumber, but also shows a high level of iron.

Similarities and differences within the longitudinal keel assembly and among individual transverse floors and futtocks were determined by comparing fingerprints from different specimens. A comparison of chemical data from four sites along the length of the keelson indicates their commonality. However, one fingerprint shows a high iron content. That segment of the keelson of *Sparrow-Hawk* corresponds to the location of the mast step. In one keelson fingerprint, magnesium appears. In others, iron and chloride are elevated. Cobalt is detected in one fingerprint, while titanium and manganese are absent from that specimen. Comparison of two fingerprints of the keel indicates aluminum, but not vanadium, nickel, rubidium, zirconium or molybdenum. One keel fingerprint contains zinc and arsenic.

Comparison of three separate futtocks from *Sparrow-Hawk* show that one futtock differs from the others because magnesium and aluminum are detected. These individual differences suggest that some frames may have been replaced by different species of wood during repairs made in either 1626 or 1865.

The analysis of historic wooden ship components from *Sparrow-Hawk* indicates that commonly appearing elements are sulfur, chlorine, potassium, calcium, titanium, manganese, iron, zinc, arsenic, rubidium, strontium and lead. Other elements are infrequent or absent.

A 2D PCA plot of ship frames shows definite clustering, but clearly indicates that there are some differences among the wooden components (Figure 4). Two of the fingerprints fail to cluster with the others. These disparate wooden artifacts have been identified from among the total distribution. The one at the top center is from the keelson and the one to the far right is from a futtock. They are distinct from one another and from the clustered specimens. Since the keelson is a single longitudinal frame, the odd fingerprint at the mast step may represent exposure to a metal object that supported the mast. The odd futtock suggests that it either was a replacement frame of another wood type or was stabilized by metal fasteners. The outlier futtock may have been repaired after construction of the ship. That repair would have been introduced in 1627 on Cape Cod or in 1865 during re-assembly for public display in Boston.

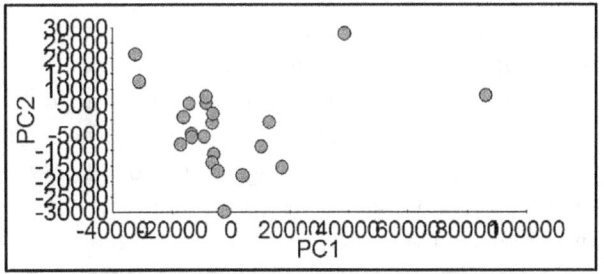

Figure 4: Two dimensional Principal Component Analysis plot of wooden shipwreck timbers from *Sparrow-Hawk*. Most of the artifacts cluster, but two are noticeably separated from the others. The outliers are a futtock (center) and one reading from the keelson (right). Within the cluster, minor variations do exist, as indicated by spaces between markers.

Discussion

Interpretation of differences among elemental chemical arrays from *Sparrow-Hawk* is difficult, if not impossible. XRF chemical data do not provide details about time or construction. Evidence to explain differences in the analytical database has not been preserved, perhaps due to the priorities of the moment or the absence of archaeological expertise.

Possible interpretations of chemical differences include the introduction of new or different wood types during repairs, contamination from contact with storage or cargo items, or the addition of metal fasteners during repair or display. Furthermore, marine plants, animals, or microbes may have attached to or been adsorbed by the timbers during more than 200 years of burial. Such organisms could have accumulated elements from seawater. Other transfers might have come from sediment of the marsh meadow or from the sand bar. Chemical exchanges could also have been introduced from stone ballast stone or bilge water contacting floor planks and futtocks. When the wreckage was assembled for public display, support materials such as ropes, metal fasteners, glues or paints may have been applied, allowing post-excavation chemical exchanges to occur.

Despite the uncertainties of interpretation indicated above, the benefits and opportunities provided by XRF analysis of historic wooden shipwrecks are obvious from the results of this study. Because of its portability, accuracy, convenience, and rapidity of analysis, x-ray fluorescence is a valuable tool for artifact analysis under field conditions, on a research boat, or in the laboratory. This technology is a significant advancement for archaeological studies of artifacts that may be discovered at a wreck site. Though not waterproof or submersible, the rechargeable, battery-powered XRF instrument is rugged and weatherproof. It can be operated on board a small research vessel and can be used to evaluate wet specimens. The complete cycle of operation takes less than a minute for each reading. Hundreds of spectral and tabular records can be stored indefinitely in the unit and subsequently downloaded as computer files.

On the Olympus Delta instrument, a camera adjacent to the x-ray emission port photographs the precise spot on the surface of an object that is analyzed. Also, an HTMI port on the unit can be used to transfer data for display of spectral or numerical data to a monitor or recording device as they are being collected. These data may be later re-organized for comparative analysis of a single element, such as Lead (Pb) or Copper (Cu), or for complete fingerprint comparisons.

XRF data confirm the presence of standard metal alloys (e.g., brass or bronze). Also, elemental ratios, such as Calcium (Ca): Strontium (Sr), may be calculated from tabular data for comparisons among specimens. Graphic displays or fingerprints of elemental arrays may be constructed from numerical data and statistical analyses may also be performed from data spreadsheets. Post-processing of descriptive analyses, interpretation, and validation of chemical characterizations are readily conducted from the numerical data (Thermo Fisher Scientific 2015).

Elemental characterization of wooden ship components with XRF provides supplementary information that is not available from supra-molecular or gross inspection of artifacts. From the elementary chemical database, specific comparisons may be made between and among components, leading to details and suggestions previously unavailable to the field archaeologist. Such information from wooden shipwreck timbers might include post-construction alterations or substitutions of wood types. Detection of differences might suggest contamination from applied sealants, paint or anti-fouling treatment used during or following original ship construction. These comparisons may also evidence impacts of biological organisms that may attach to or invade exposed wooden components during the life history of a ship or after submergence. Interpretation of chemical differentials often requires additional evidentiary records or historical documentation.

Conclusions

Results of this x-ray fluorescence analysis of the historic wooden sailing ship, *Sparrow-Hawk*, suggest that elemental chemistry is distinctive for different wooden ship timbers, for marine sediment, and for ship building wood. Since *Sparrow-Hawk* frames were secured by wooden treenails and gluts, heavy metals (Fe, Cu, Ni) were probably introduced from spikes, nails or bolts during repairs in 1827 or display in 1865.

Chemical elements are shared among similar components but vary in concentration in different ship frames. Previously unknown details about *Sparrow-Hawk* are that repaired or replaced timbers have been identified and compared to similar types of untreated wood. Wooden components of *Sparrow-Hawk* may have been disordered or replaced during recovery, display, or storage, due to disassembly and loss of the original form of each framing component.

Burial in marsh meadow mud of Pleasant Bay and in sand from Nauset Beach most likely preserved the chemical integrity of wooden artifacts. Although some chemical exchanges probably occurred due to transfer from the environment, the elemental chemical fingerprints of ship timbers have been remarkably preserved despite prolonged burial followed by outdoor exposure on Boston Commons. Periodic storage and display in museum settings probably accelerated weathering of the wooden frames, since they were never conserved with modern reagents, such as polyethylene glycol, for archaeological preservation.

Had *Sparrow-Hawk* been submerged in seawater for more than 200 years and then air dried without conservation, structural disintegration and chemical dissolution of the framing would have certainly destroyed the physical integrity as well as the chemical composition of the frames. Today's nautical archaeologists are indeed fortunate to be able to study and learn from this early historic shipwreck. We recommend that elemental analysis of intact wooden frames from historic wooden wrecks with XRF technology be considered for routine investigation of such archaeological artifacts. XRF provides uniquely detailed sub-molecular data about historic wooden ships.

Acknowledgments

The author expresses sincere thanks to many individuals who have encouraged this study and who have granted access to historical wooden ship artifacts for analysis. As for *Sparrow-Hawk*, the consent and cooperation of Director Janet Preston of the Cape Cod Maritime Museum and of Directors Ann Berry and Donna D. Curtin of the Pilgrim Hall Museum are gratefully appreciated. This study was partially funded by an academic research grant from the Olympus Innov-X Corporation in Woburn, MA, that was awarded to the author, based upon his affiliations with Howard University, Washington, DC, and the Marine Biological Laboratory, Woods Hole, MA.

References

BRADFORD, WILLIAM
1647   *Of Plymouth Plantation*, 1620-1647. Samuel E. Morrison (Editor), re-published 1979, Alfred A. Knopf, New York, NY.

CLARKE, K. ROBERT AND WARWICK, RICHARD M.
1998a   Quantifying Structural Redundancy in Ecological Communities. *Oecologia* 11:376-389.

1998b   A Taxonomic Distinctness Index and Its Statistical Properties. *J. Appl. Ecol.* 35: 523-531.

CLARKE, K. ROBERT AND RAYMOND N. GORLEY
1999   *PRIMER v5 User Manual/Tutorial.* Primer-E Ltd., Plymouth Marine Laboratory, Plymouth, England.

DALY, AOIFE
2020   Dating the *Sparrow-Hawk*. Proc. 53rd Annual Conf. on Terrestrial and Underwater Archaeology, Soc. Hist. Archaeol. Boston, MA (Abstract).

FORS, YVONNE, HAKAN GRUDD, ANDERS RINDBY, FARIDEH JALILEHVAND, MAGNUS SANDSTROM, INGEMAR CATO AND LENNART BORNMALM
2014   Sulfur and Iron Accumulation in Three Marine-archaeological Shipwrecks in the Baltic Sea: the Ghost, the Crown and the Sword. Sci. Rep. 4: 4222; DOI:10.1038/srep04222.

HOLLY, HOBART H.
1969   *Sparrow-Hawk: a Seventeenth Century Vessel in Twentieth Century America.* Pilgrim Society, Plymouth, MA.

LIVERMORE, CHARLES W. AND LEANDER CROSBY
1865   *Ye Antient Wrecke. Loss of the* Sparrow-Hawk *in 1626: Remarkable Preservation and Recent Discovery of the Wreck.* Alfred Mudge & Son, Boston, MA.

OTIS, AMOS
1864   *An account of the discovery of an ancient ship on the eastern shore of Cape Cod* (1864). J. Munsell, Albany, NY.

THERMO FISHER SCIENTIFIC
2015   *XRF Technology in the Field* (e-book), Thermo Fisher Scientific, Inc., Boston, MA, thermoscientific.com/xrf (accessed March 2020).

WARWICK, RICHARD M., K. ROBERT CLARKE, AND J. MICHAEL GEE
1990   The effect of disturbance by soldier crabs, *Mictyris platycheles*, H Milne Edwards, on meiobenthic community structure. *Exp. Mar. Biol. Ecol.* 135: 19-33.

WARWICK, RICHARD M. AND K. ROBERT CLARKE
1995   New 'biodiversity' measures reveal a decrease in taxonomic distinctness with increasing stress. *Marine Ecology Progress* Series 129: 501-305.

WILKINS, MARK C.
2011   *Cape Cod's Oldest Shipwreck*, History Press, Charleston, SC.

· · · · · · · · · · · · · · · ·

Raymond L. Hayes
1010 N. Noyes Drive
Silver Spring, MD 20910
USA

The Wreck of HMS *Erebus*: A Fieldwork and Research Update

Jonathan Moore

HMS Erebus *is situated amongst islands and reefs in Wilmot and Crampton Bay, off the west coast of the Adelaide Peninsula, Nunavut, Canada. Since the wreck's discovery in 2014, Parks Canada's Underwater Archaeology Team has completed a multi-year site evaluation, continues to carry out remote sensing and site environment studies, and has embarked upon targeted excavation. This paper presents a brief historical background, an update on archaeological activities, and recent findings from the wreck. It points to new insights into the Franklin Expedition, summarizes current research objectives, and describes substantial structural changes to the wreck brought about by site formation processes.*

Historical Background

On 19 May 1845, two state-of-the-art Royal Navy discovery ships, HMS *Erebus* and HMS *Terror*, were finally ready to head out from the Thames River en route to the Arctic. Sir John Franklin, the expedition commander, had orders to lead the Royal Navy's latest search for a Northwest Passage from the Atlantic to Pacific. Little did the men on the two departing ships know that the expedition would end in disaster. They could scarcely have imagined that Inuit, the indigenous inhabitants of what is now Canada's central Arctic, would have scoured the deserted decks of *Erebus* to scavenge useful materials before it sank.

Erebus was launched in 1826 at Pembroke Dockyard, Wales, as a *Hecla*-class bomb of 372 tons burthen, with a length of 105 ft. (32 m) and breadth of 29 ft. (8.8 m). Its slightly smaller consort *Terror* had been launched over a decade earlier at Topsham, England in 1813 as a *Vesuvius*-class bomb of 325 tons burthen. Like other bombs in a period of renewed Royal Navy Arctic exploration after the Napoleonic Wars, *Terror* had been the first to be refit as a polar discovery ship in 1835-1836 for Captain George Back's Arctic expedition of 1836-1837. *Erebus* was first refit as a polar discovery ship in 1839 prior to a successful 1839-1843 voyage with *Terror* to Antarctica under the command of Captain James Clark Ross. A final refit for both of these barque-rigged ships took place in early 1845 prior to Franklin's voyage, an important modification being the addition of auxiliary steam screw propulsion to complement the sailing rig of each (Cyriax 1939; Battersby and Carney 2011; Moore et al. 2017:11-19). Given that important elements of the 1845 expedition were geographical exploration and scientific study, the ships were equipped with the very latest instruments and each had an extensive library. Many of the crew members, including officers, had prior polar experience.

Erebus (Captain Sir John Franklin) and *Terror* (Captain Francis Rawdon Moira Crozier) first crossed the North Atlantic to the Whalefish Islands, Greenland, with the supply ship *Barretto Junior*, and after transhipping provisions in July 1845, the two discovery ships crossed into Lancaster Sound. A record later left in a cairn in April 1848 by the combined crew, and found in 1859, reported that they spent their first winter, 1845-1846, at Beechey Island. The next navigation season, following the break-up of sea ice, Franklin's ships headed south, presumably through the then uncharted Peel Sound and, as the record added, then became beset in ice north of King William Island on 12 September, 1846. Thereabouts they remained solidly trapped, yet at least one party of men carried out exploration on shore in May of 1847, the situation reported as "All well." The cairn record further detailed that soon things took a turn for the worse: Franklin died on 11 June, 1847 and on 22 April, 1848 the surviving 105 crewmembers (out of 129) under the command of Crozier, deserted the ships that were still ice-bound off King William Island. Making landfall on the island the combined crews headed south towards the North American mainland, dragging boats on sledges over the still frozen sea and land (McClintock 1860; Cyriax 1939).

What happened after the cairn record was cached in 1848 was gleaned from Inuit by subsequent searchers from 1854-1879 (Cyriax 1939; Barr 1987; Woodman 1991; Keith and Kamookak 1999). In 1854, Dr. John Rae was the first to obtain Inuit information of the demise of the Franklin Expedition and the loss of the ships, learning that the men had resorted to cannibalism on their desperate southward retreat. Rae ascertained that a ship or ships had been crushed by ice and that all of their men had died. He also brought back to England relics of the expedition collected from Inuit (Rich 2014:333-351). In 1859, Captain Francis Leopold McClintock's searching party was the first to reach King William Island, the epicenter of the expedition's demise, and found not only the cairn record outlined above, but also a trail of human remains, boats, equipment, etc., left in the wake of Crozier's 1848 escape effort. He also learned more about the fate of the ships: one of them, now known to be *Terror*, sank to the west of King William Island and the other, *Erebus*, sank at a place farther south called Ugjulik (McClintock 1860:208-237; Stenton 2014).

Charles Francis Hall, an American explorer who travelled to King William Island in 1869 determined that the Inuit place name Ugjulik (meaning "it has bearded seals") referred to the expansive region of sea ice and small islands west of the Adelaide Peninsula, some 200 kilometers to the south of the 1848 point of desertion (Hall 1869a; Keith and Kamookak 1999:1). One of Hall's informants, In-nook-poo-zhee-jook, reported that the wreck "… was very near O'Reilly Island, a little eastward of the north end of said island, between it and Wilmot and Crampton Bay" (Nourse 1879:403-405). Hall was told that *Erebus* was first spotted by a seal hunting party of Ugjulik Inuit (Ugjulingmiut) possibly in the spring of 1849: "The ice about the ship one winters make all a smooth floe & a plank was found extending from the ship down onto the ice. The Innuits were sure some white men must have lived there through the winter" (Hall 1869b, 1869c; Woodman 1991:249-250). He further determined that Inuit found "The sails, rigging, and boats — everything about the ship — was in complete order" and once satisfied the ship was unoccupied, scavenged the ship and in doing so "… broke into a place that was fastened up & there found a very large white man who was dead." Koo-nik told Hall "… the vessel [was] covered over with see-loon, that is housed in with sails or that material, not boards" (Hall 1869c; Nourse 1879:403-405). Like Rae, he too brought back many relics of the expedition that had found their way into the material culture of Inuit of the King William Island region.

Lieutenant Frederick Schwatka, another American explorer, set out on a quest for expedition records ten years after Hall. He and his party, like McClintock, carefully searched King William Island and additionally the Adelaide Peninsula in 1879. His evidence, collected from Inuit, confirmed Hall's findings regarding the Ugjulik ship. Remarkably, near the Adelaide Peninsula Schwatka met an elderly Inuk named Puhtoorok who was one of the first to have gone aboard *Erebus* before it sank (Schwatka 1878-1880:123-126; Gilder 1881:77-79; Stackpole 1965:61-63; Barr 1987:63-65).

The searches for *Erebus* and *Terror* through 1879 never found the wreck at Ugjulik, nor one west of King William Island, nor any survivors, nor any detailed expedition records other than the 1848 cairn record, nor any conclusive information as to how *Erebus* came to be in Ugjulik. No one, other than Schwatka, explored close to the actual sinking location of *Erebus*, and that was thirty years or so after the ship arrived in Ugjulik. Nevertheless, the location information gathered by Hall and Schwatka in particular defined a sizeable yet practicable search area approximately 75 by 30 kilometers (47 by 19 miles) in Ugjulik to guide modern day wreck searches for the Ugjulik wreck (*Erebus*), a search that began in the mid-1960s (Harris and Moore 2010:3-12).

Archaeological Accomplishments 2014-2018

The wreck of what proved to be HMS *Erebus* was discovered on 2 September, 2014 by members of Parks Canada's Underwater Archaeology Team (UAT) using its research vessel (RV) *Investigator*, during a sixth season of towed side-scan sonar surveying in search of the wreck (Harris et al. 2015). This discovery was the result of a renewed multi-partner search for the *Erebus* and *Terror* launched by the Government of Canada in August 2008. While there was far less available evidence for where *Terror* went down, yielding a commensurately larger search zone than that for *Erebus*, the wreck was located on 3 September, 2016 in the coincidentally named *Terror* Bay (on the southwest flank of King William Island) based on present-day information of Gjoa Haven resident Sammy Kogvik (Dagneau and Moore 2017). Collectively, the wrecks comprise The Wrecks of HMS *Erebus* and HMS *Terror* National Historic Site of Canada.

The UAT carried out the first dives to *Erebus* in September 2014 and with project partners completed four subsequent field seasons from 2015-2018 that together were termed a site evaluation. This research achieved a wide range of archaeological results (Harris et al. 2015; Moore et al. 2017; Dagneau and Moore 2018, 2019). To begin with, side-scan sonar and multi-beam echosounder (MBES) surveying of the wreck and its debris field were carried out at the time of discovery of the wreck and, thereafter, to improve MBES coverage and document site change with side-scan sonar. Up to the end of 2018, a total of 276 dives over the course of 33 diving days took place, including an April 2015 project staged from the ice that employed surface-supply ice diving methods. Three-dimensional mapping of the debris field, hull exterior and exposed lower deck were carried out using 3D photogrammetry and both the direct survey method (DSM) and baseline-offset hand mapping. All of this has been used to create integrated scale site plans, profiles and sections and to impose a provenience grid system over the site based on 2 m by 2 m sub-operations (Figure 1). A key accomplishment has been high-definition photographic and video wreck documentation as well as interior exploration of the lower and orlop decks using a micro remotely-operated vehicle and point-of-view cameras. By the end of the 2018 season, more than 64 selected artifact recoveries had been made, chiefly to gather a representative sample of artifact types, and a suite of associated material culture and analytical studies had been completed. From 2014-2018, site environment studies were undertaken, including deployment of a current meter and tide gauge, and a biological inventory completed.

Research Objectives and Approaches

Stepping back for a moment to take a wider view of the project, it is worth placing *Erebus*, as well as *Terror*, in their overall research framework. Research activities at the wreck sites are inherently multidisciplinary, collaborative and consultative given that the wrecks (generously gifted to Canada by Great Britain in 2018) are co-managed by Canada and Inuit (at present via the Franklin Interim Advisory Committee). All wreck artifacts, apart from some to be returned to Great Britain, are co-owned by Canada and the Inuit Heritage Trust (Parks Canada 2019). The work of Parks Canada and our Inuit partners on both *Erebus* and *Terror* is viewed as both historical archaeology and maritime archaeology (Muckelroy 1978; Adams 2001) that sets the wreck sites in a maritime archaeological landscape (Westerdahl 1992; Flatman 2003), encompassing water, ice and land. It has been conducted in concert with a parallel program of terrestrial archaeology carried out by the Government of Nunavut.

While aiming to gain insights into specific historical events and chronologies, the goal is to maintain a robust anthropological approach and to be mindful to explore human historical aspects of the expedition. The *Erebus* and *Terror* underwater archaeological investigation is framed around six themes expressed in a research design that evolves as work progresses. The themes are as follows:

1. Science: evidence of scientific and geographical discovery efforts that were central aims of the expedition;
2. Maritime technology: evidence of the refitting, equipping and operation of *Erebus* and *Terror*

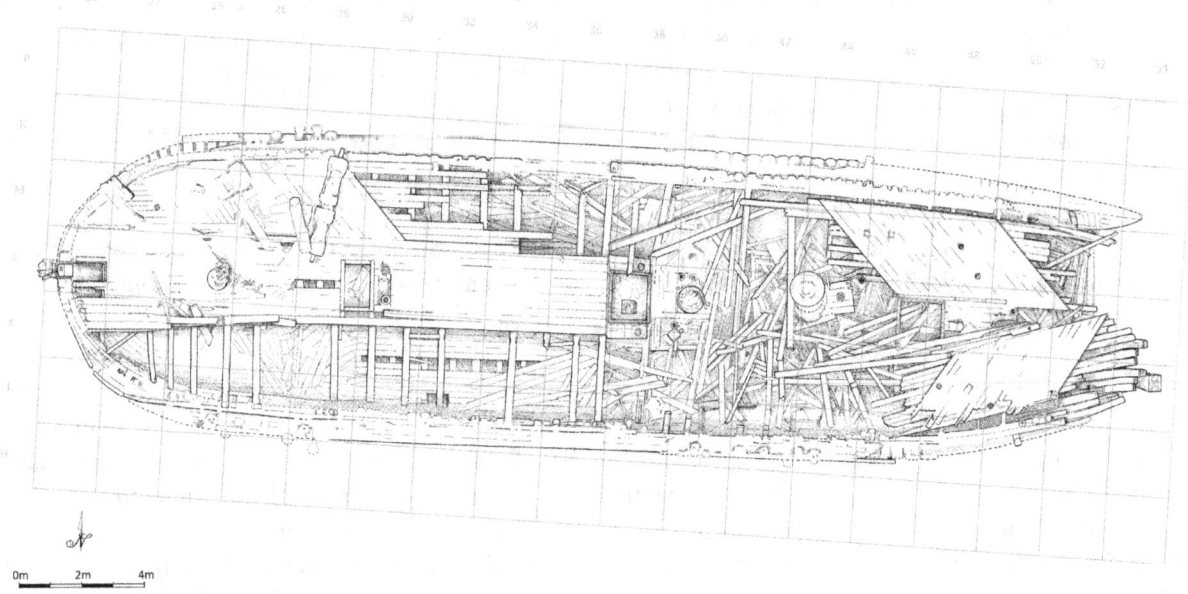

Figure 1: *Erebus* site plan as of 2016 showing the upper deck, parts of the exposed lower deck, and superimposed provenience grid (Image by Brandy Lockhart and Carol Pillar, Parks Canada, 2017).

as polar discovery ships in the wider context of contemporary Royal Navy technological advances;

3. Material culture and shipboard life: evidence of the material environment of the ships to reconstruct shipboard societies and events, understand the function of the ships and to provide direct linkages between artifacts and named individuals;

4. Cultural interaction: evidence of human interaction within the ships' onboard micro-societies through archaeological manifestations of social organization, rank, class, discipline, and politics, and any material evidence for external cultural contact with Inuit;

5. Chronology of events: evidence to reconstruct the sequence of events throughout the expedition, including relative and absolute dates; and

6. Wreck environments past and present: evidence of the local environments of both shipwrecks and of site change in order to inform site management, archaeological, conservation, and outreach efforts.

Site Setting

Erebus is situated amongst islands and reefs in Wilmot and Crampton Bay, in the Kitikmeot Region of Nunavut, Canada. The site's remoteness means that archaeological work is logistically challenging. Indeed, the site is ice-covered for about nine months of the year (from November to break-up in late July) and ice-free for about a three month period (from early August to October) thereby limiting the window of opportunity for working from vessels. Archaeological work can also be accomplished by ice diving operations that are practicable in April.

The wreck rests upright at a depth of 11 m (35 ft.) with the upper deck at 5 m (16 ft.). The hull is intact to the upper deck more or less from bow to stern (where there is significant damage) and there is an extensive debris field and scour pocket(s) around the hull perimeter. The bulwarks are missing and much of the upper deck is actively collapsing, exposing parts of the lower deck. The wreck is an artificial reef festooned with sea life requiring vegetation management to allow archaeological work. The water temperature at the site ranges from -2°C to +6°C and visibility is highly variable between 0-15 m (0-50 ft.), this range influenced by extended periods of calm winds versus high wind events, respectively. Given the absence of shipworm in the central Arctic, the wreck has not been subjected to timber decay normally associated with saltwater wrecks. It exhibits exceptionally good artifact preservation conditions largely due to the prevailing water temperatures and the physical protection afforded by ice coverage most of the year and, also, by the intact hull elements (Moore et al. 2017:49-54).

Logistical Preparations to 2019

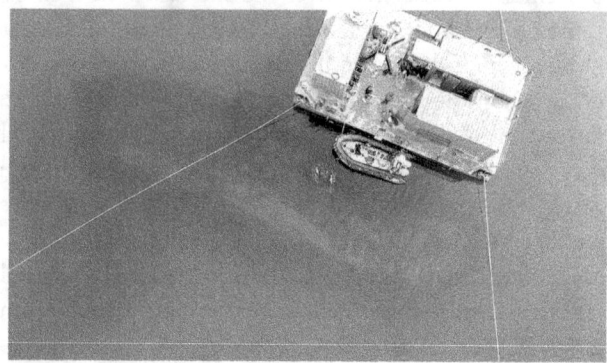

Figure 2: Parks Canada barge *Qiniqtirjuaq* moored atop the wreck of HMS *Erebus* at the outset of fieldwork in 2019. The wreck's bow is to the right (Photo by Thierry Boyer, Parks Canada, 2019).

For five years following the discovery of *Erebus*, logistical preparations were in constant motion with the aim of being able to carry out extended periods of excavation. Between 2016-2018, Parks Canada acquired and refit the 100 ft (30-m) RV *David Thompson* and commissioned construction of the diving and excavation support barge *Qiniqtirjuaq* (Figure 2). The latter mounts a crane and three containers housing:

1. a dive control container with a hyperbaric recompression chamber and associated compressed gas supplies;
2. an equipment container with generator, compressors, hydraulic power supply and storage; and
3. an artifact processing lab.

The archaeological team of up to nine resides on the RV *David Thompson*, which anchors near the site, and all team members perform shipboard duties to complement the core professional crew of five.

The RV *David Thompson* made its first voyage to the wreck site with the barge in 2018 and while the RV *David Thompson* travels to and from the Arctic annually, the *Qiniqtirjuaq* overwinters at Gjoa Haven, the nearest community to the wrecks. The installation of a four-point mooring system for the barge was completed in 2019 from which both surface-supply and Scuba diving can be carried out. In terms of the former, the UAT employs a range of commercial diving equipment configurations depending on individual dive requirements, including hot water suits that allow for long and effective dives (up to 3.5 hours) in the frigid water. In summary, the RV *David Thompson* and *Qiniqtirjuaq* combination provides a highly mobile, adaptable, and appropriately-scaled platform to both safely access and work at *Erebus* (as well as *Terror* in future) under challenging logistical constraints and highly changeable weather conditions.

Test Excavations in 2019

Archaeological and logistical preparations for test excavation were completed by late August 2019, with the aim to explore artifact potential, determine preservation conditions of artifacts in sealed or partially sealed contexts, and to expose more completely interior partitions and fitted furniture. A number of zones including the stern cabin were initially targeted for excavation. However, actual excavation took place only in two cabins on the port side amidships that are freely accessible to non-penetration diving.

In 2019, a total of 93 dives were completed over the course of 16 days on site, with 7 other days lost to weather when the ship and barge had to evacuate the site and shelter from high winds. The majority of the dive time was devoted to excavation of the lowermost sections of fitted storage compartments in the Captain's Steward's pantry (sub-operations 38J/K and 40J/K) and two drawers of the bed place in the adjacent Third Lieutenant's cabin (sub-operations 40J/K and 42J/K) (Figures 3 and 4). In addition, the UAT undertook mapping and surface collection of a concentration of artifacts at the Officers' Mess skylight (sub-operation 46L).

Collectively, more than 355 artifact recoveries were made by excavation and surface collection, with the vast majority coming from the Captain's Steward's panty. The 2019 excavation confirmed the high number and density of in-context finds and the excellent prevailing preservation conditions. For instance, two (of four) drawers in the presumed Third Officer's cabin, one atop the other, were found to be filled with compacted sediment evidently transported on account of currents and wind-generated waves that when deposited largely encapsulated the drawers' artifact contents. The upper

Figure 3: Presumed Third Lieutenant's cabin (facing the bow) during 2019 excavation showing a drawer under the bed place that has just been opened (below archaeologist) exposing an unexcavated drawer (at middle left) that contained a box of epaulettes encapsulated in sediment (Photo by Thierry Boyer, Parks Canada, 2019).

drawer contained a number of items that clearly fell into it from above, for instance some rigging elements and small ship fittings. Once completely excavated and emptied, the drawer could actually slide open to reveal the closed drawer below (Figure 3). It was virtually devoid of artifacts, except for a box of epaulettes. The adjacent Captain's Steward pantry exhibited exceptionally dense artifact concentration at the base of the fitted cabinetry to the extent that artifacts were generally more prevalent by volume than sediment, many were completely physically intact, and many items were in their original stowage positions.

In comparison with the wreck of *Terror*, the upper portions of the (originally fragile) lower deck cabin partitions are no longer in situ. In future, complete exposure of their bases will aid in understanding cabin spacing, sizes, and boundaries. At the Officers' Mess skylight, a cohesive assemblage of intact glass bottles still survived, despite the significant collapse of the upper deck at this location.

Structural Damage

At the time of discovery of the *Erebus* in 2014, natural site formation processes had already significantly damaged much of the upper deck and all of the masts were down. Whereas the deck at the starboard bow extending aft to amidships was in situ, a large section of laminated deck planking from the port bow was dislocated and rested on the seabed off the port side. The upper deck amidships was largely dislocated and collapsed in a seeming jumble. The deck at the stern had deflated into a V-shape in cross section that was propped up along the port and starboard margins of the hull, more or less sealing the lower deck below, including the cabins and mess of the senior officers (Harris et al. 2015; Moore et al. 2017:60-66).

Throughout the 2008-2014 search period and subsequent on-site work, the UAT regularly experienced gale-force winds in Wilmot and Crampton Bay, which on occasion forced project vessels to either seek shelter or curtail operations. In 2015, the extent to which the site is actively affected by wind-generated waves first came to light, when following a strong gale with gusts to 45 knots the upper deck at the bow was seen to lift up and down on account of a ground swell that lingered after the gale (Moore et al. 2017:29, 123). The storm also shifted exposed artifacts lying directly atop the lower deck within the hull. In 2018, a large section of upper-deck planking at the starboard bow was found to have been lifted, flipped, and shifted aft by wind-generated waves and/or swell which in turn displaced the massive windlass barrel (Dagneau and Moore 2019).

Examination of the construction of the upper deck has revealed that despite its very heavy timbering, with diagonal doubled construction, it is relatively lightly affixed to the deck beams. Indeed, it is fastened by vertical dump bolts into blind holes and is not, so far as can be determined, through-bolted to the beams.

While this construction arrangement suited the ship well while afloat in order to resist the crushing forces of ice, no doubt as the Royal Navy's shipwrights conceived, evidently it does little to resist the lifting forces of water movement. What is more in 2019, significant change to the scour pocket around the hull perimeter was observed, in that there was significant deflation of sediment (increased scour depth) to the extent that more of the lower hull was exposed and that previously unseen artifacts and timbers in the debris field were exposed.

Every indication is that climate change will lead to longer seasonal periods of open water in Wilmot and Crampton Bay; consequently, it is presumed that there will be a greater frequency and intensity of wind storms at *Erebus* that will pose a significant threat to what Parks Canada terms its commemorative integrity (Parks Canada 2019). The result is that there is now added impetus for the archaeological program to focus on the excavation of zones that have the highest potential to meet the research design aims.

New Insights into the Franklin Expedition

While on the one hand the discoveries of *Erebus* and *Terror* have answered the longstanding question of their locations, they have equally ushered concomitant questions. For instance, did the ships travel from their 1848 desertion point to their sinking locations due to

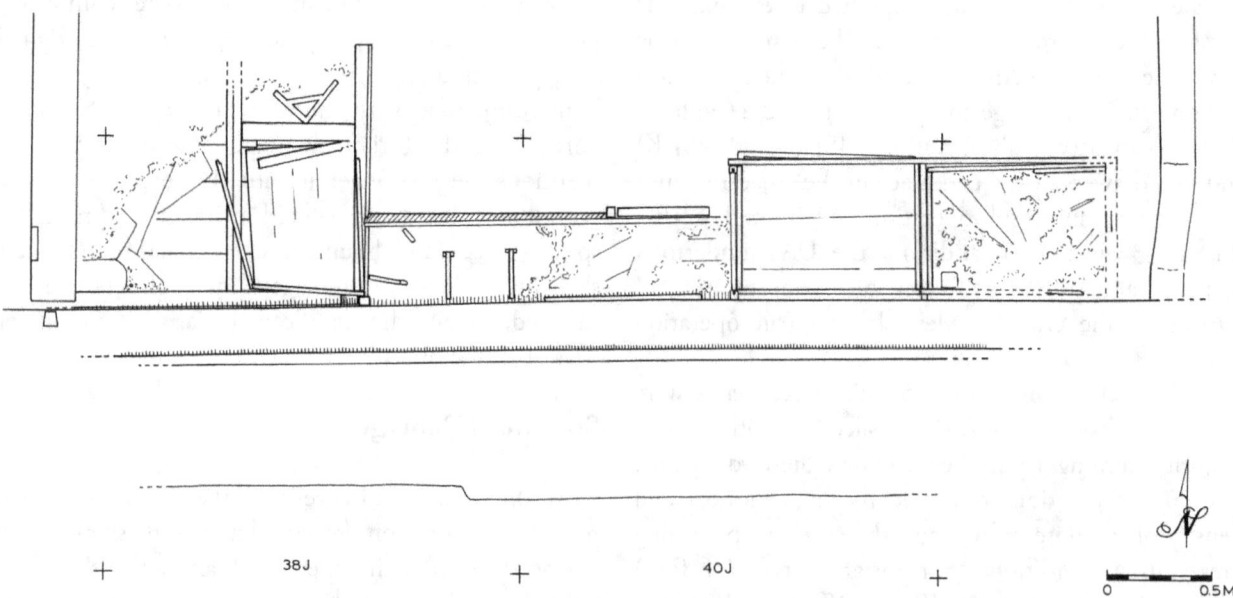

Figure 4: Preliminary plan of partially excavated sub-operations 38J and 40J showing selected fitted furniture on the port side of the lower deck. The bow is to the left. The presumed Captain's Steward's pantry is at the middle left and the presumed Third Lieutenant's bed place and its chest of drawers is at right (Drawing by Carol Pillar, Parks Canada, 2020).

wind, currents, ice floes, the actions of any crew members aboard, or any combination thereof? Who were the last men aboard either ship and in what state did they leave them? How exactly did they sink? While it is not yet possible to completely answer these and other questions, some insights about *Erebus* that speak to the research themes maritime technology and cultural interaction are put forward here as examples.

The hull of *Erebus* survives intact to the extent that its form and polar adaptations are preserved, including its: distinctive ice channels; doubled hull planking (naked given the absence of copper hull sheathing); iron bow sheathing; propeller aperture and trunk; laminated upper deck planking; two propellers (one primary on one spare) in the debris field; and interior features such as watertight bulkheads and coal bunkers (Moore et al. 2017). This archaeological evidence of course complements contemporary ship construction records and, especially, due to *Erebus*' partial collapse, exposes many construction details, fittings and equipment. For example, one of the ship's Massey patent pump heads was recovered in 2019. The fact that its two bower anchors, now lying at the heel of the stem and still attached to their stud-link chain, had evidently been catted prior to falling to the seabed demonstrates that the ship had not been anchored in the traditional sense in open water prior to sinking, if indeed anyone was on board to anchor the ship in that way. Further, the tiller was unshipped and the rudder is not in place (Moore et al. 2017:85, 126). Perhaps collectively, this and other evidence indicates that the ship was in a winter quarters configuration. Given the very poor state of preservation of the standing and running rigging, and the upper deck in general, it is not possible to make many definitive statements, especially as to whether it was housed prior to sinking as reported by Inuit in the nineteenth century.

Since the discovery of *Erebus* in 2014, a rewarding part of our work has been to look afresh at the contemporary Inuit descriptions of their discovery of and interaction with the ship while it was afloat upon its arrival at Ugjulik. *Erebus*' archaeological record accords closely with Inuit oral histories recorded in the mid to late nineteenth century by Hall and Schwatka noted above, from the wreck's sinking location and its depth to the detailed observations of Inuit who boarded the ship before it foundered as early as 1849. There is consistent evidence in the Inuit accounts that salvage efforts were incomplete before the ship sank, that its masts projected out of the water after it went down and that it was later much broken up by ice. The Utjulingmiut found flotsam from the wreck, including books, casks, and rigging as well as the remains of one boat (Moore et al. 2017:127-128). The Inuk Puhtoorok (noted above) told that Inuit "… went all over and through the ship and found also many empty casks. They found iron chains and anchors on deck, and spoons knives forks, tinplates, china plates, etc. below" (Schwatka 1878-1880:125-126). He added "They also saw books on board, and left them there. They only took knives, forks, spoons, and pans; the other things they had no use for" (Gilder 1881:78-79). The casks, iron chains, anchors and chains on deck, plates and many other features all check with the archaeology; what is more, to date, no cutlery has been observed on the wreck with the exception of one spoon and a pair of sugar tongs. Puhtoorok's information regarding books is a tantalizing prospect and reminder of what written material, whether mundane records or personal correspondence, could reveal about all aspects of the Franklin Expedition.

Conclusion

Given the prevailing preservation conditions of *Erebus* and *Terror*, Parks Canada and its partners earnestly recognize their archaeological potential to rewrite chapters in the story of Franklin's 1845 expedition. The UAT relishes tackling historical questions about the chronology of events aboard the ships as well as probing the experiences of their crews. The test excavations of *Erebus* in 2019 ably demonstrated the extent to which artifact assemblages in primary contexts are intact and many more remain to be explored in the coming years. Whereas *Terror* may offer far better overall preservation condition, the advantage of *Erebus* is that given the opening up of its upper deck and its shallower depth make it more archaeologically accessible. On the other hand, natural site formation processes at *Erebus* pose a serious threat and lend urgency to ongoing archaeological work and site management by Parks Canada and our Inuit partners.

References

ADAMS, JOHN
2001 Ships and Boats as Archaeological Source Material. *World Archaeology* 32(3):292-310.

BARR, WILLIAM (EDITOR)
1987 *Overland to Starvation Cove: With the Inuit in Search of Franklin 1878-1880*. University of Toronto Press, Toronto, Ontario, Canada.

BATTERSBY, WILLIAM AND PETER CARNEY
2011   Equipping HM Ships *Erebus* and *Terror*, 1845. *International Journal for the History of Engineering & Technology* 81(2):192-211.

CYRIAX, RICHARD J.
1939   *Sir John Franklin's Last Arctic Expedition: A Chapter in the History of the Royal Navy.* Methuen & Co., London, UK. Reprinted 1997 by The Arctic Press, Plaistow, United Kingdom.

DAGNEAU, CHARLES AND JONATHAN MOORE
2017   HMS *Terror* Archeological Survey April 2017. Wrecks of HMS *Erebus* and HMS *Terror* National Historic Site of Canada. Underwater Archaeology Team, Parks Canada, Ottawa, Ontario, Canada.

2018   Underwater Archaeology Research Bulletin No. 1: HMS *Erebus* Underwater Archaeological Survey 2017. Underwater Archaeology Team, Parks Canada, Ottawa, Ontario, Canada.

2019   Underwater Archaeology Research Bulletin No. 2: HMS *Erebus* Underwater Archaeological Survey 2018. Underwater Archaeology Team, Parks Canada, Ottawa, Ontario, Canada.

FLATMAN, JOE
2003   Cultural Biographies, Cognitive Landscape and Dirty Old Bits of Boat: "Theory" in Maritime Archaeology. *The International Journal of Nautical Archaeology* 32(2):143-157.

GILDER, WILLIAM H.
1881   *Schwatka's Search; Sledging in the Arctic in Quest of the Franklin Records.* Charles Scribners's Sons, New York, New York. Reprinted 1996 by Abercrombie & Fitch, New York, New York.

HALL, CHARLES FRANCIS
1869a Notebook 22, May 2, box 11, folder 4, Charles Francis Hall Collection 2157.103, Smithsonian Institution, National Museum of American History Archives Center (NMAHA), Washington, DC.

1869b Notebook 24, May 4, box 11, folder 4, Charles Francis Hall Collection 2157.103, NMAHA, Washington, DC.

1869c Notebook 28, May 9, box 11, folder 4, Charles Francis Hall Collection 2157.103, NMAHA, Washington, DC.

HARRIS, RYAN AND JONATHAN MOORE
2010   *Erebus* and *Terror* National Historic Site of Canada Remote Sensing Search 2008. Underwater Archaeology Team, Parks Canada, Ottawa, Ontario, Canada.

HARRIS, RYAN, JONATHAN MOORE, AND MARC-ANDRÉ BERNIER
2015   Wrecks of HMS *Erebus* and HMS *Terror* National Historic Site Remote Sensing Search 2014 and Discovery of HMS *Erebus*. Underwater Archaeology Team, Parks Canada, Ottawa, Ontario, Canada.

KEITH, DARREN AND LOUIE KAMOOKAK
1999   Franklin Oral History Project October 12-19, 1998. Manuscript, Underwater Archaeology Team, Parks Canada, Ottawa, Ontario, Canada.

MCCLINTOCK, FRANCIS LEOPOLD
1860   *The Voyage of the Fox in the Arctic Seas. A Narrative of the Discovery of the Fate of Sir John Franklin and His Companions.* Ticknor and Fields, Boston, Massachusetts.

MOORE, JONATHAN, CHARLES DAGNEAU, MARC-ANDRÉ BERNIER, RYAN HARRIS, THIERRY BOYER, FILIPPO RONCA, BRANDY LOCKHART, AND JOE BOUCHER
2017   HMS *Erebus* Underwater Archaeological Surveys 2015 and 2016. Wrecks of HMS *Erebus* and HMS *Terror* National Historic Site of Canada. Underwater Archaeology Team, Parks Canada, Ottawa, Ontario, Canada.

MUCKELROY, KEITH
1978   *Maritime Archaeology.* Cambridge University Press, Cambridge, United Kingdom.

NOURSE, J.E. (EDITOR)
1879   *Narrative of the Second Arctic Expedition Made by Charles F. Hall: His Voyage to Repulse Bay, Sledge Journeys to the Straits of Fury and Hecla and to King William's Land, and Residence among the Eskimos during the Years 1864-'69.* Government Printing Office, Washington, DC.

PARKS CANADA
2019   Wrecks of HMS *Erebus* and HMS *Terror* National Historic Site of Canada Commemorative Integrity Statement. Parks Canada, Gatineau, Québec, Canada.

RICH, E.E. (EDITOR)
2014   *John Rae's Arctic Correspondence, 1844-1855, reissue of 1953 edition John Rae's Correspondence with the Hudson's Bay Company on Arctic Exploration, 1844-1855,* TouchWood Editions, Surrey, British Columbia, Canada.

SCHWATKA, FREDERICK
1878-80 Journal, miscellaneous volume 163, Manuscripts Collection, G.W. Blunt White Library, Mystic Seaport Museum, Mystic, Connecticut.

STACKPOLE, EDOUARD A.,
1965   *The Long Arctic Search: The Narrative of Lieutenant Frederick Schwatka, U.S.A., 1878-1880, Seeking the Records of the Lost Franklin Expedition.* The Marine Historical Association, Mystic, Connecticut.

STENTON, DOUGLAS R.
2014   A Most Inhospitable Coast: The Report of Lieutenant William Hobson's 1859 Search for the Franklin Expedition on King William Island. *Arctic* 67(4):511-522.

WESTERDAHL, C.
1992   The Maritime Cultural Landscape. *The International Journal of Nautical Archaeology* 21(1):5-14.

WOODMAN, DAVID C.
1991   *Unravelling the Franklin Mystery: Inuit Testimony.* McGill-Queen's University Press, Montreal, Québec, Canada.

. . . .

Jonathan Moore
Underwater Archaeology Team
Parks Canada Agency
1800 Walkley Road
Ottawa (Ontario), K1H 8K3, Canada

Seeing Life in 3D: Digital Recording of HMS *Erebus*

Thierry Boyer, Brandy Lockhart

This paper describes the digital photogrammetry methodology used by Parks Canada to collect and process primary data to model the wreck of HMS Erebus *in 3D. It outlines how spatial models are integrated with a range of geomatic and site plan data sets using complementary photogrammetry and GIS/CAD software. It demonstrates how the combined use of different recording methods, both 2D and 3D, provide the opportunity to evaluate photogrammetry results and effectively juxtapose 3D photogrammetric models with data derived by other recording techniques. In Parks Canada's experience, this method allows for systematic and continuous post-fieldwork data analysis to meet research and outreach aims.*

Introduction

The use of 3D digital recording methods in underwater archaeology is now commonplace and one of the established and accessible methods is without a doubt single point digital photogrammetry (Costa 2019; McCarthy et al. 2019; Radic Rossi et al. 2019). Fortunately, Parks Canada's Underwater Archaeology Team (UAT) had embraced this method the year prior to the discovery of HMS *Erebus* in 2014 as it was considered the best way to record a freestanding 3D structure in a remote environment which places significant limitations on field time (Rzhanov 2014). This paper introduces the use of photogrammetry and digital 3D modelling software in the archaeological recording, analysis and digital record keeping of the wreck of HMS *Erebus*. It demonstrates how the UAT combined photogrammetry with other recording methods, both 2D and 3D, such as multi-beam echosounder (MBES), the direct survey method (DSM) and traditional hand mapping. Furthermore, it discusses the use of 3D photogrammetric models in archaeological cataloguing, artifact provenience control, site reconstruction, and record keeping.

Archaeological Context and Methodology

The hull of HMS *Erebus* is approximately 30 m (98 ft) long by 10 m (33 ft) in breadth and stands 5 m (16 ft) off the bottom in 11 m (36 ft) of water in Wilmot and Crampton Bay, Nunavut, Canada. It is surrounded by an extensive debris field comprised of collapsed hull elements, anchors and rigging components. The intact and freestanding wooden hull is atypical of saltwater wrecks that usually have completely collapsed and lie flat on the seafloor, sites that generally pose fewer complications arising from depth and elevation recording. Therefore, given the wreck's three-dimensionality the UAT had to devise a recording methodology that allowed for accurate yet efficient documenting of the third dimension. To accommodate this, photogrammetry was added to the list of recording techniques to be employed on the wreck that ran the gamut from hand mapping to trials of 3D laser scanning (Moore et al. 2017:41-47).

To generate a digital photogrammetric model using the single point method, multiple photos of the same subject must be taken from different positions and different angles. What is used here is the umbrella approach, according to our invented terminology. In other terms, it means to aim the camera towards the same central point while moving between photos along the ribs of the fictive umbrella. This is fairly simple for underwater archaeologists as they can swim above the site; as on land, it would require an unmanned aerial vehicle. There must be a large overlap between each of the photos to allow the processing software to detect identical points on multiple photos and thereby generate a model. However, this large overlap also raises another important issue in that the greater the number of photos the greater the required computer processing time. UAT's compromise was to employ a minimum overlap of 50%, but not to exceed 70%.

Initially, over 3,800 photos were taken to produce the comprehensive photogrammetric model of *Erebus*. Typically, photos were taken using a Nikon D4 with 14-24 mm lens or a Nikon D300 in their respective Aquatica housing with glass dome and two Ikelite DS161 strobes. The images were captured in stages during three different field projects: the port side of the wreck in April 2015; the debris field and upper deck in August 2015; and the starboard side of the wreck in August-September 2016. To photograph this side satisfactorily proved to be most problematic. Among the many challenges encountered during the photogrammetry recording was the fact that the wreck is positioned with its bow pointing west, with the starboard side facing directly due north. As a result, this side is never exposed to direct sunlight and is perpetually shadowed. This would not necessarily have been a problem if it were not for the fact that the upper part of the wreck, photographed with direct sunlight; this generated very high contrast compared to the starboard side, therefore requiring a lot of successive trials on the starboard side to gather enough usable images to generate a somewhat consistent model. Another factor that affected the work was the prolific plant life that grows on site. The principal problem was undeniably kelp with its long fronds move with the current and waves. Given it is close to impossible to generate a photogrammetric model when subject points move from one photo to another, the wreck eventually had to be cleared of kelp prior to wholesale photogrammetric recording. The vast majority of this careful clearing took place in April and August 2015. Otherwise, underwater visibility conditions at the wreck are generally good (and can be excellent) thereby facilitating orderly recording and engendering unblemished photos.

Data Processing and Model Creation

Once the necessary photos were acquired, the wreck could be reproduced on a computer. The photogrammetric software employed is Agisoft Photoscan Professional Edition (now Metashape). The first batch of photos obtained in April 2015 were processed while the UAT was still staged on seasonal ice cover atop the wreck site. At this time, many areas were still obscured by kelp and the resulting upper deck portion of the model was consequently blurry. Subsequently after each dive

Figure 1: 3D model of the HMS *Erebus*, a compilation of the photogrammetric models created in the first years of survey, port side hull, sea floor surrounds and upper deck (Image by Thierry Boyer, Parks Canada, 2015)..

and project, new images were added into the software to produce models of various wreck sections, slowly building the complete model. In doing so, this ensured that all required images were taken before leaving the site during a given fieldwork episode.

The procedure used to generate the model follows closely the Agisoft software manual and will not be discussed here (Agisoft 2015). Whereas the initial model produced by the software has no intrinsic positioning information, relative distances were available between the different structures and artifacts on and around the wreck to allow co-registration of separate models. The three models created during the first three field episodes in 2015-2016 had to be aligned to one another in order to create a single united model within Agisoft photoscan (Figure 1). To accomplish this, a minimum of three common reference points found on at least two models were selected for each of the alignments. To ensure no mistakes could come from the software calculation of these positions, these points were accurately positioned in every photo used in the model in which they could be seen, or removed if the point was not clearly visible or if it was located in a shaded area. It was then possible to produce a model that covered over 95% of the entire site in a single photogrammetric model. Once this step was completed, poor quality (i.e. too dark or blurry) and redundant images were manually removed and the computer processing resumed.

This second iteration of the model used 2,500 of the 3,800 photos originally taken and produced a point cloud comprising over 125 million points, each having X-Y-Z and R-G-B values. The sheer quantity of raw photographic data demanded a dedicated dual-processing engineering workstation with multiple solid-state hard drives and large amount of RAM. Even with this processing power, model processing time was measured in days and weeks, not hours and minutes, excluding the human hours required in model creation. However, lower resolution models could be created in the meantime: with faster processing times, these could be completed in order to ascertain that all required images were available to produce a high-resolution model.

Photogrammetry Model Validation

To validate the model and ensure the accuracy of its relative information, it was geo-rectified against a 2014 MBES model of the wreck, the site's primary geomatic model. To accomplish this, several feature points were selected on the wreck according to the ease with which

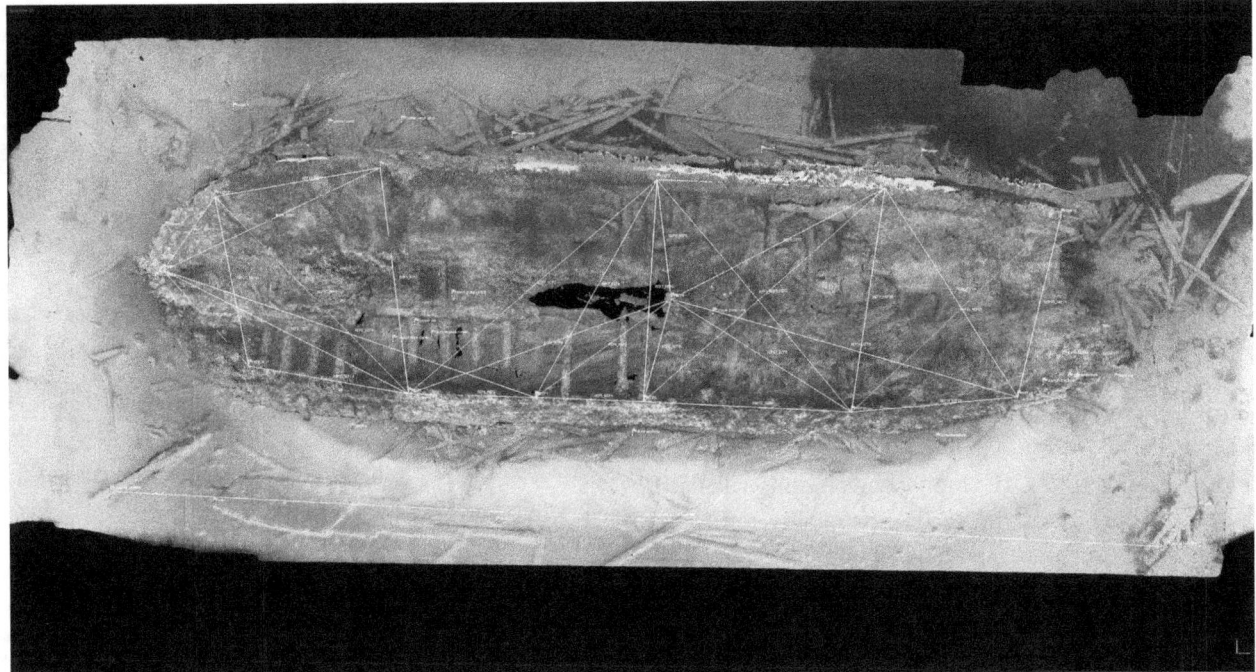

Figure 2: 3D photogrammetric model of HMS *Erebus* with the DSM web recreated over its deck using datum markers visible within the model (Image by Thierry Boyer, Parks Canada, 2016).

they could be linked to their corresponding points on the MBES model; these included: the top of the main mast stub; the tip of the bow; and the center of a wooden pump tube. The corresponding Inertially Aided Post Processed Kinematic positions (IAPPK) extrapolated from the MBES data set for each point were then entered into the Agisoft software, thereby georectifying the model and providing it with a geographic scale.

As an independent check to ensure the model was spatially accurate and to be able to use the model to take exact measurements, it was also cross-referenced against measurements made by DSM. It is worth pointing out that a DSM model was created using 3H Consulting Site Surveyor 4 software, which was calculated by the software to be internally accurate. For the photogrammetry validation step, we digitally positioned the 18 primary reference (DSM) points affixed to the wreck that are clearly visible in the photogrammetry model, created scale bars in Agisoft Photoscan Professional, and compared the recorded measurements of both sets (Figure 2). According to these observations, there were a few discrepancies between the measurements obtained by DSM and photogrammetric model, which were between +8 cm and -6 cm with an average of 1.5 cm error. While the horizontal (X-Y) values were fairly accurate, the elevations (Z values) created greater initial discrepancies evidently due to the inherent difficulty of measuring elevations on site by DSM. The absolute depth for one DSM reference point, that served as a benchmark, was determined from MBES depth data and for the other points by using a handheld digital diver's depth gauge (10 cm resolution); although compensating for tidal depth changes, this overall approach left a fair margin of error for the Z values from DSM alone.

The differences of the horizontal measurements (X and Y) on the 3D model and those taken during the DSM work were less than 10 cm. These can be easily attributed to some distortion of the measuring tapes. When these tapes are stretched over distance above 10 or 20 meters, the current could easily put tension on the tape and modify the reading.

As a further check to prove the model, the photogrammetry point cloud model and DSM model were integrated into Bentley Map Enterprise (now Bentley OpenCities Map Enterprise) software. In 2015, UAT selected this versatile and powerful software (with both CAD and GIS functionality) to serve as the primary digital site mapping platform. Based on a comparison of the photogrammetry and MBES point clouds, a small correction to the photogrammetry model's georectification had to be applied to perfectly place the wreck geographically. Using the Bentley software to accomplish this, cross sections were sliced through the two models and they were compared section by section at different angles to ensure that the scale and geographic location were accurate and in perfect agreement; any distortion within each model appeared very minimal and is attributed at the resolution difference between the MBES and the photogrammetric models. Furthermore, this final check demonstrated the X-Y accuracy of the DSM model; the differences between the X-Y distances between the primary reference points determined by DSM versus MBES were between 0.4 cm and 2 cm. However, this comparison also confirmed problematic depth measurements determined by DSM with discrepancies between 1.8 cm and 35 cm.

Agisoft Metashape has an internal tool, which takes into account the information it has on the model it just generated, to estimate the margin of error within a model, taking. This estimation of precision is calculated based on the size of the model, its quality (i.e. point cloud resolution), and the quantity and the resolution of the photos used to build the model. For our *Erebus* model, this yielded an estimated measurement precision of better than 0.5 cm for X-Y-Z values. In the final analysis, one could not reasonably hope for more given that the model records a 30m-long site in an underwater context.

Model Integration and Archaeological Applications

Outside the obvious public outreach uses of this type of model, photogrammetry is an incredible archaeological tool. It allows archaeologists to bring an accurate, scaled version of the wreck to the surface, in a non-destructive fashion and, thus, allowing them to continue their analysis of the site well beyond the UAT's extremely short Arctic field season. Continued analysis of the model is carried out within Bentley OpenCities Map Enterprise software and on scaled print outs of the entire site (or subsets such as the debris field) to analyse visible artifact distribution and help to plan future onsite activities for instance. For example, 10 to 15 hours spent in the office studying and deriving measurements from the scale model of the debris field surrounding the wreck could represent 4 to 8 days of field work on site to accomplish the work through diving. Furthermore, the model allows for a large-scale perspective of the entire site at once which is not possible when diving.

Within the Bentley software, the point cloud wreck model is used as a scaffold upon which historic information, newly acquired data and newly created models of wreck sections can be incorporated. This allows for interpretation and analysis using multiple data sets and a constantly growing model. This model is not

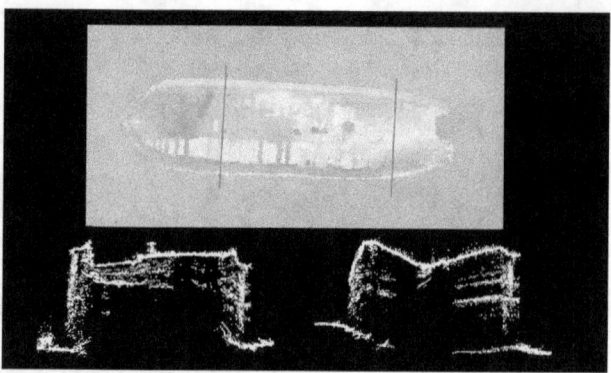

Figure 3: Multibeam Echo Sounder point cloud data (top) with 2 cross sections through different locations of the wreck showing the variation in the extent of collapse of the upper deck, with an increase in the damage to the upper deck towards the stern (right) (MBES data from Canadian Hydrographic Services. Image by Brandy Lockhart, Parks Canada, 2017).

only 3D, but also 4D, as it can display changes to the site through time.

The software allows for the rapid processing and manipulation of large point cloud data; as noted above, it has integrated computer aided design (CAD) capability as well as a geographic information system (GIS) framework. The point cloud density of the current model is high enough that it was possible to isolate the heads of the bolts used to affix the primary datum tags on the upper deck from the attached numbered tags themselves. This level of detail has allowed for accurate measurements of features on the wreck using the model alone.

The Bentley software allows for the easy creation of sections through the model. This can provide a clearer understanding of the condition of the wreck and differences (sometimes subtle) from bow to stern (Figure 3). Cross sections can be created in any orientation producing the in situ equivalent of waterlines, station lines and buttock lines as well as other useful angles and measurements. For example, using this method the heel and pitch of the wreck were determined. Some of the data incorporated into the model includes the original 1839 Admiralty ship plans of *Erebus* (National Maritime Museum 1837a, 1837b, 1839a, 1839b, 1839c, 1839d). These are not just layered over the 3D model, but are actually incorporated within their spatially-correct position and angle in three dimensions, in that the lower deck plan slices through the wreck model at the level of the lower deck and so on. Using these images, the "as built" design can be compared with the current locations of features such as hatches, deck illuminators and cabin locations. These images have also been used to determine measurements, such as the depth of the hull within the sediment, by comparing the plans and the point cloud model.

Within Bentley, it is possible to isolate individual points within the point cloud and classify them. With this tool, features can be grouped within the site such as deck beams, pumps, deck planks, and visible artifacts; these can then be viewed independently and compared to one another. This tool will become more important as excavation proceeds. Changes to the site are tracked by recording, isolating and classifying deck planks or debris that have been removed during yearly excavation. This allows for the integration of the 4D data, change over time, by viewing the site through different phases of the excavation process and allowing for digital re-excavation as required.

The fact that the hull is intact and stands proud of the seabed creates archaeological challenges, including the placement of the site provenience grid (based on 2 m by 2 m units or sub-operations), something more easily accomplished over a flattened or collapsed hull. Using the model, a virtual grid has been imposed which can be applied to the physical site on a unit by unit basis. The virtual provenience grid aligns with baseline markers placed on the site. Verification of the exact location of each grid unit can be ascertained by extracting the grid unit from the 3D model and viewing unit features from multiple angles (Figure 4).

Another data set currently being integrated into the model is that of the locations of recovered artifacts which have been placed in their 3D location in the point cloud. Using the software's GIS framework, this allows for the visualization and analysis of artifact distribution not only from bow to stern, but also stratigraphically, and between the different decks. This permits the automatic updating of the model when new artifacts are recovered and entered into an external relational artifact database. Once the location of the artifact within the 3D provenience grid has been entered into the database, a marker will appear automatically within the model indicating the location and providing metadata of the artifact. The marker can also be selected automatically from predefined symbols related to either its function or name. Possible future markers include scaled 3D models

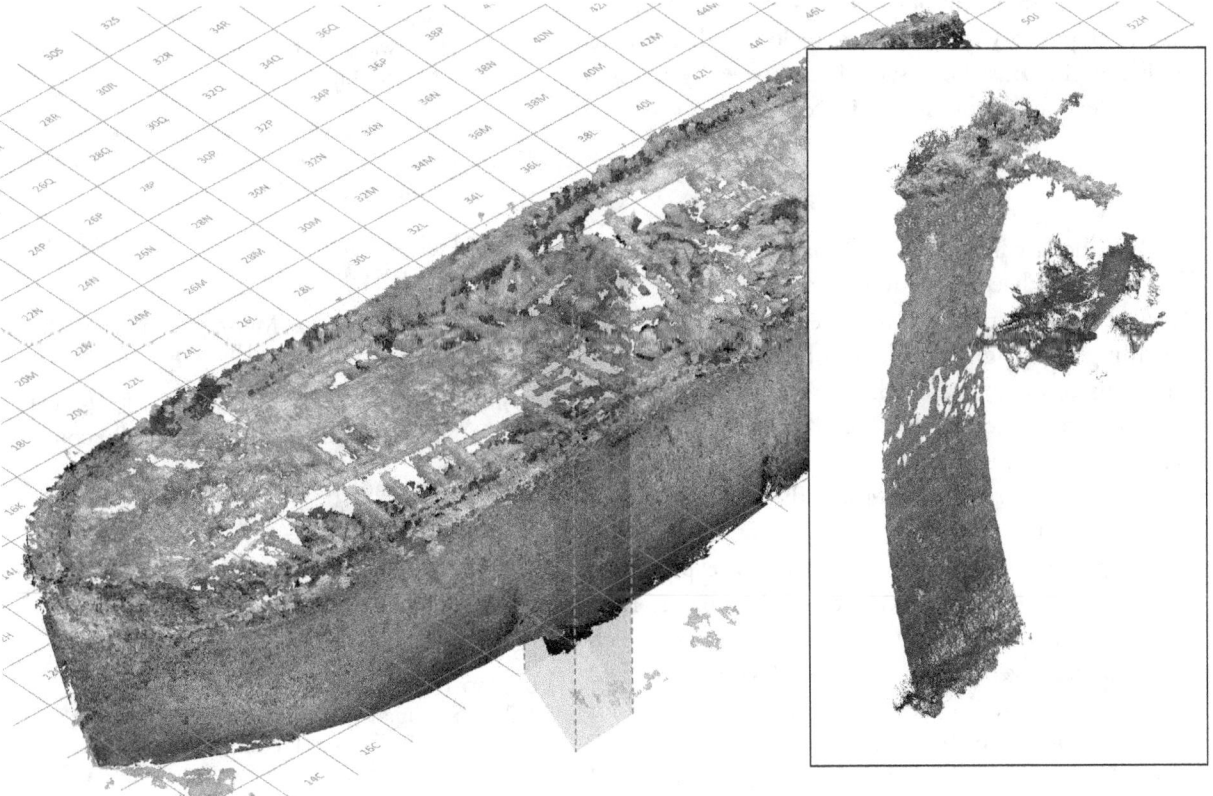

Figure 4: Virtual provenience grid over the site of HMS *Erebus* indicating the location of a specific grid unit through the model (left) and the isolated grid unit portion of that model at lower right (inset) (Image by Brandy Lockhart, Parks Canada, 2017).

of individual artifacts, placed back into the point cloud, in their original in situ orientation.

Future applications of the 3D photogrammetric model include a virtual reconstruction of the site. For example, upon the wreck's discovery in 2014, the UAT observed a dislocated portion of the upper deck of the *Erebus* resting on the seafloor off its port side. This deck section has been isolated within the point cloud model and was digitally moved back to its original location and orientation on the upper deck. This same method can be used to place the collapsed deck beams back onto the beam shelf, or to replace missing structural elements with those modeled from the original plans.

Notwithstanding our extensive use of the 3D modelling for archaeological study of *Erebus*, traditional manual methods are still employed during survey and excavation, including hand-drawn scale sub-operation excavation drawings made underwater, and hand drawn site plans and artifact drawings. Indeed, a series of site plans and a hull cross section were drawn by the UAT's archaeological illustrator based largely on the photogrammetry and MBES models. As with other data, these completed illustrations have been incorporated back into the 3D model within the Bentley software. The model thereby not only acts as a source of data, but also as a repository for other data, including that of non-digital origin. This allows such data to be easily accessed and understood within its spatial context.

Conclusion

Over the last five years, UAT has created the multi-faceted 3D archaeological model of the wreck of HMS *Erebus*. This has provided a powerful new method of recording, studying, and presenting this remarkable wreck site. This technology is both relatively straightforward and far more efficient than hand mapping, especially when the site's three-dimensionality is considered. It is thereby more cost-effective given the very substantial savings in dive time to complete a comprehensive site mapping task that may otherwise have proven to have been wholly impractical. It rapidly provides large quantities of demonstrably highly accurate data which can be poured over for months in the office after the field season is complete. In themselves, these models are not only excellent sources of data, but are also a framework into which other sources of data can be imported and held as an interactive and evolving repository, and a powerful tool for comparative and spatial analysis.

References

AGISOFT
2015   Agisoft Photoscan User Manual https://www.agisoft.com/downloads/user-manuals/. Accessed November 15, 2015.

COSTA, E.
2019   The Progress of Survey Techniques in Underwater Sites The Case Study of Cape Stoba Shipwreck. In: *The International Archives of the Photogrammetry, Remote Sensing and Spatial Information Sciences*, Volume XLII-2/W10: 69-75., 2–3 May 2019, Limassol, Cyprus.

MCCARTHY J., BENJAMIN J., WINTON T., VAN DUIVENVOORDE W.
2019   The Rise of 3D in Maritime Archaeology. In: McCarthy J., Benjamin J., Winton T., van Duivenvoorde W. (eds) 3D *Recording and Interpretation for Maritime Archaeology*. Coastal Research Library, vol 31. Springer, Cham, Switzerland.

MOORE, JONATHAN, CHARLES DAGNEAU, MARC-ANDRÉ BERNIER, RYAN HARRIS, THIERRY BOYER, FILIPPO RONCA, BRANDY LOCKHART, AND JOE BOUCHER
2017   HMS *Erebus* Underwater Archaeological Surveys 2015 and 2016. Wrecks of HMS *Erebus* and HMS *Terror* National Historic Site of Canada. Underwater Archaeology Team, Parks Canada, Ottawa, Ontario, Canada.

NATIONAL MARITIME MUSEUM, GREENWICH
1837a   Plan of the *Terror* Lower Deck. ZAZ5676 (J1410), Admiralty Collection.

1837b   Profile of the *Terror*. ZAZ5675 (J1406), Admiralty Collection.

1839a   *Terror* and *Erebus*, Midship Section. ZAZ5678 (J1412). Admiralty Collection.

1839b   *Terror* and *Erebus*, Plan of Lower Deck (As Fitted). NPC3135 (J8650), Admiralty Collection

1839c   *Terror* and *Erebus*, Plan of Upper Deck (As Fitted). ZAZ5675 (J1409). Admiralty Collection.

1839d   *Terror* and *Erebus*, Profile (As Fitted). ZAZ5673 (J1413). Admiralty Collection.

RADIC ROSSI, IRENA, JOSE CASABAN, KOTARO YAMAFUNE, RODRIGO TORRES AND KATARINA BATUR
2019   Systematic Photogrammetric Recording of the Gnalic Shipwreck Hull Remains and Artefacts. In: McCarthy J., Benjamin J., Winton T., van Duivenvoorde W. (eds) 3D *Recording and Interpretation for Maritime Archaeology*. Coastal Research Library, vol 31. Springer, Cham, Switzerland.

Rzhanov Yuri, H. Hu, and T. Boyer,
2014   Dense Reconstruction of Underwater Scenes from Monocular Sequences of Images, in OCEANS 2014 - TAIPEI, Institute of Electrical & Electronics Engineers (IEEE).

. . . .

Thierry Boyer
Underwater Archaeology Team
Parks Canada Agency
1800 Walkley Road
Ottawa (Ontario), K1H 8K3, Canada

Brandy Lockhart
Underwater Archaeology Team
Parks Canada Agency
1800 Walkley Road
Ottawa (Ontario), K1H 8K3, Canada

HMS *Erebus* Material Culture: Reaching Out to the Individuals

Charles Dagneau

The study of HMS Erebus *and HMS* Terror *promises long-waited answers to some of the lingering mysteries surrounding the 1845 Franklin Expedition. The initial study and excavation of* Erebus, *in particular, has great potential for feature and artifact group discoveries from sealed contexts. This exploratory paper aims to identify and study individuals aboard* Erebus *through the interpretation of material culture in conjunction with historical evidence. Depending on archaeological context, ceramics, clothing articles, and personal items are linked to specific ranks and/or individual crew members from the Franklin Expedition.*

Introduction

Parks Canada's investigations into the 1845-Franklin Expedition is articulated around six themes, three of which are particularly pertinent to this paper: science; maritime technology; and material culture and shipboard life. The first two can be used to understand the motivation behind this polar expedition, exploration activities carried out during the voyage, as well as the vessels themselves. This paper focuses on the third theme listed above. It examines the different ways in which identities are expressed through material culture aboard *Erebus*. The main objective is to identify distinct crew members from the expedition using both archaeological and historical evidence. Knowledge pertaining to these people will be valuable in reconstructing the final phases of the Franklin Expedition. However, the following paper should be considered as a preliminary and exploratory work given that the study and excavation of *Erebus* and *Terror* are only in their initial stages.

Sources

Despite some gaps, there is an abundance of historical and anthropological sources related to the Franklin Expedition. Contemporary documentation includes paintings, sketches, correspondence, daguerreotypes, dockyard records, and multiple sets of ship plans (Dagneau and Moore 2017; Moore et al. 2017). Inuit oral accounts collected in the 19th century and present-day Inuit knowledge add to the corpus of data available for interpretation (Hall 1879; McClintock 1860; Schwatka 1878-1880; Woodman 1991; Keith and Kamookak 1999; Moore 2015). One of the most important set of documents regarding the expedition is certainly the muster lists for both vessels, containing the name, rank, position, and birthplace of the individual crew members (Muster Book of Her Majesty's Ship '*Erebus*' 1845; Muster Book of Her Majesty's Ship '*Terror*' 1845).

Peter Carney (2016) reconciled archival records to create a list of officers and crew members of the expedition that we can draw from for this study (Table 1). According to this list, *Erebus* departed the Whalefish Islands, Greenland, in July 1845 with 67 men on board, including 16 officers, 22 petty officers, 20 able seamen, 7 Royal Marines, and 2 boys. Able Seaman John Hartnell and Royal Marine Private William Braine died and were buried at Beechey Island in 1846 (Beattie and Geiger 1988). While Sir John Franklin died on 11 June 1847, sources indicate that nine other officers and 15 men from the expedition (*Erebus* and/or *Terror*) had lost their lives before 25 April 1848 (Cyriax 1939:94,158–159; Woodman 1991). However, very little is known after that date and up to the final loss of the wreck. Importantly,

Name	Qualities
Sir John Franklin	Captain
James Fitzjames	Commander
Graham Gore	Lieutenant
Henry T.D. Le Vesconte	Lieutenant
James W. Fairholme	Lieutenant
Robert O. Sergeant	Mate
Charles F. Des Vœux	Mate
Edward Couch	Mate
James Reid	Master (Acting)
Stephen S. Stanley	Surgeon
Charles H. Osmer	Paymaster & Purser
Harry D.S. Goodsir	Surgeon (Acting)
Henry F. Collins	Second Master
Thomas Terry	Boatswain, 3rd Class
John Weekes	Carpenter, 2nd Class
John Gregory	Engineer, 1st Class

Table 1: List of officers aboard *Erebus* after it departed the Whalefish Islands, Greenland, July 1845 (After Carney 2016).

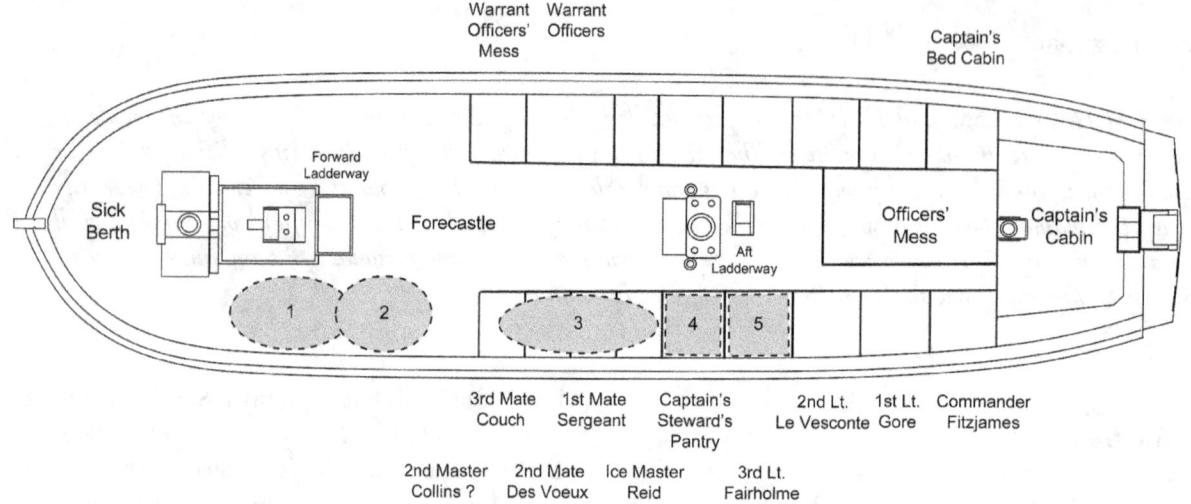

Figure 1: Reconstruction of possible lower deck configuration and selected cabin assignments on *Erebus* in 1845, with five artifact clusters discussed in this paper. This sketch is derived from an 1845 *Terror* lower deck plan drawing by Matthew Betts. Doorways and hatches not depicted (Image by Author, Parks Canada, 2020; After Matthew Betts 2016).

it is not yet known if one or both vessels drifted unmanned from their known desertion point in April 1848, or if they were re-manned and navigated to their final destination (Dagneau and Moore 2017:26–27). Thus, any attempts to link artefacts and archaeological features to specific individuals from the expedition has to cope with a high level of uncertainty.

Another key document is the *Terror and Erebus, Plan of Lower Deck (as Fitted)* showing *Terror* with modifications dating from 1837-39 (National Maritime Museum [hereafter NMM] 1839). According to Matthew Betts (2016), we know that the same document also shows pencil drawings and annotations displaying modifications from 1845, including the division of living space on the lower deck, and the cabin layout and assignments by rank. At this stage of the project, it is assumed that most of the 1845 lower deck modifications to *Terror* would have also been applied to *Erebus* with some adjustments.

These historical records, considered together, represent a powerful tool for the interpretation of archaeological data. They provide a means of linking ship areas and/or groups of artifacts to specific individuals from the expedition, thereby a means of reaching out to the individuals, so to speak, something that is not always possible in archaeology. Thus, *Terror*'s lower deck plan can be coupled with the abovementioned muster list and other archival sources to determine the officer most likely to have been assigned to a given cabin on *Erebus*.

Indeed, each of *Erebus*' commissioned officers (military and civil) were assigned individual bed cabins; they worked and ate in the officers' mess, if not invited to the captain's table. The three warrant officers (boatswain, carpenter, and engineer) shared the same cabin and small mess room. All of the other seamen onboard slept in the forecastle area (including the sick berth) and had their meals on a series of mess tables along both sides of the vessel (NMM 1839; Betts 2016).

It is known from contemporary accounts that Sir John Franklin's bed cabin was at the starboard quarter of the lower deck, while Commander James Fitzjames' was at the port quarter cabin normally assigned to the 1st Lieutenant (Fitzjames 1845b; Illustrated London News 1845a; 1845b). We also know that 3rd Lieutenant James Walter Fairholme was assigned the port side cabin opposite the aft ladder way (Fairholme 1845b). From this, one can extrapolate a possible 1845 *Erebus* cabin layout and assignments (Figure 1).

* * * * *

The discussion below focuses on five artifact clusters located on the lower deck of *Erebus*, two of which are located in the forecastle area, the lower ranks' living quarters, and three in the port-side officers' cabins area. For each group, we hypothesize possible owner(s) or occupant identifications based on the available

Figure 2: Selected ceramic assemblage from the forecastle (bottom) and suspected Captain's Steward's pantry (top right). Examples of graffiti and cut marks on a dinner plate (89M99X1-12) from the forecastle (top left) (Drawing by Carol Pillar, Parks Canada, 2016; Photos by Thierry Boyer and Marni Wilson, Parks Canada, 2016 and 2019).

historical sources and the archaeological contexts of the clusters (See Jonathan Moore, this publication, Figure 1 for a detailed site plan of the *Erebus* wreck site with provenience grid).

Ceramics from the Forecastle and the Captain's Steward's Pantry

The first artifact group in this study includes ceramic dishes from the forecastle (sub-operations 28J/K and 30J/K), as well as from what is believed to be the Captain's Steward's pantry (38J/K and 40J/K) (Figure 2). Five whiteware and one pearlware dinner plates, as well as a service bowl are part of the forecastle assemblage, five of which have a common blue willow pattern (Miller 1991:8–9). Two of these examples have a maker's mark attributed to William and Samuel Edge, Staffordshire (Godden 1991:229). A single "Whampoa" flow blue dinner plate is part of the group, marked William Ridgway, Staffordshire (Godden 1991:538). Most interestingly, three ceramics show graffiti on their reverse sides: a broad arrow, an anchor and a number "4". Four plates and the bowl also bear different numbers of cut marks on their foot rings (Moore et al. 2017:89–92). Table 2 summarizes the marks found on different artifacts. Similar cut marks are often found on

Artefact Number	Shape & Decor	Maker's Marks & Stamps	Graffiti	Foot Rim Cuts
89M30J200-6	Bowl, Blue Forest and Fern	Forest C	4	2
89M30K200-1	Dinner plate, Blue Willow	WARRANTED STONE CHINA W & S E 3 [Crown]	-	3
89M30K200-2	Dinner plate, Blue Willow	-	-	3
89M30K200-3	Dinner plate, Blue Willow	-	-	6
89M99X1-12	Dinner plate, Blue Willow	WARRANTED STONE CHINA W & S E [Crown]	Broad Arrow	5
89M99X1-13	Dinner plate, Blue Willow	STAFFORDSHIRE [WAR]RANTED CHINA [Royal Arms]	[Anchor ?]	-
89M99X1-11	Dinner plate, Whampoa	OPAQUE GRANITE CHINA W R & Co WHAMPOA [Royal Arms]	-	-

Table 2: List of graffiti marks and foot rim cut marks on ceramics from *Erebus*' forecastle.

ceramics in military contexts for example, this occurs on the HMS *Swift* and *Infatigable* wreck sites, as well as at Fort Wellington, Ontario (Sussman et al. 1994; Elkin et al. 2011:197–199; Diego Carabias 2016, pers. comm.).

It is believed that the graffiti and cut marks probably relate to specific messes and/or individuals within mess units aboard *Erebus*. The relatively low value of these plates and their presence in the forecastle suggests these were ship's property used by the ratings, probably stored along the ship's sides as seen inside *Terror*.

On the other hand, a set of 47 ceramic wares were found in 2019, well stacked in a compartment within what is believed to be the Captain's Steward's pantry, on the port side amidships. The entire set consists of whiteware dishes with "Whampoa" flow blue design. Although most of the pieces are by W. Ridgway, different potters' marks, and multiple batches of variable quality are observed. The assemblage includes 22 dinner plates of 2 shapes, 8 soup plates, 4 serving bowls, 3 lids, 6 platters, and 4 strainers. No cut marks or graffiti are present on any of these artifacts. As opposed to the ceramics found in the forecastle bearing marks and likely used by the crew, those found in the presumed Captain's Steward's pantry may have been owned by Sir John Franklin and used for day-to-day meals at his table with his officers.

Royal Marines Equipment from the Forecastle

The second group of finds from the forecastle (Figure 1) includes Royal Marines equipment, or artifacts related to their duties (sub-operations 30-32J/K). A Royal Marines brass shoulder belt plate (89M32J200-1) is the key artifact of this group. It is decorated with a typical lion and crown crest, and two banners (Figure 3) (Parkyn 2014:242; Rawlinson 2014:288–191). This badge comes from the uniform of one of the 13 marines from the Woolwich Division on the expedition. Although there is not enough evidence to make any firm individual association at this point, based on its design and quality, it was probably owned by a higher ranking, non-commissioned officer such as a sergeant, since privates and corporals used lesser grade plates (Rawlinson 2014:288–191). Given that both vessels had a contingent of three to four privates, a corporal and a sergeant, this artifact likely belonged to Sergeant Daniel Bryant of *Erebus* (and less likely Sergeant Solomon Tozer from *Terror*). We know from the muster list that he was 31 years old when *Erebus* left England in 1845 and came from Shipton Montagu, Somerset, England. He enlisted at Woolwich on 30 October 1828, and signed his attestation form himself, something that speaks to a certain level of literacy (Lloyd-Jones 2004). Sergeant Bryant is mentioned in expedition correspondence when Commander James Fitzjames writes from the Whalefish Islands, Greenland that he "sent [Lieutenant] Gore and the Sergeant of marines below, and searched the whole deck for spirits" (Fitzjames 1845a). In addition to the belt plate, two Royal Marines buttons (89M99X1-9 and 10) are included in this group, along with 40 percussion caps, and a few lead shots. A pharmacy bottle and the 19 small shots it contained can also be added, as the bottle is believed to have been re-used as a shot flask (Moore et al. 2017:95–97, 100–102).

Lower Ranking Officers' Cabins

The third artifact cluster relates to *Erebus*' lower ranking officers (Figure 1). It includes artifacts mostly found loose on the port side of the lower deck (sub-operations 34J/K-38J/K), where the cabin structures are severely truncated and collapsed, with little sediment accumulation. This area corresponds to the foremost cabins on the port side, believed to be assigned to the master(s) and the mates. Among other finds, a naval officer's sword was found next to a pestle, a fire broom, and an artificial horizon roof. A sextant, a wool garment and a pair of boots were found slightly farther aft, with

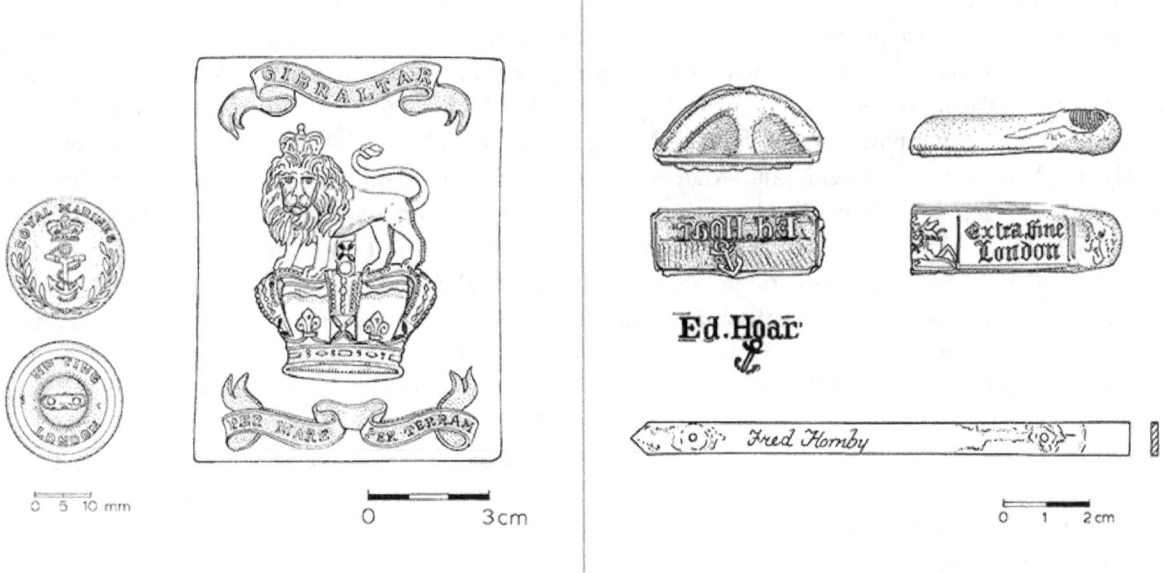

Figure 3: Royal Marines shoulder belt plate (89M32J200-1) and button (89M99X1-9) from the forecastle (left). Lead stamp marked "Ed. Hoar" (89M38J201-43), sealing wax (89M38J200-26), and unidentified instrument part marked "Fred Hornby" (89M38J201-5) from suspected Captain's Steward's pantry (right) (Drawings by Carol Pillar, Parks Canada, 2017 and 2019).

a complete artificial horizon box set. All of these objects are associated with officer ranks and duties.

The sextant and mercurial artificial horizon would have been used in conjunction to determine latitude, if the horizon was blocked, for instance, by ice floes. The sword hilt (89M34K200-5) corresponds to an 1827-pattern naval officer's sword (McGrath and Barton 2013:43–44). It is made of gilt brass and decorated with a crown and fouled anchor badge, with its pommel in the shape of a lion's head. The sword knot is made of silk with gold-plated silver threads woven in, and blue median strings. This sword was no doubt owned by one of the naval officers.

Equally of interest is a pair of fashionable custom-made winter boots (89M38J200-8) with wool gaiters and seal fur lining that, on account of their high quality, probably belonged to one of the officers. One boot was found in 2016, the other in 2019. Samples were collected inside the former and sent for human DNA extraction and sequencing at the Lakehead University Paleo-DNA Lab. It was anticipated that some human skin fragments may be found in the boot. Fortunately, a mitochondrial DNA profile was retrieved. The DNA profile does not match any known profiles from skeletal remains found to date on land sites (Stenton et al. 2017; Stenton 2018). As more DNA material is collected through this project, there may be the opportunity to link this artifact either to other artifacts or to a specific member of the expedition, including through their descendants.

Considering the 1845 presumed cabin assignment presented above, this artifact cluster, including the pair of boots, could have originated from one or perhaps two of the Mates' cabins, and possibly that of the Ice Master: namely 1st Mate Robert Sargent, 2nd Mate Charles Des Vœux, or Ice Master James Reid respectively. Interestingly, much is known about these officers through Royal Navy documents, personal correspondence and, in some cases, family records. Indeed, these men and the other officers from *Erebus* sat for daguerreotype portraits prior to departure in 1845 (NMM 1847).

Captain's Steward's Pantry

One of two cabins excavated in 2019 is believed to be the Captain's Steward's pantry, in sub-operations 38J/K and 40J/K. Although the excavation of this discrete ship space was only partially completed, the artifact assemblage gathered thus far is consistent with our identification (Figure 3). The base of a storage compartment (lots 38J201/40J203) in particular contained the abovementioned set of 47 ceramic pieces, as well as an accordion, mitten, numerous buttons, coins, clothing articles, and many other objects still being studied. A writing kit, including natural and manufactured lead pencils, slate pencils, ink pens, and an associated box and an ink bottle were also discovered in the same cabin. It is believed that they may have been used for teaching lessons or scientific work aboard *Erebus*. Other artifacts include a pitcher, a mustard pot with residual contents, some food bottles, a toothbrush, and corked bottles of different types. A hairbrush is of particular interest due to human hairs discovered trapped within its bristles. It is hoped that these hairs could provide valuable insight into its user's or users' health during the last months of the expedition and, possibly, allow DNA sequencing and individual identification.

A key artifact of this cabin space, also found in the same storage compartment, is a lead stamp (89M38J201-43) bearing the inscription "Ed. Hoar" with an anchor motif below. According to the muster list, Edmund Hoar was Sir John Franklin's steward (Muster Book of Her Majesty's Ship '*Erebus*' 1845). It is hypothesised that his pantry was mainly used (not occupied) by Hoar and, possibly, the Subordinate Officers' Steward John Bridgens, who would have served the combined lieutenants' and mates' mess (Figure 1; Table 1).

More puzzling is an unidentified object, possibly part of a navigational or scientific instrument (89M38J201-5), marked "Fred Hornby" that was also found in the compartment. This is a particularly interesting artifact; according to the muster books, Frederick Hornby was 2nd Mate of *Terror* (Muster Book of Her Majesty's Ship '*Terror*' 1845). This find suggests that Hornby and/or the object shifted ships at some point during the expedition. This a distinct possibility considering the deaths of nine officers by April 1848 (Millar et al. 2013; Millar et al. 2016; Park and Stenton 2019).

While not much is known about Edmund Hoar, other than what is in the muster list and description books, there is already a great deal known about Frederick Hornby and his family. It is known that a double sextant with his name was brought back to London by the McClintock search expedition (NMM, AAA2230) (Walpole 2011:49; Walpole 2017).

Third Lieutenant's Cabin

Immediately aft of what is believed to be the Captain's Steward's pantry is a port-side officer's bed cabin partially excavated in 2019, located in sub-operations

Figure 4: Pair of lieutenant's epaulettes (89M40J204-5 and 6), found in their box, in a drawer under suspected 3rd Lieutenant's bed place (Photo by Marni Wilson, Parks Canada, 2019).

40J/K and 42J/K. This cabin had been targeted as early as 2015 for test excavation because it showed a fairly well preserved bed place along the ship's side, thus providing the opportunity to clearly delineate a single cabin and find artifacts within a specific item of fitted furniture. Two of the four drawers under the bed were completely excavated, and contained very few artifacts compared with the Captain's Steward's pantry. The bed frame and its lee board were missing, meaning the bed place's chest of drawers was exposed. The upper excavated drawer contained a mix of artefacts, including rigging material that had fallen from the upper deck. The closed lower drawer presented a completely sealed context and was largely empty, except for a pair of epaulettes, still in their box (Figure 4).

The epaulettes (89M40J204-5 and 6) are composed of gold (gilt silver) laces over sheet metal. The strap and crescent are edged with twisted gold purl, alternating bright and dark, and bordered on either side with small twisted gold wire. Twenty-one (21) large bullions are attached to the bonnet on the outside and 20 small bullions on the inside. The Royal Navy button on the strap is made of gilt brass. According to the dress regulations of the day, this model corresponds to the rank of lieutenant (May et al. 1974; Miller 2007:140). There is no owner's name or identifier on the epaulettes or the box.

It is believed that this cabin was initially occupied by 3rd Lieutenant Fairholme and, based on available evidence, the epaulettes belonged to him. In a letter to his father sent from the Whalefish Islands in 1845, Fairholme (1845b) complained about the cool air coming down the aft ladderway opposite his cabin doorway. While one might have expected these very epaulettes to have been depicted in Fairholme's 1845 daguerrotype portrait (NMM 1847), he mentions in a letter home that out of convenience he actually sat for his portrait wearing Fitzjames' dress coat and not his own (Fairholme 1845a; Ryan 2017).

The fact that the two bed drawers were mostly empty is interesting. If this proves to be the case for the rest of the cabin furniture, it could indicate that the occupant (presumably Fairholme) may have been alive upon desertion of the ships in 1848 and took many or most of his belongings, such as clothing. While we must be prudent not to draw conclusions at this early stage of excavation, one thing is certain: the epaulettes were left aboard the ship in April 1848 as they would have served no use to anyone in the desperate southbound exodus of the crews of *Erebus* and *Terror*. It is anticipated that full excavation of this cabin will bring new evidence that could support or refute these interpretations.

Like the other officers on *Erebus*, Fairholme had a distinguished career that is fairly well documented. Three items of his personal silverware originally on *Erebus* and bearing his family crest, a dove with an olive branch and the motto "Spero Meliora," were acquired from Inuit by Dr. John Rae's search expedition in 1854 (NMM, AAA2481, 2386, and 3276). Interestingly, one of the silver spoons also bears the initials "C.H.," presumably those of Cornelius Hickey (AAA2386), Caulker's Mate of HMS *Terror* (Walpole 2011:28).

Conclusion

The nascent excavation of *Erebus* has thus far focused on some of the most accessible areas of the lower deck and represents a very small sample of the totality of artifacts aboard. We expect to find more artifact clusters and sealed contexts, including in the captain's cabin and his bed cabin. Archaeological interpretation of material culture coupled with historical data and DNA analysis stand to provide fascinating results in the years to come.

As a closing remark, a few passages from one of Commander Fitzjames' (1845b) letters are worth quoting, as they give substance to some of the discoveries discussed above and about their potential owners and/or users. "Fairholme," he wrote, "is a smart, agreeable companion, and a well-informed man." "Des Voeux is now a most unexceptionable, clever, agreeable, light hearted, obliging young fellow." "Sargent, a nice, pleasant-looking lad, very good-natured." "The most original character of all – rough, intelligent, unpolished, with a broad north-country accent, but not vulgar, good humoured, and honest-hearted – is Reid, a Greenland whaler."

> *"And now, good night, it is past eleven o'clock. I have written without stopping, all with the porcupine quill. God bless you!"*

Acknowledgments

The author acknowledges Parks Canada staff Despoina Kavousanaki, Louis Laflèche and Timothy Greening (Conservation Science), Flora Davidson (Conservation Services), and Shelley Rowan (Collections) for their dedicated work on the *Erebus'* artefacts. Special thanks to Alexandre Poudret-Barré, Jonathan Puqiqnak and the other members of the Underwater Archaeology Team for their work in the inventory lab during fieldwork, to Carol Pillar for site plans and artefact drawings, to Marni Wilson for specialized imagery and x-rays, to Despoina Kavousanaki (again) for her amazing analytical work. Thank you to Jonathan Moore for reviewing and editing this article, to Matthew Betts for sharing information about *Terror*'s configuration, most importantly his interpretation of 1845 *Terror*'s lower deck plans. Finally, a special thanks to material culture specialists Charles Bradley and Phil Dunning for so generously sharing some of their immense knowledge.

References

BEATTIE, OWEN, AND JOHN GEIGER
1988   *Frozen in Time: Unlocking the Secrets of the Franklin Expedition*. Western Producers Prairie Books, Saskatoon, Saskatchewan.

BETTS, MATTHEW
2016   *Terror* 1845 Lower Deck Plans with Furniture. CAD tracing. Ottawa, Ontario.

CARNEY, PETER
2016   Roll Call of the Doomed. <https://ErebusandTerrorfiles.blogspot.com/2016/03/roll-call-of-doomed.html>. In *Erebus* and *Terror* Files, 18 March 2016 (posted date).

CYRIAX, RICHARD J.
1939   *Sir John Franklin's Last Arctic Expedition: A Chapter in the History of the Royal Navy*. Methuen & Co., London, UK. Reprinted 1997 by The Arctic Press, Plaistow, United Kingdom.

DAGNEAU, CHARLES, AND JONATHAN MOORE
2017   HMS *Terror* Archeological Survey April 2017. Wrecks of HMS *Erebus* and HMS *Terror* National Historic Site of Canada. Underwater Archaeology Team, Parks Canada, Ottawa, Ontario.

ELKIN, DOLORES, CRISTIAN MURRAY, RICARDO BASTIDA, MÓNICA GROSSO, AMARU ARGÜESO, DAMIÁN VAINSTUB, CHRIS UNDERWOOD, AND NICOLÁS CIARLO
2011   *El Naufragio de La HMS Swift - 1770 - Arqueologia Maritima En La Patagonia*. Vazquez Mazzini, Buenos Aires, Argentina.

FAIRHOLME, JAMES WALKER
1845a   Letter to His Father, 1 June 1845. R14108-0-9-E (MG24-H18). Fairholme Papers fonds, Library and Archives Canada, Ottawa, Ontario.

1845b   Letter to His Father, 29 May 1845. R14108-0-9-E (MG24-H18). Fairholme Papers fonds, Library and Archives Canada, Ottawa, Ontario.

FITZJAMES, JAMES
1845a   Letter to Coningham, 16 June 1845. MS 248/380. GB 15 James Fitzjames collection, Scott Polar Research Institute, University of Cambridge, Cambridge, United Kingdom.

1845b   Letter to Coningham, 10 June 1845. MS 248/380. GB 15 James Fitzjames collection, Scott Polar Research Institute, University of Cambridge, Cambridge, United Kingdom.

GODDEN, GEOFFREY A.
1991   *Encyclopaedia of British Pottery and Porcelain Marks*. Barrie and Jenkins, London, United Kingdom.

HALL, CHARLES FRANCIS
1879   *Narrative of the Second Arctic Expedition Made by Charles F. Hall: His Voyage to Repulse Bay, Sledge Journeys to the Straights of Fury and Hecla and to King William's Land, and Residence Among the Eskimos During the Years 1864-'69*. J. E. Nourse, editor, Government Printing Office, Washington, DC.

ILLUSTRATED LONDON NEWS
1845a   Commander Fitzjames' Cabin. *Illustrated London News,* 24 May, London, United Kingdom.

1845b   Captain John Franklin' Cabin. *Illustrated London News,* 24 May, London, United Kingdom.

KEITH, DARREN, AND LOUIE KAMOOKAK
1999   Franklin Oral History Project October 12–19, 1998. Underwater Archaeology Service, Parks Canada, Ottawa, Ontario.

LLOYD-JONES, R.
2004   The Royal Marines on Franklin's Last Expedition. *Polar Record* 40(4):319–326.

May, William E., William Y. Carman, and John Tanner
1974   *Badges and Insignia of the British Armed Services.* Adam & Charles Black, London, United Kingdom.

McClintock, Francis Leopold
1860   *The Voyage of the Fox in the Arctic Seas. A Narrative of the Discovery of the Fate of Sir John Franklin and His Companions.* Ticknor and Fields, Boston, Massachusetts.

McGrath, John, and Mark Barton
2013   *British Naval Swords & Swordsmanship.* Seaforth Publishing, Barnsley, United Kingdom.

Millar, Keith, Adrian W. Bowman, and William Battersby
2013   A Re-Analysis of the Supposed Role of Lead Poisoning in Sir John Franklin's Last Expedition, 1845-1848. *Polar Record* 51(3):224–238.

Millar, Keith, Adrian W. Bowman, William Battersby, and Richard R. Welbury
2016   The Health of Nine Royal Naval Arctic Crews, 1848 to 1854: Implications for the Lost Franklin Expedition. *Polar Record* 42(4):423–441.

Miller, Amy
2007   *Dressed to Kill: British Naval Uniform, Masculinity and Contemporary Fashions, 1748-1857.* National Maritime Museum, Greenwich, United Kingdom.

Moore, Jonathan
2015   Inuit Qaujimajatuqangit at Its Best - Finding the Lost Franklin Expedition Ship HMS *Erebus*. In *The Land Is Our Teacher: Reflections and Stories on Working with Aboriginal Knowledge Holders to Manage Parks Canada's Heritage Places,* Parks Canada, Editor, pp. 21–24. Parks Canada, Gatineau, Québec.

Moore, Jonathan, Charles Dagneau, Marc-André Bernier, Ryan Harris, Thierry Boyer, Filippo Ronca, Brandy Lockhart, and Joe Boucher
2017   HMS *Erebus* Underwater Archaeological Surveys 2015 and 2016. Wrecks of HMS *Erebus* and HMS *Terror* National Historic Site of Canada. Underwater Archaeology Team, Parks Canada, Ottawa, Ontario.

Muster Book of Her Majesty's Ship '*Erebus*'
1845   Muster Book of Her Majesty's Ship '*Erebus*', Commencing 3 March, Ending 19 May 1845. The National Archives of the United Kingdom, ADM 38/672, Kew, United Kingdom.

Muster Book of Her Majesty's Ship '*Terror*'
1845   Muster Book of Her Majesty's Ship '*Terror*', Commencing 3 March, Ending 17 May 1845. The National Archives of the United Kingdom, ADM 38/1962, Kew, United Kingdom.

National Maritime Museum [NMM]
1839   *Terror* and *Erebus*, Plan of Lower Deck. (as Fitted). Admiralty Collection (Ship Plans), NPC3125 (J8650), National Maritime Museum, Greenwich, United Kingdom.

1847   Portrait Photographs of the Officers of HMS *Erebus* (1826) and the Captain of HMS *Terror* (1812). Polyester negative by Richard Beard (Original daguerreotypes 19 May 1845). National Maritime Museum P4470, Greenwich, United Kingdom.

Park, Robert W., and Douglas R. Stenton
2019   Use Your Best Endeavours to Discover a Sheltered and Safe Harbour. Polar Record. 1-12. <https://Doi.Org/10.1017/S0032247419000573>. Accessed 4 January 2020.

Parkyn, Major H. G.
2014   *Shoulder-Belt Plates and Buttons.* Naval & Military Press, Uckfield, United Kingdom.

Rawlinson, John
2014   *Personal Distinctions. 350 Years of Royal Marines Uniforms and Insignia.* Royal Marines Historical Society Special Publication 41. The Royal Marines Historical Society, Esplanade, United Kingdom.

Ryan, Karen
2017   Remembering the Franklin Expedition — The Lieutenant Fairholme Collection. https://www.historymuseum.ca/blog/remembering-the-franklin-expedition-the-lieutenant-fairholme-collection/. Canadian Museum of History Blog, 15 June 2017 (Posted date).

Schwatka, Frederick
1878-1880   Journal. Miscellaneous Volume 163, Manuscript Collection, G.W. Blunt White Library. Mystic Seaport Museum, Mystic, Connecticut.

Stenton, Douglas R.
2018   Finding the Dead: Bodies, Bones and Burials From the 1845 Franklin Northwest Passage Expedition. *Polar Record* 54(3):197–212.

Stenton, Douglas R., Anne Keenleyside, Stephen Fratpietro, and Robert W. Park
2017   DNA Analysis of Human Skeletal Remains from the 1845 Franklin Expedition. *Journal of Archaeological Science* 16:409–419.

Sussman, Lynne, Charles Bradley, Stephen Davis, Phil Dunning, Gérard Gusset, Catherine Sullivan, Joe Last, and Suzanne Plousos
1994   Material Culture of the Royal Canadian Rifle Regiment: Artefacts Found in the Latrine at Fort Wellington, Prescott. Microfiche Report Series No 529. Parks Canada, Ottawa, Ontario.

WALPOLE, GARTH
2017 *Relics of the Franklin Expedition : Discovering Artifacts from the Doomed Arctic Voyage of 1845.* Russell Potter, editor, McFarland & Co, Jefferson, North Carolina.

2011 *The Search for, and an Analysis of, the Relics of the Franklin Expedition 1848-1880.* Undergraduate thesis, Bangor University, Bangor, United Kingdom.

WOODMAN, DAVID C.
1991 *Unravelling the Franklin Mystery: Inuit Testimony.* McGill-Queen's University Press, Montréal, Québec.

. . . .

Charles Dagneau
Underwater Archaeology Team
Parks Canada Agency
1800 Walkley Rd.
Ottawa (Ontario), K1H 8K3, Canada

A Personal Snapshot: An Abridged Comparative Analysis of the Emanuel Point, Padre Island, and *Santa Clara* Shipwrecks (1554-1564)

Brandon L. Herrmann

Surviving artifacts from the crew and passengers' personal possessions on the ships of the 1559-1561 Tristán de Luna y Arellano expedition assisted in developing a comprehensive analysis of material culture. A cross-comparison analysis focused on the Emanuel Point (1559) shipwrecks, as well as the contemporaneous Padre Island (1554) and Santa Clara *(1564) wrecks through the study of iconography, medical equipment, and navigational tools. Ultimately, conclusions gathered through intense study of personal possessions such as scale weights will help further contribute to a comprehensive understanding of the average seaman and his material identity among fellow crew members aboard sixteenth-century vessels.*

Introduction

The analysis of surviving personal possessions from the crew and passengers on the ships of the Tristán de Luna y Arellano expedition of 1559-1561 draws the primary focus in this comprehensive study of material culture. A focus centered on the extensive array of artifact types found on the Emanuel Point I, II, and III (1559) shipwreck collection housed by the University of West Florida in Pensacola, Florida. Next, to better illustrate the sixteenth century, the research expanded to incorporate the Padre Island (1554) shipwrecks of Texas (*Santa María de Yciar*, *Espíritu Santo*, and *San Esteban*) and the *Santa Clara* (1564), formerly known as the St. Johns Bahamas wreck. Overall, this established a 10-year research baseline between 1554 and 1564. The following analysis of these seven shipwrecks will proceed in chronological order.

The Sunken Padre Island Fleet

The earliest group of shipwrecks in the study were the Padre Island shipwrecks: *Santa María de Yciar*, *Espíritu Santo*, and *San Esteban*, which set sail on 4 November 1552, within a fleet of fifty-four vessels under Captain-General Bartolomé Carreño from Barrameda, Spain (Arnold and Weddle 1978:5). This expedition was a cursed journey from the start, as the Padre Island fleet experienced numerous stretches of foul weather and multiple disasters that resulted in the loss of several vessels. The only glimmer of hope for this journey was the flagship of the fleet, *San Andrés*, which became separated from the other vessels throughout the bad weather and was able to make it to Havana. Once there, all the passengers and cargo boarded another vessel on its way to Spain. Their luck was sadly not transferred to the *San Esteban*, *Espíritu Santo*, and *Santa María de Yciar*, which after leaving the port at Veracruz, ran aground on 29 April 1554, on Padre Island. An event precipitated by a massive storm that blew all three remaining vessels across the Gulf of Mexico from the coast of Cuba (Arnold and Weddle 1978:35-36). At the time, this was the greatest disaster ever to befall the Spanish fleet in the New World. A fleet laden with cargo bound for home and the survivors of the wrecks both passengers and crew left to die of want for food and water and attacked by natives, as they traveled along the shore in an attempt to walk back to the port of Veracruz (Arnold and Weddle 1978:37). This historical background provided a brief window into the Padre Island shipwrecks themselves, but what about the artifacts and the museum that houses them?

The Corpus Christi Museum of Science and History

In pursuit of learning more about the Padre Island Fleet and its collection of artifacts, a grant was obtained in 2018 through the University of West Florida Archaeology Institute to perform research at the Corpus Christi Museum of Science and History in Corpus Christi, Texas. The focus of the research narrowed from all three 1554 shipwrecks to the *San Esteban* and *Espíritu Santo*, as the Port Mansfield Channel dredging project so heavily damaged the *Santa María de Yciar* in the 1950s that any remaining artifacts were of little help to the overall research goal (Gearhart II et al. 1990). Research at the museum encompassed viewing the entire history of the collection via card catalogs and microfiche to get the full scope of their holdings in terms of personal possessions for future research. This task was tedious for sure, but the analysis of these new wrecks provided a plethora of artifacts to compare, such as astrolabes and enema syringes.

The Santa Clara

Next, the youngest shipwreck researched in the study was *Santa Clara*. It set sail on 9 November 1563, with the Captain-General Pedro Menéndez de Avilés of the Indies fleet at the helm and the interim viceroy Lope García de Castro on board as a passenger on their way to the New World (Malcom 2017:329). However, they soon had to turn back as inclement weather struck. They took on substantial damage, barely making it back to port. Nevertheless, a few months later, they set sail again under Pedro Menéndez's lieutenant Esteban de las Alas, who successfully sailed them to Panama, where they made a note of trading 100% of items on the ship (Las Alas 1564). The ship then stayed in Panama for a few months before moving on to Cartagena in search of more supplies. Although, on finding them scarce, they decided to make their way to Havana at the height of hurricane season no less, only to find it be inaccessible because of rough weather. As a result, they decided to try and return to Spain, only to strike a reef (*El Mime*) in the Bahama Channel on 6 October 1564. This incident forced them to abandon ship, taking only the passengers, crew, and what they could carry in the way of their Peruvian silver cargo (Las Alas 1564). The *Santa Clara* shipwreck housed numerous artifacts, such as straight pins and hand tools, which led to further research in the Florida Keys.

The Mel Fisher Maritime Heritage Museum

Another grant in 2019, from the Pensacola Archaeological Society, allowed access to the Mel Fisher Maritime Museum that houses the 1564 *Santa Clara* collection in Key West, Florida. A diverse collection of artifacts viewable from the ongoing conservation of the shipwreck included crossbows, straight pins, decorative fasteners, and even a pair of scissors. On the other hand, access to the *Santa Clara* three-dimensional database introduced artifacts that could be viewed remotely at any time in the future for additional research on everything from cannonballs to olive jar sherds. Finally, Corey Malcom, one of the original investigators of the wreck and the local expert on nautical history, provided first-hand accounts on its discovery and how he identified the wreck, but also what artifacts stood out as ideal candidates to compare with the Padre Island and Emanuel Point wrecks (Corey Malcom 2018, pers. comm.).

Florida's Lost Expedition

Tristán de Luna y Arellano and his fleet set sail from Veracruz, Mexico, on 11 June 1559, with 1,500 colonists and an ambition to finally settle what was then known as *La Florida* (Smith 2018:34). This objective assisted in establishing a settlement wrought from experience gained through numerous failures of previous Spanish expeditions to the northern coast of the Gulf of Mexico. Nonetheless, these past failures allowed Luna's colonists to be aware of the dangers that came with past *entradas* (expeditions) relying on taking food from natives either through chance or barter. To avoid this, Luna had bolstered his stores to include "more than a million pounds of solid food, including more than 600,000 pounds of corn, 300,000 pounds of hardtack, 130,000 pounds of beef, as well as beans, wheat flour, rice, chickpeas, pork, fish, cheese, and salt, and 8,300 gallons of olive oil, wine, and vinegar" (Worth and Bratten 2014). Hence, this expedition was a colonial undertaking of both vast expenditure and grand proportions, as it was unlike any carried out by the Spanish in *La Florida* and harkened back to the voyage of Christopher Columbus. Finally, Spanish colonists from Veracruz, Mexico, under the leadership of Tristán de Luna y Arellano, arrived at Pensacola Bay after a nine-week voyage in August 1559 (Priestley 1928:211-213).

The Emanuel Point Shipwrecks

The last collection in the study was the Emanuel Point I, II, and III shipwrecks, as they were the inspiration for this research and artifactually the base on to which to compare the Padre Island and *Santa Clara* shipwrecks. The collection is currently housed in Pensacola, Florida, home to the University of West Florida and the site of the Tristán de Luna y Arellano expedition of 1559-1561. A unique site further aided by the three Emanuel Point shipwrecks from the expedition found right offshore. Hence, both these sites combine to form the earliest multi-year European colonial settlement ever archaeologically identified in the continental United States.

Therefore, to ascertain more about people on this expedition and their comparative qualities to the personal possessions on all seven shipwrecks, the study first examined three specific classification groups: iconography, medical equipment, and navigational tools. This classification utilized the archaeological sample, as opposed to starting with a document-based holistic overview of "personal items" and working one's way out to classifications based on all personal possessions ever found on all sixteenth-century shipwrecks. Additionally, analysis of the collections examined artifacts of unique circumstances such as an ivory manicure set and rosary beads, to showcase the wide-ranging personal items one finds on a shipwreck. Overall, this is merely an abridged snapshot into the analysis and thus will focus exclusively on one personal possession, sixteenth-century scale weights.

Scale Weights

The sixteenth-century weights from the University of West Florida collection, shown in Figure 1, are distinctive as they showcase multiple aspects of congruity with both iconography and personal possessions since each was presumably an artifact used by one specific person on the expedition. Specifically, this includes one or more individuals who traveled over on the Emanuel Point I shipwreck for the two weights on either side, as well as another individual who lost the weight in the middle on the Tristán de Luna y Arellano Settlement (8ES1) land site. Together, these weights form an artifactual bridge between the terrestrial and maritime sites. In order to gain a better understanding of these personal possessions, a preliminary analysis of artifact composition using portable x-ray fluorescence, a state-of-the-art tool began.

Portable X-Ray Fluorescence

Under the supervision of Dr. John Worth from the University of West Florida, a portable x-ray fluorescence (pXRF) machine seemed the best way to accomplish a preliminary analysis of artifact composition. Based on Dr. Worth's knowledge of using the pXRF machine on other metal artifacts from both the Emanuel Point shipwrecks and the Tristán de Luna y Arellano Settlement, we were able to determine the composition of the weights. A task we accomplished by using a non-destructive diagnostic technique to determine the elemental composition of the materials within the weights. Therefore, pXRF analysis determines the interaction of a sample by measuring the photon energy displacement signature given off by the weight when it is excited by the primary x-ray source, and an electron breaks off to be picked up by the scanner and provides a reading of, for instance, brass (Shackley 2011). Hence, a scatter plot diagram created with three distinct shapes: circles for Emanuel Point I (EPI) brass, diamonds for the Tristán de Luna y Arellano Settlement (8ES1) brass, and triangles for 8ES1 bronze. The pXRF machine then used zinc and tin as baselines for detecting elemental similarities in metal composition for comparative analysis of both EPI brass weights (01,485 and 02,158) to the 8ES1 bronze circular weight, and 8ES1 brass objects.

The scatter plot diagram depicted in Figure 2 shows the resulting comparison of all three weights to the Tristán de Luna y Arellano Settlement (8ES1) brass using the portable x-ray fluorescence machine. Additionally, readings from the two Emanuel Point I (EPI) brass weights (01,485 and 02,158) are circles and showcase a high level of zinc, but a low level of tin. Next, diamonds depict several 8ES1 brass objects with both low levels of zinc and tin. Finally, triangles indicate a single circular 8ES1 bronze weight with high levels of tin and low levels of zinc.

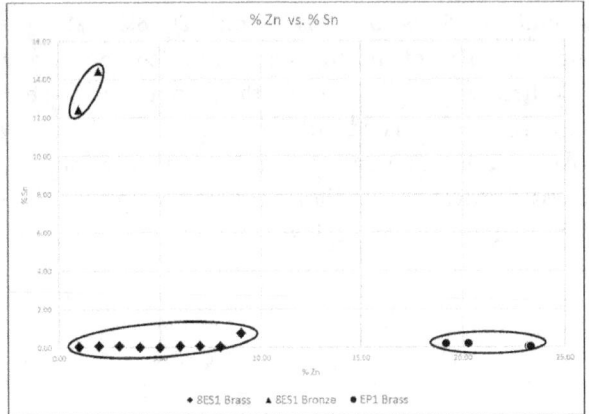

Figure 2: Portable X-ray Fluorescence Scatter Plot Diagram of Comparative Analysis between 8ES1 and Emanuel Point I Brass / Bronze Artifacts (Scatter Plot Diagram by Dr. John E. Worth and Brandon L. Herrmann, 2019).

Figure 1: Emanuel Point I and 8ES1 Scale Weights (Image by Brandon L. Herrmann, 2019).

The main takeaway from the results on the scatter plot diagram is that the two brass weights from the Emanuel Point I shipwreck have higher proportions of zinc than both the circular weight from the Tristán de Luna y Arellano Settlement land site and all the 8ES1 brass objects tested. Likewise, neither of the two Emanuel Point I weights or the 8ES1 brass objects have enough tin to be bronze, as previously thought. There is a clear distinction between the 8ES1 circular bronze weight, and the two brass weights found on the Emanuel Point I shipwreck. To learn more about the origins of the wreck weights in addition to metal composition, research needed to delve deeper into the study of the iconographic figures stamped on the front of both weights.

Religious Iconography

The two weights from the Emanuel Point I shipwreck depict common motifs from the sixteenth century. Hence, the next step was to take a closer look at the religious iconography initially described to the weights by the Florida Department of State, Division of Historical Resources in the 1990s (Smith 2018:199). The artifact on the left of Figure 3 is a rectangular-shaped brass object (field specimen 02,158) with faceted sides and two markings stamped on it, the fleur-de-lis and the other resembling what appears to be a starburst or dancing figure.

Additionally, on the right of Figure 3 is a six-sided brass object (field specimen 01,485) with a small rampant lion in the bottom right, an unidentified image on the bottom left, and a cross in the center surrounded by what appears to be a looped circle and another rope-like circle beyond that (Smith 2018:198-199). A fair assessment of the artifacts was to describe them as "apothecary" weights due to their contextually being nothing else associated with them on the wreck, such as balance scales. However, through more recent analysis, it was discovered that they were scale weights used in conjunction with gold coins.

This determination came after taking a closer look at the iconographic description provided by the Florida Department of State, Division of Historical Resources for the "apothecary" weights in conjunction with the new photographs in Figure 1. At first, in studying the iconographic depictions on the weights, it appeared that they were the same as those described in the conservation process of the late 1990s. On a second look at field specimen 01,485, a lowercase italicized "h" was noted in the bottom center portion of the scale weight, which led to the reign of a king named "Henry" from the sixteenth century, as linked with the Latin cross in the center and the 1559 Emanuel Point I shipwreck. However, this still did not explain the "rampant lion" on the right side of the coin, or after closer observation, the fleur-de-lis on the left side. That is until the discovery of a common misconception for heraldry during the sixteenth century that portrayed the passant leopard as a rampant lion. New information that then refined the search to a time when both England (passant leopard) and France (fleur-de-lis) appeared in conjunction with a Latin cross, thus placing it firmly under the rule of King Henry VI of England (North 2018).

Salut D'or

The discovery of a passant leopard led to only one inevitable conclusion, that field specimen 01,485 was a scale weight for a gold salut d'or from 1422-1453! The salut d'or coin itself is depicted in Figure 4, showcasing the reverse side of the coin as the same found on the scale weight with a Latin cross above a lowercase italicized "h," a fleur-de-lis, and passant leopard to either side within the ten tressure of arches. In contrast, the obverse depicts Mary standing behind the coat of arms of France facing the Archangel Gabriel, who is standing behind the quartered coat of arms of France and England, handing her a scroll (Gardiner and Allen 2005:260). The inscription on the obverse translates into, "Henry,

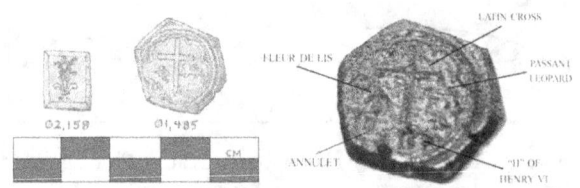

Figure 3: Sketch and Illustrative Diagram of Emanuel Point I Scale Weights (Sketch and Illustrative Diagram by Brandon L. Herrmann, 2020).

Figure 4: Henry VI Salut D'Or Coin (1422-1453) (Image by Brandon L. Herrmann, 2019).

by the grace of God king of France and England" (Friedberg and Friedberg 2003:173). Additionally, coins at this time bore no physical date, distinguished only by various privy marks, such as the annulet or small circle on the bottom left portion of the scale weight, which indicated it was Henry VI's coinage from 1422-1427 (North 2018).

Furthermore, after extensive archival and comparative research of field specimen 02,158, there are currently no other known examples. However, in researching scale weights and their coin counterparts, the closest representation seems to be an ecu d'or au soleil. A coin minted under the reign of Louis XII from 1498-1515 because of its close approximation in time to the salut d'or scale weight (01,485) and the prominent six-sided sunburst above a fleur-de-lis on the obverse side of the coin (Friedberg and Friedberg 2003:190-192). In conclusion, this places field specimen 01,485, or the salut d'or brass scale weight, 132-137 years earlier than the Emanuel Point I shipwreck of 1559 itself and replaces the Henry IV of Castile and León blanca from 1471-1474 to make it the oldest artifact to date found on the wreck.

Conclusion

This research has the potential to form a connection that will further tie artifacts from these shipwrecks found in the New World to their artisans and places of manufacture throughout the Old World. A connection based on introspection of material traces left behind on the Emanuel Point (1559), Padre Island (1554), and *Santa Clara* (1564) shipwrecks, as to better link the person with the artifact using state-of-the-art techniques like the portable x-ray fluorescence machine. Moreover, as the study continues, it will delve further into analyzing the assortment of personal possessions found on the seven shipwrecks, but also broader categories of iconography, medical equipment, and navigational tools. Finally, conclusions gathered through intense study of personal possessions, such as scale weights, will help further contribute to a comprehensive understanding of the average seaman and his material identity among fellow crew members aboard sixteenth-century vessels.

References

ARNOLD III, J. BARTO, AND ROBERT WEDDLE
1978　*The Nautical Archeology of Padre Island: The Spanish Shipwrecks of 1554.* Texas Antiquities Committee Publication, No. 7, Austin, TX.

FRIEDBERG, ARTHUR L., AND IRA S. FRIEDBERG
2003　*Gold Coins of the World: From Ancient Times to the Present: An Illustrated Standard Catalogue with Valuations,* 7th edition. The Coin and Currency Institute, Inc., Clifton, NJ.

GARDINER, JULIE, AND MICHAEL J. ALLEN (EDITORS)
2005　*Before the Mast: Life and Death Aboard the Mary Rose,* Vol. 4, Archaeology of the Mary Rose. Mary Rose Trust, Portsmouth, UK.

GEARHART II, ROBERT L., STEVEN D. HOYT, AND CLELL L. BOND
1990　*Remote-Sensing Survey, Diver Verification and Cultural Resource Assessment Port Mansfield Entrance Channel and Vicinity, Willacy County, Texas.* Espey, Huston, & Associates, Inc., Austin, TX.

LAS ALAS, ESTEBAN DE
1564　Letter to Philip II, 5 December. Legajo 36, Archivo General de Simancas, Spain.

MALCOM, COREY
2017　*Solving a Sunken Mystery: The Investigation and Identification of a Sixteenth-Century Shipwreck.* Doctoral dissertation, Department of Music, Humanities, and Media, University of Huddersfield, UK.

NORTH, JEFFREY J.
2018　*English Hammered Coinage, Edward I to Charles II: 1272-1662.* Vol. 2. Spink Books, London, UK.

PRIESTLEY, HERBERT INGRAM (EDITOR)
1928　*The Luna Papers, 1559-1561.* Vol. 1. Florida State Historical Society, Deland, FL.

SHACKLEY, M. STEVEN (EDITOR)
2011　*X-Ray Fluorescence Spectrometry (XRF) in Geoarchaeology.* Springer, New York, NY.

SMITH, ROGER C. (EDITOR)
2018　*Florida's Lost Galleon.* University Press of Florida. Gainesville, FL.

WORTH, JOHN E., AND JOHN R. BRATTEN
2014　The Materials of Colonization: Archaeological and Documentary Traces of Tristán de Luna's Colonial Fleet. Paper presented at the 79th Annual Meeting of the Society for American Archaeology, Austin, TX.

∙ ∙ ∙ ∙ ∙ ∙ ∙ ∙ ∙ ∙ ∙ ∙ ∙ ∙ ∙ ∙

Brandon L. Herrmann
Historical Archaeology Graduate Student
University of West Florida
201 Freedom Lane,
Waterville, OH 43566

Aviators Down! Tuskegee Airmen in Michigan

Wayne R. Lusardi

During World War II, Michigan was selected by the U.S. Army Air Corps for advanced training of African-American graduates of the Tuskegee flight program. Although many Tuskegee aircraft were involved in accidents, the material remains were almost always recovered, leaving little, if any, trace of the resultant disaster. Aircraft that went missing are a notable exception. Two airplanes, both Bell P-39Q Airacobras, have been discovered in the Great Lakes. At least three additional aircraft flown by Tuskegee Airmen remain to be discovered in Lake Huron. Ongoing efforts are being made to locate, document and preserve Tuskegee aircraft in Michigan waters.

Aviation Archaeological Potential in Michigan

More than 7,100 aircraft were lost and 15,530 U.S. Army servicemen killed in aviation training accidents on American soil during World War II (Mireles 2006). Nearly 200 military aircraft were lost in the Great Lakes during the war. The vast majority of accidents occurred in lower Lake Michigan where U.S. Navy aviators qualified to take off and land on aircraft carriers (Somers 2003). Norwegian, British and Royal Canadian Air Force planes and flight crews were also lost during training exercises over Canadian waters. U.S. Army pilots and aircraft went down in Lake St. Clair and Lake Huron, some flown by Free French aviators training in the United States, others flown by Tuskegee Airmen.

The potential for Tuskegee Airmen-related archaeological sites worldwide is very low. Outside of Tuskegee Army Airfield in Alabama, very few places where Tuskegee Airmen trained, fought or occupied are conducive for archaeological research. Although many Tuskegee aircraft were involved in accidents that resulted in loss of the pilot and airframe, the material remains were almost always recovered, leaving little, if any, trace of the resultant disaster. Aircraft that went missing are a notable exception. Two airplanes, both Bell P-39Q Airacobras, were recently discovered in Michigan waters. Both were lost in training accidents and both were hidden beneath the water for many decades. At least three additional aircraft flown by Tuskegee Airmen remain missing in Lake Huron.

Tuskegee Airmen in Michigan

President Franklin D. Roosevelt began preparing the United States for war after Germany's invasion of Poland in September 1939. The President's advisors urged him to increase the production of arms and aircraft, and to reinstate the draft. As part of this preparation, the Civil Aeronautics Authority organized a civilian pilot training program (CPTP) throughout the United States. African-American colleges, including Tuskegee Institute in Alabama, were encouraged to participate, and many established CPTPs to teach young men and woman how to fly airplanes. With increasing political and social pressure, the United States Army reluctantly agreed to allow African-Americans to enter the Army Air Corps, though on a segregated basis (Francis 1988:5-14).

On 21 March 1941, the United States War Department announced the creation of the 99th Fighter Squadron, the first African-American pilots to fly for the United States military (McKissack and McKissack 1995:54-55). The 99th Fighter Squadron remained at Tuskegee adding pilots to its ranks until April 1943 when it deployed to North Africa. Pursuit or fighter pilots of the 100th, 301st and 302nd Fighter Squadrons, collectively under the 332nd Fighter Group, earned their wings at Tuskegee, but received their advanced training in Michigan starting in March 1943. Weather and geographical conditions that approximated what aviators could expect to encounter in Europe, encouraged the military to use airfields at Selfridge northeast of Detroit, and at Camp Skeel near Oscoda (Homan and Reilly 2008:69; Lusardi 2014:7; Maurer 1982:366, 493-494).

Beginning in September 1943, the primary aircraft used by Tuskegee Airmen over Michigan was the P-39Q Airacobra. Manufactured by Bell Aircraft Corporation of Buffalo, New York, the Airacobra was 30 feet 2 inches in length, 12 feet 5 inches in height, and had a wingspan of 34 feet. The single seat airplane had a range of 650 miles, could reach speeds of 385 mph, and could climb to 35,000 feet (Angelucci and Matricardi 1977:27; Munson 1985:59). The Airacobra was armed with machine guns in the wings and forward fuselage, and a cannon that fired through the propeller hub. Airacobras were the first aircraft in the U.S. arsenal equipped with tricycle landing gears. These aircraft were used throughout World War II to attack armored vehicles, infantry, motorized columns, locomotives and tanks (Caidin 1944).

Unfortunately, dozens of training accidents occurred resulting in the loss of both aircraft and crewmen. Six pilots of the 332nd Fighter Group lost their lives while training over water in Michigan, and nine pilots were lost in the state as a result of land crashes or mid-air collisions. One of these pilots, Frank Herman Moody, was born at Castle, Oklahoma on 18 December 1921. He graduated in Class 44-B-SE at Tuskegee on 8 February 1944, and was commissioned a 2nd Lieutenant in the U.S. Army Air Corps. Following graduation, Lt. Moody was transferred to Selfridge Field, Michigan. On 11 April 1944, Lt. Moody's Bell P-39Q Airacobra (42-21226) was part of a four-ship flight from Selfridge Field on a strafing exercise over lower Lake Huron. His airplane crashed in the lake 7 miles north of Port Huron, and Lt. Moody was killed instantly. Several months later his body came ashore near the mouth of the St. Clair River. According to investigators:

> "The formation had just flown up to the gunnery range was in level flight approximately 50 to 100 feet above the water, flying abreast with the flight leader slightly ahead, when the accident occurred. Lt. Moody had just fired two bursts into the water when small pieces were seen coming from the front right side of his ship. According to the testimony of witnesses, Lt. Moody's ship gave off a trail of black smoke, raised its nose slightly, but then cart-wheeled into the lake" (Mireles 2006:750).

On 11 April 2014, David Losinski, a helicopter pilot with the Oakland County Sheriff's Department, and his son Drew Losinski, discovered the disarticulated remains of a Bell P-39Q Airacobra in Lake Huron. The radio call number on the forward instrument panel (42-21226) confirmed the identity of the aircraft as the one flown by Lt. Frank H. Moody. Lieutenant Moody's aircraft was the second Tuskegee airplane found in Michigan waters. The first wreck site, also a Bell P-39Q Airacobra (42-21249), was piloted by Flight Officer Nathaniel Porter Rayburg. It crashed in Lake St. Clair on 12 December 1943 and was found by divers in 1995 (Stayer and Stayer 2012). Michigan's State Maritime Archaeologist Wayne R. Lusardi (author) visited both aircraft wreck sites, and organized an expedition to document Moody's aircraft in August 2015 (Grulke 2015:1C; Lusardi 2019b:14-15; Patel 2015:20). The project resulted in a site plan (Figure 1), photographs of all visible objects, and detailed drawings of many aircraft components.

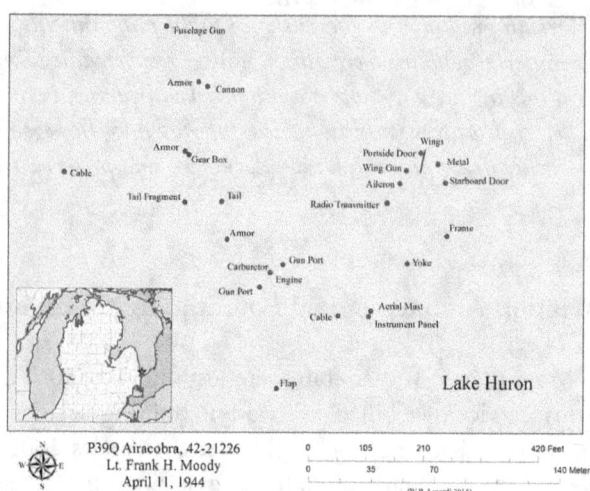

Figure 1: Bell P39Q Airacobra artifact distribution (Map by author, 2015).

Lt. Frank H. Moody's Bell P-39Q Airacobra (42-21226)

Airframe: The Airacobra's wings (Figure 2) are fairly intact, though missing portions of the flaps, ailerons, starboard wing tip, and several access ports. A five-pointed white star in a field of blue, and traces of the red insignia bar remain visible on the upper wing surface. The red, teardrop-shaped plastic running light is positioned near the portside wing tip. An opening for a wing gun port exists though the P-39Q was not equipped with guns mounted in the wings but rather in fairings beneath the wings. Loose fuel cells can be seen through the wing's access ports. Both landing gears are retracted into the wing and the starboard side rubber tire remains intact and appears to be filled with air. The framework between wings holds a collection of aircraft components including a Prestone® coolant radiator top plate, a fragmented aluminum piece of the canopy frame, two oil cooler cylinders, and the forward armored glass windshield. The empennage consists of the port and starboard side horizontal stabilizers, and a section of the vertical stabilizer. The rudder and elevators are missing. The starboard side door is located southeast of the wings and features a roll down window, document case, and manufacturers' placards. The portside door, designated for emergencies only, is located beneath the portside wing.

Power Plant: The Allison V-1710 engine slid forward off its mounts and is separated some distance, but still in line with the carburetor shutter. The engine has fallen over to its portside and is loosely attached to the engine bed framework and central chassis web. Considerable rubber, aluminum and steel sheathed tubing and hosing extend from the stern end of the engine, and two small motors or pumps are still mounted and wired to the complex. A box-shaped aluminum carburetor intake shutter housing remains in place. The engine was mounted behind the pilot; both sections of steel drive shaft required to connect the engine to the forward gearbox, are located near the wings. The gear box, nose cone, and one of three propeller blades are located northwest of the engine.

Armament: A 37mm cannon and three of the four Browning M2 machine guns have been located on the lake bottom. One of the wing guns remains mounted in its aluminum wing fairing. Another gun features a charging handle indicative of the starboard fuselage mounted machine gun. The portside fuselage gun is missing. Several dozen live .50cal. bullets, some individual, others on belts of three to a dozen or more, were found scattered about the site. The turnover bulkhead steel armor plate and several sections of gear box armor are located between the wings and propeller.

Instruments: Two brass levers with ball handles, the throttle control and the mixture control, are loosely held within a steel gearbox located abaft of the framework between wings. The throttle control, the longer of the two levers, also features a microphone control button on the side. The forward instrument panel contains openings for nine gauges (tachometer, coolant, engine gauge unit, oil pressure gauge, carburetor thermometer, fuel, suction gauge, radio clock, unknown) and two pull handles (parking break, unknown) in the lower portion. Two of the lower gauges and both pull handles are missing, one gauge is broken, though the remaining six still have glass faceplates. Seven gauges (altimeter, remote indicating compass, artificial horizon, compass, air speed indicator, vertical speed indicator, and bank and turn indicator), two knobs and the radio call number, 221226, are located in the upper portion of the panel. A radio transmitter case and wooden aerial mast are also present on site.

Preliminary investigation of Bell P-39Q Airacobra 42-21226 has provided valuable information about the airframe, many of its components, and the condition and distribution of aircraft wreckage on the bottom of Lake Huron. Although highly fragmented and dispersed over a considerable area, many of the Airacobra's pieces and parts are very well preserved. Markings and color schemes are evident on several components. The radio call sign attached to the forward instrument panel is clearly readable and served to positively identify Lt. Frank H. Moody's aircraft. Several gauge faceplates are also readable, as are several gauge indicator needles. The cause of the crash of Lt. Moody's Airacobra, however, is not immediately evident in the archaeological assemblage. There is no obvious sign of preexisting structural or mechanical damage. It is currently assumed that all broken parts resulted from the initial impact with water and subsequent site dynamics over the last seven decades. The guns do not seem to be jammed. The

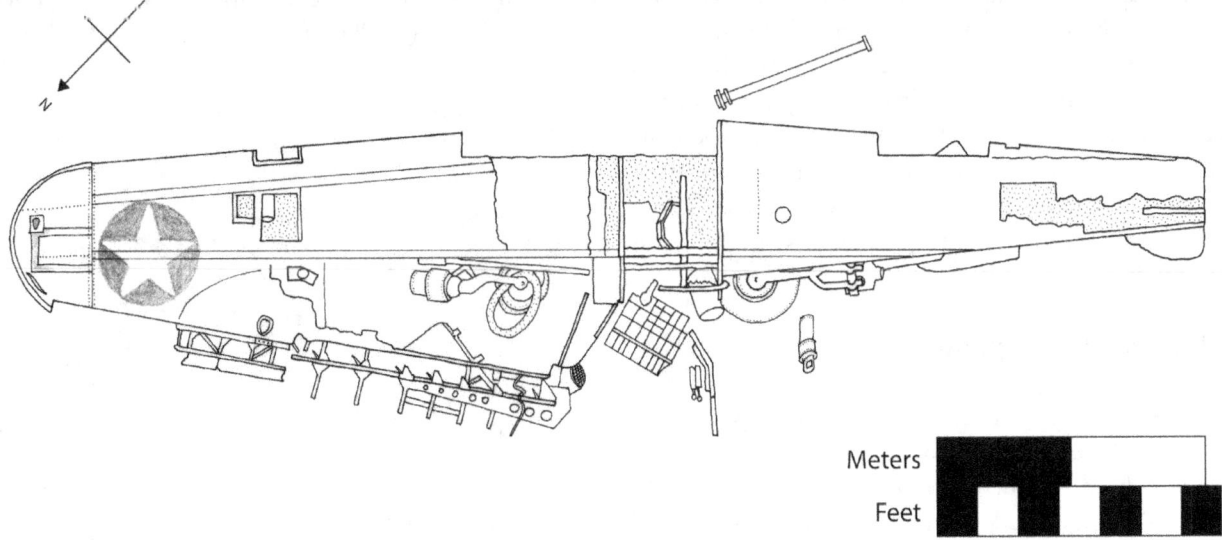

Figure 2: Bell P39Q Airacobra wings (Drawing by author, 2015).

munitions are all live and unfired. There is no evidence of explosion or fire damage.

The distribution of airframe components on the lake bottom is complex and difficult to interpret. An aircraft that was originally only 30 feet 2 inches in length with a wingspan of 34 feet is now spread out over 487,500 square feet. Objects that were closely associated on the airframe before the crash are now located hundreds of feet apart in directions opposite similarly paired materials. Paraphrasing Muckelroy (1978:169), an aircraft flying over water is a complex machine containing a large number of constituent parts arranged in a specific order to ensure airworthiness, ease of handling, and other desirable qualities. From the moment of impact, however, that high degree of organization begins to break down, until the remains are assimilated into the lakebed in some degree of disorder. This constitutes the "wrecking" process. Very often a catastrophic event occurs to an airframe or its propulsion system that causes the accident in the first place, with pieces of the aircraft becoming disarticulate and deposited prior to, and great distances away from, the primary impact area. Site survey and documentation before salvage is the only means of saving valuable information that may otherwise be lost during the recovery process. The survey of an aviation archaeological site is one of the first steps in a long process aimed at fully understanding a historic event and its material remains.

A State of Michigan archaeological recovery permit issued to the National Museum of the Tuskegee Airmen in Detroit authorized documentation, excavation and recovery of the entire P-39 aircraft. In July 2018, seven objects were brought to the surface and transported to Michigan's Maritime Archaeological Conservation Laboratory in Alpena. The artifacts include the starboard door, both sections of steel drive shaft, a wooden aerial mast, the forward instrument panel, a flap actuator, and the armored windshield glass. Additional components will be systematically excavated on an annual basis until the entire aircraft is recovered. Following conservation, the artifacts will be exhibited at the Tuskegee Museum in Detroit.

Additional Investigations

Other military aircraft were lost in Michigan waters. In 2018, NOAA's Office of Ocean Exploration and Research funded a survey to look for additional World War II airplanes in Lake Huron. A geospatial analysis of historical records determined five areas of the lake within and adjacent to Thunder Bay National Marine Sanctuary where military aircraft were lost in training accidents. A Republic P-47D Thunderbolt, piloted by Free French Sgt. Francois Messinger, crashed 17 September 1944 off Sturgeon Point. A Bell P-39Q Airacobra, piloted by Tuskegee Airman 2nd Lt. William E. Hill, was lost 22 November 1943 off Harrisville. A Curtiss P-40F Warhawk, piloted by Tuskegee Airman 2nd Lt. Wilmeth Sidat-Singh, was lost 9 May 1943 off East Tawas. A Vultee BT-13A Valiant, piloted by Tuskegee Airmen 2nd Lt. Nathaniel M. Hill with weather observer 2nd Lt. Luther L. Blakeney on board, crashed off Oscoda on 16 June 1943. Portions of this aircraft were recovered immediately after the accident. Post-war accidents in the area include a Republic P-47D Thunderbolt, piloted by Georgia Air National Guardsman 2nd Lt. Louie A. Mikell, that crashed off Greenbush on 1 June 1948 during the filming of *Fighter Squadron*, a Hollywood production about the war. On 16 March 1957, a U.S. Air Force Lockheed F-94C-1-LO Starfire jet, with pilot 1st Lt. Henry Charles Nicolay and navigator 1st Lt. Harold A. Lewis on board, went missing off Oscoda on a flight from Bunker Hill Air Force Base to Wurstmith Air Force Base in Michigan (Lusardi 2018b).

Five survey areas were defined using ArcGIS and uploaded to HYPACK (Figure 3). The NOAA ship R/V *Storm*, equipped with a Kongsberg Multibeam sonar, a Klein 3000 side scan sonar, and a Geometrics G-882 cesium-vapor magnetometer, were used to conduct the remote sensing survey of Lake Huron off Alcona and Iosco Counties in Michigan over 19 calendar days from 27 June 2018 to 26 September 2018. A total of 583 acoustic and/or magnetic anomalies were recorded during the survey. Of the 92 targets that were ground truth by divers (15.8% of the total), all but two were

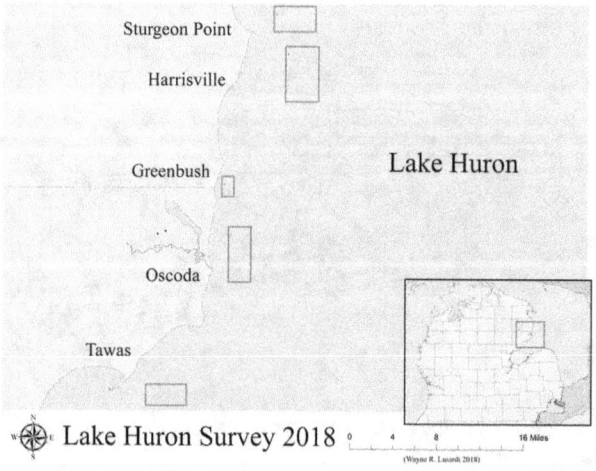

Figure 3: Lake Huron search areas (Map by author, 2018a).

geological features including glacial clay deposits, angular boulders, and bedrock outcrops (Lusardi 2018a; Lusardi 2019a:122).

One acoustic and magnetic anomaly consisted of the ground tackle (anchor, windlass and chain) from a 19th-century vessel. The artifacts were not associated with other wreckage and may not be representative of a shipwreck, but rather a loss of equipment. Another acoustic and magnetic anomaly consisted of a military tow target manufactured in 1956 by Schweizer Aircraft Corporation of Elmira, New York (Figure 4). Positive identification of the Aero X-27A was made following discovery of the aircraft data plate. Targets, like the Aero X-27A, were towed using piano wire several thousand feet behind jets and used for target practice over Lake Huron. The aluminum targets replaced the older style cloth banners used over the lakes beginning in World War I. The Aero X-27A tow target more closely simulated aerial combat and could be landed to assess number of hits. Although the wreckage is broken and largely buried in soft sediments, it retains its original red paint on the fuselage and variable pitch wings.

Additional remote sensing survey of Lake Huron will be conducted in 2021 to complete the five survey areas. All acoustic and magnetic anomalies recorded in 2018 and 2021 will also be investigated to determine whether or not they originated from previously undiscovered World War II aircraft.

The Lake Huron Tuskegee Airmen Project, dubbed *Red Tail 2* by the divers that helped document an Airacobra crash site, was much more than an archaeological investigation of a wrecked aircraft. It was a dive into history – and into a man's life. Lieutenant Frank Herman Moody was tragically killed while training in a Bell P-39Q Airacobra on 11 April 1944. He was only 22 years old. Lieutenant Moody was part of the now famous Tuskegee Experience, often referred to as Red Tails. He was one of less than 1,000 African-American men that were trained to fly Army aircraft during World War II. Lieutenants Frank H. Moody, William E. Hill, Wilmeth Sidat-Singh, Nathaniel M. Hill and Luther L. Blakeney, and Flight Officer Nathaniel P. Rayburg, were preparing to fight for their country; a country that did not want them to fight; a country that considered them physically and mentally incapable of flying airplanes; a country's military that refused to integrate. Tuskegee was designed to segregate. It was a place to keep black men, and women, out of mainstream military service. The Tuskegee Experience was designed to fail. But it did not fail. The Tuskegee Airmen persevered. They overcame unimaginable obstacles. They learned to fly. They became officers and leaders of men. They soared!

References

Angelucci, Enzo and Paolo Matricardi
1977   *World War II Airplanes, Volume 2*. Rand McNally and Company, Chicago, IL.

Caidin, Martin
1944   Air Tech Presents the Bell P-39 Airacobra. *Air Tech* 5.2 (August):17-23, 68.

Francis, Charles E.
1988   *The Tuskegee Airmen: The Men Who Changed a Nation*. Branden Publishing Company, Boston, MA.

Grulke, Nicole
2015   Plunging into History: Team Dives Site of World War II Plane Crash in Lake Huron. *The Alpena News* (19 September):1C.

Homan, Lynn M. and Thomas Reilly
2008   *Black Knights: The Story of the Tuskegee Airmen*. Pelican Publishing Company, Gretna, LA.

Lusardi, Wayne R.
2014   Michigan was Home to Several African-American Air Combat Units. *Voyage to Discovery Newsletter* 1.1 (September):7.

2018a   Aviators Down: Survey Summary. NOAA Ocean Exploration and Research <https://oceanexplorer.noaa.gov/explorations/18aviatorsdown/welcome.html>. Accessed 12 February 2020.

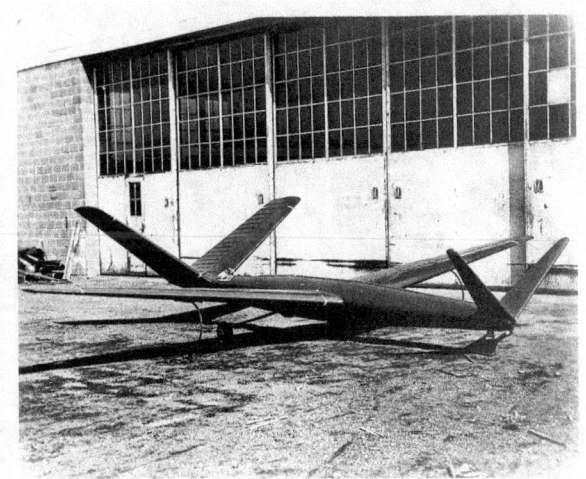

Figure 4: Schweizer Aero X-27A tow target (Schweizer Aircraft Photo Archives).

2018b   World War II Aircraft Lost in the Great Lakes. NOAA Ocean Exploration and Research <https://oceanexplorer.noaa.gov/explorations/18aviatorsdown/history.html>. Accessed 12 February 2020.

2019a   Aviators Down! The Search for Tuskegee and Free French World War II Aircraft in Lake Huron. *New Frontiers in Ocean Exploration*, 32.1, Supplement (March):122.

2019b   Honoring the Tuskegee Airmen. *Earth is Blue* 4 (June):14-15.

MAURER, MAURER
1982   *Combat Squadrons of the Air Force-World War II.* U.S. Government Printing Office, Washington, DC.

MCKISSACK, PATRICIA AND FREDRICK MCKISSACK
1995   *Red-Tail Angels: The Story of the Tuskegee Airmen of World War II.* Walker and Company, New York, NY.

MIRELES, ANTHONY J.
2006   *Fatal Army Air Forces Aviation Accidents in the United States 1941-1945.* McFarland & Company, Inc., Jefferson, NC.

MUCKELROY, KEITH
1978   *Maritime Archaeology.* Cambridge University Press, Cambridge, UK.

MUNSON, KENNETH
1985   *US War Birds from World War I to Vietnam.* New Orchard Editions, Poole, UK.

PATEL, SAMIR S.
2015   Last Flight of a Tuskegee Airman. *Archaeology* 68.6 (November-December):20.

SOMERS, PAUL M.
2003   *Lake Michigan's Aircraft Carriers.* Arcadia Publishing, Charleston, SC.

STAYER, JIM AND PAT STAYER
2012   *Tuskegee Airacobra Down!* Out of the Blue Productions, Lexington, MI.

· · · · · · · · · · · · · · · ·

Wayne R. Lusardi
Michigan State Maritime Archaeologist
Thunder Bay National Marine Sanctuary
500 W. Fletcher Street
Alpena, MI 49707

Mystery Rocket Recovered from Lake Ontario: Avro Arrow or Other Cold War Relic?

Nancy E. Binnie, Erin Gregory

In 2018, a delta winged object was recovered from Lake Ontario, under archaeological permit, by the OEX Recovery Group Incorporated. It was hoped that this was one of nine 1/8th scale Avro Arrow free flight models launched from the Point Petre CARDE firing range in Prince Edward County between 1954-1957 and thought to be resting on the lake bed amid boosters and other vehicles. This object was provisionally identified as a Delta Test Vehicle. This paper details the process of recovering, conserving, and understanding the significance of the DTV and what it could mean for aviation heritage in Canada.

Introduction

On 12 August 2018, a small delta winged test vehicle (DTV) identified as Target 84 was recovered under archaeological permit from Lake Ontario by the OEX Recovery Group for the Canada Aviation and Space Museum (CASM) and the National Air Force Museum of Canada. The Canadian Conservation Institute (CCI) has been working with this team during survey and planning and has carried out the conservation of the object. OEX hoped to recover of one of nine precision 1/8th scale Avro Arrow free flight models (AAFFMs) of the Avro Arrow CF-105 interceptor aircraft produced in Malton, Ontario between 1954 and 1957. However, the object recovered in 2018 was not an AAFFM. Instead, it may be a unique test vehicle from the related Velvet Glove (VG) missile development program, and one of the few objects related to the development of the iconic Canadian CF-105 not held in private or public collections.

Between 1952 and 1957, nine AAFFMs and hundreds of other test vehicles were launched by rocket boosters or ballistic guns from the Point Petre Canadian Armament and Research Development Establishment (CARDE) range. These vehicles carried telemetry equipment that relayed pertinent flight data back to engineers at ground stations at Point Petre and the nearby Picton radar base. Like the delta test vehicle in question (Target 84), having served their purpose while in flight, they were never recovered.

Background

Avro Arrow CF-105 Program

During the peak of the Cold War, the Canadian government initiated a project to design and build an all-weather, supersonic interceptor fighter to replace the Avro CF-100 Canuck for the Royal Canadian Air Force (RCAF). The new aircraft would be capable of carrying guided missiles including the Canadair Velvet Glove, the American-designed AIM-4 Falcon or AIM-7 Sparrow II active radar guidance missiles, or unguided AIR-2A Genie nuclear rockets (Leversedge 2014). The program was in response to the anticipated threat of high-speed, high-altitude nuclear bombing runs launched from the Soviet Union travelling into Canadian airspace from the Arctic. Preliminary studies for this new interceptor began in 1952-1953, wind tunnel testing began along with extensive computer simulation studies, and the first production drawings were issued mid-1954 (Floyd 1958).

Hundreds of test models were produced including 1/120th, 1/30th, and 1/6th scale models fabricated from plastic, aluminum or steel (Valiquette 2011a; Waechter 2017). These were used for aeroballistics and wind tunnel tests at locations in Ontario, Quebec, Virginia, Maryland and New York. At that time, Canada did not have a supersonic wind tunnel (Leversedge 2014) and was limited in the tests they could carry out without one. Eleven 1/8th scale AAFFMs of length 2.79 m, wingspan 1.905 m, and weight about 217 kg were fabricated from magnesium and aluminum alloys. The AAFFMs had no internal engine and were launched using NIKE booster rockets. Nine AAFFMs were launched from the CARDE test range between 14 December 1954 and 10 January 1957, and then the CARDE range was permanently closed. Two others, the 6th and 7th in the series, were launched from the National Advisory Committee on Aeronautics (NACA) Wallops Island test range in Virginia on 9 and 15 May 1956. AAFFMs 1-4 were crude models used to resolve general problems associated with firing procedures and tracking, while AAFFMs 5-11 were accurate scale models used to determine aerodynamic derivatives for structural design improvements for the CF-105 (Valiquette 2011a).

The first completed, full size CF-105 Arrow was rolled out to the public on 4 October 1957. Unfortunately, this event was eclipsed by the launch of Sputnik 1 the same day. Flight-testing of the CF-105 Arrow began on 25 March 1958, and on its third flight, the first Arrow Mk 1 RL 201 flew at Mach 1.7. While still awaiting completion of the Canadian-made Iroquois engine designed for the Arrow, the fighter met most of its performance requirements (CASM 2017). By early 1959, five planes had been produced, a sixth was ready for testing, and another 31 planes were on the production line (RCAF 2018).

Then came Black Friday, 20 February 1959. John Diefenbaker, Prime Minister of Canada, announced the total shut down of the program. Fearing that the technology might fall into enemy hands, the RCAF ordered the disposal of materials relating to the program (Valiquette 2011b). This included destruction of the assembly line, existing airframes, and all plans. Many records survive from this program purely because Canadians ignored the RCAF and Diefenbaker's orders, but all planes were destroyed. The Arrow free flight models, test missiles, and booster rockets fired from the CARDE range lay forgotten and undisturbed on the bottom of Lake Ontario for over 40 years until rival heritage groups began expressing an interest in finding and recovering them.

Velvet Glove Missile Program

The Velvet Glove missile (VGM) was a short-range, semi-active radar homing air-to-air missile designed by the CARDE for use with the CF-100 Canuck and CF-105 Arrow. The missile (Figure 1) was almost the same size as Target 84 (Table 1), about 3 m long, weighted about 200 kg, and was powered by a solid rocket motor (Pickler 1998). A typical wing-mounted configuration had a conical nose cone, four squared mid-body wings, and four smaller offset tail fins used for steering. Quebec's Canadair assumed control of the development

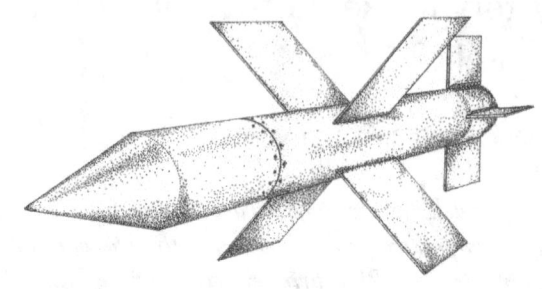

Figure 1: Velvet Glove Missile (Drawing styled after photograph of missile mounted under the wing of an AVRO CF-100 (Pickler 1998).

of this missile in 1951. Between December 1951 and December 1953, 28 missiles were ground fired from the CARDE range (Dugelby 1997). Mid-air launches from a CF-100 Canuck, flying out of nearby RCAF Trenton and tracked by the CARDE range, took place between 1952 to 1954.

Following the 1954 crash of CF-100 RCAF 18117, being used as a VG test platform near Navan, Ontario (Walker 2005), fears of dropping a missile on the inhabitants of Prince Edward County relocated testing in 1955 to CFB Cold Lake. This allowed exclusive use of the CARDE range by Avro and the AAFFM program until its closure in 1957 (Beadle 2002). Westinghouse built the radar guidance unit for the VG, as well as the microwave radar proximity fuse that would fire its 60 pound (27 kg) warhead.

In order to validate range procedures, more than 50 test track vehicles (TTVs) including three identified as 'Delta Test Vehicles' (DTVs) were launched during the AAFFM and VG programs (Taylor 1955; Ewart et. al. 1957; Landry 1954a, 1954b). Tracking of the high-speed targets was carried out by at least four methods: (1) conventional S band tracking radar with mounted cameras to record azimuth, elevation and boresight data; (2) C band Doppler radar; (3) 35 mm Kine theodolite cameras recording at 5 frames per second; and (4) standard FM/FM telemetry (Beadle 2002). The CARDE range operators obtained poor tracking results because of poor equipment siting. Information has not yet been found which specifies the aerodynamic configuration or launch methods for most TTVs. However, it is likely they were fired on a similar trajectory to the AAFFMs within the range boundaries over Lake Ontario. The DTVs were launched using a single Demon rocket booster with 8,000 lbs thrust for 2.8 seconds, compared to the AAFFMs NIKE booster with, typically, 59,000 lbs of thrust for 2.3 to 3.0 seconds. The DTVs contained an internal solid fuel LAP sustainer motor which provided an additional 4,500 lbs of thrust, used to initiate separation from the Demon booster.

Public Archaeology and Search for the AAFFMs

Several times in the last 20 years, CCI has been asked to provide conservation plans for field recovery operations by heritage groups, like Arrow Recovery Canada and the Aerospace Heritage Foundation of Canada, each hoping to find and recover the AAFFM models for public and museum display. In Ontario, the Ministry of Heritage, Sport, Tourism and Culture Industries issues permits for archaeological survey and recovery. The Ministry requires a conservation plan and project funding to be in place prior to recovery, as well as a repository designated to hold and curate the artifacts recovered under permit. During these and other previous surveys, the wreckage of many NIKE and VG booster rockets have been located and viewed by ROVs or divers in the waters south of Prince Edward County.

In 2017, CCI was contacted by Scarlett Janusas Archaeology Inc., the OEX Recovery Group's "Raise the Arrow" team, and the CASM to produce an updated conservation plan prior to the start of survey operations. CCI's archaeological conservators were also asked to carry out the conservation of recovered objects on behalf of the CASM. The OEX Recovery Group funded this current initiative as a Canada 150 collaborative project, supported by a group of Canadian mining companies and several financial institutions (Calder 2018). This group has received the support and assistance of the Royal Canadian Air Force (RCAF), the Royal Canadian Navy and Fleet Diving Unit Atlantic. Underwater survey and diving operations have been carried out by Kraken Robotics Inc., Shark Marine, the Royal Canadian Navy (RCN), and General Diving Contractors. To aid in the search, the RCN provided the survey team with the results of a 2004 sidescan survey undertaken by the HMCS *Glace Bay*, the HMCS *Kingston*, and the Fleet Diving Unit Atlantic (Binnie 2004).

	Target 84	Delta Test Vehicle No. 3 (DTV-3)	Velvet Glove Missile	Avro Arrow Free Flight Models
Designer & fabricator	Unknown, no unique airframe identifier	RCAF	CARDE from 1948; Canadair 1953-1956	Avro Canada Ltd, Milton, Ontario
Purpose	Unknown	Structural design development	Air to air missile development	Structural design development
Launch site	CARDE range	CARDE range	CARDE range; Cold lake	CARDE range
Launch dates	Unknown; before 1957 when range was closed	20-Oct-1954	1952-54 from CARDE range	Between 14 December 1954 and 10 January 1957
Length	About 3.18 m (damaged forebody)	3.18 m	3.25 m	2.79 m
Wingspan design	1.54 m, mid-body delta 70° cutback, aluminum plate	1.54 m, mid-body delta 70° cutback, aluminum plate, bulkhead and stringer construction	About 1 m span, cruciform design with offset mid-body and tail fins	1.905 m, delta 70° cutback
Fuselage diameter and shape	0.254 m, circular	0.254 m, circular	0.25 m, circular	Diameter not specified, rounded rectangular fuselage
Weight	117 kg after conservation	126 kg	144 kg	About 217 kg
Afterbody diameter and tail fin design	0.203 m, 45° delta fins, two control fins and one larger tail fin	0.203 m, 45° delta fins, two control fins and one larger tail fin	Four 90° fins located mid-body, four control fins (smaller than mid-body fins)	45°
Nose cone	30° cone, mild steel	30° cone, mild steel	30° cone	
Interior engine or propulsion system	0.127 m inside diameter/0.133 m outside diameter sustainer rocket motor	0.127 m inside diameter/0.133 m outside diameter liquid ammonium perchlorate (LAP) sustainer rocket motor, 4,500 pounds thrust for 1.55 seconds	32 kg internal sustainer motor, Aerojet solid fuel	No engine, separation from booster rocket achieved by force of drag after launch
Launched by	Unknown booster rocket; sabot mount like DTV-3	Single DEMON booster rocket, 8,000 pounds thrust for 2.8 seconds; sabot mount	Air or rocket launch; 7,600 pounds thrust	Solid fuel NIKE booster rocket, around 59,000 pounds of thrust for 2.3 to 3.0 seconds
Telemetry	Yes – functions unknown; General Communications Company model no. 4	Four channel telemetry signal sent by radio signal to ground station - longitudinal and pitch acceleration, yaw	X-band semi active pulse radar	Up to 16 devices sending out telemetry signals by radio to ground stations; telemetry specifications within each FFM are known
Materials of construction	Aluminum alloys for wings and attachment angles; steel for nose and tail section, small amounts of other materials like wood, rubber, paint	Aluminum alloys for wings, steel for nose and tail section, small amounts of other materials like wood, rubber	Not specified	Magnesium alloys for wings, fins, fuselage castings, ramp, fairings; aluminum alloys for telemetry door, centre and aft door, fuselage duct, upright portion of tail fin, attachment angles; also wood, fiberglass

Table 1: Characteristics of Target 84, DTV-3, VG missile, and AAFFMs.

Wreck Location and Survey Methodology

Target 84 (Borden number AkGg-1) was recovered from Lake Ontario, south-east of the Point Petre CARDE firing range located at the westerly tip of Prince Edward County. The Point Petre range is still in use today as a military transmitter site. It is also the site of a search and rescue helipad.

Kraken deployed its ThunderFish® Autonomous Underwater Vehicle (AUV) with Aquapix® Synthetic Aperture Sonar system from the harbor at the Quintes Isles Campground, just north east of Point Petre or from the workboat *John T. Cooper*. Shark Marine used its "Barracuda" ROV unit, equipped with Looking Forward Sonar and HD video and a Total Navigation System, to ground truth targets from their survey vessel. When no AAFFMs had been located by mid-August 2018, the decision was made to recover Target 84 (Figure 2), a test vehicle of similar size and shape to the AAFFMs and believed to be associated with the AAFFM and VG programs.

In preparation for recovery, three lift cradles were designed and fabricated by Mike Fletcher and Rich Wolters (Detail Steel). Two large (3.1 x 2.1 x 0.1 m) and one smaller stackable cradle were constructed from recycled steel cargo boxes, rated for a half ton load (450 kg). One side of the larger cradles was hinged to form a loading ramp and reinforced corner lift points were installed for rigging attachment. The stacking height could be modified with adjustable extension tubes or wood blocking. The cradles were painted yellow for better visibility underwater and were designed so that they could be used as water-filled holding tanks with pool-liner installed during later conservation work. To prevent loss of fragile elements during lift through the water column, the cradle was lined with heavy duty plastic mesh and fine Nylon window screen. The interior bottom and side ramp were also lined with white ¼-in Coroplast® to prevent the object from being marked by the steel lattice. A cargo net could be rolled in from one side to secure the load.

The week before recovery, the lift cradle was loaded on the self-propelled barge *Wilson T. Cooper* and divers installed a temporary mooring and marker buoy to assist positioning the workboat. Recovery operations were carried out by commercial surface-supply divers, a requirement of the archaeological permit. On the morning of 11 August 2018, the lift cradle was lowered to site and positioned adjacent to the wreckage. Two divers were readily able to lift Target 84 off the lake bottom and into the cradle where it was secured using cargo straps padded out with pieces of open cell polyurethane foam. The excess white Coroplast® around the object was cut away to reduce lift resistance and allow water to drain more efficiently through the bottom of the cradle.

Conservation staff were onboard for the lift operations and were given the opportunity to view the secured load and suggest modifications to padding or rigging prior to lift. No changes were required – the load had been secured exactly as planned. Divers observed the load during the lift to ensure it remained secure. During daytime transit and overnight, the wreckage was covered with wet cotton towels and frequently soaked down with sprinklers. Target 84 and the lift cradle were off loaded by crane onto a flatbed trailer at CFB Trenton the morning of 12 August 2018 and unloaded in the parking lot of the old seaplane terminal for a brief unveiling and public viewing. It was then moved by forklift into the temporary field conservation lab.

In Situ Environment and Structural Observations

The wreckage of Target 84 was found with the fuselage lying horizontal on the lake bottom in an upside-down

Figure 2: Side scan sonar image (upper) and photograph (lower) of Target 84 (Courtesy of Kraken Robotics Systems, Inc.).

orientation (defined as the upper tail fin bracket pointing downwards). Most of the upper surface was coated with a thick layer of biofouling composed of quagga mussels (*Dreissena rostiformis bugensis*) mixed with fine sediment. This layer obscured the details, dimensions and color of the shape which was similar in overall length and delta-wing configuration to that expected for an AAFFM. As characterized elsewhere in Lake Ontario on wreck sites (Binnie 2009), the quagga mussel is better adapted to the deeper cold waters of freshwater lakes than the zebra mussel (*Dreissena polymorpha*).

Under layers of biofouling, upward oriented surfaces retained significant quantities of yellowish-orange paint and grey primer applied to all surfaces, as well as a greenish-grey primer applied along edges and seams. Biofouling was left undisturbed on the surface during recovery to allow for later removal in a more controlled environment. The lower layer of mussels was securely attached to the surface by their proteinaceous byssal threads and could not be removed easily without disrupting paint and corrosion layers. The sediment below was 10 cm or less in depth above a rock surface. The periodic shifting of sediment with current had eroded away most paint off the underside of the wings and fuselage creating an environment unsuitable for colonization by mussels.

Surface damage was revealed after cleaning (Figure 3). The steel nose cone was intact with the outer surface depressed inwards along rivet lines indicating an internal reinforcement structure. The nose cone also had a reinforced circular orifice and bracket offset to one side, possibly for pressure equalization. The aluminum alloy forebody was crumpled, cracked, and bent towards the left (proper) wing; this damage likely caused by high speed impact with the lake surface. The left wing was damaged with losses from the top and bottom surfaces along the leading edge, revealing the interior U-channel and rivet construction. The right wing was essentially intact, except for a small loss at the trailing edge of the wing tip. Both left and right control fins and the larger central tail fin attached to the steel afterbody were missing. Prior to recovery, a bottom search located one control fin (22.3 x 10.2 x 1.0 cm) about 10.3 m away from the main target.

Fuselage wing surface brackets holding the wing in place, fasteners, and interior U-channel were all composed of various aluminum alloys that had corroded differentially. Aluminum alloy brackets holding the three tail fins were still attached to the afterbody, but with some losses and deformations likely caused when the tail fins were removed on impact. The fuselage had two access ports – one centrally located to access the interior telemetry unit just aft of the forebody and another located centrally and offset behind a thermal bulkhead at the leading end of the sustainer motor. The sides of the fuselage were depressed inwards where unsupported by interior reinforcement bands or bulkheads as indicated by rivet lines. The nose cone and afterbody (both iron alloys) were uniformly corroded. The wing surface was highly corroded, with large carbuncular formations and pitting visible when the soft corrosion was disturbed. The forebody and fuselage were free of the carbuncular corrosion seen on the wings.

Sediment, water samples, and biofouling collected from the underwater site the day of recovery were analyzed later in the field lab, at a local environmental testing lab, or at the Canadian Museum of Nature. The sediment slurry from the lake bottom (95% solids) had a pH of 7.3 and 30 ppm chloride. Water had a pH of 7.8, 25 ppm chloride, 120 ppm total hardness as $CaCO_3$, 160 ppm total dissolved solids, 0.4 mg/L total nitrogen, 37,600 µg/L calcium, and 1,865 µg/L potassium. These water parameters are optimal for *Dreissena* colonization.

Conservation

Target 84 was moved into a containment area in the field lab created from pool liner and 10 x 10 cm timbers. This shallow "tank" structure was designed as a quarantine area to contain wastewater, mud and mussels to avoid contamination of the floor drains or environment. Over the course of three days in Trenton, the CCI team carried out photographic documentation, removed sediment and bulk biofouling, and prepared the object for shipping to Ottawa. They also conducted tests to remove the mussel byssus and corrosion using a variety of hand tools and a dry ice abrasive unit. In total, over 15 kg of sediment and mussels were removed from the exterior and, later in Ottawa, another 10 kg of sediment was removed from the interior after the nose section and forebody were removed. This was almost a quarter of the mass of the object after cleaning was completed (117 kg).

At the end of the week, the object was packed and shipped to the CASM restoration hanger for further conservation. A full report on the details of treatment, stabilization, and associated scientific investigations will be presented elsewhere. The main components of this work were: (1) condition assessment; (2) photographic documentation; (3) removal of biofouling and sediment from the exterior including below paint layers that had lifted, with retention of original paint; (4) reduction of exterior corrosion; (5) facing of paint layers to protect them during subsequent treatment; (6) removal of two access ports, removal of the nose cone/forebody section, and extraction telemetry equipment; (7) removal of sediment and water from interior (retained for hazardous waste disposal); (8) cleaning and remediation of telemetry and battery units; (9) desalination in water bath; (10) consolidation of paint; (11) drying; (12) radiography of fuselage in field lab Trenton; (13) radiography of telemetry board at CCI; (14) materials analysis (metals, corrosion, paint, other components); and (14) a structures investigation with technical drawings. After completion of conservation, Target 84 was revealed to the public on Canada Day, 1 July 2019, at the CASM in Ottawa.

The fine particulate sediment which had made its way into the interior through small cracks in the forebody proved to be sufficiently contaminated by heavy metals that it had to be treated as hazardous waste. The sediment was contaminated with cadmium, copper, chromium, lead, nickel, tin, and zinc, while wash water was contaminated with cadmium, manganese and zinc. These substances are thought to have been leached out of the telemetry equipment. While no mercury was detected in the sediment or water, opened battery packs were found to contain free liquid mercury; this was also removed for disposal.

Discussion - Identification of Target 84 Delta Test Vehicle

After the public unveiling in Trenton, RCAF historian Richard Mayne provided copies of four incomplete reports found in the National Research Council Library's special collection in Ottawa (Landry 1954a; 1954b). The reports describe the configuration of three boosted test vehicles, DTV-1, DTV-2 and DTV-3, launched as part of the VG missile development project. No other delta wing test vehicles are known to have been fired from the CARDE range, other than the AAFFMs. These reports also listed the personnel attending the firing trials for DTV-2 and DTV-3. On 20 October 1954, 54 people were present during the firing of DTV-3. Four of these were representatives of A.V. Roe. Two test tracking vehicles (TTVs) were also fired on the same date as DTV-2 (Landry 1954a).

The reports, written by Landry, describe the purpose of DTV-2 and DTV-3 was to determine structural adequacy, launch stability, and characteristics. In addition, DTV-2 would be used to determine the effect of tolerance misalignments on the trajectory, and roll and yaw stability. DTV-3 would be used to verify the method of separation and initiation of the sustainer motor and to determine aerodynamic derivatives as a function of control deflection during supersonic flight. The announcement of firing reports (Landry 1954a, 1954b) include a general description of the test vehicle and defined the responsibilities of CARDE personnel, the Trials Coordinator and Safety Officer, including: (1) airframe design and ground camera operation during firing trials; (2) airframe fabrication; (3) assembly and testing of the telemetering system including antenna, transmitter, power supplies and control systems; (4) inspection and preparation of the booster assembly for launch including installation explosive bolt detonators responsible for the first stage (test vehicle)-second stage (booster) separation; (5) preparation and firing of launcher, and (6) reduction of data received by ground stations.

The two announcements of firing reports also include the same generic test vehicle drawings (Figure 4) similar in dimension to Target 84, and both refer to CARDE drawings A/54051401/E and A/54051549/E for test

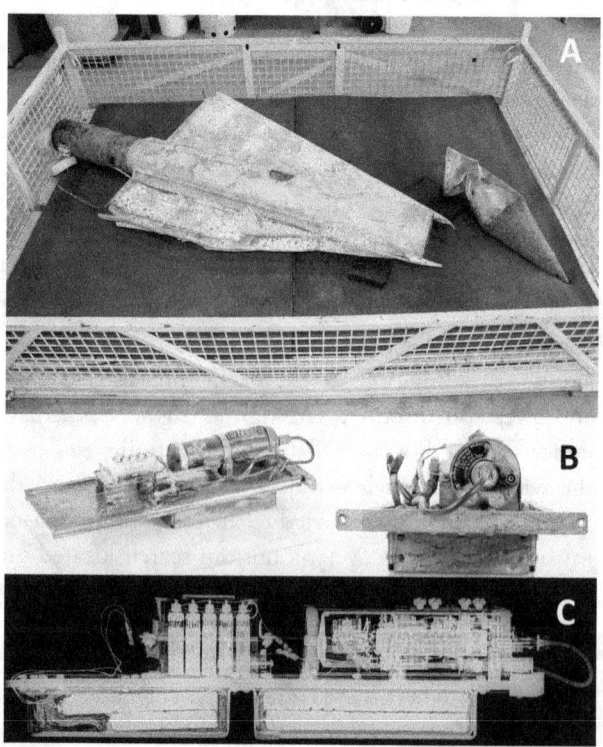

Figure 3: Target 84 Delta wing test vehicle after treatment (A), telemetry unit during treatment (B), and radiograph (C).

vehicle and booster assembly, respectively. The latter two drawings have yet to be located in any archival collection. Many details from the structural descriptions for the DTVs correlate closely to those of Target 84 (Table 1). DTV-1 and DTV-2 had two large 45° delta tail fins top and bottom with two smaller fixed 45° delta control fins in plane with the wings, while DTV-3 had only one top large fin with two control fins. The wings of DTV-1 and DTV-2 were built up by bonding ¼ in aluminum plate onto plywood sheet, with leading and trailing edges of the wings formed by strips of machined aluminum bolted to the edges of the ¼ inch plate. Wing structure for DTV-3 is not described in the general description of test vehicle.

Target 84 had two control fins and only one tail fin, and the wings were constructed from aluminum plate riveted to U-channel; no interior plywood except a thin shim between the leading and trailing wing edges, and a fretting strip where the wings attach to the body. The tapered wing edge was formed by bending the wing plate and riveting over top of a triangular shim, not by the addition of machined aluminum strips bolted to the edges. The size of fuselage and afterbody, wing shape and size, and the presence of an internal 5 inch diameter sustainer motor also match the known structural information for DTV-3.

The telemetry equipment removed from the interior of Target 84 (Figure 3) may eventually provide diagnostic features to match the equipment listed for DTV-3 (Landry 1954b); it was not a Westinghouse product. An engraved plaque attached to the forward end of the radar transponder was engraved with "REC-XMTR, RADAR, P/O RBX SER. NO. 4, GENERAL COMMUNICATION COMPANY." A circa 1956 vintage catalog (General Communication Company, c.1956), purchased on eBay, shows what appears to be the same transponder unit, Radar Beacon Model RBX, and describes its properties and performance characteristics. The transponder unit and batteries have been radiographed at CCI revealing the structure in good detail, but individual electronic components or devices have yet to be identified as to function. In particular, the transponder unit is slightly longer than that described in the catalog and appears to contain additional devices that have a resemblance to a force (acceleration) measuring device patented in by the General Communications Company filed in 1958 (Burt 1961).

Conclusion

The recovery and conservation of this vehicle has provided an opportunity to establish solid practices for the eventual retrieval of an AAFFM. The project team continues to carry out research to establish a definitive identification of Target 84, as well as a link between this object, the VG missile program, and the AAFFM program. In Britain, Avro produced other similar test vehicles such as wind tunnel models for the Avro 720 (Science Museum Group 2020a; 2020b). Avro Canada operated separately and independently from Avro in the United Kingdom.

Canadians are fascinated with the Avro Arrow CF-105 fighter and that fascination takes many different forms. Some lament the permanent damage to the aviation industry in Canada and the subsequent "brain drain" which saw many of Avro's best and brightest hired by NASA and British Aerospace. Others are technophiles who obsess over the technological superiority of the CF-105 and maintain that it would stand up even against some of the modern fighters from the 1980s and 1990s. Still more indulge in anti-American conspiracy theories about the United States government and lobby groups forcing the Canadian government to shut down the program. No matter the reason, one thing is clear: Canadians mourn the loss of this aircraft, and as a result, any mention of it will undoubtedly make headlines. There are more books about the Avro Arrow than about any other single Canadian Cold War story or event. It inspired a CBC movie, a heritage moment commercial, and countless articles. This is why the recovery of Target 84 last year and the continuing search for the free flight models (AAFFMs) has generated so much interest. They are the last remains of this program and as such, have become a kind of holy grail; they are a testament to the lost potential of the Canadian aviation industry.

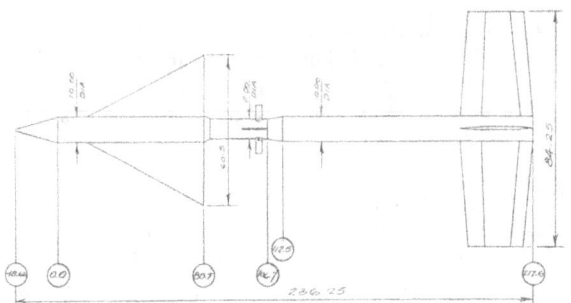

Figure 4: Delta Test Vehicle with single Demon booster rocket, dimensions of body, afterbody, and wingspan in inches (Landry 1954).

Acknowledgements

The authors would like to thank the OEX Recovery Group for providing funding for this project. The National Air Force Museum of Canada, Royal Canadian Air Force, Canada Aviation and Space Museum, Canadian Conservation Institute, and the Department of Canadian Heritage supported this research. Scarlett Janusas Archaeology Inc. provided leadership as project archaeologist. Dr. Richard Mayne, Royal Canadian Air Force and Dr. David Waechter contributed historical research. Kraken Robotics Inc. and Shark Marine Technologies carried out the survey work. Diving operations were carried out by the Royal Canadian Navy and General Diving Contractors of Dundas, Ontario. Jackie Madill, Dr. André Martel, and Dr. Jean-Marc Gagnon of the Canadian Museum of Nature provided identification of biofouling species.

References

BEADLE, PETER
2002 Avro Engineering: Picton Test Range. < http://www.avroarrow.org/ffm/pictonrange.html>. Accessed 18 April 2017.

BINNIE, NANCY E.
2004 Trip report and Field Notes (observations) for the search for the Avro Arrow Models, July 5-7, 2004. Manuscript, Canadian Conservation Institute, Department of Canadian Heritage.

2009 Overloaded? Mussels, Biofouling, and Material Condition Observations for the Hamilton and Scourge Shipwreck Site. ACUA Underwater Proceedings.

BURT, WILLIAM G.
1961 Force Measuring Instrument. US 2,992,561 United States Patent Office.

CALDER, JOANNE
2018 "Raise the Arrow" team recovers first artifact from Lake Ontario. The Maple Leaf, Royal Canadian Air Force. <https://ml-fd.caf-fac.ca/en/2018/08/18277>. Accessed 15 September 1018.

CASM
2017 Collection Highlights: Avro Canada CF-105 Arrow 2. Canada Aviation and Space Museum. <http://casmuseum.techno-science.ca/en/collection-research/artifact-avro-arrow-2.php>. Accessed 28 February 2020.

DUGELBY, THOMAS B.
1997 The Avro Arrow, Chapter 1. Thomas B. Dugelby, Freelton, Ontario. Accessed at the NRC Library, Ottawa.

FLOYD, J.C.
1958 The Fourteenth British Commonwealth Lecture: The Canadian Approach to All-Weather Interceptor Development. The Journal of the Royal Aeronautical Society 62 No. 576: 845-866.

GENERAL COMMUNICATION COMPANY
Circa 1956 Catalog, Radar Beacons, Coaxial Switches, Radar Test Equipment, Pulse Powered Calibrators, Electronic Engineering Services. General Communications Company, Boston, MA.

LANDRY, R.J.
1954a Technical Letter No. N-44-284 Velvet Glove Project Air-To-Air Guided Missile, Delta Test Vehicle No. 2 Experimental Aerodynamic Configuration, Part I Announcement of Firing and Part III Firing Report. RCAF, Canadian Armament and Development Establishment, Defence Research Board.

1954b Technical Letter No. N-44-327 Velvet Glove Project Air-To-Air Guided Missile, Delta Test Vehicle No. 3 Experimental Aerodynamic Configuration, Part I Announcement of Firing and Part III Firing Report. RCAF, Canadian Armament and Development Establishment, Defence Research Board.

LEVERSEDGE, T.F.J.
2014 Avro Canada CF-105 Arrow RCAF Serial 25206 (Nose Section & Components). Canada Aviation and Space Museum. <https://documents.techno-science.ca/documents/CASM-Aircrafthistories-AvroCanadaCF-105Arrownose.pdf>. Accessed 26 February 2020.

PICKLER, RON
1998 1959 Missiles. Canadair the First 50 Years, Canadair History Website. <https://sites.google.com/site/canadair50otherproducts/1959missiles>. Accessed 26 February 2020.

ROYAL CANADIAN AIR FORCE
2018 CF-105 Arrow. Historical aircraft of the Royal Canadian Air Force, Canada. <http://www.rcaf-arc.forces.gc.ca/en/aircraft-historical/cf-105.page>. Accessed 24 February 2020.

SCIENCE MUSEUM GROUP
2020a Avro 720 Wind Tunnel Aircraft. Y1988.250.4. Science Museum Group Collection Online. <https://collection.sciencemuseumgroup.org.uk/objects/co8417468/avro-720-wind-tunnel-aircraft-model-representation>. Accessed 28 February 2020.

2020b   Wind Tunnel Model for the Avro 720 Rocket Fighter. 1993-2597. Science Museum Group Collection Online. <https://en.wikipedia.org/wiki/Avro_720#/media/File:Blythe_House,_Science_Museum_10_-_windtunnel_model.JPG>. Accessed 28 February 2020.

SHARK MARINE
2017   Avro Arrow Expedition 2017, Raise the Arrow 2017. Shark Marine Technologies Inc. <http://www.sharkmarine.com/avro-arrow-expedition-2017/>. Accessed 27 February 2020.

VALIQUETTE, MARC-ANDRÉ
2011a   *Destruction of a Dream, the Tragedy of Avro Canada and the CF-105 Arrow, vol. 1 A.V. Roe Canada's "Per Ardua Ad Astra"*. Friesens Corporation, Altona, Manitoba, Canada.

2011b   *Destruction of a Dream, the Tragedy of Avro Canada and the CF-105 Arrow, vol. 4 Master in Our Own House?* Friesens Corporation, Altona, Manitoba, Canada.

WALKER, R.W.
2005   Canadian Military Aircraft Serial Numbers. <http://www.rwrwalker.ca/RCAF_18101_18150_detailed.html>. Accessed 26 February 2020.

WAECHTER, DAVID
2017   Aeroballistics Range Tests of the Avro Arrow, A Lesser-known Investigation. *Canadian Aviation Historical Society Journal* April 2017: 150-153.

. . . .

Nancy E. Binnie
Canadian Conservation Institute
Department of Canadian Heritage
1030 Innes Road
Ottawa, ON K1B 4S7
Canada

Erin Gregory
Canada Aviation and Space Museum
11 Aviation Parkway
Ottawa, ON K1K 2X5
Canada

"The highest tribute to the dead is not grief but gratitude."

Thornton Wilder

Memorial: Richard Allan Gould (1937–2020)

David L. Conlin

Richard Allan Gould died at his home in Honolulu, Hawaii, after losing his fight with a particularly nasty brand of cancer on Friday March 13th — an ironic day and date that probably pleased him to no end. He was 80 and his wife of almost 60 years, Betsy, was at his side when he passed. Dick was a highly original thinker, a talented didact, and a mentor to several generations of American and Australian ethno-, historical, prehistoric, and underwater archaeologists. His career included significant contributions to ethnoarchaeology, historical archaeology, the anthropology of hunters and gatherers, Northern European historical archaeology, archaeological theory, and underwater archaeology, to name just a few. A teacher to the end, he donated his body to the University of Hawaii School of Anatomy for medical study.

A kind and brilliant man, who took immense pride in the accomplishments of his students and colleagues, he will be missed by many.

Biographical Information

Richard Allan Gould was born in 1939, in Newton, Massachusetts, and was an only child. His father served in the Pacific during WWII on the aircraft carrier USS *Yorktown* (CV-10) and after the war spent a career in higher education as President of Antioch College, Chancellor of the University of California at Santa Barbara and, ultimately, Chancellor of the State University of New York (SUNY). During the war, his first-generation Finnish mother worked at a shipyard in Massachusetts and Gould grew up in a bilingual household.

Gould graduated with a B.A. (cum laude) in anthropology from Harvard University in 1961, and followed with a Ph.D. in anthropology from the University of California at Berkeley in 1965.

Gould's initial interest in archaeology was sparked by a meeting with the former Chair of the University of Chicago Department of Anthropology, Fay Cooper-Cole, who had retired to California and was a family friend. Through Cooper-Cole, Gould was introduced to one of Cole's former graduate students, Jessie Jennings, who was leading the southern section of the Glen Canyon Project — a vast public archaeology undertaking that was to catalogue and excavate key sites along the Colorado River that would be submerged by the construction of Glen Canyon Dam. Gould worked under the exacting tutelage of Jennings during field seasons in 1961–1962 and came to appreciate the value of science and intellectual rigor as applied to archaeological work.

While at Berkeley, Gould wrote a Ph.D. thesis on Northern California Tolowa ethnoarchaeology. The work addressed questions of cultural continuity and change that were tested via excavations at the Point Saint George Site (CA-DNO-11) (Gould 1965, 1966a, 1966b). Gould's thesis advisor, John Rowe, was a prominent Peruvian scholar, and though he did not become an Inca specialist, Gould was drawn to Rowe by his expertise in ceramic analysis and culture history, which he applied to other areas throughout his professional life. During his Ph.D. research: "…Gould worked closely with Tolowa elders who were extremely knowledgeable about the history of the site. A key argument of his study was that the 'direct historical approach,' or the use of ethnographic and historical data to interpret pre-contact lifeways, if carefully applied, could be employed by archaeologists under certain circumstances" (Tushingham 2019).

Following graduation from Berkeley, Gould took a curatorial position in North American Archaeology at the American Museum of Natural History in New York (1965–1971). After his time at the museum, Gould accepted a position at the Department of Anthropology at the University of Hawaii, Honolulu (Associate Professor 1971–1974; Professor 1975–1981). After their time in Hawaii, the Goulds returned to the mainland in 1981 where Dick served the remainder of his professional career as Professor of Anthropology at Brown University in Providence, Rhode Island (1981–2009).

Subsequent to his graduate work in California, Gould and his wife Elizabeth (Betsy) did groundbreaking work in ethnoarchaeology with the Aborigines of the Western Australian Desert. Continuing a theme established in Dick's Ph.D. research, and drawing on ethnoarchaeology and the careful application of the direct historical approach, the Goulds proposed the concept of a Western Desert Culture — a discernible amalgamation of the ideas of cultural continuity drawn from John Rowe coupled to the culture area theories of Jessie Jennings (Gould 1968, 1969).

After work in Western Australia, Gould looked to his mother's homeland of Finland where he studied the historical processes of farm abandonment and the material residues that were left behind as Finnish families reacted to varying degrees of socio-economic stress after the Russo-Finnish War and WWII (Gould 1988). The work focused on the physical byproducts of farm abandonment and adaptation by Finnish farmers and looked for patterning in abandoned farms, the basic conditions under which abandonment occurs, and how this plays out in the material record.

In 1977, while on sabbatical to Cambridge University to work on his ethnoarchaeology book *Living Archaeology* (1980), Gould met maritime archaeologist Keith Muckelroy. Muckleroy sparked a long-term interest in the subject of underwater archaeology in Gould, and in 1981 he chaired a School of American Research Seminar dedicated to the subject. From this seminar came the highly regarded book *Shipwreck Anthropology* (1983), one of the first volumes to advocate for an explicitly anthropological approach to underwater archaeology. The seminar began a long, productive professional relationship between Gould and National Park Service underwater archaeologists Daniel Lenihan, Larry Murphy, Matthew Russell, Brenda Lanzendorf, and David Conlin (Figure 1). The ideas and approach in the volume moved across the Pacific to Australia where scholars such as Graeme Henderson, Jeremy Green, Michael McCarthy, Ian McCloud, Mark Staniforth, Nathan Richards, Corioli Souter, and Jennifer McKinnon continue to push the field in an anthropological approach to underwater archaeology. Following the seminar, Gould expanded his research interests to include underwater work in Dry Tortugas (Figure 2), Florida, and Bermuda. In 2000, he continued his contributions to the field with his volume *Archaeology and the Social History of Ships* (Gould 2000).

After the September 11, 2001, terrorist attacks, Gould realized that the techniques of archaeology could provide insights into mass-casualty events and bring closure to the families of those who died. Gould's initial efforts at the destroyed World Trade Center were followed, in 2003, by a much larger examination of a tragic fire at "The Station" nightclub in Warwick, Rhode Island. This work tied in with his commitment to a "knowable past" and an empirical approach in line with the standards of modern crime-scene forensics (Gould 2004).

Gould retired from his position in the Department of Anthropology at Brown University in 2009 and lived in Honolulu, Hawaii, with his sweetheart and wife of 57 years Betsy Gould (neé Barber).

Figure 1: Richard Gould (left foreground) with NPS Archaeologist Larry Murphy at Fort Jefferson, Dry Tortugas National Park, 1989.

Figure 2: Richard Gould recording features on the Bird Key Brick Wreck, Dry Tortugas National Park, 1989.

Major Accomplishments

After completing his Ph.D. in Anthropology at Berkeley, Gould embarked on a diverse examination of different subjects, all tied together by the common thread of human cultural and behavioral adaptations to stress, risk, conflict, and uncertainty (Philosopedia 2012). Gould's career blossomed during the transition in American archaeology from cultural-historical particularism to the scientific/ecological focus of the New Archaeology in the late 1960s and 1970s, and he remained heavily involved in the field during the period of paradigmatic confrontation between Post-Processual and Processual archaeology in the mid to late 1990s.

Intellectually, Gould's lineage draws from Jessie W. Jennings and through Jennings anthropological ecologist Julian Stewart, a student of Franz Boas. Other intellectual influences include John Rowe for his ideas of cultural continuity, and Mike Schiffer for his theories of archaeological formation processes and the physical changes that happen to an archaeological site over time. Gould saw the past as knowable with varying degrees of certainty and noted that a large amount of human behavior, even in some surprising instances, could be tied back to adaptive responses to risk, conflict and uncertainty. As an example, the well-known concept of "songlines" of the Australian Aboriginal peoples can be seen, according to Gould, as a geographical mnemonic that helps retain knowledge, even for areas at a great distance, and this facilitates human movement in time of resource stress. The incorporation of ideational aspects of culture in archaeological interpretation differed in small but important ways from the harder bioecological approach of the New Archaeology of the 1960s and 1970s; and, although Gould avoided much of the rancor of the paradigmatic clash between classificatory-historical archaeology and New Archaeology, he did produce cogent and important theoretical insights that helped develop the field as the New Archaeology reached maturation in the late 1970s and 1980s (Gould 1982, Gould 1985).

Gould's definition of "culture" shades closely to a "bio-cultural mechanism of adaptation" that combines elements of both biological and non-biological aspects of human experience as opposed to an ideational notion of culture defined as a "negotiated system of symbols." Gould often worked in a stepwise approach to cultural adaptation from human symbology in a feedback loop of systemic relationships that connected ideational and biological behavior in unusual ways. As such, this focus on the bio-adaptive characteristics of human behavior sometimes put him at odds with archaeologists focusing more closely on negotiated social meaning in the Post-Processual movement as it moved into maturity in the 1990s.

Gould's writings are fundamentally scientific and carry a theme of a "real past" that is knowable in some of its facets via the careful application of science and the scientific method. Gould's approach was to apply standards of evidence akin to courtroom testimony (i.e., empiricism, logical connection, minimal assumptions, and rigorously argued linkages between the observed material to inferred behavioral causes) to the results of his research. His mass casualty work came as a result of his emphasis on science, and the notion that in some instances there is a single answer that adheres most closely to the facts and is at least "provisionally true pending additional evidence to the contrary." Gould privileged statements about the past that carried with them minimal assumptions, yet he also argued from particular instances, such as the shipwrecks of the Spanish Armada and the salvage of WWII aircraft during the Battle of Britain, towards more generalized statements of human behavior responding to risk, stress, and conflict that have broad applicability over time and space. Gould claimed that anomaly, not analogy, should be used to explore the dissonance between ethnographic, archaeological, or ecological observations and current laws, generalizations, or regularities (Saggers 2020), and he derived considerable professional satisfaction by offering insights into the past derived from the dissonance between historical and archaeological evidence.

Gould argued that human behavior, even in some surprising instances, can be linked to adaptive responses to the environment. In this he defines "environment" as encompassing both the physical environment and the larger socio-economic forces that shaped human decisions in the past. He was a strong proponent of a stepwise approach to the study of cultural adaptation that encompasses multiple feed-back loops combining a systemic relationship of both the ideational and biological aspects of human experience. In this Gould advocated for the use of both "emic" (i.e., internal, socially constructed categories of thought and meaning such as local religion) and "etic" (i.e., external categories of thought and meaning such as the application of the Western scientific method).

While Gould lived a vibrant life of the mind, he received great fulfillment from the application of his studies for the betterment of the communities in which he worked. Here his work in disaster archaeology as well as the use of his research in Northern California and Australia to assist the communities connected to the archaeology of their respective regions for social justice and legal remedy stand out. Through his words and actions, Gould showed us all that the past remains relevant to the future for many people and that we have both a professional and a moral obligation to tread respectfully and diligently into the histories and prehistories that define our field.

References

GOULD, R.A.

1965   An Introduction to Tolowa Prehistory: Archaeology and Ethnology along the Northwestern California Coast. Doctoral dissertation, Department of Anthropology, University of California, Berkeley.

1966a   Archaeology of the Point St. George Site and Tolowa Prehistory. Vol. 4, *Publications in Anthropology*, University of California Berkeley.

1966b   The wealth quest among the Tolowa Indians of northwestern California. *Proceedings of the American Philosophical Society* 110(1):67-89.

1968   Living Archaeology: The Ngatatjara of Western Australia. *Southwestern Journal of Anthropology* 24(2):101-122.

1969   *Yiwara: Foragers of the Australian Desert*. Charles Scribner's Sons, New York, and William Collins, Ltd., London and Sydney. Reprinted 1971, 2nd edition. Chapter 5 reprinted 1976 in *Ritual, Play and Performance*, Richard Schechner and Mandy Schuman, editors, Seabury Press, New York.

1980   *Living Archaeology*. Cambridge University Press.

1982   A Dialogue on the Meaning and Use of Analogy in Ethnoarchaeological Reasoning, R. A. Gould and Patty Jo Watson, authors. In *Journal of Anthropological Archaeology* 1(4):355-381.

1983   *Shipwreck Anthropology*. R. A. Gould, editor. University of New Mexico Press.

1985   The Empiricist Strikes Back: Reply to Binford. *American Antiquity* 50(3):638-644. (Reprinted in *Readings in American Archaeological Theory: Selections from American Antiquity 1962-2002*, compiled by Garth Bawden. SAA, 2003, pp. 67-74).

1988   Life Among the Ruins: The Ethnoarchaeology of Abandonment in a Finnish Farming Community. *The Social Implications of Agrarian Change in Northern and Eastern Finland*, Tim Ingold, editor, pp. 99-120. Suomen Antropologinen Seura, Helsinki.

2000   *Archaeology and the Social History of Ships*. Cambridge, Cambridge University Press.

2004   Disaster Archaeology at the West Warwick, Rhode Island, Nightclub Fire Scene. The SAA *Archaeological Record* 4(1):6-11.

PHILOSOPEDIA

2012   Richard A. Gould. Philosopedia <http://philosopedia.org/index.php/Richard_A._Gould>. Accessed December 2012.

TUSHINGHAM, S.

2018   *SCA Harrington Recommendation Letter*. Society for California Archaeology Board and Award Review Committee

SAGGERS, S.

2020   *Richard Allan Gould Obituary* (in press). Australian Archaeology Journal.

Further Readings

1973   *Man's Many Ways: A Natural History Reader in Anthropology*. R. A. Gould, editor. Harper and Row, New York. Revised 1977.

1977   *Puntutjarpa Rockshelter and the Australian Desert Culture*. Anthropological Papers of the American Museum of Natural History 54(1).

1978   *Explorations in Ethnoarchaeology*. R. A. Gould, editor. University of New Mexico Press.

1978   Tolowa. In *Handbook of North American Indians* Vol. 8: California, Robert F. Heizer, editor, pp. 128-136. Smithsonian Institution, Washington, D.C.

1981   *Modern Material Culture: The Archaeology of Us*. R.A. Gould and M. B. Schiffer, editors. Academic Press, New York.

1984   *Toward an Ethnoarchaeology of Modern America*, Research Papers in Anthropology No. 4., R. A. Gould, editor. Brown University, Providence.

1990   *Recovering the Past*. University of New Mexico Press.

2007   *Disaster Archaeology*. University of Utah Press.

Papers and Articles
(Peer Reviewed Journals Marked *)

1963   Aboriginal California Burial and Cremation Practices. *Reports of the University of California Archaeological Survey* 60:149-168. Reprinted 1991 in *Spanish Borderlands* Sourcebooks, David Hurst Thomas, editor. Garland Publishing.

*1964   (Jack Brown and R. A. Gould) Column Chromatography and the Possibility of Carbon-Lens Migration. *American Antiquity* 29(3):387-389.

1964 Exploitative Economics and Culture Change in Central California. *Reports of the University of California Archaeological Survey* 62:123-163.

1964 (R.A. Gould and Theodore Paul Furukawa) Aspects of Ceremonial Life among the Indian Shakers of Smith River, California. *Kroeber Anthropological Society Papers* 31:51-67.

*1966 The Wealth Quest among the Tolowa Indians of Northwestern California. *Proceedings of the American Philosophical Society* 110(1):67-89.

*1966 Indian and White Versions of 'The Burnt Ranch Massacre.' *Journal of Folklore Institute* 3(1):30-42.

1966 Some Stone Artifacts of the Wongkonguru of South Australia. *American Museum Novitates* 2249:1-9.

1967 Notes on Hunting, Butchering, and Sharing of Game among the Ngatatjara and Their Neighbors in the West Australian Desert. *Kroeber Anthropological Society Papers* 36:41-66.

1968 Chipping Stones in the Outback. *Natural History* 77(2):42-49. Reprinted 1976 in T*he Evolution of Human Adaptations,* J. Poggie, G. Pelto, and P. Pelto, editors. Macmillan, New York, pp. 143-151.

1968 Masculinity and Mutilation in a Primitive Society. *Medical Opinion and Review* 4(1):58-75.

1968 R.A. Gould and E. B. Gould) Kunturu: An Aboriginal Sacred Site on Lake Moore, Western Australia. *American Museum Novitates* 2327:1-17.

*1968 Seagoing Canoes among the Indians of Northwestern California. *Ethnohistory* 15(1):11-42.

1968 Archaeology of the Mayan Caves, Alta Verapaz, Guatemala. *Explorers Journal* 46(3):164-167.

*1968 Preliminary Report on Excavations of Puntutjarpa Rockshelter, near the Warburton Ranges, Western Australia. *Archaeology and Physical Anthropology in Oceania* 3(3):161-185.

1969 (R. A. Gould and E. B. Gould) Songs of the Western Desert Aborigines. *Asch Mankind Series Recording* AHM 4210 (45 min., 31 sec.) with 5 pp. accompanying notes.

*1969 Subsistence Behavior among the Western Desert Aborigines of Australia. *Oceania* 39(4):253-274.

*1969 Puntutjarpa Rockshelter: A Reply to Messrs. Glover and Lampert. *Archaeology and Physical Anthropology in Oceania* 4(3):220-237.

1969 Una Aproximacion Etnográfica para la Clasificacion de Instrumentos de Piedra. "MesaRodonda de Ciencias Prehistoricas y Antropologicas, Vol. 2", *Publicaciones del Instituto Riva-Aguero, No. 58B, Peru*, pp. 66-72.

1970 Spears and Spear-Throwers of the Western Desert Aborigines of Australia. *American Museum Novitates* 2403:1-42.

1970 Journey to Pulykara. *Natural History* 79(10):56-67. Reprinted 1974 in *Aborigines, Race and Racism*, Humphrey McQueen, editor, Penguin Books, Ltd.

1970 (Don E. Crabtree and R.A. Gould) Man's Oldest Craft Recreated. *Curator* 13 (3):179-198.

*1970 (Richard A. Gould, Dorothy A. Koster, and Ann H.L. Sontz,) The Lithic Assemblage of the Western Desert Aborigines of Australia. *American Antiquity* 36 (2):149-169.

1971 Australia. In Peoples of the Pacific, Margaret Mead and Preston McClanahan, editors. *Natural History* 80(5):39; 48-49.

*1971 Uses and Effects of Fire among the Western Desert Aborigines of Australia. *Mankind* 8(1):14-24.

1971 The Old Stone Age. *Man, Culture, and Society*, Harry L. Shapiro, editor, pp. 47-94. Oxford University Press.

*1971 The Archaeologist as Ethnographer: A Case from the Western Desert of Australia. *World Archaeology* 3(2):143-177.

1972 A Radiocarbon Date from the Point St. George Site, Northwestern California. *Contributions to the University of California Archaeological Research Facility* 14:41-44.

1972 (R.A. Gould and Jeffrey Quilter) Flat Adzes: A Class of Flaked Stone Tools from Southwestern Australia. *American Museum Novitate* 2502:1-14.

1972 Progress to Oblivion. *The Ecologist* 2(9):17-22.

*1972 (Richard A. Gould, Don D. Fowler, and Catherine S. Fowler) Diggers and Doggers: Parallel Failures in Economic Acculturation. *Southwestern Journal of Anthropology* 28(3):265- 281.

1973 Australian Archaeology in Ecological and Ethnographic Perspective. *Warner Modular Publications Module* 7:1-33.

1973 Use-Wear on Western Desert Aborigine Stone Tools: A Reply to Messrs. Hayden and Kamminga. *Newsletter of Lithic Technology* 2(1-2):9-13. Reprinted by Bobbs-Merrill.

1974 Some Current Problems in *Ethnoarchaeology*. *Ethnoarchaeology*, Monography IV, Institute of Archaeology, U.C.L.A., C.B. Donnan and C.W. Clewlow, Jr., editors pp. 29-48, Reprinted 1977 in *Experimental Archaeology*, D. Ingersoll et. al., editor. Columbia University Press.

1974 (R.A. Gould and Elizabeth B. Gould) Burial Caves of Eastern Polynesia. *Explorers Journal* 52(3 and 4):136-141.

*1975 Ecology and Adaptive Response among the Tolowa Indians of Northwestern California. *The Journal of California Anthropology* 2(2):148-170. Reprinted 1976 in *Native Californians: A Theoretical Retrospective*, Lowell J. Bean and Thomas C. Blackburn, editors. Ballena Press.

*1976 A Case of Heat Treatment of Lithic Materials in Aboriginal Northwestern California. *The Journal of California Anthropology* 3(1):142-144.

1977 Numbers, Names, and Nonagnates: Anthropological Problems in Genealogical and Census Data Collecting. *Asian and Pacific Census Newsletter* 2(3):4-6.

1977 The Archaeologist as Ethnographer. In *Horizons of Anthropology*, Sol Tax and Leslie G. Freemen, editors, pp. 151-170. Aldine, Chicago.

1977 Discovering the Australian Desert Culture. *Pacific Discovery* 30(1):1-11.

1977 (Patrick C. McCoy and R.A. Gould) Alpine Archaeology in Hawaii. *Archaeology* 30(4):234-243.

1977 Ethno-archaeology; Or, Where Do Models Come From?. In Stone Tools as Cultural Markers, R.V.S. Wright, editor, pp. 162-8 *Australian Institute of Aboriginal Studies*, Canberra.

1978 From Tasmania to Tucson: New Directions in Ethnoarchaeology. In *Explorations in Ethnoarchaeology*, R.A. Gould, editor, pp. 1-10. University of New Mexico Press.

1978 Beyond Analogy in Ethnoarchaeology. In *Explorations in Ethnoarchaeology*, R.A.Gould, editor, pp. 249-293. University of New Mexico Press.

*1978 The Anthropology of Human Residues. *American Anthropologist* 80(4):815-35.

1978 James Range East Rockshelter, Northern Territory, Australia: A Summary of the 1973 and 1974 Investigations. *Asian Perspectives* 21(1):86-126.

1979 Exotic Stones and Battered Bones. *Archaeology* 32(2):28-37.

1981 Quatre-vingt Annees d'Ethnoarcheologie. *Nouvelles de L'Archeologie* 4:11-16.

1981 Comparative Ecology of Food-Sharing in Australia and Northwest California.In *Omnivorous Primates: Gathering and Hunting in Human Evolution*, Robert S.O. Harding and Geza Teleki, editors, pp. 422-454. Columbia University Press.

1981 Brandon Revisited: A New Look at an Old Technology. In *Modern Material Culture: The Archaeology of Us*, Richard A. Gould and Michael B. Schiffer, editors, pp. 269-281. Academic Press.

1982 To Have and Have Not: The Ecology of Sharing Among Hunter-Gatherers.In *Resource Managers: North American and Australian Hunter-Gatherers*, Nancy M. Williams and Eugene S. Hunn, editors, pp. 69-91. AAAS Selected Symposium 67, Washington, D.C.

1982 'Indoor' vs. 'Outdoor' Living: Preliminary Comparison of Habitation Residues in Stratified Open-Air and Rockshelter Sites in the Australian Desert.In *Oceanic Studies: Essays in Honor of Aarne A. Koskinen*, pp. 241-252 and Fig. 1-3. Suomen Antropologinen Seura, Helsinki,.

1982 Getting Off the Gold Standard. *Early Man* 4(4):41-44.

1983 Looking Below the Surface: Shipwreck Archaeology as Anthropology. In *Shipwreck Anthropology*, R.A. Gould, editor, pp. 3-22. University of New Mexico Press.

1983 The Archaeology of War: Wrecks of the Spanish Armada of 1588 and the Battle of Britain, 1940. In *Shipwreck Anthropology*, R.A. Gould, editor, pp. 105-142. University of New Mexico Press.

1983 Ethnoarchaeology in the Service of CRM. *CRM Bulletin* 6(4):10-11.

1984 Rock Pools and Desert Dances. *Natural History* 93(3):62-70.

1984 (R.A. Gould and Parker B. Potter) Use-Lives of Automobiles in America: A Preliminary Archaeological View. In *Toward an Ethnoarchaeology of Modern America*, R.A. Gould, editor, Research Papers in Anthropology, 4:69-93.

1985 'Now Let's Invent Agriculture...': A Critical Review of Concepts of Complexity among Hunter-Gatherers. In *Complexity Among Prehistoric Hunter-Gatherers*, T. Douglas Price and James A. Brown, editors, pp. 427-434. Academic Press.

*1985 (R.A. Gould and Sherry Saggers) Lithic Procurement in Central Australia: A Closer Look at Binford's Idea of Embeddedness in Archaeology. *American Antiquity* 50(1):117-136.

1985 (Duncan Ritchie and R.A. Gould) Back to the Source: A Preliminary Account of the Massachusetts Hill Quarry Complex. In *Stone Tool Analysis: Essays in Honor of Don E. Crabtree*, Mark G. Plew, James C. Woods, and Max G. Pavesic, editors, pp. 35-53. University of New Mexico Press, Albuquerque.

1985 The Indians of Northwest California. *Masterkey* 59(2 & 3):12-21.

1986 Cave Art of Australian Desert Aborigines. In *Ancient Texans*, Harry J. Shafer, editor, pp. 204-209 (with photographs on pp. 196-199). Texas Monthly Press, Austin.

1986 Blue Water Archaeology. In *The Marine Research Community and Low-Cost ROV's and Submersibles: Needs and Prospects*, Lynne C. Hanson, editor, pp. 29-33. Center for Ocean Management Studies, University of Rhode Island, Kingston.

*1987 (Richard A. Gould and John E. Yellen) Man the Hunted: Determinants of Household Spacing in Desert and Tropical Foraging Societies. *Journal of Anthropological Archaeology* 6(1):77-103.

1987 The Semi-Submerged Dockyard. *Bulletin of the Institute of Maritime History and Archaeology*, Bermuda Maritime Museum, 9:7-11.

1987 H.M.S. Vixen, An Early Ironclad Ram. Bulletin of the Institute of Maritime History and Archaeology, Bermuda Maritime Museum, 10:13-14.

*1987 The Ethnoarchaeology of Abandonment in a Northern Finnish Farming Community. *Nordia* 21(2):133-152.

*1987 Archaeological Survey by Air: A Case from the Australian Desert, *Journal of Field Archaeology* 14(4):431-443.

1988 Kennelle Historia Kuuluu? ("To Whom Does History Belong?"). *Varelia* no. 1:30-31. Turku, Finland.

1988 The Experimental Armada. *Earthwatch* 7(4):30-34.

1988 The 1988 Field Season on H.M.S. Vixen. *The Bermuda Maritime Museum Quarterly* 1(1):38-39.

1988 The U.S.S. *Monitor* Project Research Design. In *Naval History: The Seventh Symposium of the U.S. Naval Academy*, William B. Cogar, editor, pp. 83-88. Scholarly Resources, Wilmington, DL.

1988 Vanha Panssaripuskulaiva Burmudassa ("An Early Ironclad Ram in Bermuda"). *Helsingin Urheilusukeltajat ry, Jäsentiedote* 4. (Helsinki Sport-Divers' Association Journal 4), pp. 6-9.

1989 Archaeological Frameworks for Evaluating Site-Formation Processes. In *The Physical-Chemical-Biological Processes Affecting Archaeological Sites*, Christopher C. Mathewson, editor, pp. 12-26. Report EL-89-1, U.S. Army Corps of Engineers, Vicksburg.

*1989 Ethnoarchaeology and the Past: Our Search for the 'Real Thing. *Fennoscandia Archaeologica* 6:3-22, Helsinki.

*1989 H.M.S. Vixen: An Early Ironclad Ram at Bermuda. *Bermuda Journal of Archaeology and Maritime History* 1:43-80.

1989 H.M.S. Vixen: An Early Ironclad in Bermuda. In *Underwater Archaeology Proceedings from the Society for Historical Archaeology Conference, Baltimore*, J. Barto Arnold III, editor, pp. 124-129.

1990 The Case of the 'Two Gibraltars' in Nautical History. In *Underwater Proceedings from the Society for Historical Archaeology Conference, Tucson*, Toni Carrell, editor, pp. 21-26.

*1990 Underwater Construction at the Royal Naval Dockyard, Bermuda. *Bermuda Journal of Archaeology and Maritime History* 2:71-86.

*1991 (Richard A. Gould and John E. Yellen) Misreading the Past: A Reply to Binford Concerning Hunter-Gatherer Site Structure. *Journal of Anthropological Archaeology* 10:283-298.

*1991 (F. Donald Pate, John T. Hutton, Richard A. Gould and Graeme L. Pretty) Alterations of in vivo elemental dietary signatures in archaeological bone: evidence from the Roonka Flat Dune, South Australia. *Archaeology in Oceania* 26:58-69.

*1991 The Archaeology of HMS Vixen, an Early Ironclad Ram in Bermuda. *The International Journal of Nautical Archaeology* 20(2):141-153.

*1991 (Richard A. Gould, Edward C. Harris and John R. Triggs) The 1991 Archaeological Field Season at Fort Cunningham, *Bermuda. Bermuda Journal of Archaeology and Maritime History* 3:65-88.

*1991 Arid-Land Foraging as Seen from Australia: Adaptive Models and Behavioral Realities. *Oceania* 62:12-33.

1991 Ngatatjara. Encyclopedia of World Cultures, Vol. II, Oceania, Terence Hays, editor, pp. 238-241. Human Relations Area Files.

*1992 (Richard A. Gould, Edward C. Harris, and John R. Triggs) The 1992 Archaeological Field Season at Fort Cunningham, Bermuda. *Bermuda Journal of Archaeology and Maritime History* 4:21-57.

1993 Bird Key Harbor Wreck (FOJE 029) 1990 Fieldwork. In *Dry Tortugas National Park*, Larry Murphy, editor, pp. 333-351. National Park Service, Santa Fe, NM.

*1993 (Stephen A. Mrozowski and Richard A. Gould) Ethnoarchaeology and Historical Archaeology: A Comparative Examination of Marginality and Farm Abandonment. *Northeast Anthropology* (formerly Man in the Northeast) 46:77-97.

1994 Technical Report: Richard A. Gould and Grant E. Hearn, "Modeling and Simulation." In *Anglo-US Meeting on Cooperation for Cleaner Seas,* James W. Bales and James G. Bellingham, editor, pp. 2-5. M.I.T.

1994 Food Sharing. *The Encyclopedia of Aboriginal Australia* Vol. 8, David Horton, editor, pp. 383-384. Australian Institute of Aboriginal and Torres Straits Islanders, Canberra.

1994 (Richard A. Gould and Donna J. Souza) Floating Dock *Bermuda. Maritime Archaeological and Historical Society* (MAHS) News 6(6):1, 8-11.

*1995 Archaeological Survey by Air: An Update for the 1990s. *Journal of Field Archaeology* 22:257-261.

*1995 The Bird Key Wreck, Dry Tortugas National Park, Florida, *Bulletin of the Australian Institute for Maritime Archaeology* 19(2):7-16. Reprinted in Florida Keys Sea Heritage Journal, 7(4):1-14.

*1996 (Richard A. Gould and Donna J. Souza) History and Archaeology of H.M. Floating Dock, *Bermuda. The International Journal of Nautical Archaeology* 25(2):4-20.

*1996 Faunal Reduction at Puntutjarpa Rockshelter, Warburton Ranges, Western Australia. *Archaeology in Oceania* 31:72-86.

1996 Ethnoarchaeology. In *The Oxford Companion to Archaeology*, Brian Fagan, editor, pp. 207-208. Oxford University Press.

*1997 (Peter Veth, Richard Fullagar, and Richard Gould) Residue and use-wear analysis of grinding implements from Puntutjarpa Rockshelter in the Western Desert: Current and proposed research. *Australian Archaeology* 44:1-3.

1997 Contextual relationships (pp. 108-110), Research Design (pp. 344-345), Shipwreck Anthropology (pp. 377-380), and H.M.S. Vixen (pp. 459-460). In *Encyclopedia of Underwater and Maritime Archaeology*, James P. Delgado, editor. British Museum Press.

*1999 (Richard A. Gould and David L. Conlin) Archaeology of the Barrel Wreck, Loggerhead Reef, Dry Tortugas National Park. *The International Journal of Nautical Archaeology* 28(3):207-228.

2000 Ethnoarchaeology (pp.181-187), and Remotely-Operated Vehicles (ROVs) (pp.519-521). In *Archaeological Method and Theory,* Linda Ellis, editor. Garland Publishing.

*2000 Beyond Exploration: Underwater Archaeology after the Year 2000. *Historical Archaeology* 34:24-28.

2001 From Sail to Steam at Sea in the Late Nineteenth Century. In *Anthropological Perspectives on Technology*, Michael B. Schiffer, editor, pp. 193-223. University of New Mexico Press.

*2001 (Balme, Jame, Glenn A. Garbin, and Richard A. Gould) Residue Analysis and Paleodiet in Arid Australia. *Australian Archaeology* 53:1-6.

*2002 (Gould, Richard A., S. O'Connor, and Peter M. Veth) Bones of Contention: reply to Walshe. *Archaeology in Oceania* 37:96-101.

2002 WTC Archaeology: what we saw, what we learned, and what we did about it. *The SAA Archaeological Record* 2(5):11-17

*2002 The Wreck of the 'North Carolina', New Years Day, 1880. *Bermuda Journal of Archaeology and Maritime History* 13:28-56.

*2005 The Wreck of the Barque, 'North Carolina,' Bermuda, 1880: An Underwater Crime Scene? *American Antiquity* 70:107-128.

2005 Archaeology Prepares for a Possible Mass-Fatality Disaster. *The SAA Archaeological Record* 5:10-12.

2005 Identifying Victims after a Disaster. *AAA Anthropology News* 46:22-23.

2006 In His Own Words: Disaster Archaeology. In *Archaeology*, David Hurst Thomas and Robert L. Kelly, editors, pp. 474-476. Thomson/Wadsworth, 4th edition

• • • • • • • • • • • • • • • •

David L. Conlin, Ph.D.
National Park Service Submerged Resources Center
12795 West Alameda Pkwy.
Lakewood, CO 80228

Memorial: María del Pilar Luna Erreguerena (1944–2020)

Toni Carrell, Margaret Leshikar-Denton, Dolores Elkin, Roberto Junco

Traveler There is No Road...

Traveler, your footprints
are the only road, nothing else.

Traveler, there is no road;
you make your own path as you walk.

As you walk, you make your own road,
and when you look back
you see the path
you will never travel again.

Traveler, there is no road;
only a ship's wake on the sea.

This poem by Antonio Machado (1912), more than anything else, epitomizes the spirit and incredible life's journey traveled by Pilar Luna. This excerpt, from a longer poem, was one of her favorites and when there were choices to be made or paths to choose, she always chose her own.

Early Years

Pilar was a native of Tampico, Mexico, and was the youngest of five children. Born to Spanish parents, she was baptized in the Cathedral of Tampico between the Mexican and Spanish flags on the anniversary of Columbus's arrival in the New World. Perhaps reflecting the blending of her family's roots spanning the old and new worlds, Pilar studied languages and general culture at the Stella Viae School in Rome, Italy, and was fluent in Spanish, English, French, and Italian.

Indeed, Pilar may have been destined to become an underwater archaeologist. She was born with a love of the sea. As a youth, she loved to swim for hours just for the pleasure of it. In her early twenties, she was the first person in Mexico to teach children with Downs Syndrome how to swim. In 1975, she won two championships in underwater navigation and two gold and four silver medals in an underwater techniques competition.

Although they did not always understand her passion, her family faithfully encouraged her studies and supported her decision to pursue archaeology.

As a student in the National School of Anthropology and History in the early 1970s, Pilar took an interest in underwater archaeology, realizing that Mexico has a tremendous variety and wealth of such sites, from cenotes with Maya ceremonial sites to shipwrecks off Mexico's coasts. She obtained her Bachelor's Degree in Archaeology from the National School of Anthropology and History in 1975. That same year, she participated in her first underwater archaeology project at Chunyaxché Lagoon, Quintana Roo, Mexico, with Dr. Harold Edgerton under the direction of Dr. Nancy Farris. This early experience and her love of the sea set her lifelong path.

Pilar returned to terrestrial work, and in 1978, while a young professional working on the excavations in downtown Mexico City, in the Templo Mayor of the former Aztec city of Tenochtitlan, she made a unique discovery, unearthing an enormous conch shell carved in precise detail without the use of metal tools, out of pink and gray andesite, a volcanic stone. The artifact is so unique and rare that in 1980 it became the central piece of the first exhibit of pre-Columbian art held in the National Palace of Fine Arts in Mexico City. Today, it is prominently displayed at the Templo Mayor museum and was featured on the ten thousand peso bill.

Underwater Archaeology in Mexico

In 1978, Pilar convinced the authorities of the National School of Anthropology and History to sponsor a series of lectures on and exercises in underwater archaeology. In the words of Donald Keith, "During this class we discussed how to grow underwater archaeology in México, which we quickly perceived was more than Pilar's professional ambition, it was her passion" (Figure 1).

In 1979, Pilar traveled to Turkey to gain field experience with the Institute of Nautical Archaeology (INA) under George Bass, on two ancient shipwrecks from the Hellenic and Byzantine periods at Serçe Limani. It was a life-changing experience. She emerged from this experience even more committed to the cause of underwater archaeology in Mexico.

Figure 1: Pilar Luna at the January 1979, Laguna de Media Luna fieldwork exercise during the first underwater archaeology class held in Mexico. Photo Donald Keith.

Long before travelling to Turkey, Pilar and three students prepared a proposal to create a program dedicated to underwater archaeology and presented it to the General Director of Mexico's National Institute of Anthropology and History (INAH). Historian Flor Trejo called this the "foundational document" of the program. Pilar labored unrelentingly to get a formal program established, often vigorously opposed, criticized, and even threatened by treasure-hunters, bureaucrats, prejudiced scholars, and Navy officers. She had to win over scores of officials in Mexico's sprawling bureaucracy, ranging from oceanographers to admirals in the Navy. It took Pilar eight years of passionate lobbying to convince INAH to create the Department of Underwater Archaeology to which she was appointed director in 1980.

INAH's Department of Underwater Archaeology

Pilar wasted no time in getting involved in numerous projects. Among the first were: surveys and test excavations of 16th- and 18th-century shipwrecks on Cayo Nuevo Reef (Figure 2) in the Bay of Campeche (1979–1983); surveys in Media Luna Spring (1981–1982); test excavation of an early 16th-century shipwreck site in Bahia Mujeres (1983–1984, 1990); and the survey of Chinchorro Reef (1984), among others. Of that first project on Cayo Nuevo Reef, Donald Keith remarked:

> *It could be argued that Mexican underwater archaeology was born during that first expedition to Cayo Nuevo in late November 1979. Far from the classroom, it was not a simple, safe, learning exercise. It is just as well that we did not know the Bay of Campeche is not a good place to be in winter. Pilar saw recovery of the bronze cannon as an opportunity to draw attention to her efforts to jump-start underwater archaeology in México, and was willing to lay everything on the line to stage a high-profile raid on Davy Jones' locker. It was the first of what eventually became three expeditions to Cayo Nuevo and the crucible in which Pilar's mettle was tested. For that matter, we were all tested — but Pilar had the most at stake. A lot of important people were looking over her shoulder.*

In addition to projects in Mexico, Pilar worked internationally in the Cayman Islands with Roger C. Smith (1980), Jamaica with Donny L. Hamilton (1983), and with Donald Keith in the Bahamas (1986) (Figure 3), and Panama (1990).

In the midst of these accomplishments, Pilar presented her Master's thesis in 1982, entitled, "Underwater Archaeology," which was accepted *Cum Laude* and recommended for publication.

Never one to sit on her laurels, Pilar understood that to ensure the future of underwater archaeology in Mexico, she needed to train Mexican students and engage other professionals in related fields. In 1994, Pilar engineered an intensive Master's level course in underwater archaeology offered through the National School of Anthropology and History and open only to applicants already holding or nearing degrees in archaeology or

Figure 2: Pilar Luna briefing PEMEX saturation divers aboard the diving vessel *Mercurio del Golfo* at Cayo Nuevo during the November 1979 recovery of the 16th century bronze cannon. Photo Donald Keith.

Figure 3: Pilar Luna checking the grid orientation during the September 1986 Highborne Cay Wreck test excavation, Bahamas. Photo KC Smith.

conservation. She invited colleagues Donald Keith, Jack Hunter, and Monica S. Hunter from the U.S. and Steve Willis from Canada to teach and provide their insights into the practice of underwater archaeology. The first of its kind in Mexico, the course was a tremendous success and, as a result, Pilar's Department was upgraded within INAH to become the Underwater Archaeology Vice-Directorate in 1995.

INAH's Underwater Archaeology Vice-Directorate

Soon after becoming a Vice-Directorate in 1995, three major research projects were started: the 1630–1631 New Spain fleet research project; the inventory and analysis of submerged cultural resources in the Gulf of Mexico, and the Underwater Archaeological Atlas for recording, studying, and protecting cenotes in the Yucatan Peninsula. Other projects that followed included: researching a Manila Galleon wreck site in Baja California; surveys of two lagoons in the crater of the Nevado de Toluca volcano; and survey of underwater cultural heritage at the Biosphere Reserve of Banco Chinchorro in Quintana Roo and seeking its nomination as a World Heritage Site on the basis of natural and cultural criteria.

In 2003, the Underwater Archaeology Vice-Directorate initiated five special programs: (1) attention to public reports of cultural material findings; (2) dissemination of information about UCH; (3) training; (4) conservation of archaeological material recovered from submerged sites; and (5) agreements for national and international collaboration.

More recently, the landmark Hoyo Negro project in the Yucatan Peninsula excited Pilar. A Paleoindian site inside a sinkhole, Hoyo Negro is a treasure trove of Pleistocene fauna. Pilar was especially fond of Naia, the remains of a woman who lived 13,000 thousand years ago and is one of the oldest most complete skeletons in the Americas. Perhaps, it is fitting that a woman from Mexico has once again excited the imagination and is furthering underwater archaeology. The work stemming from this project is a model of collaborative research and international recognition.

Training the Next Generation

Pilar's ongoing commitment to training Mexican underwater archaeologists was evident throughout her career. Every year, she invited renowned specialists from different parts of the world to give mini-courses and share their knowledge and experience with Mexican underwater archaeologists, as well as conservators, biologists, historians, students, divers, and fishermen, among others. Chris Amer, former State Underwater Archaeologist of South Carolina, observed that, "Pilar has been instrumental in bridging the gulf between professionals and watermen by engaging them in the process of discovery, identification and registration of shipwrecks and other submerged cultural resources."

A third course in underwater archaeology, "Research and Management in Underwater and Maritime Archaeology," took place in Campeche from 27 September to 8 October 2010. Sponsored by UNESCO and INAH, 20 countries in Latin America and the Caribbean were invited to send participants. Of these, 14 countries sent 27 professionals from the fields of archaeology, anthropology, law, conservation, cultural resource management, and undergraduate students in archaeology and conservation. One of the important outcomes was the creation of a region-wide Organización Latinoamericana de Arqueología Subacuática. Its goals were identified to establish a regional network of professional support and to work towards the adoption and implementation of the 2001 UNESCO Convention on the Protection of the Underwater Cultural Heritage (UNESCO Convention) throughout the region.

Pilar's contribution to maritime archaeology in Latin America continued through courses and other initiatives aimed at archaeologists and other professionals from various countries of the region. The last course she promoted, with support of UNESCO, took place in 2019, again in Campeche. With the financial support of

Spain, the course included participants from Argentina, Bolivia, Chile, Costa Rica, Cuba, Dominican Republic, Ecuador, Guatemala, Honduras, Nicaragua, Panama, Paraguay, Peru, Uruguay, and from Mexico as host country, all of whom received training from specialized professors from Mexico and Spain.

International Collaboration

With growing respect among Mexican and international scientific circles, Pilar expanded her influence by actively consulting with other Central and South American nations and offering advice on how to establish programs to protect their submerged cultural resources. Dolores Elkin, Director of the Underwater Archaeology Program in Argentina's National Institute of Anthropology remarked:

> *I first met Pilar Luna in Montevideo in 1994, when she was invited to lecture on underwater cultural heritage in the context of Uruguay's national archaeology conference. At that time, there were virtually no maritime archaeologists in South America .... I was instantly impressed by this woman who was a pioneer in such a male-dominated environment ... Pilar's model was ... enough for me to decide to become involved in maritime archaeology and to try to follow in her steps ... and putting together a team ... capable of studying and protecting the underwater cultural heritage ... Twenty five years down the road it is fair to say that, directly or indirectly, the achievements of the Argentinean Underwater Archaeology Program at the National Institute of Anthropology are thanks to Pilar Luna.*

Matthew Russell expressed the sentiments of many of Pilar's colleagues in highlighting that "Through her international activities, Pilar serves as a powerful example of how a single, committed individual can influence national policies and steer a nation towards a preservation ethic."

Service

Pilar led the Underwater Archaeology Vice-Directorate in increased participation in international forums held by organizations such as the Society for Historical Archaeology (SHA), the International Council on Monuments and Sites (ICOMOS), UNESCO, and the World Archaeological Congress (WAC). She served as chair of the Underwater Archaeology Scientific Committee for ICOMOS Mexico and as one of the four international advisors for the National Geographic Society.

Pilar served on the Mexican delegation during development of the 2001 UNESCO Convention and was instrumental in Mexico's ratification of the UNESCO Convention on 5 July 2006. She served as Vice-Chairperson of the First Meeting of the Scientific and Technical Advisory Body (STAB) to the States Parties, held in Cartagena, Spain, in June 2010. Lyndel V. Prott, former Director of the Cultural Heritage Division of UNESCO wrote:

> *During the negotiations, [Pilar] was one of the most active and influential figures. She often represented the interests of the Latin American States and she was a most knowledgeable source of information .... She also proved to have considerable diplomatic skills, being able to persuade with both arguments and humor ... I believe it is fair to say that, without her participation, the text of the Convention as adopted would not appear as it now does.*

Pilar first attended an SHA conference in 1980, making international and professional connections and raising awareness of underwater archaeology in Mexico. In recognition of her pioneering role, in 1982 Pilar was invited to join the Advisory Council on Underwater Archaeology (ACUA), becoming its first woman member, and was elected to emeritus status in 2002. She also served on the SHA UNESCO committee, providing an important international perspective to the society.

Friends and colleagues regularly sought out Pilar's perspective. Robert Grenier, former Chief of Underwater Archaeology at Parks Canada and Past President of ICOMOS ICUCH wrote of her innate wisdom:

> *I often had to rely on advice from respected colleagues in periods of crisis. None could equal Pilar as my most reliable advisor; her incredible judgement, her overall vision, her well-balanced sense of values and her indefatigable rigor made her advice irreplaceable.*

She also served on the Ships of Discovery Board of Directors (1989), ICOMOS International Committee on Underwater Cultural Heritage (ICUCH) (1992), and the Waitt Institute for Discovery's Advisory Committee (2006).

A Tireless Advocate

In an effort to create a national and international consciousness regarding the importance of submerged cultural patrimony in Mexico and beyond, Pilar presented numerous lectures, wrote articles, and gave interviews on radio, television, and in the popular press. These activities included the scientific community, diving groups, fishermen, and the public. Francisco Alves, former Head of Portugal's Nautical and Underwater Archaeology Branch, expressed his "...admiration of her professional, scientific and leadership skills, her tremendous human personality, and her talent as an engaging and clear communicator."

One of Pilar's most relevant publications is *Underwater and Maritime Archaeology in Latin America and the Caribbean* (Left Coast Press, 2008). It was co-edited with Margaret Leshikar-Denton. It was inspired by a symposium on the subject at the Fifth World Archaeological Congress (WAC-5), held in Washington, DC, in 2003. Lyndel Prott particularly commended the work:

> *This book has long been needed and is a very valuable demonstration of the variety and significance of the underwater heritage of this region. Its appearance contributes to the understanding and the debate on ratification of the 2001 Convention at a time when many States are working towards its acceptance.*

Honors

Pilar was recognized for her advocacy and international influence in the field of underwater archaeology on several occasions. These include awards from the Society for Historical Archaeology. She twice received the Society's Awards of Merit. In 1997, for her efforts in underwater archaeology in Mexico and, again, in 2016 for her work in promoting and the adoption of the UNESCO 2001 Convention on the Protection of Underwater Cultural Heritage. In 2011, Pilar received the Society's prestigious lifetime achievement J. C. Harrington Medal. Pilar was the first Latin American woman and only the second underwater archaeologist to receive it. It was fitting that Pilar received the award at the Society's annual conference in Austin, Texas, a location near the border to Mexico that provided Pilar's family members and Mexican friends and colleagues the best opportunity to attend and share in the joyous occasion.

On 1 February 2020, Pilar received the prestigious Alfonso Caso medal, given on the 124th anniversary of Caso's birthday. Caso is one of the founding figures of Mexican archaeology and anthropology and was the founder of the National Institute of Anthropology and History in 1940. Pilar was recognized for her 40 years of work on underwater archaeology. This award is given only to those researchers who have played a significant role in development of INAH, such as Matos Moctuzuma, Pilar's teacher and one of Mexico's leading archaeologists.

Mentorship and Legacy

In spite of physical ailments including a near-fatal bout with histoplasmosis acquired during a cave excavation in the Yucatán and a back injury that occurred during the abandonment of a sinking ship in Alaska, Pilar succeeded in no small measure because of her kindness and sincerity and her attitude about life. Pilar was a generous, warm, and committed mentor and friend (Figure 4).

When Pilar was elected to the ACUA in 1982, she was already a legend among the comparatively few women actively involved in underwater archaeology. Toni Carrell said:

> *When I met Pilar in 1980, I knew that she was someone special. Against all odds, she had achieved tremendous recognition in her home country and*

Figure 4: Pilar Luna overlooking the sea in Veracruz, 2016. Photo SAS-INAH; Underwater Archaeology Vice Directorate.

it was clear she had a passion for underwater archaeology. Within minutes, I felt I had known Pilar my whole life; she quickly became my hero, my mentor, and my very dear lifelong friend. I could always count on her to listen and give generously of her time and affection. I try to follow her example and, when faced with a decision or asked for advice, I often ask myself what wise words of comfort and guidance Pilar would give. One of my fondest memories are the times we spent in Paris during the UNESCO Convention negotiations. It was the honor of my life to share the SHA Award of Merit with Pilar in 2016.

It may be fitting to mention that during the Paris 2001 UNESCO Convention negotiations, the professional and personal network of Pilar Luna, Toni Carrell, Dolores Elkin, and Margaret (Peggy) Leshikar-Denton, was given the bold name of Las Chicas Radicales by Francisco Alves from Portugal, who recognized the commitment, diplomacy, and tenacity of this team. Las Chicas shared the SHA 2016 Award of Merit for their work toward ratification of the UNESCO Convention.

Peggy Leshikar-Denton met Pilar in 1980 at the Albuquerque SHA Conference, where Pilar encouraged and, later, supported her MA research into Mexica-Aztec watercraft at the Museum of Anthropology in Mexico City. Peggy shared that:

Pilar and I had the good fortune to work together on the 1980 Cayman Islands Project with Roger Smith, where we developed a lasting personal and professional bond that continued over the next four decades. Pilar invited me to join INAH projects in Mexico and we cherished our time as roommates at SHA Conferences and the Paris 2001 UNESCO Convention negotiations. As ICUCH members, we traveled to meetings around the world, always working for the protection of underwater cultural heritage, and taking a few extra days to enjoy cultural experiences along the way. We shared our professional passion as organizers of the Latin American and Caribbean symposium at WAC-5 (2003), resulting in its publication (2008). It was a privilege to share the 2016 SHA Award of Merit. Pilar was wise and calm, prepared equally for challenge or success; she deeply influenced my life. In spite of her worldly accomplishments, Pilar's philosophy was that when we leave this earth, we take with us only what we have become as human beings. Godspeed Pilar Luna. Fair winds and calm seas.

Dolores (Loli) Elkin took to heart Pilar's call to leadership and established Argentina's Underwater Archaeology Program. Loli reflected on Pilar's strength of character:

Well beyond her professionalism as an archaeologist and heritage manager, Pilar was simply a wonderful human being. Extremely talented but never arrogant, tenacious and with strong convictions yet respectful and willing to listen to those who disagreed with her, passionate but also calm and wise, entertaining and funny but always class. Incredibly generous, sympathetic, sensitive, loving and ready to help at any time. Words seem not enough to describe such an amazing person. I will be forever grateful to Pilar for having been my mentor in maritime archaeology, but the greatest privilege was that she was my friend.

Helena Barba-Meinecke, responsible for underwater archaeology in the Yucatan Peninsula under the Vice-Directorate, recalls Pilar's impact on her life:

I met Pilar when I was 19, when she visited my Uncle Román and Aunt Beatriz. From that first moment, I was captivated. She was always my example to follow and since then I considered her as a warrior woman ahead of her time. She has left us an invaluable legacy and an example of life; she is my mentor and friend. Pilar was a great woman who knew how to communicate, always with great affection, a sense of teamwork, dedication, and a strong passion for the life. She will always be present through all who follow in her footsteps.

Flor Trejo was an early team member and was involved in one of Pilar's most notable projects, the search for *Nuestra Señora del Juncal*. Flor has continued in the Vice-Directorate and is a maritime historian and project manager of the 1630–1631 New Spain fleet research project.

I first met Pilar in 1996, when she began to build a team of young researchers in order to launch one of her most complex projects, finding the remains of Nuestra Señora del Juncal, *sunk in 1631. This ship was sought-after by treasure hunters because of the amount of precious metals it carried. Pilar defended this site from salvage for many years. In the 2012 campaign, a 45-day geophysical survey, I saw all the challenges she managed to solve day by day. Nothing bent her. Her legacy and her holistic approach to work, committed but enlightened by human insight, will remain always in our memories.*

Laura Carrillo was also an early team member, beginning in 1994 at an underwater archaeology course. Today she continues to work in the Vice-Directorate.

I had the good fortune to meet Pilar during the Underwater Archeology course in 1994. Those of us whose paths crossed on this excellent program, met a strict Pilar, but with that warmth and human quality that always characterized her. A year later, she invited me to participate in the Nuestra Señora del Juncal *project, predecessor to the New Spain Fleet of 1630-1631 project, later offering me the opportunity to develop the archaeological project at Chinchorro Bank. Pilar was a very important person for me, both professionally and personally, always empathetic and interested in the life stories of the people around her, always supporting and encouraging us to be better. Infinite thanks dear Pilar, your remembrance and teachings will remain in our memory, navigate happily through that unknown sea.*

To Roberto Junco, tasked with leading the Vice-Directorate after Pilar's retirement in 2017, she was more than just an admired professional colleague:

Most of the people she met will agree there was an aura around her in the way she talked and treated everyone. Personally, it was a privilege to work with her for so many years. Like many of us, we will always be indebted to Pilar for her kindness and interest in us as human beings, our personal situations, our dreams and desires. A bit of a mother figure and a mentor, she gave many of us the tools to continue our dreams of a professional career in underwater archaeology. I cannot thank her enough for believing in me more than I believed in myself. I feel a great responsibility to occupy her place at the Subdirección de Arqueóloga Subacuática since 2017. She is always on my mind when it comes to decision making. Her departure is a big loss. I am grateful to have had her as my boss and friend all those years.

On March 15, 2020, María del Pilar Luna Erreguerena once again embarked on her own road.

Caminante, son tus huellas
el camino y nada más;

Caminante, no hay camino,
se hace camino al andar.

Al andar se hace el camino,
y al volver la vista atrás
se ve la senda que nunca
se ha de volver a pisar.

Caminante, no hay camino
sino estelas en la mar.

References

Machado, Antonio
1912 [2007] Caminante, son tus huellas. In Campos de Castilla. Renacimiento, Madrid. *Fields of Castille*, Stanley Appelbaum, translator, pp. 94-95. Dover Publications.

. . . .

Toni L. Carrell
Ships of Discovery
39 Condesa Rd.
Santa Fe, NM 87508

Margaret Leshikar-Denton
Cayman Islands National Museum
P.O. Box 30702
Grand Cayman KY 1-1203 Cayman Islands

Dolores Elkin
Instituto Nacional de Antropología y Pensamiento Latinoamericano
3 de febrero 1378 - 1426
Buenos Aires, Argentina

Roberto Junco
Instituto Nacional de Antropología e Historia
Moneda 16, Col. Centro
Cuahatemoc, Mexico City, CP, Mexico 06010

In Memoriam - Dr. Roger C. Smith (1949–2020)

Della A. Scott-Ireton, Christopher E. Horrell, Chuck Meide

Figure 1: Dr. Roger C. Smith (3 May 1949 - 5 February 2020): colleague, teacher, mentor, dive buddy, friend.

The winds and waves are always on the side of the ablest navigator.
- *Edward Gibbon, historian*

Dr. Roger C. Smith (Figure 1) was truly one of the few people who may be considered pioneers in the field of underwater archaeology. Roger was born in Salt Lake City, UT, on 3 May 1949. Roger began his college career at the University of Virginia, completing his BA in 1971. In 1973, Roger began training as a commercial diver in Wilmington, CA, where he met Karen Christine "KC" Westburg, and the two married in 1976.

Roger's career in underwater archaeology began in 1974, working with the South Carolina River Survey. At the completion of this project, his interest shifted to Florida. From 1975 to 1978, Roger served as a Field Agent for the State, where he saw first-hand the effects of treasure hunting and recorded the 1733 *flota* wrecks before they were further impacted. In 1978, Roger entered the Nautical Archaeology Program at Texas A&M University (TAMU) focusing his research on the maritime heritage of the Cayman Islands. Completing his MA in 1981, Roger continued to lead and participate in projects including: Highborn Cay Wreck, located in the Bahama Islands; Molasses Reef Wreck in the Turks & Caicos Islands; Bahía Mujeres Wreck offshore of Quintana Roo, Mexico; and multiple projects in Florida. From 1982 to 1985, Roger directed the Columbus Caravels Project in St Ann's Bay, Jamaica. To further his knowledge of the Age of Exploration, Roger enrolled in TAMU's History Department, completing his PhD in 1989. His dissertation research became the seminal volume *Vanguard of Empire* (Smith 1993).

In 1987, Roger accepted a position with the State of Florida's Division of Historical Resources, Bureau of Archaeological Research (DHR, BAR), as State Underwater Archaeologist. Roger's tenure in Florida was characterized by a string of successes, including the Pensacola Shipwreck Survey (1990-1995), which ultimately led to the discovery and excavation of the first Emanuel Point Shipwreck (Smith et al. 1995; Smith et al. 1998). Roger also completed multiple surveys and studies of other Spanish colonial sites throughout the state, including a vessel called the Mystery Wreck in the Florida Keys (McKinnon and Scott-Ireton 2006).

While the Spanish colonial period was certainly Roger's forte, he also had a keen interest in other aspects of Florida's submerged archaeological resources. Never missing an opportunity to explore unknown sites, Roger often stated, "I am constantly amazed at what you find underwater." Perhaps one of the most significant contributions is the Underwater Archaeological Preserve program. Begun in 1988, this state-wide system of shipwreck parks provides opportunities to engage and educate the public (Scott-Ireton 2003). Roger was instrumental in the creation of the Florida Maritime Heritage Trail, which grew from his publication, *An Atlas of Maritime Florida* (Smith et al. 1997; Smith 2007). In 2004, Roger and his team helped to develop the 1733 Galleon Trail as an underwater park (McKinnon 2007). One of his last major projects with the State was the Panhandle Shipwreck Trail (Smith (L.) 2014).

Roger was prolific as a researcher and author, publishing five books, more than 100 peer-reviewed articles, popular publications, book reviews, and research reports. Upon his retirement from the State of Florida in 2016, Roger donated his extensive and amazing library to the University of West Florida (UWF). Before his passing on 5 February 2020, Roger completed the publication of the Emanuel Point I book, *Florida's Lost Galleon*, as well as a compendium of underwater archaeology in Florida, *Submerged History* (Smith 2018a, 2018b).

Roger Smith's contribution to the field of underwater archaeology and to the State of Florida is immense. But perhaps his greatest gift is the lasting impression that he left on the maritime archaeological community. What follows are stories and memories that illustrate the impact Roger, among the ablest of navigators, had on his colleagues, co-workers, students, and friends. They are in alphabetical order by contributor; take a look at all the people, agencies, organizations, and groups that Roger had a hand in shaping, and see how his legacy lives on.

Brenda Altmeier, Florida Keys National Marine Sanctuary

Roger is one of the quintessential founders of Florida's underwater heritage story as we know it today, a well-assembled, organized history of Florida's maritime people, places, and things. He addressed his work with satisfaction, opened his door to collaborations, and nurtured those willing to listen. In doing so, he helped to elicit research ideas in the underwater archaeology community that bolstered the existing storyline.

I knew Roger's name in relationship to much of the archaeological work in Florida Keys waters when I began working for Florida Keys National Marine Sanctuary in 1993. It was not until later that we met in person. I would listen intently to every word that he said. Roger always had a thoughtful, decisive way of elaborating his knowledge, explaining his considerations and reasons behind his decisions. I feel this part of his personality contributed to his well-respected reputation.

I was fortunate to participate in four separate three-week field projects with Roger, earning a place along with his name as a collaborator on those final reports (Smith et al. 2006). In my observations, both professional and personal, Roger fully participated in life, which provided for great lunchtime stories and thoughts. On a project in 2008, the Bronze Pin Wreck (Shefi et al. 2009), Roger pondered over the primary feature on the site, an iron frame emerging from the sand at a 45-degree angle with a prominent copper alloy fastener protruding through it. The copper was rubbed smooth and shiny and the iron frame was curved, exposed with no growth. He came to the conclusion that sea turtles were using the frame and fastener to rub their shells, knocking off barnacles as they swept under the shipwreck feature. A gift came towards the end of the project as we sat in the boat having lunch. It was a flat calm day and a slight drift brought the vessel to sit silently over the wreck lying just 10 feet below us. Noticing movement, a glance over the side of the boat revealed a sea turtle rubbing its shell under the frame, just as Roger had suspected. What an exciting moment, the experience of which forever trained my eyes to notice the slightest curve, exposed metal, or unusual wear marks found on underwater sites.

I will never forget the sound of his voice, cadence of his speech, and how he could talk about anything. He had a laugh that made you feel good. Roger was a mentor, friend, and contributor to the story that connects us all (Brenda Altmeier 2020, pers. comm.).

Michael Beach, University of Miami Rosenstiel School of Marine and Atmospheric Science

It was a hot day on Florida's "treasure coast," in the vicinity of the wreck of the 1715 fleet ship *Urca de Lima*, Florida's first Underwater Archaeological Preserve. Roger Smith and Della Scott-Ireton were my companions as we drove to inspect sites of the Preserve program that Roger championed. One of them, *Half Moon*, the seventh Preserve, was the topic of my thesis at the University of Miami. Roger was my outside committee member on paper, but much more in life. As the sun set that day, we checked into a motor lodge on A1A. That evening I enjoyed a "Roger Rant" that became a favorite and influenced me beyond words. Fair winds and following seas, Roger (Michael Beach 2020, pers. comm.).

> *"America had often been discovered before Columbus, but it had always been hushed up."*
> -- Oscar Wilde

John Bratten, University of West Florida Department of Anthropology

My first meeting with Roger Smith was in 1994. Roger called Donny Hamilton at TAMU seeking a conservator for the Emanuel Point Shipwreck discovered in Pensacola in 1992. For the project, Roger established a team of four, Jim Spirek, Della Scott-Ireton, Chuck

Hughson, and myself, for the excavation and study of the 16th-century Spanish colonization vessel. As Florida's State Underwater Archaeologist, Roger divided his time between Pensacola and BAR in Tallahassee. When Roger was required at BAR, we provided him updates from the field. One of the many things he impressed me with was his ability to identify artifacts over the phone. One day, Chuck discovered a concreted iron object off the stern of the vessel. All of us looked at the object and formulated our own ideas of what it might be. Based on our descriptions, Roger easily identified it as an armor breastplate before we had even recovered it. We continued to work together on the project through 1998. I always respected Roger's insistence that we not identify the vessel as part of Tristán de Luna's fleet until we had uncovered every piece of evidence needed to support the identification with absolute assurance. Roger continued to remain an essential advisor to UWF when we discovered the second Luna ship in 2006 and the third in 2016.

I have a very fond memory of seeing how happy Roger was at the conference "Shipwrecks of America's Lost Century" in Beaufort, SC, held in April 2019. Roger delivered a wonderful presentation related to the excavation and analysis of the first Emanuel Point Shipwreck and gave praise to every participant of the project. He shared several photos that many of us had never seen. Roger reveled in the gathering of his many colleagues and former schoolmates including Don Keith and Barto Arnold. This conference and his almost simultaneous publication of *Florida's Lost Galleon* and *Submerged History* were surely among Roger's proudest moments, which occurred at the culmination of his long and devoted career in maritime archaeology. He was both a teacher and a friend (John Bratten 2020, pers. comm.).

Melanie Damour, U.S. Dept. of the Interior, Bureau of Ocean Energy Management

I first met Roger around 1997 when I was an undergraduate student in the Florida State University (FSU) Department of Anthropology's Program in Underwater Archaeology. Later, as a graduate student in the Department, I volunteered on several projects led by Roger and BAR in the early 2000s, including the historic dugout canoe in the Wakulla River and the Flintlock Site in the Apalachicola River.

I attended my first Society for Historical Archaeology Conference in 2001. Roger was kind enough to walk me around and introduce me to many of the big names in underwater archaeology as an "up-and-coming" graduate student. I was thrilled to meet so many pioneers of our field whose work I had read about. But, it was Pilar Luna (who sadly passed away only weeks after Roger) of whom I was the most star-struck. Roger introduced me to Pilar and I shook her right hand with so much excitement and enthusiasm that the glass of red wine in her left hand accidentally spilled…all over her expensive white cashmere scarf. I was horrified and embarrassed and wanted to melt into the floor and disappear. Pilar, with grace and humility, brushed it off as no big deal. Roger responded by simply giving me a comforting pat on the back and then ushered me off to meet other well-known underwater archaeologists (probably hoping I did not embarrass him any further!). I always appreciated Roger taking the time to help me begin networking within our archaeological community.

Later that year, Roger agreed to serve on my master's thesis committee. I vividly remember bringing a draft of my thesis to his office for his review. He brandished it in one hand, grabbed a red pen in his other hand, and in his Roger way said, "I will take this red pen and write all over it. I will tear it apart." I nervously looked forward to hearing his feedback and advice on how to make it better. A couple of weeks later, I received his copy of my thesis expecting every page to resemble a murder scene. Instead, I was relieved to see he had only written on a few pages with minor corrections and thoughtful suggestions. In my graduate career and even later in my professional career, Roger was a continuous source of support, advice, and encouragement, and for that, I will always be grateful (Melanie Damour 2020, pers. comm.).

James "Jim" Dunbar, Florida Bureau of Archaeological Research (retired)

In the spring of 1977, Roger Smith and I were assigned to be State Field Agents on a treasure hunter's boat looking at a site in the Florida Keys. Roger and KC, and my wife Patricia and I traveled to the often-bizarre world of life in the Keys. I say that because, once there, we encountered the Iguana Man, who owned a taxi cab and always had his three "pet" iguanas on leashes strung to the rearview mirror. Then there was a local fisherman who delighted in selling barracuda to tourists, which can be toxic if eaten. I remember the Seven Mile Bridge being shut down more than once as law enforcement officers perused the bridge from top to bottom for things like explosives.

The contractor we were assigned to had a boat named *Cajun Queen*, an old wooden Navy skiff of about 50-feet. It had a history of being used by different treasure hunters, then passed along. While we did some work with the contractor, it did not last long. The leaky, dilapidated boat soon sank at its mooring, which delayed offshore operations so Roger had the contractor contact Sonny Cockrell, who was State Underwater Archaeologist. Cockrell was informed that the boat was in dry dock and would be ready to go in about two weeks. Two weeks came and went several times, but we remained stationed in Big Pine Key just in case *Cajun Queen* was fixed and the salvor's offshore work resumed. Roger spearheaded the situation in a positive direction, which is how the 1733 Spanish Plate Fleet Survey came to pass (Smith and Dunbar 1977; Smith 1988) (James Dunbar 2020, pers. comm.).

Mary Glowacki, on behalf of the Florida Division of Historical Resources

Dr. Roger Smith, retired State Underwater Archaeologist and esteemed colleague, served the Florida Division of Historical Resources for more than three decades, greatly contributing to our understanding and appreciation of historic shipwrecks in Florida waters. During the height of shipwreck "treasure" salvage, Roger redirected the State's efforts to the scientific pursuit of shipwrecks, his most notable project being the Emanuel Point Shipwreck in collaboration with UWF's archaeologists. He also fostered Florida's Underwater Archaeological Preserves, a series of historic shipwrecks in Florida that were identified, recorded, and promoted in partnership with local coastal communities.

We will always be grateful to Roger for his unwavering support and advocacy of Florida's underwater archaeological sites. His legacy lives on in the digital archives of the Florida Bureau of Archaeological Research Underwater Program and State archives (Mary Glowacki 2020, pers. comm.).

Christopher E. Horrell, U.S. Dept. of the Interior, Bureau of Safety and Environmental Enforcement

In 1999, I began the PhD program at FSU's Department of Anthropology Program in Underwater Archaeology. Soon after my arrival, I showed up in Roger's office looking for potential dissertation topics related to Florida's submerged archaeological resources. During this meeting, I encountered Roger's unique ability to "reason" with people (the word 'reason' was always over-enunciated for emphasis). Roger convinced me to focus my attention on Florida's forgotten coast.

In 2001, a position opened with BAR for an underwater archaeologist to assist with the program and, two days following September 11, Roger offered me the position. I accepted and began working for Roger the following week. My time at BAR was during a period of tremendous upheaval within state government, and though this presented numerous challenges, Roger always found ways to make projects happen. Such is the case with the Flintlock Site located in the Apalachicola River (Horrell et al. 2003; Horrell et al. 2009). Reported to BAR by river divers and avocational archaeologists, we documented the site during two field seasons. What stands out in my mind regarding this project was Roger's enthusiasm and dedication to the resource. Moreover, Roger trusted his staff, providing us the opportunity to conduct research, do requisite analysis, and discuss findings, allowing us to expand our horizons.

Roger had an innate ability to laugh at situations that could be stressful or even absurd. There was the time he was helping his boss, the Bureau Chief, into a wetsuit but accidentally directed him to put his leg in the sleeve, getting him stuck, and then asked if it would impact his performance evaluation. Or the time a treasure hunter showed Roger a coin and, after pausing to examine it, Roger put it in his pocket and started to walk off. He subsequently gave the coin back, but not after shocking the treasure hunter and explaining the "trouble with treasure." Sometimes jarring and always quick with a descriptive name, Roger could make any circumstance brighter with his unique brand of humor.

Roger was an incredible source of knowledge, a mentor, and friend. The sheer volume of knowledge and insight he shared with me and others will continue to be passed on to future generations of underwater archaeologists (Christopher E. Horrell 2020, pers. comm.).

James Hunter, Australian National Maritime Museum

I met Roger in 1997, during excavation of the Emanuel Point Shipwreck's bow. I was a first-year master's student at UWF and knew practically nothing about shipwrecks or maritime/underwater archaeology. I did, however, have a very keen interest in Spanish colonial history and archaeology, and no doubt drove Roger absolutely bats**t crazy with an endless litany of questions on that topic. Luckily for me, he had limitless patience, and always took the time to answer my queries, as well as offer valuable insight and advice that has served me well over the course of my career.

During the 1997 investigations, Roger was often accompanied by esteemed "research associate" Rudy Vizsla, a furry, four-legged ball of seemingly endless energy who was *always* keen to make the project team's acquaintance and "review" what everyone was doing. In. Great. Detail. And almost always with his nose and big slobbery tongue leading the way. To his credit, Roger tried to rein Rudy in, but his commands—delivered in the softly spoken, heavily enunciated monotone for which he was well known—just did not seem to have the desired effect:

"Rudy."
"Rudy. No."
"Rudy."
"Rudy."
"Rudy. No."

In most instances, Roger would have to physically remove Rudy from whatever thing/individual/place had aroused his interest, and we would all eventually get back to work…

until something else caught Rudy's attention! (James Hunter 2020, pers. comm.)

Donald Keith, Ships of Discovery, Inc.

I met Roger and KC in 1977 at TAMU when the Nautical Archaeology Program was still being formed with only eight or nine students. We studied and worked together for the better part of a decade. Roger and KC were inseparable and mutually supportive, doing fieldwork, research, and writing together. Although not formally a student in the Nautical Program, in addition to being a great photographer, KC soon became known as "KC Wordsmith" for her writing and editorial skills. They were a uniquely formidable pair.

Having worked previously as a Field Agent in Florida, Roger came with experience and first-hand knowledge of underwater archaeology, exploration, and treasure hunting the rest of us graduate students lacked. As a result, he knew what he wanted to study before he got to TAMU: the under-researched and under-appreciated Iberian ship type known as the caravel.

In 1980, I learned about the Molasses Reef Wreck in the Turks & Caicos Islands from Roger. At the time, I was working on a dissertation about the Chinese Age of Exploration and Discovery, but changed course when asked to direct excavation of the site in 1982 and bring the artifacts back to TAMU for conservation and study. Largely due to Roger's enthusiasm for the history and ships of the European Age of Exploration and Discovery and now with a large collection of artifacts to research, a small group of Program students formed the Ships of Exploration and Discovery Research (SEDR) group. Over the next six years we located, recorded, or test-excavated the earliest known European shipwreck sites in the New World. In the end, SEDR produced six master's theses, three PhD dissertations, three books, and more than 100 scientific and popular articles and book chapters.

I learned a lot from Roger and KC, and not just about the Discovery Period. I was surprised to find myself learning more from my fellow students than from my professors. More about thinking outside the box and challenging conventional wisdom. More about scientific diligence and the responsibility every archaeologist has for dissemination. And, perhaps most importantly, about maintaining a zest for life no matter what adversity presents itself.

After Roger left TAMU for Tallahassee, our lives went their separate ways and we fell out of contact, but I was honored when he visited me for a week in July 2019. We reminisced over the old days, the adventures we had, our accomplishments and failures. He knew he did not have much time left, but seemed to be at peace, perhaps largely due to the knowledge that the two books he had devoted his last years to, *Florida's Lost Galleon* and *Submerged History*, were published (Donald Keith 2020, pers. comm.).

Margaret "Peggy" Leshikar-Denton, Cayman Islands National Museum

While a graduate student at the University of Texas in Austin, also taking a course at TAMU and working for the Texas Historical Commission, I met Roger Smith. When Roger invited me to join his 1980 Cayman Islands Project team, I jumped at the chance to focus on Caribbean and Latin American archaeology. I learned a tremendous amount from Roger and KC that summer, about underwater survey methods in clear water, inventory and documentation of shipwreck sites, and oral history research, while contributing skills in artifact analysis and illustration. I also met my future husband, Dennis Denton, and first worked with my soul-mate

Pilar Luna. The 1980 Cayman Islands Project crew emerged as a tight-knit team that forged lasting bonds.

Roger influenced the direction and development of cultural heritage protection in the Cayman Islands and the Caribbean region, both by his pioneering project and by his inspiration that led me to continue his legacy. In 1986, I moved to the Cayman Islands and, in 1990, I joined the Cayman Islands National Museum. The rest is history as I have been promoting the protection of underwater cultural heritage in Cayman and the Caribbean ever since.

In December 2019, I reached out to thank Roger for his review that appears in *Cayman's 1794 Wreck of the Ten Sail: Peace, War, and Peril in the Caribbean,* my book inspired by a shipwreck disaster, whose archaeological remains I first encountered during Roger's Cayman Islands Project (Leshikar-Denton 2019). He replied that he had received his copy and commented, "All that research that you did brings this episode alive in perpetuity in a major historical narrative of maritime Cayman. My best compliments to you…KC and I probably won't make it to Boston; we're saving up for Lisbon…" I was able to express to him how interesting this all turned out, after he and KC first invited Dennis and me to participate in the 1980 project. Meanwhile, he had just received the rebound edition of his book, *The Maritime Heritage of the Cayman Islands* (Smith 2000). These two books are natural companion volumes, so I assured him we would carry them together in the Cayman Islands National Museum Shop.

As I reflect, it is as though the planets aligned at the close of the 1970s, for the many pioneers in our generation who came into the emerging field of underwater and maritime archaeology at that time, and who worked on multiple projects around the world over the next four decades. It surprised and saddened me to learn that Roger Smith and Pilar Luna left us so suddenly in February and March of 2020; I am comforted that Pilar knew of Roger's vanguard passage, as I had shared the news with her, while also sensing that she was fighting the good fight herself (Margaret Leshikar-Denton 2020, pers. comm.).

Godspeed Roger Smith! And Many Thanks!

Jeff Lockwood, Lockheed Martin Corp.

On 23 March 1993, I received a phone call. I remember the day well because it was my birthday. Dr. Roger Smith was calling to ask me if I would be interested in joining his team at the Pensacola Shipwreck Survey as a Field Technician for the beginning of the first Emanuel Point Shipwreck excavation. Trying not to sound too excited, I croaked out a nervous acceptance of his offer and could not wait to begin.

Over the ensuing months, I found working with Roger to be a combination of an invaluable education in maritime history with some poignant proclamations. My favorite of the latter was a discussion one day about Key West and my youthful desire to go. Roger's response: "Key West is lost forever thanks to Jimmy Buffett." Ouch.

During work on Emanuel Point, I made the comment to Roger that I would get a tattoo of a Spanish ship if he would announce that the wreck was, in fact, one of Tristán de Luna's from 1559. He laughed, but said it was not quite time to make that announcement. Eventually funding for the project ran its course and I was let go from the Shipwreck Survey. The day finally came when the announcement was made that EPI was one of Luna's fleet. Some time later, there was a gathering at the bayside which overlooked the wreck site and Della Scott-Ireton invited me to attend for the dedication of a historical marker signifying the Luna shipwrecks. Roger was there and when I went over to say hello he asked me if I was going to get that tattoo now. I smiled and told him, "You fired me. Get your own tattoo." With that rounded-cheek chuckle of his, he slapped me on my shoulder and said, "Jeff, don't ever change."

I haven't, Dr. Smith. Thank you for a great opportunity (Jeff Lockwood 2020, pers. comm.).

Jennifer McKinnon, East Carolina University

Having worked for the State of Florida as an underwater archaeologist between 2004-2006, I shared many adventures with Roger. I first met Roger as a graduate student at FSU, volunteering on projects in the Suwanee River. At the time, a job with the state as an underwater archaeologist seemed like a dream; little did I know a few years later I would land that very job. Without a doubt, that was my favorite job I have ever held.

Roger provided me with many opportunities to grow, fail, and learn. Roger liked to challenge me, and others, in ways that were often unspoken, but obvious. For example, Roger confirmed my first job was to clean and inventory the dive locker, a momentous and dirty job that likely had not been undertaken since the move into the building. I know this because I found objects that were by state law considered artifacts. Nevertheless, I persisted. This job was followed by Roger proclaiming that I oversee the purchase and outfitting of the state's next new research vessel. Again, a challenge I accepted with nervous delight. Had I ever purchased or even owned a boat before? No, but did that stop Roger in challenging me to accept the task? Certainly not. Nevertheless, I persisted.

Over the years, Roger challenged me on several more occasions for which I am forever grateful. I think, as he already knew, that these experiences would allow me to grow as an archaeologist and person. Perhaps the biggest challenge that Roger presented me with was when he hired Jason Raupp, who assisted us in the summer of 2004 on the 1733 Galleon Trail project in the Florida Keys. Little did I know that this would be the longest-running challenge I would accept from Roger, one that became officially recorded in a marriage certificate, and one that continues to today! Despite being vehemently opposed to the idea of partnering with another underwater archaeologist, I accepted the challenge nevertheless, and we persisted (Jennifer McKinnon 2020, pers. comm.).

Chuck Meide, LAMP, St. Augustine Lighthouse & Maritime Museum

I was an intimidated undergraduate when I first met Roger, but he would become not just a mentor but a friend. We worked on shipwrecks together from the Suwannee to St. Augustine, and enjoyed cross-country biking with our dogs Rudy and Noaa. Over the years, I heard many of Roger's stories. I heard about the time off Cayman (pronounced as only Roger could) when his small boat was adrift in ripping currents with a dead outboard engine, and upon ordering his shipmate to throw the anchor out he promptly did—without checking to note that there was no line attached to it. The only way to keep from drifting out to sea was to remove the outboard and use it as an anchor before the water became too deep to save themselves. I heard of his recruitment of psychics and dowsers to find shipwrecks. I heard how he put his own life at risk by stepping out into his street in front of speeding cars, arm outstretched to slow them down. I remember when he was not yet ready to assert that his galleon was definitely Tristán de Luna's, but described it as "looking very Lunate." I learned from him that you never say "trunnel", but always "treenail." I learned from Roger the grooming habits of sea turtles that used historic anchors to scratch their backs. I heard and witnessed stories which should not, and will not, be repeated here, but will be remembered for a long time to come by the generations of archaeologists he inspired.

It is cruel that so shortly after Roger retired, we lost him. He had much more to teach and write. I treasure that he signed and inscribed his first book for me, when I was young and up-and-coming, and his last, a year ago, at his final public appearance, the "Shipwrecks of America's Lost Century" conference. In these two books, which never get dusty on my shelves, are his two messages to me, one to an aspirational student and one to a colleague whose career has matured, which span our careers and friendship. I am a better person and archaeologist from that friendship, and I lament his loss even as I celebrate his legacy (Chuck Meide 2020, pers. comm.).

Jeff Moates, Florida Public Archaeology Network

I had a short stint working for Roger beginning in 2005 and am grateful for the time spent with him. He offered me a job and, without a second thought, I accepted. I learned a lot of new things during those couple of years, some archaeology things, but mostly other sorts of things, such as Roger's appreciation for the techno-musical group Tangerine Dream and electronic music, his habit of telling the octopus-on-his-head story just about every time we stopped for a buffet lunch, scooters, and his dogged approach to projects.

In summer 2006, Roger had a boat of three rookies, including myself, at a shipwreck site. I jumped in first, amazed and confused by the exposed timbers and marine life below. The other two followed, equally captivated. Roger was last in and last out. We had not the first clue, except there was wood exposed. He took our scribbled-on mylar and sketched out a simple, organized depiction of the long-sunken vessel's disposition. Instantly, we understood.

I had more than a couple opportunities to ask Roger about his life, learning about KC and what he would have liked to be if not for a career in history and archaeology. His answers to me always included a tug boat captain and a bulldog. That is how I will choose to picture him, a bulldog captain of his own inner-harbor tug, pushing big boats around (Jeff Moates 2020, pers. comm.).

Jason Raupp, East Carolina University

I worked with Dr. Roger Smith on several different projects over the years. Without a doubt, my favorite among them was a 2004 mission to relocate and document the wrecks of the 1733 Plate Fleet lost in the Florida Keys. This project was a follow-up to one undertaken by Roger, Jim Dunbar, and Larry Murphy in 1977 to inventory the sites which are scattered along the Upper and Middle Keys. Many of those wrecks were under permit to the various treasure hunters operating at the time and the team believed it crucial to inspect them before they were (potentially) destroyed. The stories of how they worked–clandestinely and when time from their day jobs as State Field Agents permitted–to locate and record the remains of 12 of the 13 wrecks were inspiring. Flash forward nearly 25 years to when Roger again set out to relocate the 1733 Fleet sites, only this time with the goal of studying impacts that occurred over that time and better understanding the value that such sites have to the various stakeholders. Being fresh out of graduate school at UWF, I was contracted by BAR to join the Underwater Archaeology Team for the summer. Over those three months, Roger led the team in documenting the 1733 wrecks using the same methods as those employed in 1977, researching numerous other sites along the Keys, and travelling around south Florida to work with archaeologists at various agencies and organizations–all while dodging three major hurricanes!

Over the years, I was fortunate to spend many hours talking with Roger about the discipline of maritime archaeology, his vast research experience, and life in general. Roger was undoubtedly a pioneer in our field, but he was also a mentor and friend who encouraged me to further my education and career. I am lucky to have known him and will forever appreciate his incredible impact on Florida archaeology (Jason Raupp 2020, pers. comm.).

Michael Scafuri, Clemson University Warren Lasch Conservation Center

I first met Roger Smith in the summer of 1994 when I had the opportunity to participate as an intern on the first Emmanuel Point Shipwreck project with the Florida BAR. As a young graduate student, I learned quite a bit from him about how projects actually functioned, including dealing with weather delays, boat problems, and everything else that can happen with projects of this kind. In fact, while I do not think that we ever managed to do any archaeology on the shipwreck that summer (as happens), I did gain many formative experiences. During the course of the internship, Roger gave me lots of good professional advice that I would often recall as my career in nautical archaeology progressed. Getting to know Roger and KC was a true pleasure and they made me, on my first real project, feel welcome.

As a part of the internship, we were required to give a public presentation towards the end of the summer. I was asked to present some of the latest work that had been done by BAR in Pensacola in an open forum. This was a little intimidating for me since I had never delivered a public presentation at that point. While I prepared as best I could, I was unfamiliar with the subject matter since I had not directly participated in it. About 2/3 of the way through the presentation, I began to receive very pointed questions about some of the work that 'we' were doing around Pensacola. Apparently, there was some controversy about it and I had no idea how to respond. Given the situation and my inexperience, I froze and could not answer the questions. After a minute of badgering, Roger, sitting in the front row, calmly stood up and came to my defense at the podium. He responded to the questions from the audience while explaining that I had not actually participated in the work in question. Afterwards, Roger looked at me and said (to paraphrase), "Sorry about that. I didn't know they would grill you, but sometimes you have to think on your feet." I often wonder if he knew there might be trouble and wanted me to learn, but I have never forgotten the experience and his advice has stayed with me ever since. Sometimes you do have to think on your feet (Michael Scafuri 2020, pers. comm.).

Della Scott-Ireton, Florida Public Archaeology Network

I met Roger when he taught UWF's first underwater archaeology class in 1989. Enthralled, I joined UWF's first maritime field school that summer, led by Roger, investigating the lower hull of a British sloop-of-war (Smith 1990). Soon after I graduated, Roger offered me a job with the Pensacola Shipwreck Survey, for which I had been volunteering. That started my career and many years of working for, learning from, and diving with Roger.

Through more than a decade of working with Roger, he and I dived on sites all over the state. The first Emanuel Point wreck in Pensacola was his favorite; I remember his excitement after his first dive on it, shaking his head and saying, "I can't believe it!" Roger also taught me how to share our findings with the public. Florida's Underwater Archaeological Preserves, the 1733 Galleon Trail, the Maritime Heritage Trail, and the Panhandle

Shipwreck Trail are his legacy; these museums in the sea are a triumph of public engagement and education.

Roger became one of my favorite dive buddies. Once, we were deep in Pensacola Bay, where the mud is thick and the visibility poor. We were circle-searching for a mag target and finally found it—one of the creepiest things I've ever seen under water, this object was about 15 feet long, cigar-shaped, and covered in weed, although no fish were around it. I was loaded with the tape, slates, and camera, while Roger was holding the probe. We swam around it, not too close, and looked at it warily. I finally motioned to Roger to probe it. He looked at me, looked at it, looked back at me and tried to hand me the probe, in addition to all the other stuff in my hands! I just stared at him, then realized he was laughing, eyes squinted and puffs of bubbles from his regulator; I could almost hear his characteristic "heh, heh, heh." He poked at it a bit and we got creeped out and left it alone. Roger dubbed the thing "the evil cocoon" and we often laughed about it. Still do not know what it was.

Roger taught me so much, always giving of his knowledge and experience to students and anyone who wanted to know more. Many of my friends and colleagues I met or got to know as a result of Roger. All these people who Roger influenced in some way.... I know he was so proud (Della Scott-Ireton 2020, pers. comm.).

Deb Shefi, Western Australian Museum

For a short few years, I had the pleasure of working under Dr. Roger Smith at the Florida BAR. His creative approaches to working within the system taught me about lateral thinking and ambiguous boundaries, lessons I am sure have guided careers for decades. When I reminisce, memories of Roger's love for KC, Vizsla dogs, and scooters comes to mind, as well as his keen ability to convince others that living on a boat in the Florida Keys for three weeks whilst undertaking fieldwork was "hard work." He also had a knack for finding the most obscure "watering hole," Cuban food, and great BBQ. Above all else, there is one Roger-ism that has embedded itself into my daily practice: "Two is one, and one is none," a phrase that has saved me more times than not! Rest well, old friend. You are missed but not forgotten (Deb Shefi 2020, pers. comm.).

Clifford Smith, Sarasota (FL) County Government (no relation to Roger)

In the spring of 1994, I applied for a paid internship with the Pensacola Shipwreck Survey. I was not selected. So, in the fall of 1994, I called Roger Smith directly and told him I had to have an internship and I would do it for free. Roger, always willing to help and keen to draft a willing volunteer, said ok. He offered me a 15-week internship working on the Emanuel Point Shipwreck site. Needless to say, I had no idea what to expect.

My first impressions and introduction to real underwater archaeology was Roger picking me up that first morning in his truck with Rudy, a very excited red puppy, for the trip down to the boat. I am not sure who was the most excited that morning, me or the dog. Over the following 15 weeks I not only learned about underwater archaeology, but also what they do not tell you in the journal articles: the never-ending battle to keep everything working. Sometimes, we started our day by refloating the work barge that had sunk overnight. Never put off by these small setbacks, Roger would have us push on with the work. During one of these raising of the barge episodes, Roger came to me and said he felt he had to pay me; he had found the funds to create a paid internship to support my semester's stay. Working for Roger was always real, and I always felt he was there for me, then and in the future, as he was a true mentor in the finest sense of the term (Clifford Smith 2020, pers. comm.).

Irina Sorset, U.S. Dept. of the Interior, Bureau of Safety and Environmental Enforcement

I worked with Roger at the BAR in Tallahassee, FL, first as an intern in 2005 and later as the Underwater Program Coordinator in 2007. I am thankful for everything I learned during my experiences with the BAR. Roger went out of his way to mentor me during my early career with advice including job opportunities, career paths, work/life balance, and the optimal family pet - a Vizsla. He cautioned me that my pet Beta fish, Sebastian III, was far from ideal, yet shockingly jumped at the chance to adopt him before I departed for graduate school. Roger even made Sebastian the unofficial mascot of the underwater team. Throughout the years, Roger and I stayed in touch via email and conferences. In addition to sharing his wealth of knowledge about the field, he also took the time to get to know me as an individual, not just as an employee. I will be forever grateful for Roger's genuine mentorship during my beginning years in the field of underwater archaeology (Irina Sorset 2020, pers. comm.).

James "Jim" Spirek, South Carolina Institute of Archaeology and Anthropology

Shared by many of my fellow memorialists, Roger proved instrumental in launching our careers by guiding us from "wannabes" to "respectable" underwater archaeologists. My career took a fortunate turn after meeting Roger during an East Carolina University underwater archaeological expedition to Mobile Bay and Pensacola Bay in the summer of 1991. We spent several days with the Pensacola Shipwreck Survey team documenting and ground-truthing several targets. We also went to see the wreck of USS *Massachusetts*, BB-2, which Roger planned to add to the state's Underwater Archaeological Preserve system. During those hours of boating, diving, and after-hours socializing, I spent valuable time with Roger discussing the days' work, my thesis topic, and other subjects. That visit accelerated my trajectory from graduate student to young professional. When, a few weeks later, I wrote a letter offering to volunteer on the project for a month, he instead responded by offering me the job as Field Director of the second phase of the Shipwreck Survey. Roger issued a simple directive: here is a boat, a magnetometer and a crew, now go find shipwrecks, especially one from the 1559 Luna expedition, but first map *Massachusetts*. Then began a 3-1/2 year underwater archaeological odyssey accomplishing those tasks and others, working closely with Roger and alongside my fellow team members. While we had many adventures and tribulations on, off, and under the water, perhaps the one thing I really remember from this time is Roger's hearty laugh in response to a funny story, recollection, or incident, a laugh readily conjured up in my mind.

From my perspective, garnered from working with and maintaining contact over these many years, Roger had two great gifts: teaching and identifying future colleagues. First and foremost, Roger was an educator. Whether talking in formal or informal settings with elected officials, the general public, volunteers, or students, he was persistent in advocating for the preservation of underwater archaeological sites, particularly exemplified by the Preserve system. As for college students, I believe he never met a young mind that he did not want to shape and cultivate, and that is the cruel irony with his untimely passing. Retired from navigating state bureaucracy, he was poised to share his many years of management, research, and experiences with the students at UWF. Another of Roger's talents was identifying upcoming leaders in the field, attested by a review of professionals who started out in Florida. Some have stayed in the state, others have moved on to other parts of the world, but all serve as evidence of Roger's unswerving desire to promote the field of underwater archaeology through the development of his colleagues, as well as his contributions to the scholarship of the discipline. I think the greatest testament to Roger are the folks writing these memorials and all the others influenced by his guidance and leadership (James Spirek 2020, pers. comm.).

Brenda Swann, St. Augustine Lighthouse & Maritime Museum

Roger was the stuff of legends, providing material for countless stories at parties and gatherings of archaeologists far and wide. The things he would say, and the way he would say them! To this day, those stories bind me to my colleagues and friends in the profession. In truth, this jesting is done largely out of respect for his contributions to the field of archaeology. He popularized the notion of site protection by starting Florida's Underwater Archaeological Preserve program. He wrote numerous popular publications on shipwreck archaeology. His efforts led to the discovery of the oldest shipwreck in North America and the subsequent study of that first attempt at settlement. I was fortunate to have him both as an instructor while a graduate student at UWF and a co-worker at the Florida BAR.

As I was writing this, so many memories came to mind, but an early one stands out. Coming back to shore after a day of working on Emanuel Point I in winter of 1998, the fog was so thick you could barely see past the end of the boat. The weather and Roger at the wheel with a cigarette created a scene that compelled him to go on one of his well-known philosophical journeys. He asked everyone on the boat (most of us grad students) who we thought would actually have a successful career in archaeology and what did that mean anyway? Well, Roger, you showed us! Thanks for getting us safely back to shore that day and for guiding so many in this field (Brenda Swann 2020, pers. comm.).

Ryan Wheeler, Robert S. Peabody Institute of Archaeology

I worked with Roger Smith between 2004 and 2011 when I was Florida's State Archaeologist. Roger was the state's Underwater Archaeologist. He ably headed the state's underwater section and spent much of his time promoting Florida's amazing subaqueous cultural heritage.

We spent the bulk of our time together, however, dealing with treasure hunters. State and federal law permitted—and still permits—the salvage of historic shipwrecks by private interests. During my tenure as State Archaeologist, we had to appear in federal court several times to protect sites from seizure. People were attempting to live out their dreams of getting rich quick, but mostly it was a nightmare, with few real discoveries.

As a Field Agent for the state in the 1970s and '80s, Roger had a front-row seat to the archaeologist-salvor battlefield. I needed Roger's expertise, and he gave it, but Roger did not like spending time on the salvors. Sometimes we talked about the big ideas and issues. Most of the time we pored over ancient files or strategized how to respond to specific situations.

Our adventures with the salvors came to a climax when the Department of State's attorneys learned that Florida's treasure hunting rule had remained unchanged for decades. Roger and I worked together on the revision, mostly contending with the demands of the treasure hunters and their attorneys. In the end, we developed a revised rule that made managed areas off-limits to treasure hunting and replaced the antiquated contract system with permits. When the dust settled, everyone was relatively content, though I am positive Roger would have preferred to see it all go away.

Roger and I also lived around the corner from each other. We shared a passion for dogs, all-you-can-eat sushi, as well as oddball TV shows and movies from the 1980s. Occasionally one of Roger's Vizsla hounds would come and stay with me. Roger had many specific instructions for the dogs, including early morning walks. I ignored these and found that the dogs enjoyed sleeping in as much as I did! When one of Roger's Vizslas passed on, I shared Pablo Neruda's poem, *A Dog Has Died*. With Roger's passing, I thought of Neruda's meditation *And How Long?*

How long does a man live after all?
Does he live a thousand days, or only one?
A week, or several centuries?
How long does a man spend dying?
What does it mean to say 'for ever'?

Neruda's words are particularly evocative for an archaeologist, who measures time for a living. I learned a lot from Roger, about shipwrecks, public archaeology, dogs, and cheap sushi. Thinking about Roger, the memories come easily. I will certainly carry them with me for my "for ever" (Ryan Wheeler 2020, pers. comm.).

References

Horrell, Christopher E., Della A. Scott-Ireton, Roger C. Smith, James Levy, and Joseph Knetsch
2009   The Flintlock Site (8JA1763): An Unusual Underwater Deposit in the Apalachicola River, Florida. Journal of Maritime Archaeology 4(1):5-19.

Horrell, Christopher E., Roger C. Smith, Della Scott-Ireton, and James Levy
2003   The R. W. Scott Site (8JA1763): An Underwater Deposit in the Apalachicola River near Chattahoochee, Florida. Florida Archaeological Reports 16. Florida Department of State, Division of Historical Resources, Bureau of Archaeological Research, Tallahassee.

Leshikar-Denton, Margaret E.
2019   *Cayman's 1794 Wreck of the Ten Sail: Peace, War, and Peril in the Caribbean.* Maritime Currents: History and Archaeology Series. University of Alabama Press, Tuscaloosa.

McKinnon, Jennifer F.
2007   Creating a Shipwreck Trail: Documenting the 1733 Spanish Plate Fleet Wrecks. In *Out of the Blue: Public Interpretation of Maritime Cultural Resources,* John H. Jameson, Jr. and Della A. Scott-Ireton, editors, pp. 85-94. Springer, New York, NY.

McKinnon, Jennifer F., and Della A. Scott-Ireton
2006   Florida's Mystery Wreck. *The International Journal of Nautical Archaeology* 35(2):187-194.

Scott-Ireton, Della A.
2003   Florida's Underwater Archaeological Preserves. In *Submerged Cultural Resource Management: Preserving and Interpreting Our Sunken Maritime Heritage,* James D. Spirek and Della A. Scott-Ireton, editors, pp. 95-106. Kluwer (now Springer), New York, NY.

SHEFI, DEBRA G., ROGER C. SMITH, DANIEL P. MCCLARNON, AND BRENDA S. ALTMEIER
2009 Archaeological and Biological Examination of The Bronze Pin Wreck (8MO1879) off Grassy Key, Monroe County, Florida: an Interim Report. Florida Division of Historical Resources, Bureau of Archaeological Research, Tallahassee.

SMITH, LINDSAY S.
2014 The Florida Panhandle Shipwreck Trail: Promoting Heritage Tourism in the Digital Age. In *Between the Devil and the Deep: Meeting Challenges in the Public Interpretation of Maritime Cultural Heritage*, Della A. Scott-Ireton, editor, pp. 109-118. Springer, New York, NY.

SMITH, ROGER C.
1988 Treasure Ships of the Spanish Main: The Iberian-American Maritime Empires. In *Ships and Shipwrecks of the Americas: A History Based on Underwater Archaeology*, George F. Bass, editor, pp. 85-106. Thames and Hudson, New York, NY.

1990 Marine Archaeology Comes of Age in Florida. In *Underwater Archaeology Proceedings from the Society for Historical Archaeology Conference*, Tucson, AZ, Toni L. Carrel, editor, pp. 110-116. Society for Historical Archaeology, Pleasant Hill, CA.

1993 *Vanguard of Empire: Ships of Exploration in the Age of Columbus*. Oxford University Press, New York, NY.

2000 *The Maritime Heritage of the Cayman Islands*. University Press of Florida, Gainesville.

2007 Florida's Maritime Heritage Trail. In *Out of the Blue: Public Interpretation of Maritime Cultural Resources*, John H. Jameson, Jr. and Della A. Scott-Ireton, editors, pp. 52-63. Springer, New York, NY.

SMITH, ROGER C. (EDITOR)
2018a *Florida's Lost Galleon: The Emanuel Point Shipwreck*. University Press of Florida, Gainesville.

2018b *Submerged History: Underwater Archaeology in Florida*. Pineapple Press, Sarasota, FL.

SMITH, ROGER C., JOHN R. BRATTEN, J. COZZI, AND KEITH PLASKETT
1998 The Emanuel Point Ship: Archaeological Investigations, 1997-1998. University of West Florida, Pensacola, and Florida Department of State, Division of Historical Resources, Bureau of Archaeological Research, Tallahassee.

SMITH, ROGER C., AND JAMES S. DUNBAR
1977 An Underwater Archaeological Survey of Eight Spanish Merchant *Naos* of the 1733 New Spain Fleet. Florida Master Site File Report 13489. Florida Division of Archives, History and Records Management (now Division of Historical Resources), Tallahassee.

SMITH, ROGER C., JAMES J. MILLER, SEAN M. KELLEY, AND LINDA G. HARBIN
1997 *An Atlas of Maritime Florida*. Florida Heritage Series. University Press of Florida, Gainesville.

SMITH, ROGER C., DELLA SCOTT-IRETON, JENNIFER MCKINNON, STEPHEN BECKWITH, BRENDA ALTMEIER, AND LAURI MACLAUGHLIN
2006 Archaeological and Biological Examination of "The Mystery Wreck" (8MO143) off Vaca Key, Monroe County, Florida. Report submitted to Florida Keys National Marine Sanctuary. Florida Division of Historical Resources, Bureau of Archaeological Research, Tallahassee.

SMITH, ROGER C., JAMES D. SPIREK, JOHN R. BRATTEN, AND DELLA A. SCOTT-IRETON
1995 The Emanuel Point Ship: Archaeological Investigations, 1992-1995, Preliminary Report. Florida Department of State, Division of Historical Resources, Bureau of Archaeological Research, Tallahassee.

• • • • • • • • • • • • • • •

Della A. Scott-Ireton
Florida Public Archaeology Network
207 East Main Street
Pensacola, FL 32502

Christopher E. Horrell
U.S. Dept. of the Interior, Bureau of Safety and Environmental Enforcement
1201 Elmwood Park Boulevard
New Orleans, LA 70123

Chuck Meide
St. Augustine Lighthouse Archaeological Maritime Program (LAMP)
St. Augustine Lighthouse & Maritime Museum
81 Lighthouse Avenue
St Augustine, FL 32080

www.ingramcontent.com/pod-product-compliance
Lightning Source LLC
Chambersburg PA
CBHW081443070526
44586CB00019B/2215